The People of Glengarry

To Anne & Angus
with fond regards
Don & Enid
Nov 20, 1994

McGill-Queen's Studies in Ethnic History
Donald Harman Akenson, Editor

The People of Glengarry

Highlanders in Transition, 1745–1820

MARIANNE McLEAN

McGill-Queen's University Press
Montreal and Kingston • London • Buffalo

©McGill-Queen's University Press 1991
ISBN 0-7735-0814-7 (cloth)
ISBN 0-7735-1156-3 (paper)

Legal deposit fourth quarter 1991
Bibliothèque nationale du Québec

∞

Printed in Canada on acid-free paper
First paperback edition 1993

This book was first published with the help of a
grant from the Social Science Federation of Canada,
using funds provided by the Social Sciences and
Humanities Research Council of Canada. Funding
was also received from Multiculturalism Canada

Canadian Cataloguing in Publication Data

McLean, Marianne
    The people of Glengarry: Highlanders in transition,
1745–1820

(McGill-Queen's studies in ethnic history; 9)
Includes bibliographical references and index.
ISBN 0-7735-0814-7 (bound) –
ISBN 0-7735-1156-3 (pbk)
1. Glengarry (Ont.) – Emigration and immigration –
History. 2. Highlands (Scotland) – Emigration and
immigration – History. 3. Immigrants – Ontario –
Glengarry – History. 4. Scots – Ontario – Glengarry –
History. 5. Highlands (Scotland) – History. I. Title.
II. Series.

JV7285.S3M34 1991   971.3'750049163   C91-090222-4

Typeset at University of Toronto Press in 10/12 Palatino

Jacket illustration: *Lock Jurn*, Moses Griffith, del.,
P. Mazell, sculpt., (private collection); *Colonel Alastair
MacDonell of Glengarry* by Sir Henry Raeburn, (National
Gallery of Scotland, NU 420).

For all the people of Glengarry

Contents

Tables and Maps

Preface

This study of the origins of Glengarry County, Ontario, has its roots in my curiosity about emigration, its effect on individuals, and its meaning for the country which the emigrants built. All of my father's family were Scottish Highlanders who belonged to Glengarry. But my father is a Canadian. When and how did his people become Canadian, and what survives of their former culture? The origin of this particular part of the Canadian identity clearly lies in the Highlands of Scotland and in Glengarry County; the experience of emigration, which formed the new community, was crucial in shaping the Highlanders' life in the new world. But what did the Highlanders, or any other group, preserve of their old identity when, after several generations, they considered themselves Canadian? Questions of cultural transfer are not easy to answer. This book represents only the first stage in an examination of the cultural change that marked the historical experience of one ethnic group in Canada. Nevertheless, in charting why and how certain Gaelic-speaking Scots came to Canada two hundred years ago, I have begun to define the cultural legacy which their descendants share and which is part of the Canadian heritage.

When I began work on this book, I had studied Canadian history and had heard of Glengarry County from family tradition, but I knew neither the history nor the country from which these emigrants came. Over the course of twelve years, beginning in 1973, I visited western Inverness half a dozen times. I walked the valleys, crossed the passes, and climbed the mountains in several of the districts described in this book. The scattered settlements and near wilderness that exist in western Inverness today offer a stark contrast to the populous communities and active farms described in the historical record. The stone houses and dykes these migrants left behind them, and the flocks of sheep and herds of deer that now graze on the hills, testify to the economic transformation that overtook this region more than two hundred years ago. The people whom I met in western Inverness shared their knowledge of the past with me and contributed substantially to my understanding of the Highlands.

I have written this book most particularly for the people of Glengarry, whether in Scotland, in Canada, or elsewhere, for those whose lives are remembered here, and for all their families. I may surprise some who read this book by the argument I make about the clearances and emigration. I emphasize that the creation of sheep farms and the clearance of some families were among the causes of these emigrations; I do not argue that landlords forced people to leave. While I disagree with much of J.M. Bumsted's *The People's Clearance*, we share common ground in believing that Highland emigrants of the period before 1815 chose to leave Scotland over the protests of their landlords. Once in Canada, the emigrants to Glengarry County proudly built a new Highland community. Even today, Glengarry County has special meaning for the descendants of those emigrants.

Two comments should be made concerning the text of this book. First, insofar as possible, I have generally written the names Macdonald and Macdonell as they most commonly appear in the historical record. There are, however, many variations of orthography including capitalization and the use of Mc or Mac. Not only do different people spell these names differently, but the same person may spell even his own name differently over time. I have therefore left the spelling of names inside quotations unchanged, even if this does not accord with the usual spelling, and I have tried to use consistently one spelling for an individual's name. Second, I have described the settlement of Glengarry County as occurring in only two townships, Lancaster and Charlottenburgh, and not in the four townships into which the county was ultimately divided. I made this choice because the original two townships were only divided after the initial settlement – which is the focus of my work – was complete; concessions 10–18 of Lancaster became concessions 1–9 of Lochiel in 1818, and concessions 10–18 of Charlottenburgh became concessions 1–9 of Kenyon in 1798.

The maps presented in the book were prepared by Vic Dohar and Jo-Anne Froescul. Molly Wolf edited the text with her usual precision and flare.

Many individuals also gave me encouragement and assistance in the research and writing of this book. In an earlier version, it was accepted as a doctoral thesis at the University of Edinburgh, thanks to the patient advice of my advisors, Philip Wigley, T.C. Smout, Eric Cregeen, and Margaret Mackay. The staff of the Scottish Record Office, the National Library of Scotland, the Public Record Office, the National Archives of Canada, the Archives of Ontario, the Kingston Archdiocese Archives and the Archives de l'Archevêche de Québec all provided friendly guidance to a demanding researcher. In Scotland, Sir Donald Cameron of Lochiel and Mrs. Loraine Maclean of Dochgarroch kindly let me use family papers. In Canada, the late Mrs. Florence Macdonell and Mr. Ewen Ross, as well as Mr. Alexander Fraser, Mrs. Harriet MacKinnon, Mr. and Mrs. John MacLeod, Mrs. Sybil McPhee, and Mrs. Mary Beaton, all gave generously of their knowledge of Glengarry County. Many other Glengarry people opened their homes to a stranger and described the history of their families and neighbourhoods to me; I hope that this book repays in part my debt to them.

In 1988–9, the National Archives of Canada granted me a period of professional development leave, which I used to revise the thesis manuscript. During these weeks, my colleagues in the Manuscript Division of the National Archives, Patricia Birkett, Peter Delottinville, Patricia Kennedy, and Ron Kuhnle, generously took over my duties there. I have benefited from the comments of Bruce Elliott and in particular from the careful scholarly criticism which Dana Johnson gave this manuscript. But the debt which I cannot repay is to my husband, Philip Goldring. For fifteen years Philip has listened to my ideas and commented on my work, becoming something of a Highland enthusiast himself; I could not have completed this book without his loving support.

Ottawa, Ont.
March 1990

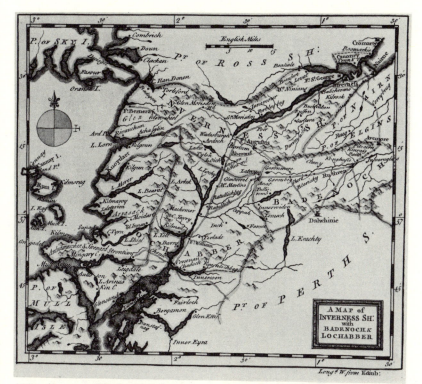

A Map of Inverness Sh[ire], with Badenoch
& Lochabber [c. 1749]. (private collection)
Neither cartographers nor lowland
Scots possessed detailed information
about the geography of western
Inverness in the mid-eighteenth
century. Note the north–northwest
rather than east–west orientation of
"L. Arkek" (Loch Arkaig), the
placement of the Isle of Skye too far to
the north, and the inaccurate drawing
of several west coast peninsulas.

Archibald McDonald of Barrisdale,
Aged 29, by Blaikie. (Scottish National
Portrait Gallery, H5731)   This portrait
of Barisdale presents Macdonell as
an eighteenth-century gentleman;
contrast it to the image of Glengarry
painted by Raeburn a half century
later.

Lock Jurn [Loch Hourn], Moses Griffith, del., P. Mazell, sculpt. (private collection)
The mountainous, forbidding character of the north side of Knoydart is evident in
this print depicting the fisheries in Loch Hourn. Note the small patches of arable
land visible as parallel sets of wavy lines near the water's edge to the right of the
centre of the print.

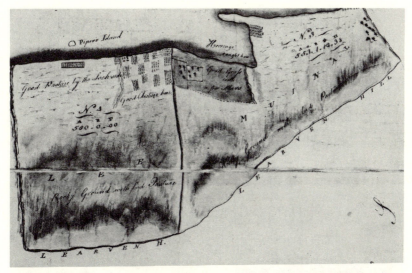

Plan of ... Barrisdale; no. 3, Muniell, William Morrison, c. 1771. (Scottish Record Office, RHP 112)   Southern officials used Morrison's surveys to plan the economic improvement of the forfeited estates; Muniall may well be the farm whose arable land is visible in the sketch of Loch Hourn by Griffith and Mazell.

Scoor Eig on the Isle of Eig, drawn and engraved by William Daniell, published 1 April 1818. (private collection)   The dramatic ridge known as the Sgurr of Eigg offered the Eigg emigrants a last glimpse of home as they sailed west in 1790.

Quebec from Point Levi, watercolour by George Heriot, September 1793. (National Archives of Canada, c-12751)   Most of the Highlanders passed through the port of Quebec on their way to the new settlement in Upper Canada; the spectacular setting of the city is seen here in a view painted from the opposite shore of the St Lawrence.

Loch Tay looking towards Killin, by Alex Campbell, c. 1802. (National Gallery of Scotland, D-4424)   The parishes of Killin and Kenmore lie on the northern shore of Loch Tay on the right of this sketch. While the mountains are high, they are not as steep and forbidding as those of the west coast.

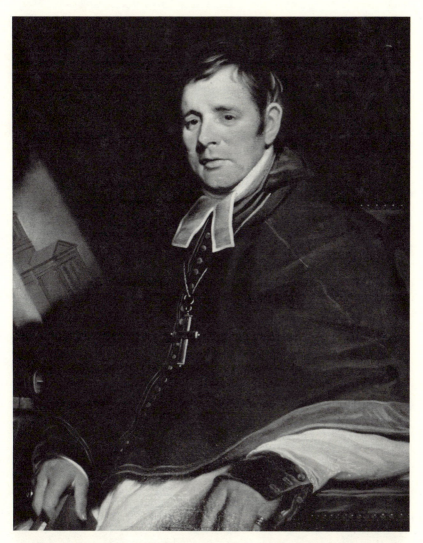

The Right Reverend Alexander Macdonell, first bishop of Upper Canada, oil painting by an unknown artist. (National Archives of Canada, C-11059) Alexander Macdonell served as a missionary in both Scotland and Canada, as well as military chaplain in the Glengarry Fencibles and bishop of Kingston; he is arguably the best known of the Glengarry emigrants. While a member of the elite by virtue of his clerical position, Macdonell shared many of the attitudes and activities of his parishoners.

Colonel Alastair MacDonell of Glengarry, by Sir Henry Raeburn. (National Gallery of Scotland, NU420) The Glengarry chief, Alexander McDonell, was a champion of Highland culture and tradition as this portrait testifies with its elaborate Highland dress and weapons of war. But to live in such a grand style, McDonell raised estate rents dramatically; many of his tenants refused to pay and instead chose to emigrate to Canada.

Glengarry House, sketch by Mrs. John Graves Simcoe. (Archives of Ontario, MU 2782, B-3, diaries 4 and 8, Sept.–May 1796). *Macdonell of Greenfield, Glengarry, Scotland now of Canada*, bookplate. (National Archives of Canada, C-8762) These two illustrations underscore the presence of the highland gentry in the new Glengarry community. Most dwellings were built of logs in this period so John Macdonell of Aberchalder's substantial stone house, called "Glengarry House," testified to his position in the community. The bookplate belonged to the Greenfield Macdonell family, organizers of the 1792 emigration; it underlines the transfer of the family, with its status intact, to Upper Canada.

Kenyon, 12 September 1846, pencil sketch by the Rev. Jacques Frederic Doudiet. (National Archives of Canada, c-127635)   In spite of the early settlement of Glengarry and its proximity to the well-travelled St. Lawrence waterway, few visual images of the community survive from its first sixty years. Thus, this sketch by J.F. Doudiet, a Swiss Presbyterian who ministered to Highlanders in the northern quarter of the county, offers a rare view of the small clearings and dense forests that dominated the early years of settlement in all parts of Glengarry.

Mr. McKillican, Breadalbane, Upper Canada, 19 June 1845, pencil and crayon sketch by Jacques Frederic Doudiet. (National Archives of Canada, c-127644)   Breadalbane was the name given to the community settled in the concessions 16 and 17 of Lancaster by the 1815 settlers from Perthshire. Thirty years after their arrival, many of the emigrants' farms probably resembled the farmstead pictured here: a one-and-one-half storey house with several small outbuildings, all built of logs, and with small open fields lying in a gently rolling country.

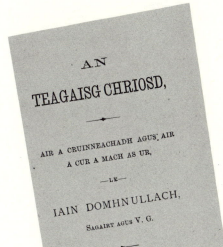

An Teagaisg Chriosd (Toronto, 1871), title page and preface. (Private collection) This small forty-four page pamphlet was prepared by Father John Macdonald who emigrated to Glengarry as a child in 1786. His claim that the pamphlet presented the teachings of the Roman Catholic church as handed down in oral recitations in the Scottish highlands underlines the richness of the cultural baggage carried by the emigrants to Glengarry.

PREFACE.

This Edition of the Gaelic Catechism is authorised to be printed by His Lordship the Right Reverend Bishop Horan, of Kingston, and presented as true Catholic doctrine by John Macdonald, Priest and V. G.

The principal part of the material has been taught and handed down from one generation to another among the Roman Catholics of the Highlands and Islands of Scotland, and collected from oral recitations, carefully compared with the teachings of the Church, and found to contain sound doctrine, good and pious counsels, good instructions and admonitions, as well as being more smooth and harmonious than anything at present accessible in the Gaelic language.

CONTENTS.

The People of Glengarry

CHAPTER ONE

Introduction

Over the past 400 years, millions of men, women, and children have emigrated from Europe to the Americas. This movement created new nations in the western hemisphere, but it also influenced the development of the modern European states. The emigrants thus stand in a pivotal role in both the Old and the New World. Questions of who these people were, why they left, and what sort of communities they created should be of interest in both Europe and America.[1]

Some of the emigrants left their homelands because political or religious conflict forced or persuaded them to go. The great majority, however, emigrated to America for its economic and social opportunities. One such migration that can be traced in detail is the movement of Highlanders from northwest Scotland to Glengarry County, Upper Canada (now Ontario), in the late eighteenth and first half of the nineteenth century. This book examines the origin and formation of the Highland community in Glengarry County and the place of these emigrants in both Scottish and Canadian history.

Glengarry County is arguably the best-known county in Canada. Located on the southeastern boundary of the province of Ontario, Glengarry stretches for twenty miles along the north shore of the St. Lawrence River. Its original two (now four) townships reach twenty-two miles inland, taking in fertile lowlands, gentle hills, and the stone-covered fields seemingly beloved by Highland farmers everywhere.

Pride in the county itself and in its Highland inheritance has marked the inhabitants of Glengarry from the first years of settlement. Glengarry expatriates carried the name of the county across North America; the most famous of these, Ralph Connor, caught and popularized the spirit of Glengarry and its Highland people some eighty years ago in his best-selling novels. Even today, Canadians whose parents and grandparents left the county a generation or two ago still explain with pride that Glengarry is a special place. County historians Royce MacGillivray and Ewan Ross argue forcefully that Glengarry was a nation "with its own intense sense of cohesion and of separation from the outside world, its own customs and values, its own awareness of having its own heroic past separate from that of the country of which it has been a part, and for a time, even its own language."[2] This extraordinary sense of the special character of Glengarry County is not just an extreme case of local boosterism; it resulted from the particular experience of the emigrants who created the new Highland community.

Between 1773 and 1853, close to 3,500 people emigrated to Glengarry County from a few districts in the Scottish Highlands. The emigrants came principally from the districts of Lochiel, Glengarry, Knoydart, and Glenelg, in the mountainous western rim of mainland Inverness-shire. Many of the clansmen of this region had been fervent supporters of the Jacobite cause in 1745; the Camerons of Lochiel and Macdonells of Glengarry followed Prince Charles Edward to bitter defeat at Culloden. All the inhabitants of western Inverness suffered the full effect of the military suppression of the revolt and then endured the government's efforts to "civilize" the region in the generation that followed. No longer did the chiefs wield legal power over the clansmen; nor did possession of their estates depend on the military numbers of their followers. But as the clansmen struggled to adapt to the new social order, dramatic change occurred in the local economy as well. Landowners sought the highest possible return on their estates and looked to agriculture to make a profit rather than to support a numerous tenantry. The clansmen were introduced to modern agricultural organization, including crop rotation, fertilizing, and fencing, and they increased their production of cattle for distant markets. Ultimately, large-scale sheep farming yielded the best returns, but the ordinary clansmen could not amass the capital needed to finance such activities.

The Highlanders of the late eighteenth century were a people in transition from a clan-based society and agriculture to a modern commercial society. For many Highlanders, however, this social and economic transformation accompanied a second change, equally dramatic: they emigrated from Scotland to North America. The relationship between these two transitions is one of the keys to Highland history and social development over the last 200 years. J.M. Bumsted has recently argued that the emigrations of 1770 to 1815 were not the result of clearances to create sheep farms but rather an attempt by the clansmen to avoid change and thereby preserve traditional life.[3] Bumsted's focus on the leaders of the emigrations, and his failure to examine the communities that produced the emigrants, have led him to underestimate the effect of clearances for sheep and to misinterpret the clansmen's motive for emigration. The case of the Glengarry emigrants suggests something different. The clansmen who left western Inverness for Upper Canada *had* made certain accommodations to the new society emerging in the Highlands. When, however, the new order fundamentally threatened social life or their economic status – in particular when land began to be cleared for sheep after 1780 – the clansmen chose to emigrate. The confident new community of Glengarry is testimony to their successful passage through the two transitions. The Glengarry settlement did not originate in a desire to retreat to the past but from a willingness to take advantage of new opportunities available in Canada.

Emigration from western Inverness to Glengarry County followed a distinct pattern. The clansmen generally organized their own sailings across the Atlantic, travelling in related family groups from neighbouring communities in western Inverness. Their departures spanned three-quarters of a century, but most emigrated in the seventeen years from 1785 to 1802.

The first clansmen to reach Glengarry County came from the new United States during and just after the Revolutionary War; they had actually left Scotland for the colony of New York, mostly in 1773. The largest group of these families was led by three Macdonell brothers, Aberchalder, Collachie, and Leek, originally tacksmen from the Glengarry estate. The American Revolution transformed the emigrants into Loyalist refugees whose Canadian refuge became the nucleus of the new Highland community. No sooner had the Loyalists obtained land in Glengarry County in 1784 than they were joined by friends and relatives, who organized five sailings from Scotland within nine years. Military officers such as Alexander McMillan and Miles Macdonell, tacksmen such as Alexander Macdonell of Greenfield and Kenneth McLeod of Glenelg, religious leaders such as Father Alexander McDonell of Scotus, and substantial tenants such as Angus Ban Macdonell of Muniall, led the departures. After a lull, created by the outbreak of war in 1794, two groups of close to a thousand clansmen emigrated to Glengarry in the brief peace of 1802. Finally, under government sponsorship at the end of the Napoleonic Wars in 1815, the last large group of emigrants left western Inverness for Glengarry County. Throughout these years, and more particularly in the four decades which followed, smaller groups and individual Highland families reached Canada from the same districts or neighbouring ones, almost rebuilding whole western Inverness communities in Glengarry.

The clansmen's emigration to Glengarry County is part of a distinct flow in the movement of Europeans to America. This was an emigration of *families* intending to settle, not of individuals, who might intend to return to their native country. Most undertook the voyage as part of a group, and both groups and single families travelled to join someone they knew. In terms used by immigration historians, the peopling of Glengarry was the result of both chain and group emigration. This pattern of movement across the Atlantic is rather an exaggerated example of one of the two streams of emigration recently identified by American historian Bernard Bailyn in his analysis of English and Scottish emigrants in the 1770s. Bailyn's first or "metropolitan" stream consisted mostly of young single men from southern England who indentured themselves to pay for their passage. The second or "provincial" stream was made up of families, including children, paying their own fares and leaving, often in groups, from northern England and Scotland.[4] The Glengarry emigrants fit this provincial model perfectly; indeed they exhibit its characteristics, not just for one decade but over an extended period. The creation of the Highland community of Glengarry County was one of the ways in which the provincial stream of emigration shaped Canadian society.

The dramatic changes which took place in the Scottish Highlands in the hundred years after the Rebellion of 1745 have long captured the public imagination. From Dr Johnson to John Prebble, popular writers have stirred their readers with accounts of social and economic turmoil in the Highlands. Recently, scholars such as Malcolm Gray, James Hunter, and Eric Richards have probed many of the problems which plagued the Highlands in this period and have debated the significance of the courses followed by landlords and clansmen.[5] A study of the districts which sent such a focused stream of emigration to Glengarry County offers an opportunity to review the findings of these scholars in detail. What changes occurred in western Inverness after 1745? When did they happen? And how did the clansmen react? How, for example, did the Highlanders come to subsist only on small plots of land in the nineteenth century when they had jointly farmed substantial holdings in the eighteenth? We know (to take one instance) that in

1755 tenants in Knoydart farmed, on average, 350 acres of land per family; one hundred years later, the average holding was only a few acres for each crofting family.[6] Michael Flinn and Eric Richards have both emphasized the demographic crisis which developed in the late eighteenth century, resulting in the subdivision of holdings and a dependence on potatoes and on wages from collecting kelp or serving in the army.[7] But they fail to examine the effects of clearances on the clansmen's fortunes. The case of the Glengarry and Lochiel estates gives important insights into the Highlanders' willingness to adapt to the new order, and it documents the choice made by some of the clansmen as they faced the transition to a modern society and economy.

Any discussion of the clansmen's reaction to the transformation of their society quickly becomes bound up with the issue of emigration. The relationship between the two experiences is complex and long-standing, and scholars are still trying to produce a simple statement of events, as well as a convincing interpretation of their meaning. This uncertainty is partly because two fundamentally opposed ways of looking at change and emigration dominate writing about Highland emigrants.

The first, or positive, viewpoint sees emigration as the ideal and inevitable solution to the problems created by population growth and socioeconomic change in the Highlands after 1745. Lord Selkirk popularized this idea at the beginning of the nineteenth century, and although Highland landlords at first strenuously opposed it, by mid-century they were enthusiastically promoting emigration from their estates.[8] In this century, scholars have often focused on the demographic aspects of Highland development, pointing out the substantial growth in population that made emigration necessary. Michael Flinn, the most forceful proponent of this viewpoint, argues that emigration, first to a modest and later a significant extent, eased the pressure of growing numbers on limited resources. The second view of Highland emigration focuses primarily on the negative aspects of the movement. Emigration was a tragedy; people were forced to leave first their farms, then their country. Population pressures (this argument claims) were irrelevant, since the land they vacated was most often turned over to sheep farmers.[9] James Hunter presents this argument as the crofters' view of events, and most popular accounts of the clearances share this perspective.

One of the simple questions about the emigrants that remains unanswered concerns the identity and number of those who left northern Scotland. For one group, the tacksmen, who served as middlemen between the clansmen and their chief, the reasons for emigration seem well established. The agrarian transformation of the Highlands left the tacksmen without an economic role and, as Eric Richards has most recently pointed out, many tacksmen made their escape by leading an emigrant group to America.[10] It was not just tacksmen however, but clergymen, military officers, and substantial tenants who led the Glengarry emigrants, and their motives for leaving are not well understood. Also unclear is the relative importance of tenants and of poorer members of Highland society in the pre-1815 migrations. Were the clansmen who remained in the Highlands in 1815 poorer because the better-off had already emigrated, or did their impoverishment result from the clearances, from the postwar economic slump, from the demographic crisis, or from some combination of these factors? Another less simple question concerns the rate at which people emigrated, or the significance of this level of departures. Malcolm Gray has argued that comparatively few clansmen emigrated, and Eric Richards also emphasizes the slow rate at which emigration from the Highlands occurred.[11] An analysis of the Glengarry emigration reveals the importance of both community leaders and tenants generally in making up the emigrant parties, as well as the high rate of emigration in the limited periods in which movement across the Atlantic was feasible.

The question of why the clansmen left the Highlands is controversial, and writing on this issue seems either highly partisan or inconclusive. All commentators agree that the Highlanders emigrated in order to obtain land, but *why* they needed land is the subject of dispute. Michael Flinn and Eric Richards argue that the clansmen emigrated because the high rate of population growth strained the resources of the Highland economy to the breaking point. When the number of people increases in any agricultural community, the immediate result is, of course, increased competition for land. In the Highlands, however, people vied for land not just with each other but also with sheep. But Richards denies that clearances for sheep farms led many tenants to emigrate before 1815, an argument which J.M. Bumsted emphatically repeats. Echoing Selkirk, Bumsted proposes that the clansmen emigrated because they could not adapt to the new order which emerged in the Highlands after 1745.[12] The rhetoric found in tacksmen's letters about recreating the feudal Highlands in America provides him with a seemingly adequate explanation for their departures. But is his explanation right? The case of the Glengarry emigrants demonstrates that such conservatism was not the primary motivation for the people's departure; instead, their migration was largely triggered by the introduction of sheep farming and clearances.

Twentieth-century people take the vast stream of emigration across the Atlantic for granted; it seems always to have been the obvious solution to Europe's demographic and economic problems. Historians, too, sometimes seem to have forgotten that people had first to see emigration as the most viable of all options before the movement could reach its eventual high tide.[13] The decision to emigrate is a radical choice, one which expresses clearly the emigrant's preference for life elsewhere than in the homeland. In the case of the Highland Scots, whose attachment to their native glens and communities was legendary, unprecedented number of people chose to go – a devastating critique of the new order. Agrarian transformation and population growth alone do not explain why after 1745 some of the clansmen left for America and others stayed behind. To explain the clansmen's decision, the historian must take into account not just general social and economic trends in the Highlands but also the particular timing and impact which these trends had on communities and individuals. Changing conditions in America also influenced the flow of people.

Were the clansmen pushed out of the old country or pulled by the new? They did receive some support from the colonial government and substantial land grants in Canada. This powerful pull was strongly reinforced by the ties of kinship and community that later migrants had with the new settlement and that made the transition easier and less traumatic. The clansmen's economic and social position in Scotland was at best marginal, at worst seriously threatened by economic transformation – an equally powerful push. The truth probably lies in the middle: in the case of Glengarry County, the clansmen emigrated in large numbers between 1773 and 1815 because social and economic conditions in *both* western Inverness *and* in Canada combined to make emigration both very attractive and possible. The story of the Glengarry emigrants illuminates the complexity of the causes of this movement, and should be of interest both to those who study the clansmen who left and those who study the people who stayed.

James Hunter has argued that the clearances psychologically devastated the clansmen. Their world was turned upside down when their erstwhile leaders suddenly jettisoned ancient social values and substituted individual self-interest for the common good. The Highlanders who experienced the transformation of their society and, in particular, the betrayal of the clearances were, according to Hunter, demoralized and unable to mount an effective resistance to their landlords until they rebuilt their confidence through the religious revivals of the first half of the nineteenth century.[14] But if Hunter and others who take this line are correct, how are we to explain the quite different attitude of the Glengarry settlers? The community of Glengarry County was extraordinarily self-confident, a fact that argues that at least some of the clansmen had quite a different experience.

The people of western Inverness who emigrated to Upper Canada found themselves dealt a poorer or losing hand by the agricultural transformation of their native glens; in these circumstances they chose to emigrate communally so as to obtain land for their families and at the same time maintain community ties. In the words of one emigrant, Anna McGillis, the clansmen "obtained townships for themselves ... [with] firm title from the king."[15] No longer did the well-being of the community depend on the goodwill of its landlord chiefs. The creation of a Highland settlement in Upper Canada was an ambitious alternative to the crofting and kelping settlements developed by the landlords of western Inverness. The conception and realization of this alternative was a remarkable achievement; it was this accomplishment which gave birth to the clansmen's pride in their Glengarry.

Writing the story of the emigrant clansmen has been a rewarding but not an easy task. The actions and thoughts of ordinary people are too often poorly documented. This is, of course, even more the case when most of the people whose story is being told could not write and left no papers of their own. As a result of the transformation of western Inverness, little oral knowledge seems to have survived in Scotland of the condition of the clansmen before 1800. I therefore experienced some difficulty in establishing the human links between Scotland and Canada and in locating complementary historical records. In one instance, the significance of a district as a major source of emigrants to Glengarry was not emphasized in the published histories of the county.[16] Nevertheless, scattered through Scottish estate records, religious archives, the Canadian public record, and many small private collections or published material is a considerable amount of information about the Glengarry emigrants.[17]

Two major archival collections with information about western Inverness in the second half of the eighteenth century provided much of the Scottish data analysed in this book. The Forfeited Estates papers, preserved in the Exchequer records at the Scottish Record Office (SRO), offer a detailed account of the administration of the estates of Lochiel and Barisdale (in Knoydart) between 1747 and 1784. These papers provide an overview of economic (and occasionally social) life on the two estates; they also detail the attempts of government agents Mungo Campbell and Henry Butter to modernize agricultural and social practices. The Scottish Catholic Archives has preserved letters written by Roman Catholic missionaries in Glengarry and Knoydart, and these offer quite a different perspective on their parishoners. The priests recorded basic data, such as the number of people to whom they ministered, but they also discussed the events leading up to the emigrations from a viewpoint more sympathetic to the clansmen than that of land-lords and government officials. The Fraser – Mackintosh collection in the SRO documents change on a number of west Highland estates, including Glengarry and Knoydart. The archival record provides the data necessary for an analysis of economic change in western Inverness during this period, and it allows us a glimpse of the effect which such change had on the people.

In Canada, government records provide considerable information about the experience of the emigrants. The British Crown controlled land that could be granted to incoming settlers; their requests for land and the response of colonial officials together make it possible to identify and chart the settlement of many Glengarry County settlers. Government involvement with these Highlanders went beyond the usual granting of land, and this too is documented in surviving colonial and imperial records. Perhaps surprisingly in view of the number of "gentlemen" concerned with the Glengarry emigrants, only one, Archibald McMillan of Murlaggan, left a substantial collection of private papers describing the emigration and settlement in any detail. As in Scotland, the papers of Roman Catholic clergymen concerned with the Glengarry clansmen provide important family information and insights into events and their causes. County traditions, oral or collected in writing (for example, by George Sandfield Macdonald in the 1880s) add substantially to knowledge of the emigrants. From small details concerning family relationships to epic poems describing the emigrations, the oral record presents crucial elements in the history of the Glengarry emigrants.

Relying on historical records from two nations has produced a work that will likely seem to its Canadian readers to discuss Scottish history and to its Scottish readers to chart Canadian development. But any effort to tell the emigrants' story must encompass the history of both countries. The focus of this study is on the emigrants themselves. It is on those clansmen whose lives encompassed the years of crumbling certainties after 1745, the momentous decision to emigrate, and the establishment of a new, avowedly Highland community in Upper Canada. Their experience forms a single history, and temporarily unites the history of western Inverness and that of eastern Upper Canada. The effect of the clansmen's emigration to Glengarry County was to divide certain small Highland communities into two parts. For a period, those communities continued their joint existence on two continents, and a steady flow of information and people across the Atlantic joined the two halves of the community. As in the case of the Englishmen who emigrated to New England, it was the passage of time and the long-term effect of different social and economic forces, not emigration alone, that severed communities in Europe and North America.[18]

The story of the Red Piper illustrates both this division of communities and the joy which the clansmen felt when families were reunited in Glengarry.[19] Duncan McDonald joined the British army as a piper, and after some years his family was informed of his death in India. But Duncan had not died, and he returned to Scotland to learn that his family had emigrated to Glengarry County. After working to earn his fare, he too crossed the Atlantic and on reaching the Highland settlement, walked the last fifteen miles north to join his family.

The family had just sat down to their evening meal when they heard music floating down the trail. The air was familiar: "Lochaber No More." ... Near and nearer came the music and soon they saw a kilted figure, travel-stained and weary, approaching the house. They scarcely knew him after twenty-one years of service, tall, broad in shoulder, bewhiskered. Yet they did recognize him and threw themselves upon him in an abandonment of happiness and thankfulness.

Such joy was surely experienced again and again in Glengarry as families divided by emigration came together again.

This study of the Glengarry emigrants – their experience of agrarian and social change, of migration, and of settlement in Canada – surveys a whole cycle in the clansmen's history. It takes in their painful adjustment to the new regime in the Highlands and their complex transition to become Highlanders in Upper Canada. It follows them until their new Glengarry was strong enough to attract and shelter the kin they had left behind. Taken separately, these narratives of agrarian change, migration, and the formation of new communities might be only of local interest. But to determine the larger patterns we must follow in detail the fortunes of small groups of people over time. Historians sometimes fall short of appreciating the distinct experience of particular groups and perhaps fail to make clear the significance of the movement of people. As a case study, the peopling of Glengarry County offers an opportunity to test the findings of earlier writers in detail and to analyse in a single study the clansmen's experience of economic development, emigration, and settlement in America.

CHAPTER TWO

Western Inverness-shire after 1745

The roots of Highland emigration lie in the transformation which so profoundly altered Highland society in the second half of the eighteenth century. In 1745, the Highlands stood poised on the edge of dramatic change, whether or not Jacobite fought Hanoverian on Culloden Moor. The 150 years preceeding the Jacobite Rebellion had brought growing involvement with southern Britain, particularly for Highland leaders; northern Scotland was steadily being drawn into southern social and economic structures. Nevertheless, the clansmen remained substantially untouched by these developments in 1745, and the radical shift from a near-feudal community to a modern commercial state was accomplished after that date. But 1745 is more than a convenient reference date. In reaction to the rebellion, Parliament passed laws that changed social and economic life in the Highlands. Southern law was more determinedly enforced there and, perhaps most significantly, southern leaders became convinced of the necessity of integrating Gaelic Scotland into the United Kingdom. The effect of the rebellion was to hasten the achievement of this integration; the years immediately after 1746 represent the point when the tide of change turned decisively against traditional society in the Highlands.

It was from the heart of eighteenth-century Gaelic Scotland that the largest number of emigrants to Glengarry County came. Western Inverness-shire lies almost in the middle of what was the Gaidheal-tachd, the Gaelic-speaking part of Scotland. To the north are Sutherland and the joint county of Ross and Cromarty; to the east, on the mountainous spine of Scotland, are Badenoch and Atholl; to the south are Argyllshire and Morvern; while off to the west are the Hebrides. With all Highlanders, the people of western Inverness shared the Gaelic inheritance of a kin-based agrarian society with a

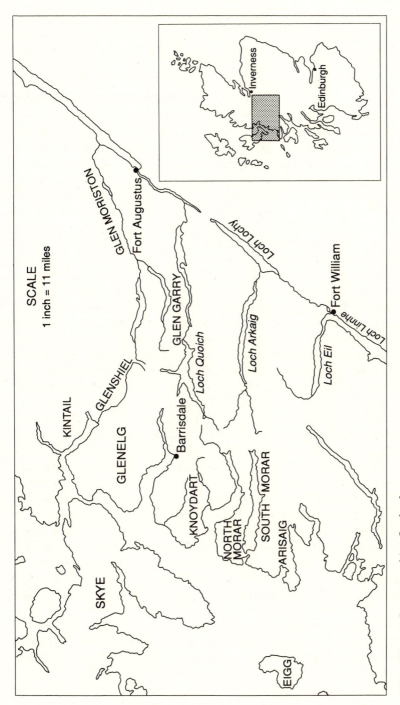

Map 1 Western Inverness-shire, Scotland

rich musical and oral literary tradition. Two clans were the most prominent in settling Glengarry County: the Macdonells of Glengarry and the McMillans of Loch Arkaig. The Macdonells, who considered themselves the heirs of the Lords of the Isles and were thoroughly Jacobite, controlled not only the Glengarry district but also Knoydart and North Morar. The McMillans and their related clansmen the McPhees and McMartins supported Cameron of Lochiel, a no less fervent believer in the Stuart cause. The periphery of western Inverness also furnished emigrants for Upper Canada. McLeods came from Glenelg, McKenzies and McLennans from Kintail, Grants from Glen Moriston, Chisholms from Strathglass, and Macdonalds from Clanranald's lands in South Morar and Eigg.

In the eighteenth century, western Inverness was considered one of the most rugged and lawless parts of the Highlands. Typical of the landscape is the area around the watersheds of Loch Arkaig and Loch Quoich, known as the "Rough Bounds," a high, flat upland in prehistoric times that was eroded by rivers and glaciers into the present east-west system of valleys and mountain ridges. Since the watershed lies near the west coast, the rivers and valleys of Knoydart, Glenelg, and Kintail are short and steep, while those of Lochiel and Glen Garry are longer and more gently graded. The old plateau remains in the many summits over 3,000 feet, with their subsidiary hills and ridges. The only land under 1,000 feet in altitude lies in narrow strips along the coastline and up the river valleys. Good arable land is therefore widely scattered and scarce.

The climate varies across western Inverness, principally with the altitude. Land along the coast of Morar, Knoydart, and Glenelg is subject to the warm currents of the North Atlantic Drift. The climate here is mild and wet, with little difference between winter and summer temperatures and an annual average of 60–100 inches of rain. The mountains and higher hills, which lie within Glenelg and Knoydart and divide Glengarry from Lochiel, have more extreme seasonal temperatures and are even wetter – up to 170 inches of rain per year in the watershed area. The inland valleys along Glen Garry, Loch Arkaig, and Loch Eil have milder temperatures than the mountains around them and rainfall drops to 80 inches or less in their eastern bounds. Geography and climate thus combine to create a rugged, spectacular land in western Inverness-shire.[1]

At the time of the 1745 uprising, society throughout this area was still based on the organization and values of the clan. The clan chiefs led their people and owned most of the clan lands. The Glengarry family estate included Abertarff on the east side of Loch Ness, the long valleys of Glen Quoich and Glen Garry together with the hills to their north and south, and the peninsulas of Knoydart and North Morar. The sale in 1769 of the Abertarff and North Morar properties to repay the greater part of Glengarry's debts marked the first step in the loss of Macdonell family lands and followers.[2] Although Glengarry owned much of Knoydart directly, roughly one-third of the peninsula was in the possession of Macdonell of Barisdale on a wadsett (a sort of mortgage)[3] from Glengarry. McDonell of Scotus owned another smaller estate in Knoydart outright. Both Barisdale and Scotus had received their lands in Knoydart as descendants of younger sons of previous Glengarry chiefs.

To the east of Knoydart, the McMillans dominated Loch Arkaig, the northern third of Cameron of Lochiel's estate. Their chief also held the land from Glen Garry south to Loch Lochy, the River Lochy, and Loch Eil, as well as the lands on the eastern shore of Loch Linnhe as far south as Ballachulish.[4] North of Knoydart was Glenelg, the mainland possession of the MacLeods of Dunvegan, Skye. MacKenzie of Seaforth, who had forfeited his lands in Kintail and Glenshiel after the 1715 rebellion, regained them in 1726. In Strathglass and Glenmoriston, the Chisholm and the Laird of Grant maintained their ancient estates. The year 1745, then, marked a time when the clans of this area still lived under the direction of their chiefs; these men were no mere landowners but paternal rulers around whom revolved economic affairs, the right to justice and much social life.

Next to the chief in social position were the tacksmen, his immediate kinsmen, who traditionally served as the chief's military lieutenants in war and as his estate managers in peace. When given a tack, or lease, usually on favourable terms, the tacksmen farmed part of the land with the help of servants and rented the remainder to subtenants; the rent paid by these subtenants generally more than paid the tacksmen's rent to the chief. Throughout the eighteenth century, however, the tacksmen's role was changing. With the decline of the clan as a fighting force, particularly after 1745, the chief came to see the tacksmen merely as an unnecessary middleman, creaming off rents that the chief could easily enjoy. Some tacksmen managed to become property owners in their own right, often by taking advantage of a chief's financial weakness, but most tacksmen were obliged to accept new leases on more rigorous terms as Highland chiefs began to rent directly to their tenants. In 1745, the tacksmen were the class of Gaelic society both most capable of benefiting from change (by virtue of their education and social position) and, paradoxically, most immediately threatened by it.

At the base of the social pyramid were the clansmen, the great majority of the Highland population. Within this group there was considerable variation in economic and social status. The chief tenants were prosperous men of standing in the community, renting substantial farms. Below them were the joint tenants and sub-tenants, who held correspondingly smaller amounts of farmland, while landless cottars and servants were the poorest element in the community. Although in the eye of Scottish law, land belonged to the chief who had legal title to it, the people believed that the chief held his property on behalf of the entire clan. Each clansman believed in his right to the use of a piece of land appropriate to his social standing and resources, somewhere on the chief's holdings.

The economic backbone of this traditional social order was a subsistence agriculture based on cattle. Blackadder's description of the economy of Skye and North Uist, although written some fifty years later, is true of this area at the time of the rebellion:

At present every Family in the Country is a Kind of independent Colony of itself, They turn up what part of the Soil is necessary to support them with Meal ... , take their own Fish, Manufacture, and make the most of the own cloaths and Husbandry utensils. Their cows supply them in Summer with Butter and Milk, after which a few of them are sold to pay for the small spot on which they live.[5]

The large estates were divided into farms of varying sizes and quality. A farm could be held by one man or, more commonly, shared by a number of tenants. Almost all of these farms had only a small amount of land suitable for growing grain; the remaining acreage was given over to pasture.[6] Each farm had rough pasture, including summer grazings known as shielings in the hills at some distance from the farmhouse. Small shelters or bothies were built on the shielings for the use of those who herded the cattle there during the short grazing season. Agricultural tools were simple and home-made. Because of the steepness of the terrain, the spade or *caschrom*, rather than the plow, was used to dig the soil. Few of the area's inhabitants had access to a mill; instead they ground their grain by hand in stone querns. Their houses were simply constructed of thatch and turf with a few pieces of homemade furniture inside.[7]

However archaic these conditions might seem now, Highland society and agriculture in fact were well adapted to the clansmen's needs. As Malcolm Gray has pointed out, older farming practices represented a balance between the physical environment and possible farming techniques on one hand and social considerations on the other. Since a large population was a military necessity, labour-saving practices in an area with no alternate employment were pointless. Instead, "any device, however laborious, that would increase ... yield [per acre] was justified."[8] The arable patches were too small for improved agrarian practices, and the climate, varying from the overwhelmingly wet and mild to the subarctic, set further limitations on agricultural technique. Traditional Highland agriculture had achieved a relatively successful balance between the needs of the people and the availability of resources.

Equally, Gaelic cultural life blossomed in the eighteenth century as older literary forms, favoured by the aristocratic bards, were succeeded by a development of the song tradition by poets and the clansmen themselves. While external social pressures in the sixteenth and seventeenth centuries had forced a major disruption in Gaelic cultural life, certain continuities were evident between Gaelic literature of the late Middle Ages and that of the pre-emigration period. The poets of the eighteenth century used the same images, close observation, and extensive detail, and expressed the same love of nature and strong religious belief as had the earlier bards.[9] In this renewal of the Gaelic cultural tradition can be seen the thread of continuity during a time of social change that so characterizes Highland society.

The precise implications for Highland development of the Jacobite rebellion of 1745 might be up for debate, but not the severe reprisals that immediately followed the revolt. The final defeat of Prince Charles Edward's army at Culloden left western Inverness-shire wide open to the victorious Hanoverian army. Most of the region's inhabitants were Jacobite in sympathy and they had formed the backbone of the Prince's army. London was determined to destroy the military power of the Highland chiefs and to punish the supporters of the rebellion. Parliament passed acts forbidding the wearing of Highland dress, disarming all clansmen, and abolishing heritable jurisdictions. Many men were attainted and some were executed, and the military was given considerable freedom to pursue rebels and establish control over the region. The government was clearly motivated both by fear of Highland military power and by contempt for feudal social organization, now long abandoned in the south. Even those clans that had remained loyal to King George were forced to comply with the new laws.

In western Inverness-shire, Cameron of Lochiel's estate was

particularly vulnerable to military reprisals, since the garrison at Fort William was located virtually in its centre.[10] In a list of damages submitted to the Forfeit Estates Commissioners, Lochiel's tenants and wadsetters claimed damages totalling £7,024 11s. 11d. incurred in 1746 and 1747. All but three of the thirty-seven farms on the estate complained of losses, which were especially heavy in the first year. Crops were completely destroyed, houses and furnishings burned or removed, and stock taken away by His Majesty's troops. Rich and poor suffered alike: Angus McPhie, tenant in Errocht, lost stock, furniture, and a house to the value of £16 15s., while Ewan Cameron, wadsetter of Errocht, lost seventy-nine great and small cows, three mares, four draught and two riding horses, a colt and a filly, two swans, seven pigs, eight sheep, silver plate, furnishings, and houses to a total value of £220 13s. 4d.[11] In a region where livestock was the principal wealth of the people, the loss of so much stock meant not just the inability to pay rents but, in many cases, extreme hardship and near starvation.

After the initial plundering by Cumberland's army, the continued presence of government authority, both in enforcing justice in this remote area and in administering estates annexed to the Crown, resulted in a significant break with the past for the clansmen. In 1747 the tenants of the Cameron estate seemed likely to refuse to permit government troops to be quartered among them. Donald Campbell, factor for the Duke of Argyll, intervened on behalf of the tenants. Campbell pointed out that the quartering of troops was usually prejudicial to the area concerned. He asked as well that Lochiel's tenants be forgiven any arrears of cess (rates or taxes) "in regard to the circumstances of the present possessors, and how much they suffered in consequence of the late Troubles."[12] Not all men in positions of authority were as conscious as Campbell of the Highlanders' difficulty in adapting to a new regime. The attitude of George Douglas, a sheriff-substitute at Fort William, represented the hardline approach that many officials followed. He believed that "in this Country when they have been very little accustomed to have the Laws dispensed amongst them we must keep up Authority even tho' some times I may be luyable to commit some errors in the execution of my Office."[13] Given this sort of attitude, the period of transition to the new legal order was likely to prove painful for the inhabitants of western Inverness-shire.

As usual after an unsuccessful rebellion, the estates of prominent rebels were forfeit to the Crown. In the aftermath of the '45, however, the British government's grim determination to eliminate the underlying causes of rebellion and to change the nature of

Highland society took them a step beyond mere confiscation. Thirteen estates were annexed to the Crown and revenue from them was set aside for the purpose "of civilizing the Inhabitants upon said Estates and other parts of the Highlands of Scotland, the promoting amongst them the Protestant Religion, good Government, Industry and Manufactures, and the Principles of Duty and Loyalty to His Majesty, His Heirs and Successors."[14] In western Inverness, Archibald Macdonell's Barisdale and Donald Cameron's Lochiel were both annexed, in 1752 and 1770 respectively.[15] The British government gave the task of administering the forfeited estates to the Scottish Barons of the Exchequer and the annexed estates to commissioners appointed for that purpose. These Edinburgh lawyers and Lowland gentlemen eagerly introduced the values and practices of the commercial economy of southern Britain to western Inverness. We will look at how the people of Barisdale and Lochiel responded to these changes in later chapters.

Before economic reform could begin, however, the government had to consolidate its position in the Highlands, since the defeat of the Jacobite army in 1746 did not immediately ensure complete government control of the north. The most obvious sign of this was the escape of Prince Charles Edward to France after several months' wandering through the western Highlands and islands. Knoydart remained a haven for Jacobites as late as 1753, in spite of naval patrols in the west and mobile military patrols on its eastern bounds. The freedom enjoyed by Archibald Macdonell of Barisdale incensed government supporters such as Mungo Campbell, factor of several forfeited estates in western Inverness. Campbell indignantly described the situation in Knoydart in 1753.

They have the insolence, Ever Since the Year 1746 to pay their Rents to the Attainted Barasdale who Since that time absolutely rules them, And ranges up and down that country and the neighbourhood with a band of Armed men dressed as well as himself, in the Highland habite, The insolence and Tyranny of this outlaw is already well known to the Government, and the military, to whom he has created a deal of trouble; He has augmented the number of his associates, since I have been named factor; And Since his having been informed of my ... resolution to make the Rents Effectual to the Crown, he had the good manners to send me anonimous Letters and Diverse verbal messages to be upon my guard in case I went to that Country.[16]

Barisdale was captured shortly after this letter was written, but both his seven years of freedom after the failure of the rebellion and his collection of rents on a forfeited estate illustrate the length of time it took for the government to gain effective control of this mountainous region.

Highland society was conservative, and the intensification of change which resulted from the political upheaval of 1745 took effect slowly. Yet arguably from the time of the Jacobite Rebellion, the pace of social and economic change in this region increased dramatically. The change that occurred in the Highlands was more sweeping than that experienced in Lowland Scotland or England at the same time. The defeat of the Jacobite uprising in 1746 meant that, for the first time, the Highland area was brought under the direct rule of a central government in the south. The patriarchial and traditional society of the north was to be integrated into the capitalistic, oligarchic kingdom of Great Britain. A combination of government policy and new geographic and social links were to transform the Highlands into a replica of lowland Scotland, and the north was to participate in the economic and social concerns of the southern kingdom. At the same time, however, England and southern Scotland were entering a period of social change that ultimately resulted in the emergence of the first modern industrial state. The Highlanders were subject to a part of this tremendous change at a time when their own society was still less complex and more traditionally organized than that of southern Britain. The period from 1746 to 1815 stands as a time of the disintegration of the traditional order in the Highlands and of its integration as an appendage into the modern British state.

The transformation that took place in western Inverness after the '45 did not occur easily or immediately. The conquest of the Highlands had been painful and the new rule of southern law was established slowly. Active Jacobitism may have ended, but family or group interests could still provide a focus for opposition to official policies.[17] The change and conflict found in Highland society during the second half of the eighteenth century revolved as much around cultural as economic issues. Until 1745, Lowlanders had paid little attention to the Highland people and culture; the region was inaccessible and seemingly contained nothing of value but cattle. But after sixty years of Jacobite discontent, the Lowlanders turned their attention northwards to the people who had "nearly subverted the constitution of these powerful kingdoms."[18] The letters and accounts of numerous travellers and government officials expressed a shocked distaste for the "primitive" way of life they found there. It was under such conditions of disdain for older cultural traditions that the intensely conservative society of the Highlands, weakened by the events of the previous hundred years, experienced social and economic transformation after 1745.

CHAPTER THREE

Barisdale

The transformation of the Barisdale family from Jacobite outlaws to improving farmers symbolizes the political and economic transformation that took place in western Inverness after 1750. As we have seen, Archibald Macdonell participated in the '45 and then evaded capture for seven years, taking refuge in the mountains of Knoydart. After his arrest in 1753, Barisdale was imprisoned until a pardon from King George III enabled him to serve with British forces in the Seven Years' War. (His brother Alexander served with the British army in General Fraser's regiment and fell at the capture of Quebec in 1759.)

The reduction of Archibald Macdonell's regiment to half-pay at the end of war made it necessary for him to look for another source of income to support his family. Highland tradition and perhaps personal preference pointed to agriculture, and so in 1763 Macdonell applied to the Commissioners of the Annexed Estates for a lease of several farms on his forfeited property. In his application Macdonell explained his change in outlook:

he has turned his thoughts to farming and Grazing, for which his Disposition to active life gives him a naturall turn, And humbly thinks that with the Countenance of the Board of Annexed Estates his labours might now be of use, not only for the support of his family, But also as an example to others in a quarter where Indolence and Ignorance have hitherto so much prevailed, that the Ideas of improvement are received with aversion, and which aversion might perhaps be most easily and gently overruled by the Example of a native now enlightened by Experience, and determined to duty, both by the ties of gratitude and necessity.[1]

In this application, Macdonell appealed directly to the commissioners' ambition to introduce improved agriculture to the High-lands. The request was granted; Macdonell was given possession of the farm of Carnoch on the southeastern boundary of the estate, where he still lived as an improving tenant in 1784 when Barisdale was disannexed and returned to its owner, Duncan McDonell of Glengarry.

Barisdale's "enlightenment" was by no means unique and illustrates the radical alteration in the attitudes and behaviour of many Highland gentlemen after 1745.[2] In youth, Macdonell was brought up in the Highland tradition of personal rule over an estate, with a profitable sideline in cattle rustling. In middle age he accepted government control over his property, spoke of High-landers as ignorant and lazy, and hoped to introduce agricultural improvement to his forfeited estate. This transformation shows his acceptance of three significant factors which changed the face of Highland society after 1745. First, the imposition of southern authority and law deprived Highland justice of its personal character and made unnecessary the organization of the clan as a defensive unit. Second, the active adoption of the individualistic goals and values of commercial capitalism seriously undermined the inter-dependent social and economic relationships of all the people of the clan. And third, the southern valuation of Gaelic culture as feudal and outdated was unlikely to allow for a compromise between Highland and Lowland objectives. The movement of Archibald Macdonell of Barisdale – and of many other Highland gentlemen alive in 1745, or their sons – from a commitment to traditional Highland society to an avowal of southern values and goals both reflected and contributed to the transformation of the Highlands in the second half of the eighteenth century.

In contrast, the clansmen of Barisdale responded more conser-vatively to the new social order than did the gentlemen. In the following pages, I draw a picture of Barisdale in 1755, when society and agriculture remained essentially traditional, and then analyse the reaction of the clansmen to economic and social change on the estate over the next thirty years. The officials of the Annexed Estates sought to improve agriculture and provide basic facilities such as roads, bridges, churches, and schools; the clansmen adapted readily to those changes, which were reasonably compatible with traditional objectives and were of obvious benefit to them. On the other hand, the tenants were also forced to accept a shift in authority over estate matters and questions of justice from paternal clan leaders to an impersonal, distant government. Nevertheless, local communities were left intact and in possession of ancestral lands. The people of

Barisdale adapted to the change which occurred between 1755 and 1784 because southern administrators did not threaten the existence of the community on the land.

The estate of Barisdale occupied less than half of the peninsula of Knoydart on the west coast opposite the island of Skye. Western Inverness as a whole is rugged country, and the mountains and lochs of Knoydart are spectacular. The land is alpine, rising sharply from the sea, and the eastern part of the peninsula is dominated by six peaks over 2,900 feet and their subsidiary ridges. The peninsula is bounded to the north and south by two long and very deep sea lochs resembling fjords. Four narrow river valleys, each with a small amount of flat land near its mouth, provide most of the arable ground. To eighteenth-century eyes, this wild terrain was both unattractive and menacing. Surveyor William Morison described the area near Loch Nevis's head as having "the most horrid appearance in nature and by far the most terrible in Knoydart[;] Nothing to be seen but perpendicular and projecting Rocks, one lying above another, without pile of grass."[3] Even today, the roughness of the land makes travel from place to place within the peninsula difficult and limits access to the rest of mainland Scotland. All the physical factors that made agriculture and economic development precarious in the Highlands – lack of good soil, poor climate, distance from large markets, and few mineral resources – are found together here.

In this rugged country of limited resources, considerable demographic pressure was building after the middle of the eighteenth century. In 1764 some 960 Highlanders lived in Knoydart, perhaps 450 of them on the Barisdale estate.[4] Nine years earlier, the factor of Barisdale prepared a detailed report for the Commissioners describing the thirty-eight tenants on the estate and their families;[5] these 249 people likely represented more than 50% of the population of Barisdale. The tenant population was remarkably young: 32% of the children were under ten, while another 18.5% was between ten and seventeen. Of the tenant population over seventeen, women outnumbered men 69 to 55. In contrast, Michael Flinn has shown that in Webster's 1755 census, children under twenty formed 44% of the Scottish population.[6] The higher-than-usual ratio of women to men in Barisdale may in part have been the result of the unsuccessful Jacobite campaign of 1745–6. But far more significant is the large percentage of children under the age of ten in the Barisdale community. Whatever the cause of the anomaly, this concentration of population would have resulted in dramatic population growth by the end of the century.

While tenant families were seemingly growing quickly, there is no evidence available concerning the rate of growth of the rest of the population – the cottars and servants who did not hold land at all and who worked as day labourers. Indeed, even the number of people other than tenants resident on the Barisdale estate is not known. Since the tenants had little cash income, the nontenant population was correspondingly worse off. In 1755 a labourer in Barisdale earned at best 18s. per year, two pairs of brogues, and his maintenance; in addition he was given a small plot of ground for planting oats. Servant maids earned 6s., brogues, and maintenance, while herdsmen received 32s. and the same in shoes and support. There are few references to these people in the reports and correspondence of the Annexed Estates' factor, a fact which might be a confirmation of their relatively small numbers.[7]

In 1755 Barisdale was still a close-knit, traditional Highland community. Since even second and third cousins were considered close family, kinship created a dense network of relationships among nuclear families and gave an intimate quality to daily life that the official record only occasionally reflects. In 1755, the farm of Sallachry was shared by a father and a son, and that of Glaschoille by a father and son-in-law; four tenants, three of them siblings, held Achagline and Gorsten, while three brothers rented the farm of Riddaroch. The same pattern is also evident in a 1767 list of tenants, which, through its use of patronymics, also points to the kinship ties which linked tenants of separate farms.[8] In this kin-based community, the landlord might have legal title, but the tenants believed that they had a *right* to farm the land – a belief that was strengthened by the communal practice of certain farming routines. Each tenant on a particular farm owned a number of cattle, but these were herded together and grazed freely over the entire farm and many other farm operations were carried on in common. Small villages or *bailtean* grew up on the farms and provided an ideal home for the development of a rich folk culture. The tremendous vitality and meaning given to daily life by this culture in turn provided an incentive for maintaining traditional community ties.

Like the rest of Knoydart, up to the 1750s Barisdale seemed to have existed outside of the reach of the government, religious, and educational authorities that shaped southern British society. Coll Macdonell's successful career in the 1730s (he sold protection from cattle rustling) and his son Archibald's avoidance of capture for seven years after the rebellion underline the total failure of the British government to extend the rule of law into this area. Aside from one justice of the peace, resident some twenty-four miles away by road at Glenelg, the nearest magistrate was at Fort William, more than forty miles from any part of the Barisdale estate. In these circumstances, it is not surprising that the inhabitants submitted their disputes to the arbitration of the clergy. But here also the people of Barisdale were subject to an authority not recognized in the southern kingdoms. The Presbyterian church had made no inroads here, and the people of Knoydart were all Roman Catholics. They were ministered to by two priests, Alexander Macdonell and Angus McLauchlan, worshipping openly at Dr McDonnell's home on the Loch Nevis coast. The factor reported that the priests had "the impudence to carry their influence so far as to inflict corporal punishment upon offenders, which indeed is partly encouraged by reason that there is no Sheriff-Substitute ... in the whole country."[9] Schools, which were so important a part of Lowland Scottish life, had not penetrated into Knoydart. Aristocractic Gaelic learning and education had disappeared by this time, since the gentry, whose support for education was essential, had successfully been weaned from their role as leaders of Gaelic culture. Nevertheless, Gaelic popular culture flourished in the eighteenth century, and the inhabitants of Barisdale, like other Highlanders, maintained a vital tradition of music, song, and story.

Until the middle of the eighteenth century, the people of Barisdale did not generally accept the jurisdiction of British justice; nor did they necessarily share certain of its basic assumptions. We can see the clash between two separate legal systems in southern officials' calling lawless what the clansmen regarded as justice. Even the unsympathetic Mungo Campbell acknowledged that the Barisdale residents were "the most honest commonality upon the west coast" – they never stole from each other, since people who lived close to subsistence could not tolerate pilfering among themselves. But cattle rustling was another matter; Campbell suspected that Barisdale gave refuge to some "notorious" McMillans and McPhees from a neighbouring part of the Lochiel estate. Political differences too could lead the people of Barisdale to disregard the law, as in 1748, when the Macdonell gentlemen induced their Barisdale tenants to hide part of the total rent, customarily paid to the landlord, from the Forfeited Estates' surveyor, David Bruce. Instead the gentlemen collected this part of the rent and paid it to their chief Glengarry.[10] As late as 1755, a gap existed between the customary law respected by the people of Barisdale and the laws of Parliament.

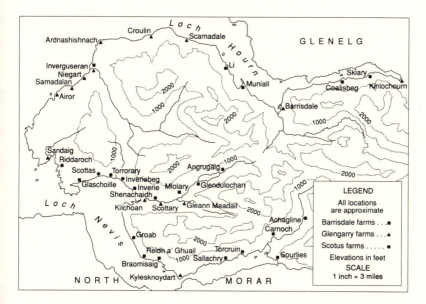

Map 2 Knoydart, c. 1771

Sources: Ordnance Survey of Scotland; SRO, RHP 112, Plan of the annexed estate of Barrisdale, William Morison, 1771; SRO, GD44/25/29, "Division and Arrangement of Knoydart"; Fraser-Mackintosh, "Macdonells of Scotus," 79–80; and AO, Father Ewen John Macdonald, box 6, envelope 2, B-1-14, list of place names in Morar and Knoydart.

Not only was social life in Barisdale very distinct from that of southern Britain, but so was work. The physical geography of Knoydart severely limits the use of land in the peninsula; the demographic layout of the Barisdale estate reflected such physical limitations as well as traditional Gaelic social values. Together these factors produced the traditional agricultural community documented by the officers of the Annexed Estates when they first surveyed the property in 1755. The Barisdale estate then consisted of sixteen farms (seventeen in 1771) with a total area of over 13,000 acres. In this mountainous region, the farmhouses and tiny plots of arable land were strung out along the coastline, while the average size of a farm was over 700 acres, reflecting both the social institution of joint farming and the difficulty of obtaining sufficient grazing land.[11]

Four of the Barisdale estate farms – Skiary, Coalisbeg, Muniall, and Li – were located on the southern side of Loch Hourn. The farms extended westward ten miles from the eastern limit of the estate near Kinlochourn, but excluded Barrisdale farm itself, which

Table 1
Estate of Barisdale, 1755

| Name of farm | No. of tenants | Acreage | | | Cattle | Sheep | Horses | Goats |
		Arable	Good pasture	Hill and moss				
Skiary	1	2	4	557	10	20	5	20
Coalisbeg	1	0.5	2	870	8	10	3	9
Muniall & Camusdoun	2	2	4	484	39	30	11	30
Li	4	4	12	534	39	42	9	50
Inverguseran and Glenguseran	1	1.5	4	76	35	12	6	12
Riddaroch	3	2	16	793	27	39	4	8
Glaschoille	1	4	4	1151	20	25	5	25
Inverie				582				
Miolary	7	10	10	575	109	70	17	62
Groab	2	2	4	300	13	25	1	21
Reidh a'Ghuail	2	2	4	468	12	16	0	23
Braomisaig	1	3	4	565	50	20	3	20
Sallachry	3	3	3	810	32	30	0	35
Torcruin	1	2	1	460	12	20	1	15
Culnacarnoch and	2	4.5	3	1100	42	35	4	45
Carnochroy	1	3	1	1100	23	20	3	20
Achagline and	2	3	2	884	35	33	4	40
Gorsten	2	2	2	884	33	30	4	45
Sourlies	2	2	4	1027	12	10	4	10

Sources: *Statistics of the Annexed Estates, 1755–6*, 4–5, with the exception of the figures for hill and moss land, which are found in SRO RHP112, Plan of the Annexed Estate of Barisdale, 1771.

was (confusingly) part of the Glengarry estate. Located on the western coast of Knoydart facing Skye, Inverguseran was isolated from the other annexed farms. Nine of the remaining farms on the estate lay along the northern coast of Loch Nevis, from Riddaroch (near the modern Torr Mor) to Sourlies at the head of the loch. Three other farms were located inland on river valleys, Miolary on the Inverie River, and Gorsten and Achagline on the Carnoch River. The Barisdale farms were not single entities neatly divided from one another. Much of the grazing land lay far from the centres of permanent settlement; hill pasture belonging to one farm might be closer to another, while a few farms had no hill grazing at all. This erratic land distribution had been created over centuries by a combination of economic, political, and geographic pressures. In general, the Barisdale farms were considered somewhat inferior to the other Glengarry farms in Knoydart – possibly because the estate of Barisdale had gone to a younger son of Glengarry at the beginning of the eighteenth century.[12]

A good picture of the agriculture traditionally practiced in this rugged land emerges from the statistics collected by Mungo Campbell in 1755 and presented in Table 1. The most striking characteristic of Barisdale agriculture is the scarcity of arable and pasture land. No single tenant farmed more than four acres of arable or six acres of good pasture, and the average holdings were much smaller than this – 1.4 and 2.2 acres respectively. Few tenants could supply their families with grain year-round, and livestock had to survive the winter on hill pasture, since no grass was saved for winter fodder. It was not made clear in Campbell's statistics whether the stock listed belonged exclusively to the tenants or if it represented the soum (or grazing capacity) of a farm and included animals owned by farm servants or cottars given free grazing rights as part of their wages.[13] Barisdale could support 551 black cattle, (tenants owned between six and fifty each) as well as 487 sheep of the small native breed kept for family use, an average of thirteen per family. The number of goats owned by each family showed the greatest range: out of a total of 490 goats, the minimum per family was three and the maximum twenty-five. Finally there were eighty-four horses on the Barisdale estate, an average of two per tenant.

As elsewhere in the Highlands, black cattle were the most important livestock kept in Barisdale. From the yearly sale of a few cattle, the tenant received his only cash income, much of which went to pay rent. In addition, cow's milk, butter, and cheese formed an important part of the everyday diet. Sheep and goats provided wool for clothing, milk and cheese, and what little meat the tenants ate. Horses were used primarily as pack animals and carried peat, fertilizer, and other loads. The quality and the amount of land and the number and type of livestock varied from farm to farm in Barisdale, but these differences were really only a question of degree; none of the tenants were wealthy men. Black cattle were their principal source of income, and in 1771 these sold for £2 at three years of age.

The yearly work cycle in Barisdale began in the spring with the planting of potatoes and a little gray oats and barley. The tenants obtained a sixfold return on each boll (or six imperial bushels) of oats and barley sown, double the yield achieved in other parts of the Highlands. This higher productivity may have been the result of the use of seaweed and seashell as fertilizer. Aside from these cereal crops, the tenants planted no gardens and grew no vegetables. There were no enclosed fields on the estate and the boundaries of farms were unfenced, since they had long been established by custom.[14] In summer and early fall, when crops were in the ground, tenants took their cattle to the better grazing of the hilltops; any milk not consumed there was made into butter and cheese. They exchanged any surplus dairy products, the only export other than cattle, in Skye for oatmeal. There was no mill on the estate, so when the tenants harvested their crops, they "set fire to the sheaves until the stalk and the grain are separated, and then they gather what of the grain remains unburnt, which they grind with a hand instrument made for that purpose called a quearn, which produces a sort of coarse meal, very bad in appearance, but which the natives reckon better than any other."[15] In winter the people cared for their cattle and spaded the fields for next year's crop; only at Inverie was the arable land flat and large enough to use a plow and horses. Herring, which filled the lochs in autumn and which the tenants salted down, supplied food for the next six months of the year. This cycle of traditional economic activity left the people of Barisdale with long periods of time with little to do. There was no spare grain left for distilling, so whisky was imported from eastern Inverness to whisky houses at Inverie and Sourlies where it was "drunk in great abundance" and contributed, according to Campbell, to the tenants' great poverty.

The traditional agriculture of Barisdale seems unsophisticated, perhaps even archaic, to twentieth-century readers, but these farming practices in fact represented a balanced use of the available resources. As critical an observer as Archibald Menzies, the general inspector of the Annexed Estates, made this point when he toured the west coast estates. Menzies, the agent of an improving landlord, commented enthusiastically on the practices of the Barisdale tenants:

It is remarkable the skill they shew in chusing their pasturages for the different seasons. It is not the local situation but the quality of the grasses they study. Every farmer is so far a botanist as to distinguish the particular season each grass is in perfection. I have seen some of their wintering ground very high and exposed and at a very great distance from the sea, when at the same time they had grassing close by the sea and where no snow lay in winter. Yet the quality of the grass as winter grass determined them to chuse the high, stormy country.[16]

Menzies noted with approval the impact of this botanical knowledge on the cattle stocks of Barisdale; he was impressed by the tenants' skill and knowledge in managing cattle, and he believed that the cattle were "of a quality [equal] to any of the West Highlands." The tenants moved their cattle regularly from one pasture to another, ensuring that all their stock had the appropriate grazing: milk cows were brought in first, store and yeld (dry) cattle next, and horses and sheep last in grazing over any particularly good field. The people of Barisdale were also experts in the breeding of cattle and in the treatment of animal disease. Since the rugged terrain and poor soil of the area did not allow for the development of arable farming, Menzies regarded the rearing of cattle as the prime agricultural activity. For all their isolation and unsophisticated farming techniques, these people were, to one experienced observer, able and conscientious farmers.

Mungo Campbell's resignation as factor of Barisdale in 1759 signaled an end to the first stage of implementing change on the estate. His successor, Henry Butter, who served as factor from 1759 until the estate was disannexed in 1784, worked enthusiastically at making effective the Commissioners of the Annexed Estates' program of civilizing the Highlands. Butter had little sympathy for either the gentlemen or the clansmen of Barisdale. He referred to the "Most Despotic Government of Barisdale" and described the people as "McDonalds formerly Dependent upon the Glengarry Family and all of them papists and too much under the Slavish Guidance of their priests."[17] Yet Butter soon claimed that the commissioners' management of the Barisdale estate was having a good effect on the disposition of the inhabitants; the clansmen were learning habits of industry and methods of agricultural improvement which would "Wean them from the former Dependence upon their Gentlemen and Leaders."

During the early 1760s Butter planned to introduce scientific farming based on English and southern Scottish models into Barisdale. A first step was to encourage tenants to build good stone houses with proper interior divisions. Butter considered such houses essential since "a person Living in a Miserable hut Without any accommodation can never be expected to enter with Spirit upon any Improvement."[18] While some of the west Highland gentry had lived in stone houses, the adoption of such structures by tenants generally was new and symptomized the influence of southern practices. The next step was to build dykes and fences between the farms to prevent cattle from wandering from one farm to another and on low ground to permit the raising of winter fodder. The factor also rationalized the number and type of cattle each farm could properly support and planned to permit no one to graze more than their soum.[19] By 1767 Henry Butter was able to introduce a plan, with the approval of the Barisdale tenants, which emphasized the orderly use of the land. The small amount of arable was strictly regulated; one-third was to be tilled each year in rotation. Between each crop of oats, a crop of pease or other green vegetable was to be grown, and potatoes were to be planted on uncultivated ground so as to increase the amount of arable land. The soil was to be manured with seaweed, if available, or with dung from nearby pastures.[20]

Butter was sufficiently pleased with the improving spirit shown by the tenants that he refused to support an application from an army officer for a lease of two of the Barisdale farms. In 1769, Lieutenant Robert MacLeod, who had studied farming in England, requested a forty-two-year lease of the farms of Li and Camusdoun and Muniall, which were (he stated) "in a rugged uncultivated State and neither proper Houses nor Inclosures upon them." Butter denied MacLeod's claim and listed the many improvements the tenants of the two farms had made. In addition to stone houses on both farms, soil dykes were being built on the boundary between them. The tenants of Muniall and Camusdoun had already made walled kale yards and brought shell sand from Glenelg to fertilize their soil. The commissioners, who refused MacLeod's request and maintained the "improving" tenants in possession of their farms, showed themselves willing to sustain local landholders, if some chance of improvement existed.[21]

The Barisdale tenants showed considerable interest in Butter's reforms. Some borrowed money from the commissioners to build fences, promising to repay the loan with interest at 5% after the first three years.[22] By 1768 the tenants of Riddaroch, Groab, and Glaschoille, like those of Muniall and Li, had built stone houses and dykes. While the factor may have exerted some pressure on the tenants, the latter found many of the changes he proposed relatively easy to accept. Improved farming made their lands more productive but did not threaten their right to a share in a farm. Indeed, one of the benefits of the Annexed Estates' administration was their introduction of leases to Barisdale. In 1776 the tenants of four farms signed twenty-one-year leases, as did those of another four farms in 1777. Lieutenant Archibald Macdonell and Jean Gordon, widow of Glengarry's brother, both obtained forty-one-year leases of their farms. Leases offered a security that, after the unrest and annexation

Table 2
Estate of Barisdale, 1771

Name of farm	Arable	Good grass (acres)	No. of houses	No. of servants	Oats/ sown/ reaped (bolls*)	Soum	Cows	Sheep	Goats
Skiary	3	—	—	—	2/6	16	—	—	—
Coalisbeg	—	2	—	—	—	—	—	—	—
Muniall	7	61	—	4	3/9	30	30	20	—
Li	3	42	—	6	3/9	40	40	few	few
Inverguseran	2	5	16 creel	—	—	—	—	—	—
Riddaroch	12	1	—	8	6/18	48	48	100	20
Glaschoille	8	6	—	3	5/15	30	30	40	40
Inverie	8	25	—	—	—	65	—	—	—
Miolary	4	—	—	2	3/10	36	36	40	30
Groab	3	204**	2 stone	4	3/8	—	28	30	—
Reidh a'Ghuail	3	—	6 creel	3	2.5/7	20	20	30	13
Braomisaig	3	—	11 creel	6	2/6	45	45	—	—
Sallachry	2	10	1 stone 10 creel	3	2/5	33	31	40	50
Torcruin	2	—	—	3	2.3/7	22	20	40	20
Carnoch	8	5	—	11	7/24	111	105	120	80
Achagline	2	—	—	"some"	2.5/7	60	50	60	80
Sourlies	5	—	—	3	1.7/6	34	31	35	30

*1 boll = 6 imperial bushels
**The remarkable number of acres in good grass in Groab cannot be explained.
Sources: SRO, E741/46 and RHP112, Plan of the Annexed Estate of Barisdale, 1771.

of the 1740s and 1750s, the Barisdale tenants had come to regard as important and that they actually preferred to cash payments for their improvements.[23]

By 1771, significant change could also be observed in the level of agricultural production in Barisdale. Statistics are available (see Tables 1 and 2) for the ten farms of Muniall, Riddaroch, Glaschoille, Groab, Reidh à Ghuail, Sallachry, Torcruin, Carnoch, Achagline, and Sourlies in 1755 and 1771. The number of cattle on these farms increased by 31% from 300 to 393 over sixteen years. The largest proportional increase was in Sourlies, where the number of cattle rose 150% from twelve to thirty-one. The largest single increase took place on Carnoch, where Lieutenant Archibald Macdonell had forty more cows, an increase of more than 60%. Since the tenants' cash income was derived principally from the sale of cattle, the larger number of cattle raised in 1771 indicated a significant increase in the return of seven of the farms.

The number of sheep kept in Barisdale rose more rapidly during the same period, from 313 to 515; this 64% increase is another indication of the change taking place on the estate. Two farms were responsible for a large part of this increase. Riddaroch had sixty-one more sheep, an increase of 156%, and Carnoch had an additional sixty-five. Only two farms carried fewer sheep in 1771 and these had minimal losses of three and ten animals. It is intriguing to speculate on the type of sheep bred in Barisdale in 1771; in his report Morison merely commented that the sheep were small-sized and hardy. In contrast, Henry Butter reported to the Commissioners in 1766 that he had "made tryal two year ago of the middle Seized Black faced Sheep from the Neighbourhood of Douglas and they have done very well; and he has reason to think that Rams of that kind of Sheep would greatly mend the breed of the Highland Sheep which are small and bad wooled."[24] It is thus quite possible that the larger herds of sheep on these farms in Barisdale were a cross between the native Highland sheep and the black-faced Cheviot. In a preview of the trend in the last two decades of the eighteenth century, the proportion of sheep to cattle thereafter began to increase. In 1755 there were virtually as many sheep as cattle on the ten farms, 313 to 300; five farms had more sheep than cattle, five had fewer. But by 1771 there were 515 sheep to 393 cattle, and nine of the ten farms had more sheep than cattle.

Little substantial change was evident in other aspects of Barisdale farming. Only Muniall and Li significantly increased their grass and good pasture acreage, Muniall from four to sixty-one acres, and Li from twelve to forty-two acres. Muniall, Riddaroch, Glaschoille, and Sourlies added three to ten acres to their arable land, perhaps as a result of new land being cultivated for potatoes. No reason is given for the decline in the yield of oats noted in 1771; the figures for that year are half those reported by Mungo Campbell in 1755 but close to the Highland average. The large number of goats still found in 1771 is surprising in light of the factor's continued requests that the tenants get rid of these forest-destroying animals. Instead, on the eight farms for which there is comparative data, the number of goats grew from 266 to 333. While the large amount of livestock on the Barisdale estate in 1771 may in part be proof of the beneficial effects of improvement, it may also reflect the increasing size of the human population of Barisdale. The greater number of cattle could provide more income with which to buy meal, while larger herds of sheep and goats might supply more food and wool.

Agricultural improvement made slow but steady progress in Barisdale during the 1760s and 1770s. Butter had to make evident the advantages of specific reforms before they were accepted, and not all of the tenants adopted the same improvements at once. Lieutenant Archibald Macdonell, who wholeheartedly managed the farm of Carnoch on "improving" principles, was an important example to the other tenants. By and large, the Annexed Estates' commissioners kept the tenants in possession of their farms throughout this thirty-year period. The commissioners removed tenants who could no longer stock or care for their farms, pay the rent, or keep peace with their neighbours, just as Highland land-lords had always done.[25] But for the most part, between 1755 and 1784, farms remained in the hands of the same tenants or their heirs, a tendency that was reinforced by the giving of leases in the mid-1770s.[26] This respect for the tenants' right to land was essential to the degree of success which the commissioners' efforts to introduce improvement enjoyed. Feeling relatively secure in the possession of their land, the tenants were able to adopt, at a modest pace, new agricultural ideas.

But agricultural reform was not the only means by which the commissioners of the Annexed Estates attempted to "civilize" the Highlands; they also paid considerable attention to the development of basic social institutions and services and of other natural resour-ces. Since with the exception of Inverness there were no villages of any size in the Highlands in 1745, the commissioners encouraged the growth of small commercial centres as part of a program of increasing manufactures and eliminating Highland "idleness."[27] Mungo Campbell suggested Inverie as the most appropriate site for a village in Barisdale, and shortly after the end of the Seven Years' War, five disbanded soldiers and sailers were settled there. Each was provided with a house, three acres of land, and a bounty; in return, all agreed to become fishermen. A few inhabitants of Barisdale, displaced by agricultural improvements during the 1760s, were given homes as "King's Cottagers" in Inverie, where they were expected to practise a trade. Plans such as this enjoyed limited success; one discharged soldier, John Macdonald who had been given the changehouse (or alehouse) at Inverie, squandered the money needed to equip the house. The changehouse was taken away from him but he still received a house and a few acres in the village. Similarly, just three years after the disbanded soldiers were accommodated in Inverie, the factor had to write to the commissioners to ask what should be done with the unused bounty and nets.[28]

Fish, seaweed, and timber were the natural resources considered most likely to provide employment in Barisdale and draw in-habitants to the new villages. Henry Butter firmly believed that the people of Barisdale and neighbouring districts could make a living from the herring fishing in lochs Hourn and Nevis, if given some assistance. The villages where the fishermen lived would in turn increase the value of the farms and provide the tenants with the capital needed to improve them. But with one exception both the inhabitants and the disbanded soldiers and sailors failed to establish a commercial fishery at Inverie. The tenants of Groab, John and Donald McDonald, were the exception; they employed two boats in the herring fishing in Loch Nevis.[29] The commissioners and the factor also encouraged forestry in Barisdale. The farm of Coalisbeg on the shore of Loch Hourn was assessed as capable of growing a fir forest; its tenant was removed to another part of the estate and over 320 acres of trees were planted by 1771.[30]

Seaware or seaweed was another product of the estate, and it existed on all farms with a shoreline. Miolary, Achagline, and Carnochroy had no seaweed, while Culnacarnoch, Inverie, and Riddaroch did not have enough to meet their requirements for fertilizer. All these farms were permitted to take the seaweed needed for that purpose from their neighbours. Once every three years, the remaining seaweed-producing farms cut the weed that grew on their shores to make kelp. In 1769 the kelp available on Barisdale was advertised for sale, but the only offer made was 10s. a ton. This was "the Common price paid formerly to the Proprietors for Kelp Shores in that Neighbourhood" and it was made by Archibald MacDonald of Achagline, the ground officer of the estate.[31]

The commissioners were saved the expense of a grist mill in Knoydart when McDonell of Scotus built one on his estate and permitted the tenants of Barisdale to use it without charge. The commissioners did, however, help pay for the building of roads and bridges in Barisdale. As early as October 1761 Henry Butter pointed out that the Inverie River, which divided the estate in two, was frequently impassable. He requested £20 from the board and promised to raise £5 locally to build the necessary bridge; by 1764 the commissioners had paid a total of £89 4s. for the Inverie bridge. Road-making was a local responsibility but the commissioners granted £10 for the purchase of tools needed for the job. Even so, the tenants considered road-building a great grievance since they had to travel long distances in order to do the work. These roads and bridges were intended both to save lives previously at risk in travelling and to give access to schools and similar institutions. "Opening an easy and constant Communication" would "Greatly facilitate the Civilizing of these Remote and Wild parts of the Highlands, and Improving the same."[32] Yet in spite of Butter's diligence in building roads and bridges, Barisdale remained isolated by its terrain;

the work of the Annexed Estates' administration was only a preliminary step towards achieving good communication with the south.

The remoteness of Barisdale had long limited access to an English education, since the tenants could not afford to send their children to the distant parish school. In 1760 Butter suggested that there was a need for a school on each of the Annexed Estates, to inculcate "the Principles of the Protestant Religion, Good Government and Loyalty to his Majesty." After some searching, Butter found a man whom he believed would be a suitable schoolmaster for Barisdale. James MacPherson had taught school for several years in Rannoch, Perthshire, and was considered a man capable of teaching "Papists." On 9 December 1762 the commissioners appointed MacPherson schoolmaster at Inverie. He was provided with a schoolhouse and a plot of enclosed ground at a cost of £25 and £10 respectively. His salary was to be larger than the usual £16 13s. 4d., because of the isolation of Barisdale and the religion professed by its inhabitants.[33] The results achieved by this investment in local education over the twenty years to 1784 were not entirely what the factor and the commissioners hoped for. In spite of this long instruction by a Protestant schoolmaster, the people remained steadfastly Roman Catholic. But the Scottish Roman Catholic clergy had abandoned their support of the Jacobite cause by the end of this period, and the Roman Catholic population was no longer associated with opposition to central government.

At the beginning of the period of forfeiture, Gaelic language and culture were the only means of communication and expression in Barisdale, since only five people on the estate spoke English. While Gaelic continued to dominate estate life, a significant change occurred when the tenants accepted formal schooling on the Lowland model. In 1755 three people in the community could read and write. Although schools were first introduced to Barisdale through the efforts of the commissioners, by March 1779 tenants from the southern part of the estate were demanding access to a school for their children. Angus Gillis and Ewen, John, Angus, Donald, and Samuel MacDonald fixed their marks to a petition pointing out that they

have a number of young Children fit for being sent to school, That they are unable to procure from their own funds any Master to their Children, That the Schoolmaster ... is altogether inaccessible to them on account of the Distance ... That a much Larger Portion of the Estate of Barasdale Lyes in the Neighbourhood of your petitioners than in the adjacencies or the present Station of the School, That in imitation of the Ambulatory rounds the Schools of the ben [*sic*] society Make for the Benefit of Children in Different parts, It is the Earnest Request of Your Petitioners that the School be Removed from Inveruiemore To Some Convenient place in this Neighbourhood.[34]

Henry Butter supported their petition, since the number of scholars at Inverie had fallen and he believed that it would be advantageous for every district of the estate to have the benefit of a school. The commissioners accepted this proposal and the tenants were asked to provide the master with a schoolhouse and grass for two cows.[35] With this petition, the tenants of Barisdale revealed a new interest in a formal English education and their willingness to accept a language originating in southern Britain.

The legal, social and economic changes set in motion after the 1745 uprising began a transformation of Highland society affecting estates owned by the government as well as those controlled by Highland chiefs. The commissioners of the Annexed Estates shielded those properties from some of the more exploitative aspects of change and exposed the estates more thoroughly to others. On the Barisdale estate, the years of administration by the commissioners (1755–84) saw significant steps taken to change that isolated, traditional Gaelic community. The very fact that it was managed for thirty years by a group of men who had no traditional ties to the estate must, in the long run, have fundamentally challenged the inhabitants' conception of the relationship between themselves, the land, and the landlord. The traditional belief was that the land belonged to the people, although the chief and his tacksmen governed and profited more directly from it. When Barisdale's land was forfeited and then administered by southern officials, the people were made aware, in the most dramatic fashion, that the land might well be taken from them. During the years of annexation, the Crown replaced the clan chief or his representative, and the relationship between landlord and tenant became essentially commercial in nature. While tending to push the tenants in the direction of improved farming, the commissioners were generally fair, and in some instances more generous than neighbouring landlords. This experience of an impersonal, commercial, landlord-tenant relationship was one of the most significant changes that the people of Barisdale experienced during this thirty-year period.

The purpose of annexation was to "civilize" the Highlands or to make them resemble the modern commercial state in the south. Thirty years was not long enough to transform a society so completely, but the commissioners made some progress towards their goal in Barisdale. The conquest of the Highlands and the thorough application of the law there forced the inhabitants of Barisdale to obey the same laws that governed lowland Scotland. Agricultural improvement brought at least partial adoption of southern forms of housing, fencing, and crop management, and the Barisdale tenants were as pleased to accept leases as their southern counterparts. Although the attempt to establish a fishing industry at Inverie failed, the settlement there did become the area's only village. The commissioners established the school as a vehicle for cultural and religious change, and although the inhabitants were not influenced by Protestant doctrine, they accepted new educational practices. This acceptance was crucial in the long term, since the bias of the school curriculum was nontraditional, English, and commercial.

The Annexed Estates' administration broke one support of traditional society – the power and authority of the clan chief – and at least threatened another, the notion of clan ownership of its own land. Other men in the community were capable of taking the place of the absent chief; the clergy and the tacksmen could be accepted as replacements, since the loss of a leader did not destroy Gaelic society's respect for authority. The effect of southern intervention in Highland life may well have been an increased reliance on the kindred and on local community leaders. The extended family had always been important in Highland life, but with traditional Gaelic society under pressure to conform to southern norms, it was kin and the community that could provide cohesion and direction to a beleaguered society. After 1745, the Barisdale people were taught to look outside the Gaelic community for their government and for standards of living and behaviour. Traditional Highland values conditioned the clansmen's response to the new beliefs and practices to which they were exposed. As long as the right of the kin to land was recognized, the people of Barisdale had to make only certain minimal concessions to the new commercial order. But if that right were denied, much more drastic change would be forced on them.

CHAPTER FOUR

Lochiel

After 1745 the people of Lochiel, like those of Barisdale, faced the transformation of their traditional community into a modern commercial society modeled on that of southern Britain. The estate of Cameron of Lochiel was one of the major clan holdings in the western Highlands. Like Barisdale, Lochiel was divided into extensive farms used for the raising of cattle, and it supported a large and culturally homogeneous population. But to a greater degree than Barisdale, the Lochiel estate was exposed to southern influence, since it was located at the western end of the Great Glen on important trade and communication routes. The Barisdale estate was only a part of the Glengarry lands, possessed by a single wadsetter who was a cadet member of the family. In contrast, the Lochiel estate, which included most of the traditional Cameron lands, was occupied by the clan chief and a large number of wadsetters and tenants. Until 1770 the Barons of the Exchequer, and then the Annexed Estates commissioners, "improved" and "civilized" the Lochiel estate without substantially changing community life or the clansmen's world view. Much of the success that officials enjoyed lay with the gentlemen tenants, who were more easily convinced of the benefits of stone houses, English schooling, or commercial agriculture. In general, the people of Lochiel preserved the essential elements of traditional life over this period, while adapting to new social and economic conditions.

The Lochiel estate was part of the civil parish of Kilmallie, which stretches north and west of Fort William, west of the River Lochy, and north of Loch Eil to Loch Arkaig. For the most part, the land is covered with high hills and cut through by glens and rivers that provide access through them. Much of the rock in the area between Loch Arkaig and Loch Eil is a soft sandstone, easily split, that shows little variation in erosion and gives rise to smooth slopes and ill-defined summits. The hills north of Loch Arkaig consist of the same rock, forming high but unimpressive grass and peat-covered tops.[1] Land of this character was ideal for raising livestock, and the river valleys had enough level ground to let the inhabitants raise at least part of their grain supply. Somewhat detached from the rest of the estate was the Mamore part of Lochiel, reaching from Fort William to Ballachulish and from Loch Linnhe to the height of land on the western side of Glen Nevis. This area forms the western flank of the Mamore mountain range, yet it had the only two corn farms on the estate, as well as several cattle farms.

The precise size of the Lochiel population is unclear, since the only statistics available cover the entire parish of Kilmallie, in which the Lochiel estate was the largest single property. Other major landowners were the Duke of Gordon, whose holdings included Fort William and the south shore of the River Lochy, and McLean of Ardgour, whose estate lay south of Loch Eil.[2] At the midpoint of the eighteenth century, the population of Kilmallie was estimated at 3,093 people; by 1793 the number had increased to 4,225 souls, and by 1801 the first British census set the population at 4,600.[3] This last figure is low, since the census did not include the considerable number of local men serving in regular or fencible regiments or those men and women temporarily employed outside the parish. An analysis of the 1801 census by district reveals that some 2,300 people, or half the parish population, then lived on the Lochiel estate.[4] No major reorganization of the Lochiel estate occurred before the census year, and while there was some emigration before 1801, the estate population was basically undisturbed in the last half of the eighteenth century. Other parts of Kilmallie had been stocked with sheep by 1793, but their inhabitants were reportedly still in the parish, presumably in the town or in crofting areas. It seems likely that roughly the same proportion of the Kilmallie population lived in Lochiel in 1755 as in 1801; thus there were possibly 1,500 people or 260 families in Lochiel in 1755.

The people who lived in Lochiel in the mid-eighteenth century formed a close-knit, hierarchical community. Unlike Barisdale, which was a small estate with few gentlemen among its tenants, Lochiel was characterized by a complex social organization with every social and economic level of traditional society. Like Barisdale, the population of Lochiel included tenants, subtenants, and cottars; Barisdale, however, seemed to lack both the very poor mentioned on several Lochiel farms and the bigger tenants and wadsetters who were so prominent in Lochaber. In 1748, 25% of the 260-odd families in Lochiel were wadsetters and tenants, while the remaining three-quarters of the population were subtenants, cottars, and servants.[5] The agricultural improvement introduced by the barons and commissioners offered different opportunities to the various classes of people found on the Lochiel estate.

The thirteen men who had acquired their farms through wadsetts were next to the chief at the top of the local social and economic ladder. In the years before the rebellion, these men had lent Lochiel a total of £2,355 sterling and were given the use of a farm in lieu of interest; their loans ranged from £55 for a farm the size of Inverskilavulin, Lundavra, or Stronlia, to £556 for Fassfern.[6] The wadsetters collected the annual rent of their farms, keeping a part proportional to the value of their wadsett for their own use and paying the balance of the rent to the chief. The considerable wealth of the thirteen wadsetters was evident in the claim submitted by the tenants of Lochiel's estate for damages suffered in 1746–7 from the looting of the Hanoverian army. Rich and poor alike experienced the destruction of stock, crops, furniture, and houses; 163 people submitted claims totalling £7,204.[7] But the ten wadsetters who submitted claims estimated their losses at £2,092 – that is, 6% of those reporting losses accounted for 29% of the total value of the claim. The wadsetters' large share of material wealth reflected their position of economic power, which the subtenants occasionally tried to limit. In 1762 Duncan Cameron, a tenant in Erocht, complained that the wadsetter of Erocht did "harass all his Tenants in many instances" and charged half again as much as was common for the conversion of casualties (or payment in kind) into money rent.[8] Duncan Cameron clearly expected the landlord, whether clan chief or Forfeited Estates, to intervene and rectify the situation. But the tone of his complaint suggests that this type of behaviour was not usual and that the wadsetters did not frequently abuse their economic power.

The tenants who possessed the other twenty-two Lochiel farms formed the next major social group on the estate. These men and women all held their land directly from the landlord and were people of some consequence in the community. There were differences, however, both in the size and quality of the farms they rented and in the tenants' social and economic status. Eleven farms were each rented by only one tenant.[9] These tenants varied in importance from such men as John McLachlan, who rented Achintore for £33 (an exceptionally large sum) and John Cameron of Fassfern, a wadsetter who also rented Kilmallie and Achnacarry for £10, down to a man like Evan McPhee who rented Kenmore for

£2 18s. The remaining eleven farms then occupied on the estate were all shared by a number of tenants. This number ranged from the two John McPhees, who held Muick for £5 16s. 1d., to the twelve men and women who rented Moy for £41 7s. 9d. While all the tenants of the estate would have enjoyed a position of social importance as a result of their land holding, it is clear that those whose rent was less than £2 per annum were hardly better off than subtenants. This is evident in William Morison's comment on the tenants of Moy, who were "supported much by working as day labourers to others, and at any publick work carrying on upon the estate."[10] On the other hand, the more prosperous tenants probably began to rival the wadsetters in economic and social influence.

Agricultural surveys of the Lochiel estate, carried out in 1762 and 1772, note the presence of impoverished subtenants and cottars, as well as tenants and wadsetters on the estate. In his testimony at the valuation of Lochiel in 1762, Donald Cameron, wadsetter of Clunes, stated that his land was subsett (sublet) to as many poor subtenants as could be accommodated and that the rents "are set as high as they can bear."[11] Ten years later, Morison also noted the large number of subtenants or cottars at Clunes, adding that "they are miserably poor and almost starving." The subtenants of other farms were mentioned as well. In Glenpeanmore, they had planted potatoes in rough ground in order to increase the amount of arable land, while in Errocht they lived permanently on two of the shielings. The inhabitants of the settlement and of the shieling of Ardnosh in Invermallie were "poor people"; the farm of Fassfern included "insignificant spots of Corn land possessed by Crofters."[12]

A majority of the Lochiel inhabitants were subtenants, cottars, and servants, who did not pay rent directly to the landlord and who lived on the farms of the wadsetters or larger tenants. The small multiple-tenant holdings of Moy or Annat obviously could not support the same number of subtenants as could Strone or Murlaggan. The distinctions made among the non-tenant population – subtenant, cottar, crofter, or servant – indicate that the group was one of considerable size and social complexity. These members of estate society depended on other members of the community for a share in the land. All social groups were mutually dependent for their livelihood from the land and for their preservation of a common culture.

The pattern of human occupancy of the Lochiel estate shows the same influence of geographic and cultural factors noted in Barisdale. The physical limits of human settlement were set first by the rough, heather-covered hills north and south of Loch Arkaig, and second by the communal nature of traditional life. The 1772 survey of the estate revealed a pattern of small local concentrations of people, a pattern still evident in road survey maps thirty years later. Houses were not evenly scattered about the various farms but rather clustered in one or (in the case of larger farms) in two or three locations. Thus the ten farm buildings in Moy were located five on either side of the Alt Coire Chraoibhe. Similarly in Glendessary thirty-nine buildings stood within a single mile on four sites.[13] Not only were domestic activities clustered on one part of a farm, but the houses built on neighbouring farms also tended to be closer to each other than to the furthest reaches of their own land. This was especially true of the Mamore farms, where arable land was completely separate from the shielings but only a few miles from the nearest neighbour.

In 1772 there were thirty-eight farms on the Lochiel estate; this number varied slightly during the years of forfeiture and annexation this as farms were joined or divided so as to accommodate tenants. The three most westerly farms on the estate, Glendessary, Glenpeanmore, and Glenpeanbeg, met Morar and Knoydart on the height of land that forms the parish boundary. Only two farms, Kinlocharkaig and Invermallie, were located on the south shore of Loch Arkaig, but the north shore was more heavily settled, with eight farms: Murlaggan, Callich, Coanich, Kenmore, Muick, Sallachan, Crieff, and Achansaul. Each farm in this group extended north to the parish boundary and Glengarry's property, with farmhouses and buildings located in small communities along the loch.[14] Five farms were found near the southern end of Loch Lochy; these included the chief's residence at Achnacarry, as well as Clunes, Kiliross, Easter Moy, and Wester Moy. Another three, Errocht, Strone, and Inverskilavulen, were located in Glen Loy, while Barr, Muirshearlich, and Banavie lay between these and Fort William.[15] Seven farms (Corpach, Annat, Achdalieu, Fassfern, Corribeg, Drimnasallie, and Stronlia) lay west of the fort along Loch Eil to the western bounds of the estate. The last seven farms in Cameron's possession, Achintore, Cornranan, Corryshenrachan, Lundavra, Culchenna, Onich, and Ballachulish, stretched south of Fort William to Loch Leven.[16]

As in Barisdale, the traditional organization of the Lochiel farms was maintained during the years of forfeiture and annexation, and small communities of men continued to occupy each farm. The valuation of the Lochiel estate made in January 1762 underlines the tenants' dependence on cattle, as well as the minimal oat crop produced on the estate; a similar picture emerges from the survey done by William Morison in 1772.[17] Since these studies describe

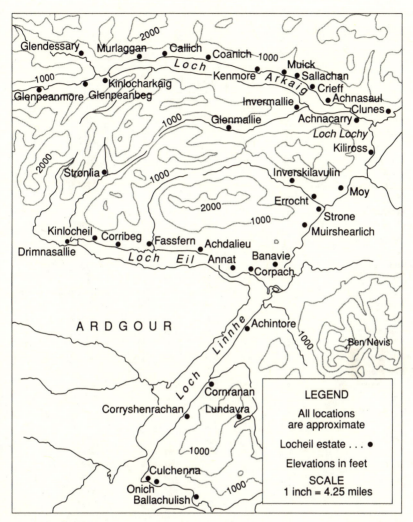

Map 3 Lochiel Estate, 1772

Sources: Ordnance Survey of Scotland; SRO, E768, RH2/8/26.

different aspects of farming in Lochiel, no comparison of agriculture on the estate between these two dates is possible, with the exception of grain yields. Nevertheless, the survey and the valuation together provide an excellent overview of agricultural organization in Lochiel during the transitional years following 1745. This information is presented in Tables 3 and 4.

The Lochiel estate was a large property totalling over 107,500 acres, 4,600 of which were under timber, planted mostly before the

Table 3
Lochiel Estate, 1772

Name of farm	Acreage					Oats: bolls sown bolls meal*	Soum
	Arable	Grass	Hill	Wood	Sheiling		
Glendessary	12	317	7103	—	—	10/40	192
Murlaggan	4	8	2779	—	—	4/15	86
Callich	4	4	1886	—	—	4/10	38
Coanich	3	2	2838	—	—	3/8	56
Kenmore	4	12	4138	121	—	4/8	28
Muick	4	20	4187	—	—	4/8	58
Sallachan	4	16	2270	—	—	4/8	49
Crieff	4	13	1276	—	—	4/8	42
Achnasaul	16	31	5423	137	—	—	92
Clunes	26	33	3673	490	—	24/50	172
Glenpeanmore	5	264	3498	—	—	6/20	100
Glenpeanbeg	10	326	2728	—	—	8/20	136
Kinlocharkaig	3	17	716	92	—	3/12	48
Invermallie	8	32	5556	1246	—	—	84
Achnacarry	—	10	985	350	—	(included with Corpach)	
Kiliross	4	3	638	69	—	—	38
Easter Moy	18	82	603	86	—	20/32	64
Wester Moy	18	60	948	135	—	20/32	64
Errocht	34	242	3815	79	—	35/72	92
Inverskilavulin	12	41	2120	147	—	—	92
Strone and Achnacarry	19	109	3126	114	—	—	120
Barr	14	78	1923	36	—	15/30	102
Muirsharlich	11	36	780	—	—	12/24	82
Banavie	14	9	1121	—	—	15/22	66
Corpach	12	50	8700	436	—	24/36	134
Annat	27	6	1868	64	—	28/50	92
Achdalieu	10	30	1589	60	—	10/20	60
Fassfern	24	40	3678	310	—	25/50	198
Corribeg	5	—	1285	—	—	6/10	52
Kinlochiel	12	37	3059	307	—	12/23	—
Drimnasallie	—	—	—	—	—	—	152
Vachan (part of Fassfern)	2	5	2688	152	—	—	—
Stronlia	4	3	2591	26	—	4/8	72
Achintore	20	129	651	—	195	—	96
Cornranan	28	182	1680	—	1078	—	152
Corryshenrachan	9	80	734	16	—	—	48
Lundavra	7	52	553	—	723	—	52
Culchenna	22	138	1584	15	1200	—	150
Onich	32	26	520	21	1281	—	76
Ballachulish	34	48	616	1	708	—	88

*1 boll = 6 imperial bushels.
Source: SRO, RH2/8/26, 15–113.

Table 4
Lochiel Estate, 1762

Name of farm	Cattle			Mares/ horses	Sheep	Goats	Oats: bolls sown bolls meal
	Great cows	2-year-olds	Stirks				
Glendessary	160	40	40	12/4	160	220	10/40
Murlaggan	70	18	18	6/2	70	120	3/15
Callich	30	8	8	2/2	30	60	4/8
Coanich	44	12	12	6/0	44	88	3/8
Kenmore	20	5	5	4/0	20	40	4/8
Muick	50	13	13	12/2	50	100	4/8
Sallachan	30	8	8	4/2	30	60	4/8
Crieff	30	8	8	4/2	30	60	4/8
Achnasaul	60	15	15	16/4	80	160	16/32
Clunes	133	33	33	12/8	150	300	22/40
Glenpeanmore	80	20	20	4/4	80	100	6/20
Glenpeanbeg	100	25	25	4/4	100	200	8/19
Kinlocharkaig	40	—	—	2/2	40	40	—
Invermallie	50	17	17	8/4	50	100	8/16
Achnacarry and Kiliross	40	13	13	0/4	40	80	8/16
Moy	96	24	—	0/16	96	192	40/64
Errocht and Glenmallie	110	27	27	12/8	160	120	24/48 11/22
Inverskilavulin	50	13	13	14/4	50	100	10/20
Strone and Achnacarry	80	20	20	12/4	80	80	18/36
Barr	60	15	15	8/8	—	120	15/30
Muirshearlich	50	12	12	4/4	50	—	12/24
Banavie	60	15	15	8/8	80	—	22/33
Corpach	40	18	18	6	70	—	20/40
Annat	60	15	15	8/8	60	60	24/48
Achdalieu	40	10	10	6/3	40	40	9/15
Fassfern	150	35	35	20/4	100	—	22/22
Corribeg	36	9	9	8/2	36	72	8/16
Kinlochiel and Drimnasallie	100	25	25	8/4	100	200	12/24
Stronlia	48	12	12	10/2	48	96	4/8
Achintore	—	—	—	—	—	—	—
Cornranan	120	30	30	8/8	150	80	—
Corryshenrachan	40	10	10	0/4	40	40	—
Lundavra	40	10	10	2/4	40	40	—
Culchenna	120	30	30	8/8	120	120	—
Onich	52	13	13	0/12	52	50	—
Ballachulish	64	16	16	0/12	64	64	—

Source: SRO, E768/7/1.

forfeiture. Three thousand acres was the average size of the thirty-eight farms on the estate, considerably more than the 800 acres common in Barisdale. The arable land on each farm averaged well over ten acres, as seen in Table 3, but most families still purchased meal for six or occasionally nine months of the year.[18] The pressure of a large and expanding population clearly tended to overburden the rather small amount of arable land. Moreover, the poor yield of the oat crop (see Table 3) underlines the limited nature of arable farming in the Highlands. In 1772, only eighteen of the twenty-four farms growing oats produced at least twice as much meal as the amount of seed sown. Glendessary and Kinlocharkaig were exceptional in achieving a fourfold increase. A comparison of the 1762 and the 1772 harvests shows that levels of oat production changed very little over ten years. In 1762, 365 bolls of oats yielded 696 bolls of meal, while in 1772, 304 bolls of oats gave 616 bolls of meal. The slightly better yield in the later year (2.02 versus 1.96) may have been the result of improved farming techniques, but the effect was hardly impressive.

Cattle breeding was the primary agricultural activity, and for that purpose the 2,591 acres of hay or good grass found on the estate were extremely important in carrying the cattle through the winter. It is clear from the widely varying figures that no standard amount of hill land was assigned to each farm; while Kiliross had a bare 689 acres, Corpach had 8,700 acres. The quality of the hill land in Lochiel differed from farm to farm, since there was no constant relationship between hill acreage and soum. Thus 148 acres were needed in Kenmore for one soum, while in Banavie the same soum required a mere 17 acres. While most of the larger farms possessed shieling land, only in the case of the Mamore farms (where the shielings were distant from the farm settlements) was the acreage listed separately.

Table 4 describes the livestock on the Lochiel estate in 1762. Thirty-five farms supported a total of 2,353 "great cows," 574 two-year-olds, and 550 stirks (one-year-olds). The same proportion of 4:1:1 between great cows, two-year-olds, and one-year-old cattle appears on most farms. Since Highland cows calved only every two years, it would seem that half the great cows were breeding stock and the other half were raised for sale or future breeding. The 2,400 sheep kept on the estate almost equalled the number of great cows; twenty-eight farms stocked precisely the same number of each, maintaining the traditional balance between sheep and cattle. Goats actually outnumbered either sheep or great cows, with a total of 3,194 found on the estate. Sixteen farms actually had twice as many goats as sheep. The stocking of so many goats seems likely the result of both geographic and human pressures. The sixteen farms carrying a large number of goats were located inland and in the more mountainous part of the estate. The steep contours that characterize Glenpean or the area north of Achnasaul and Clunes made goats the most appropriate livestock. On the other hand, the existence of a large number of subtenants and cottars dependent on these animals for food may also have contributed to the number of goats kept. In comparison only a small number of horses were raised on the estate; 232 mares and 167 horses were bred for sale as well as for local use. The balance between sheep and cattle, and the large number of goats kept indicate the survival of a significant aspects of traditional Highland agriculture in Lochiel during the early years of forfeiture.

In spite of constant effort on the part of the factor, the tenants of Lochiel only slowly implemented his simpler schemes of agricultural improvement. In the aftermath of the rebellion, the factor was at first busy getting burnt-out farms into production again and imposing a new groundwork of law and order on a previously unpoliced area. Still, Henry Butter drew up his first plan of improvement shortly after he was appointed factor of the estate in 1758.[19] By January 1760 he had won the consent of the tenants to a new series of regulations designed to improve their farms. The tenants were to build stone houses, make dykes along farm boundaries, and enclose a few acres for winter hay; upon removal from a farm, tenants would be compensated for such improvements. Butter intended these simple changes to "spirit them [the tenants] for further Improvements." Three years later he reported to the Barons of the Exchequer that many of the tenants had built houses and fences, and that such improvements were "chearfully" paid for by new tenants in the case of removal or exchange.[20]

In 1765 Butter drew up a second, more comprehensive plan of agricultural improvement for Lochiel. Once again he called for the building of stone houses, and he promised not only to have compensation paid for such improvements upon removal but also to give some financial assistance towards the cost of construction. The factor's intention was to do away with the "Timber Wattled Huts covered with Turf" in which tenants, subtenants, and cottars all lived. There were also more stringent requirements for dyke building on each farm. The tenants were to put up whatever fencing the factor thought their farms needed, to be responsible for repairs to the dykes, and to pay for such repairs if they neglected to carry them out personally. Other improvements included readjusting farm boundaries to simplify fencing and land and crop rotation; extending arable land by planting potatoes in rough ground; and draining or clearing wet and stony fields. As an enticement to begin these improvements, the tenants were offered a three-year lease with an extension promised to the industrious.[21] These plans and others that followed in the years of annexation changed agricultural practices in Lochiel very slowly, and to a substantial degree left traditional ways of life intact.

In spite of Butter's blandishments, the 1772 survey revealed that the Lochiel tenants had carried out only minor parts of his two plans of improvement. The stone houses that were an essential first step had been built on only eleven farms, in most instances only by the tenants. Thus there might be one stone house on a farm like Glenpeanbeg where there was one tenant, or several stone houses where there were several tenants, as in Muirshearlich, but the great majority of the population continued to live in creel huts.[22] In addition, the complex traditional division of farm land continued in spite of its inconvenience. "One farm has no grassing. Another has from two to six of great extent and at great distance, consequently the former had more winter Provender than necessary while the latter cannot in that Season keep his cattle from starving."[23] Butter's constant encouragement of the building of fences and dykes had achieved minimal success; only six farms had done, or intended to do, such work. Achnacarry, Culchenna, and Easter Moy had all made small garden enclosures near the farmhouse. More ambitiously, the tenant of Clunes had enclosed a meadow of seven acres with a dyke, and the tenant of Invermallie planned to enclose a field near his house. Several other fields at Invermallie, which had been reclaimed from the wild by sowing potatoes, were now fenced with wood and used for growing oats.

Yet most of the tenants and subtenants ignored the advantages of enclosed fields, at least in part because they lacked the skill needed to build fences. The Inverskilavulin tenants were among the minority who had learned the difficult task of dry-stone walling: "The one tenant digs and leads the Stones, and the other builds." Most of the tenants still had to be convinced that such hard and time-consuming labour was of any real value. The traditional practice of removing the livestock to the shielings in early summer undercut the need for fences since it gave the crops time to ripen. The tenants of Glendessary, and presumably those of other unenclosed farms, found that this journey protected their crops adequately and at the same time permitted the continuation of an agricultural tradition.[24]

While Highland tenants were aware of the need to enrich soils depleted by continuous cropping, it is not clear what role the factor's plans of improvement played in extending the use of fertilizers. Morison's survey suggests that fertilizing with ferns or seaweed was quite common in 1772, although only eight farms were specifically named as following such a program. Other improvements aimed at increasing arable production were not widely implemented. Only the farms of Strone, Glenpeanmore, Culchenna, and Invermallie tried to increase their arable land by planting potatoes in previously unused moss land. Similarly, arable land was permitted to lie fallow only on three farms: on Muick and Invermallie, oats were grown for two years and the land was left fallow for six years, while on Wester Moy three years of oats were followed by four years of fallow. Planting potatoes was the one agricultural innovation that was quite widely adopted; by 1772 eleven farms raised the new crop.[25] In spite of Butter's enthusiasm and authority, agricultural improvement proceeded slowly in Lochiel. The same agricultural improvements were suggested again and again through the late eighteenth century, yet a conservative tenantry was able to delay their introduction and force a compromise between improved and traditional farming.

The Barons of the Exchequer and the commissioners, however, made a substantial start in the task of equipping Lochiel with the infrastructure of an eighteenth-century commercial society. In 1755 Mungo Campbell pointed out that the tenants of Locharkaig, Glenloy, and Glenmallie had to burn the straw from their grain and then grind the grain by hand. To prevent the loss that this practice entailed, Campbell suggested that a corn mill be built on the Water of Arkaig in the middle of the district; four years later £28 18s .10d. was granted for this purpose. Then in 1765 the barons approved £30 to build a mill at the head of Loch Arkaig, where one had existed before the rebellion. The tenants in that district eagerly agreed to maintain the mill and pay a rent equal to the interest on the cost.[26]

The absence of bridges and roads made travel through the Highlands extremely difficult, and the need for such facilities was obvious in Lochiel, through which several major routes passed. In 1761 Butter recommended that bridges be built over rivers flowing through Glen Pean and Glen Dessary, as well as those flowing into Loch Lochy, Loch Eil, and Loch Linnhe. Estimating the cost of these bridges proved difficult. The bridge over the Kiachnish required a larger arch than had first been thought necessary, adding £100 to the original estimate of £150. Fast-flowing rivers and a very wet climate often caused disaster and the need for expensive rebuilding; in 1774 the bridge of Loy needed repairs totalling £34.[27]

The factor also made continuous attempts to see that the roads were improved. As early as 1761 Butter reported that the country services (that is, the local inhabitants) had been called out to make roads "where formerly there were scarcely footpaths." Some six years later Butter commented that while progress had been made on the country roads, the clansmen had neither spades nor other tools to do the job well. Butter requested the same £20 grant that the barons had given in previous years, since this sum went no great length in equipping two to three thousand people with tools.[28]

In addition to improvements to economic infrastructure, southern authorities attempted to induce Protestant churches and religious instruction to the previously neglected Highland region. The commissioners of the Annexed Estates firmly supported this policy, which represented one aspect of their parliamentary mandate; four times between 1757 and 1765 they recommended the subdivision of large Highland parishes whose extreme size made it impossible for the minister to serve his congregation adequately.[29] Both the commissioners and church officials believed that religion and education were closely linked. Schools were necessary to teach the English language and reading, without which it would be difficult to learn the principles of the Protestant religion. Thus the commissioners believed that the support they gave to building schools also aided the Protestant church, and they were willing to extend this support if His Majesty allowed further funds for this purpose.

Two separate efforts were made to provide the people of Lochiel with access to a school. A parish school was established at Fort William in 1760 and the factor received permission to sell up to twenty-five tons of wood from the Lochiel estate to pay for both the new school and the schoolmaster's salary. The progress that the school made was a source of pride to the factor. In 1773 he reported that Kilmallie school had 140 scholars, all of whom were doing well; the two masters taught Greek, Latin, mathematics, bookkeeping, and reading and writing in English.[30] The alien content of this program, as well as the distance of the school from most of the estate, meant that the Fort William school served a minority of the Lochiel clansmen. In October 1761 Butter recommended that local schools be started in central locations across the estate, at Onich, Corrybeg, Achnasaul, and Murlaggan; each would cost £35 for the construction of a house and the enclosure of grounds and £12 for a salary. This plan, which would have ensured relatively easy access to schools for all the inhabitants of the estate, must have been too visionary or too expensive for the barons. Only one school was approved, that at Murlaggan on Loch Arkaig in 1764.[31]

The close relationship between religion and education in the Highlands was illustrated by the work of the Murlaggan school-master, Alexander McIntosh. Previously the people of Locharkaig-side had depended on the minister of Kilmallie, who lived near Fort William, for their religious instruction, if indeed they received any. But McIntosh spent much of his time

in catechising the People, and convenning them on the Sabbath Day to Read the Scriptures; And for this purpose had meetings with them at Eight Miles Distance from his place of Residence. By his great Application in Instructing the People in the Principles of the Christian Religion, a very Remarkable Reformation is wrought among them; As family Worship is Set up in many Families, and almost [sic] Effectual Check put to Theft & Depradations for which Locharkaigside was remarkable throughout the Highlands.[32]

McIntosh's success was not surprising since the southern image of the Highlanders as an irreligious, uneducated, and lawless people was quite false. The clansmen of Locharkaigside had strong religious beliefs and a respect for learning that paved the way for the partial success of the commissioners' program; nevertheless, the focus on learning Scottish rather than Gaelic culture resulted in limited interest in the school, and most children were still miles distant from the nearest teacher.

The efficient use of the Lochiel woodland was an important part of the commissioners' attempt to improve the Lochiel estate. Highland forests had been exploited ruthlessly without thought of the future, but eighteenth-century ideas of improvement foresaw a more orderly use of this resource. In most districts, centuries of careless use by proprietors and tenants alike had stripped the hillsides and valleys of their original covering of pine, oak, birch, and hazel. Whole forests were frequently sold to timbermen for cutting and the bark was often stripped from trees for sale to tanners and the trees left to die.[33] When the Lochiel estate was forfeited, it still contained considerable forests. Within several years, however, the collector of customs at Fort William reported that the woods on the estate were steadily being cut for the private use of certain prominent men. Soldiers posted at the head of Loch Arckaig during the summer of 1753 testified that Cameron of Drimnasallie had not only cut down some oak trees but had also "destroyed a considerable number of

Young trees by peeling the bark off them." The wadsetters and tenants had, through this course of events, merely continued their traditional exploitation of Lochiel's forest wealth. Their actions also served to deny the government's authority to control the Lochiel woods and estate. The factor responded to these habits with the appointment of three woodkeepers for the estate in 1754, one at the head of Loch Eil and one on either side of Loch Arkaig.[34]

The value of the Lochiel timber was substantial: in 1760 Francis Grant offered £120 per annum for a lease of the fir woods of Locharkaigside. This figure was equal to 20% of the total agricultural rent paid by the wadsetters and tenants at that time. A few years later, John Godsman, an Inverlochy merchant, estimated the value of the timber taken from the same wood and manufactured at the estate mill at Achnacarry to be between £200 and £300 yearly. The profitability of the forests on the Lochiel estate led the factor to introduce strict rules for the management of the woods in his 1765 plan of improvement. The factor was empowered to enclose any hardwood found on tenants' land and to sequester additional acres for new plantations, while the tenants were compensated for any trees that they themselves planted and preserved.[35] Butter was willing to supply the tenants with wood needed for household and farm activities; the only bark that they were allowed would be from trees purchased for this purpose. With these regulations, the tenants enjoyed limited use of woodlands and the landlord obtained a steady supply of timber for estate use and for sale.

Government control of the Highlands after 1745 forced some change in the tenants' perception of society, but the clansmen's belief in their right to clan lands remained strong. The final escape of Prince Charles Edward and the collapse of the rebellion in 1746 did not immediately bring either peace or law and order to the Lochiel estate. Cumberland's army wreaked destruction across Lochaber, and prominent participants in the rebellion kept a low profile or fled to the hills when government forces approached. These uneasy times furnished a ready excuse, if not an actual need, for customary forays into other clans' lands in search of cattle. With Donald Cameron away in France, the people of Lochiel turned to the chief tenants and wadsetters for leadership in providing for their families.

This tendency was particularly true in the most isolated part of the estate north and west of Loch Arkaig. The area around the watershed of the loch had long been dominated by the McMillans and the McPhees, who held this border district for Lochiel against Macdonell incursions by whatever means necessary. When the king's authority was finally established around Fort William in the early 1750s, the factor and the local law officer were extremely critical of the inhabitants of Locharkaigside. Mungo Campbell expressed official opinion in a memorial to the Commissioners in 1755:

There are some McMillans on the Estate of Lochiel who are much complained of by the officers stationed in that country as Harbourers of Thieves. particularly Even McMillan at Glenpeanmore who is reackoned to be very rich and maintains a great Influence among his Clan in that Country who are mostly under bad fame. Captain Chabbert stationed last summer at Locharkaig ... has represented this Man as doing all in his power to obstruct the suppressing of theft, as well as to hinder the troops from getting provisions of reasonable rates. The Memorialist knows no more than that he's head of the Tribe McMillan and in place of assisting him to bring offenders to Justice is at great pains to support any of them that falls into the hands of Justice.[36]

The behaviour of the McMillans and their leader had a legitimate basis in traditional Highland social practice. The nature of the thefts supposedly committed by the McMillans was not revealed, but undoubtedly cattle or other livestock figured heavily. No shame was attached to stock theft in the Highlands, and a clan leader who owed his men protection would certainly not wish to betray them merely for reiving. As for "hindering the troops," the sale of provisions at inflated prices was probably a form of revenge for the losses that tenants suffered during the rebellion.

A second question of law enforcement added to the tension between the McMillan and McPhee leaders and government officials. The practice of encouraging Highlanders to join British regiments, either to escape criminal prosecution or to support their families, produced less than dedicated soldiers. In 1754 two "fellows of the Clan McFee, who had been notorious offenders, and had for a course of Years, lived on Theft and rapine" finally surrendered and enlisted in the Earl of Home's regiment. But the quite predictable occurred: "upon these Regiments being ordered to march from the Highlands, These and a great many other Highlanders deserted, and returned to their old trade of Thieving."[37] Clan leaders, who understood their duty to include protection for their people, would have to be forced to hand over their clansmen to the military enemy of ten years earlier.

The civil government, however, had the power needed to pressure local leaders to turn deserters over to the army. Lord George Beauclerk wrote to the barons in November 1758 explaining that the McMillans and McPhees should be warned to remove from their farms. Such a step, Beauclerk believed, would not only eliminate theft in the district, but would also "contribute towards making desertion less frequent for the future. I am far from being desirous that these Tenants should at any time meet with harsh or Severe usage, but as they are yet very wild and uncivilized, the making them sensible that the holding their Leases from the government must intirely depend on their good behaviour, will be a blessing to the Industrious part of the Highlands in General." The factor proposed his own solution to the problem of deserters; the McPhees and McMillans of Locharkaigside "should be intermixed with other clans less Thievishly disposed."[38] The Locharkaigside leaders knew how civil and military authorities felt about their sheltering wanted men, and they may have been informed of the threat to remove them from their farms. Late in 1758 Ewen McMillan of Glenpeanmore and Alexander McPhee of Glendessary succumbed to the realities of government and military pressure and helped Lieutenant Colonel Lambert to capture several deserters.

Lord George Beauclerk had touched Highland leaders where they were most vulnerable when he threatened to remove the clansmen from their farms. The Highlanders began to cooperate with government authorities because to do otherwise was to risk the loss of their land. While cattle lifting and irregular military service had been common for hundreds of years in the Highlands, the clansmen were willing to change their behaviour to guarantee the more important issue of their continued possession of the land. By 1770 cattle rustling had ended and deserters were no longer given refuge. Yet in spite of the forfeiture of Lochiel, the tenants continued to believe strongly in the enduring and necessary connection between the land and the people. Spokesmen for both the McMillans and the McPhees expressed this view during the valuation of Lochiel in 1762. John McMillan pointed out that he was "head of the Tribe of McMillans or McIllyvouls and he and his Ancestors have been kindly Tenants or Possessors of the lands of Muirlaggan for more than three hundred years past." Alexander McPhee of Glendessary emphasized his clan's special service; "he heard a tradition in the Country as if his Ancestor had got a better Bargain from Lochiel of this Farm than was usual; because it lay on the Confines of Glengarry's Lands; and he being Head of the Tribe of McPhees from whom personal Services were expected."[39] Other tenants echoed the conviction that 300 years of tradition and personal service to the chief were sufficient reason for a tenant to expect to keep a farm at a modest rent.

Possession of the land had never been permanent, although long occupation of a farm obviously led the tenants to believe that it should be. Clan lands had been lost from time to time by warfare or family misfortune; tenants, and particularly subtenants and cottars, were sometimes moved by the chief from one farm to another. The Annexed Estates' factor usually maintained tenants in their farms, but involvement in criminal matters could result in the loss of a share in a farm. Butter also occasionally removed to another farm or gave a smaller share in a farm to those tenants who failed to make any agricultural improvements or who attempted to prevent such improvement. In March 1772, Allan Cameron, subtenant of one-quarter, and Duncan Robertson, subtenant of one-eighth, of Achnasaul were to be removed for keeping goats against the estate regulation prohibiting such activity. Allan McMillan lost his one-eighth share of the same farm because he had been found guilty of theft.[40] The barons' and commissioners' power to remove tenants and the factor's role in determining who was to be removed was potentially the point of most serious conflict between the inhabitants of the estate and its administrators.

Events on the farm of Banavie illustrate the manner in which improvement and the tenants' attachment to the land could collide head on. The first act of the five-year conflict began in 1763 when the barons refused the factor the authority to remove any more tenants from Banavie without their permission. In the same month, Charles Stewart was confirmed in his one-quarter share of the farm after he complained of being removed by the factor, who wanted the land for his own use. (Apparently, Butter used his official position for self-aggrandizement.) The next act revolved around the question of improvements, with the factor and Charles Stewart arguing that the other Banavie tenants refused to cooperate, and Donald Cameron, Donald Boyd, Flory Chisholm, and Donald McEachan countering with a claim that the factor had overstocked the farm to his own benefit.[41] Affairs reached a violent climax in 1767 when the small tenants took justice into their own hands. Charles Stewart began to carry out improvements on his own, employing

four Soldiers of the Regiment which then lay at Fort William to build it [a dyke;] And they having wrought at it about an hour, Donald McKinnon, one of the tenants, with all the Women in the place came and offered to pull down what was built of the dyke but upon the Soldiers threatening to force them to desist, they returned to their Houses. The Soldiers went on with their work and that day finished Six Roods of the Dyke, but they no sooner left it than the said Donald McKinnon with Donald Cameron and Donald McEachan, two of the tenants of the said farm, & their Servants and Children Came and pulled down the dyke, Threw the whole seal and Earth of it into the River Lochy, which runs by it, and made the ground as Level as when the Soldiers began.

This episode resulted in an order by the barons in July 1767 that the guilty tenants be removed, but the same tenants were still there in 1768 and Butter reported that they refused to leave.[42] The rights and wrongs of the conflict in Banavie are not clear in the surviving documents but the incident reveals the determination with which tenants might defend their interests. Old Highland attitudes about the relationship between men and the land survived the years of forfeiture and, if too directly attacked, were likely to be forcibly defended.

The factor and barons or commissioners did not directly attempt to change the tenant's deep-seated belief in their right to land, but rather they set certain limitations on the circumstances in which it would be respected. In 1764 John Cameron, a lieutenant in the Second Virginia Provincial Regiment, asked for a lease for himself or his son Dougal of the farm of Strone, which his family had possessed from time immemorial. Cameron pointed out that he had built a stone farmhouse and offices at Strone and made other improvements that few of his neighbours attempted. Butter supported his application for continued possession of Strone but added to his lease an obligation to enclose three acres yearly. In another instance, the factor himself emphasized that the farm of Invermallie had been in the possession of the same family "past memory" and he urged that the petition of its occupant, Dugal Cameron, be granted since he was an improving farmer.[43] Thus, government officials and clansmen compromised over the issue of the latters' right to land; tenants were forced to accept certain agricultural improvements in return for continued possession of their traditional holdings.

In Lochiel as in Barisdale, the barons and commissioners only realized their goal of improving and civilizing the estate to a modest extent. Southern law and order were made effective throughout Lochaber within two decades of the rebellion; even the most "lawless" parts of the estate were by then noted for their honesty and good behaviour. Jacobitism died a final bloodless death, and the Lochiel tenants sent a steady stream of men to serve in the British army during the second half of the eighteenth century. Many of the tenants had been exposed to the teachings of the Protestant religion brought to them by government-supported missionaries. Highland "idleness" had been a misconception to begin with, but southern authorities applauded the programs of improvement that had promoted industrious habits in the Lochiel tenants. In the field of language and culture, progress was less apparent; the minority who learned to read and write English, for this generation at least, remained enthusiastic participants in Gaelic cultural life. The integration of the Highlands, and particularly the Annexed Estates, into the southern part of the United Kingdom had a slow, but gradually intensifying impact on northern economic life. Constant military preparedness against the incursions of other clans and fear of cattle rustling, either in home pastures or on the way to market, diminished substantially. Surplus agricultural production (which usually meant cattle) could now reach market safely, while at the same time the agricultural improvements advocated by the factor, barons, and commissioners promised to increase that production. The thirty-five years to 1784 introduced the Lochiel clansmen to the possibility of full participation in the British economy.

At the same time, the clan no longer formed an independent self-governing unit of society. The district as a whole was now subject to officials appointed in Edinburgh or London; the estate itself was administered by a factor named by southern authorities. The direction of local life was to be determined by men and ideas originating outside Gaelic society. The old belief that the land was the tenants' to farm remained intact during the years of forfeiture and annexation, when the tenants generally retained possession of their farms, albeit on new conditions. The tenants grudgingly adapted to changing social and economic ideas. Agricultural improvement was accepted very slowly at first, but a compromise between improved commercial agriculture and traditional Highland farming seemed to emerge over the long term. The old social order was not greatly changed at the farm level; many families together farmed the land, whether or not their share in the farm was formally recognized in the rental and whether or not fences divided farms and family holdings. But the tenants still had no legal right to their farms, and their continued presence on the land now depended on the landlord's judgment: could they offer the best return on the estate? The landlords of western Inverness were about to answer no.

CHAPTER FIVE

Western Inverness-shire, 1770–1800

Until the 1780s in western Inverness (later in more isolated parts of the Highlands) conflict between the new commercial society and the traditional world of the clansmen was, like European warfare in the Middle Ages, a fairly gentlemanly affair. Both sides won victories and suffered defeats; each recognized certain legimate claims of the other. As previous chapters have shown, social control passed to southern authorities and the influence of the commercial economy grew substantially after 1745, but daily life remained essentially untouched on the Annexed Estates of Barisdale and Lochiel. While events unfolded somewhat differently on estates still controlled by clan chiefs, these areas experienced a similar legal and economic integration into southern Britain. Tenants' right to land was rarely denied, although it was sometimes threatened by large rent increases in the late 1760s and 1770s. The incompatibility between agricultural production for the market, at a price competitive with the improved agriculture of the south, and the clansmen's traditional farm holdings was not yet apparent. But the tempo of development accelerated after 1780, and the conflict over the use of the land and the type of society it would support became, like modern warfare, a winner-take-all confrontation.

Shortly after 1780 in Glengarry and Knoydart, and during the two following decades in Lochiel and other parts of western Inverness, landlords took advantage of their exclusive ownership of the land and favourable market conditions to transform local agriculture and society. Landlords rented substantial parts of their estates to newcomers as large-scale sheep farms; many joint-tenant farms disappeared, while the clansmen who held the remainder were impoverished by rents set as high as the market could bear. The traditional farm economy provided the clansmen with an extremely modest standard of living and the tenants were unable to compete for long with the dramatically higher rents offered by southern graziers. Many western Inverness tenants therefore lost their share of a farm during these years. In its place, their landlords offered them at best a much smaller share in another farm or a croft with only a few acres; at worst the tenants were completely cleared from the estate. The new agricultural regime tore apart traditional communities and offered the clansmen only a pitiful share in the land.

The case of the Glengarry estate is perhaps typical of the experience of the non-forfeited estates in western Inverness in the second half of the eighteenth century. Like the clansmen of Barisdale and Lochiel, the Macdonells were made subject to southern British law, felt the effects of the commercialization of the Highland economy, and were threatened with the sale of the estate to an outsider. Glengarry's estate was not forfeited to the Crown, in spite of the Jacobitism of its inhabitants, because its politically cautious chief, John McDonell, refused to give Prince Charles Edward his open support. Cadet members of the family, however, led the clan in the Jacobite campaign of 1745–6 and McDonell himself was imprisoned in Edinburgh Castle. In the bloody aftermath of Culloden, both the tenants' and the chief's homes were burned, the estate was laid waste, and the family papers and charters were carried off.[1] After 1746 the estate was encumbered with debt as a result of John's administration before the rebellion and the long imprisonment of two successive chiefs following it.

The Glengarry estate was organized into farms along traditional lines, with settlement on each centred on the limited arable land and common grazing shared according to the soum held by each family. The right of all clansmen to land remained unchallenged on the estate before 1780. The population of Glen Garry itself stood at roughly 1,400 in 1764 and the people were, like those of Knoydart, overwhelmingly Roman Catholic. English schools reached only a minority of the population; as late as 1796 one school sponsored by the state and two sponsored by the Society for the Propagation of Christian Knowledge served the entire parish of Kilmonivaig.[2] Few children therefore received an English education, and Gaelic language and culture were the dominant means of expression in daily life on the estate.

The Glengarry estate extended from the eastern slopes of the Great Glen above the River Oich, west forty miles to the sea; it sprawled over half the width of Scotland, following the natural line of communication along Glen Garry and Glen Quoich to Knoydart and North Morar. This area contains some excellent agricultural land, and in 1750 seventy farms, traditionally organized, produced good crops of "corn" (grain) and supported large herds of cattle. The most easterly part of the estate was the Barony of Abertarff, acquired by an earlier Glengarry from the Frasers of Lovat. Abertarff was situated on either side of the River Oich and divided into nine farms of various sizes, six of which were held on wadsetts by Macdonell gentlemen. Abertarff contained the best farmland on the estate and, while somewhat short of pasture, its farms were noted for their production of excellent corn and beef.[3]

The second division of the estate, Slishmine, lay west of Abertarff on the north side of Glen Garry. There were twelve farms in the district, eight of which were held by four Macdonell gentlemen. The Slishmine farms had good arable land and pasture, but by 1768 a growing population meant that the tenants could no longer supply themselves with corn year round. A good supply of peat was located in the area and a birch wood lay along the loch. On the south side of Glen Garry lay the third division of the estate, known as Slishgarve and Achadrom. Eleven of its sixteen farms were small holdings let to single tenants or somewhat larger farms rented to several tenants. Only two of the farms were held on wadsetts, and the remaining three were rented by one gentleman, Angus Macdonell of Greenfield. The farms of Achadrom were known for their arable and grass lands, while those of Slishgarve were valued chiefly for their pastures. Peat was only available high on the mountains but birch and fir grew on most farms.

The fourth part of Glengarry's estate was North Morar, which stretched from Glen Dessary in Lochiel westward to the sea. It lies immediately south of Knoydart, bounded by lochs Nevis and Morar. Though not as high as its northern neighbour, Morar has a rugged geography that greatly limited arable farming. The farms were divided among a large number of small tenants and very few were held by gentlemen. Only two of the nineteen North Morar farms were held on a wadsett, and both of these were held by Donald Gillies. The little arable land found on the farms was cultivated with the spade and its fertility was increased by the use of seaweed and shell. Hill cattle were not of major importance in the North Morar economy, since the peninsula provided little land for pasture.[4]

The Knoydart division of the Glengarry estate (see Map 2) was roughly fifteen miles from the nearest farm in Glen Garry; Glen Quoich, which lay between, was also part of the estate, but was used only for pasture by the tenants of Slishmine. Glengarry's farms occupied over one-third of Knoydart; his cousins Barisdale and Scotus held the remainder. Of the fourteen farms held by Glengarry in Knoydart, ten were held on wadsetts by four men, three Mc-Donells and a Gillis. Glengarry's farms in Knoydart, unlike Barisdale's, had an appreciable amount of arable land capable of growing a year-round supply of corn for the tenants and an occasional surplus. The seaweed and shell sand available on the coast resulted in a "Luxuriancy in their Crops" that a visitor declared would not be believed in Speyside: "after one Boll's sowing of small Black Oats they often reap as much as produces ten Bolls of Meal."[5] The Knoydart farms also produced good hill cattle; they supported 352 milk cows and a proportionate number of yell (or dry) cattle.[6]

Knoydart's coastline added to local prosperity in several ways. The seashore provided a great variety of shellfish for only a few hours' labour, and most of the tenants were seamen who owned four-oared boats used in the rich fishing in lochs Hourn and Nevis. The sea also gave the tenants an opportunity to avoid customs officers and duties. Rum, other dutiable liquors, and contrabrand goods were smuggled from Ireland and sold inland for a profit. The trade ended some time before 1768, as a result either of the efforts of the gentlemen of Knoydart or of the presence of troops for several years after 1745.[7]

Between 1750 and 1780 the weakening of the old Gaelic social order in Glengarry was evident principally in the actions of the chief and other clan gentlemen. During the first eighteen years of this period, the self-interested behaviour of the Glengarry gentlemen reflected the emergence of southern individualism in western Inverness. Between 1721 and 1768, the chiefs of the Glengarry clan were weak, imprisoned, or minors, and effective leadership of the clan went to the chief's close male relatives. The Macdonell gentlemen took advantage of this interval without a strong chief to improve considerably their own economic and social position.[8] Many of them held wadsetts on Glengarry farms and had, in the absence of an effective chief, administered these properties for their personal benefit at the expense of the community as a whole. Andrew MacPherson summed up the state of Glengarry in 1768: "You cannot imagine any thing more grossly mismanaged than this Estate has been during the Lives of the two Last Superiors which has very near totally Extinguish [sic] the lower Class of Tenants but the Gentlemen live very much at their Ease upon it, by these Means the Present Rent is in some Part but Indifferently Paid."[9] The Glengarry estate was considered unequalled in the north for the raising of cattle, and the traditional holdings of the tenants were quite attractive in the post-1745 economic climate. The Macdonell gentlemen used their position as chief tenants and wadsetters to benefit from the productivity of the joint-tenant farms.

In 1768, the young Glengarry chief, Duncan McDonell, came of age and control of the estate shifted into the hands of a strong leader. His first priority was to clear his inheritance of debt; his second was to manage his estate to his greatest personal advantage. In accordance with tradition, the first major decision Glengarry took was made jointly with the Macdonell gentlemen, in spite of the chief's legal right to act independently. The sale of part or all of the property seemed to be the only way of relieving the debt load that the chief had inherited. The Duke of Gordon was the most likely buyer, since his lands in Badenoch bordered on Glengarry. The duke's agent acquired a detailed assessment and list of estate rents; the duke valued the property at £60,000. But feeling among the Glengarry gentlemen and their chief ran against a complete abandonment of clan lands. Although the decision to sell was legally Duncan's alone to make, "the whole Gentlemen of the Clan" met with him in Edinburgh to determine the fate of the estate.[10] Their joint decision was to sell North Morar to General Fraser. The Macdonell gentlemen for the most part lived elsewhere on the Glengarry estate; they were thus the least affected by this decision.

In 1768 it was obvious that the income produced by the Glengarry estate was disproportionately low for the estate's market value. In an attempt to forestall any more radical action by their chief, the Macdonell gentlemen in Knoydart offered to surrender their old tacks and wadsetts in 1768 and rent their old farms for a more substantial sum than had previously been paid.[11] In spite of this gesture, Duncan McDonell later concluded that many clan gentlemen still received too large a share of the estate profits. Shortly after his marriage in 1772, Glengarry relet his estate on commercial principles; the remaining wadsetters were given notice and offered tenancies on more stringent terms.[12] Although by the end of the 1770s most of the Glengarry tenants still occupied their traditional holdings, their rent was now likely to be determined by commercial values – a trend that was beginning to sweep across western Inverness and the Highlands.

By 1780, commercial agriculture had reached a turning point, not just in Glengarry but in all western Inverness. Cameron of Fassfern summed up the limitations on agrarian reform some years later with the comment that "the turn of the people for improvements is not great."[13] True, the Lochiel and Barisdale tenants had begun to adopt some of the techniques of improved farming, but this change was slow and piecemeal even among the chief tenants. In western Inverness improvers had found that a rugged geography and wet climate strictly limited the value of any improvements in arable farming. Reforms aimed at pastoral farming had been more successful; in Knoydart and in Lochiel the size of animal herds increased, partly as a result of improved farming techniques. By the late 1780s, however, the limits of improvement schemes had seemingly been met, given the existing social and economic conditions. At the same time, the burgeoning cities of southern Britain sought wool for their expanding manufactures and mutton for their new inhabitants.[14] The excellent grazing lands of Lochiel, Glengarry, and Knoydart could be made more productive, as well as extremely profitable, by the introduction of new high-yielding breeds of sheep. A niche in the new commercial economy seemed to open up for the Highlanders if they could shift the focus of agricultural production from cattle to sheep.

New breeds of sheep – in particular the famous blackfaced Cheviots – were first introduced to western Inverness in 1764. Henry Butter, the improving factor of the Annexed Estates of Lochiel and Barisdale, imported middle-sized, blackfaced sheep from Douglas and found the breed well suited to Highland conditions. Butter suggested that Cheviot rams should also be imported to improve the quality of native Highland sheep, which were "small and bad woolled"; both Barisdale and Lochiel tenants had done so by 1772. The fact that the first Cheviots were brought into western Inverness as an integral part of the traditional agricultural economy and were bred by the tenants is an indication of their willingness to adapt certain aspects of the new agriculture.[15]

Sheep farming had its remarkably disruptive effect on Inverness-shire only after 1780, as landlords began to abandon traditional agriculture and shifted to capital intensive sheep farming. The slow improvement of local flocks and the gradual establishment of Cheviots in the county was rapidly given up, and entire farms were stocked at one time with blackfaced sheep driven north from the Borders. These huge flocks completely replaced not only Highland black cattle but also many tenants and subtenants. The number of people displaced was substantial, since the scale of sheep farming resulted in the throwing together of several cattle farms to create a single, large-scale sheep farm, and since the sheep needed as winter and spring grazing the low land previously used for tenant subsistence. During the early years of large-scale sheep farming, some farms were let to the original joint tenants, but difficulties in managing the flock and in marketing made such attempts hopeless.[16] By and large, landlords concluded that only outside graziers possessed the capital and expertise needed to make these ventures successful.

The deciding factor in bringing about this agricultural revolution was the large profit to be made from intensive sheep farming. The complex economy of southern Britain would pay what Highlanders considered staggering prices for wool and mutton. Duncan McDonell of Glengarry was probably the first proprietor in western Inverness to succumb to the lure of high rents offered by incoming graziers;[17] in 1782 McDonell turned over Glen Quoich to Thomas Gillespie and Henry Gibson to be stocked as a sheep farm. The Glengarry tenants had used Glen Quoich primarily as pasture and hence no large-scale removals were necessary, but the loss of this pasture did reduce the number of cattle that the tenants could keep. The Glen Quoich sheep farm evidently proved successful since three years later there were widespread removals from farms along the twelve-mile length of the glen and river Garry. Smaller numbers of tenants were also given notice to vacate (in some cases, more than once) in 1786, 1787, and 1788. While it is not precisely clear how much of Glen Garry itself was under sheep and how much was still in the hands of the tenants, sheep certainly outnumbered black cattle by 1796. The parish of Kilmonivaig, of which Glengarry formed close to half, was stocked with 60,000 sheep and a pitiful 1,500 cattle at that date.[18]

Sheep farming also reached Knoydart in 1784, when most of the Scotus estate was stocked with Cheviots. Tenants were warned to leave three of the Scotus farms in that year, but in April 1785 the Glendulochan tenants were given leave to stay on their lands while Inveriebeg and Scottas were "planted" with sheep. The remainder of the Knoydart peninsula belonged entirely to Glengarry, since Barisdale reverted to him in 1784 when the forfeiture was lifted. Glengarry cleared tenants from the north side of Knoydart late in 1785 and again in 1788. All of the Scotus estate and a great part of Glengarry's own lands were given over to sheep farms by the time of the "Old Statistical Account" in 1796.[19]

On the Lochiel estate, by contrast, the landlord himself did not manage the introduction of large-scale sheep farming. Several of the Cameron tacksmen tried the new method of farming in order to pay the increased rents set by Donald Cameron of Lochiel in 1793. The statistical account of Kilmallie parish, prepared in that year, indicated that three-quarters of the parish was laid out in sheep farms, while the other quarter still raised black cattle. In all there were 6,000 cattle, 500 horses, 1,000 goats, and 60,000 sheep stocked in Kilmallie. A comparison of real rents to valuation (assessed rents) in the parish shows that on Lochiel's estate the ratio was 6:1 in contrast to the other properties which ranged from 9:1 to 22:1. The relatively low rental of Lochiel suggests that much of the black cattle farming carried on in the parish in 1793 was concentrated on the Lochiel estate. The change to sheep farming seems to have occurred on a farm-by-farm basis there, as successive tenants adapted to the new economy. The removal of small tenants was spread over a number of years, of which the 1804 clearance of Glendessary and Locharkaigside was the most notable.[20]

The initial stage of agricultural improvement (1750–80) was largely carried out within the traditional social order in western Inverness. The change to capital-intensive sheep farming after 1780 resulted in the eviction of tenants from their farms and was a direct denial of traditional Gaelic social values. The idea of agricultural improvement was hardly new to this area, since the Annexed Estates' factors had advocated improvement during their thirty-odd-year tenure. But the great majority of tenants, including some half-pay officers, lacked either the capital or the expertise to become successful sheep farmers. Some tried and failed. Most were not given the chance, since landowners could see no reason for renting valuable grazing land to novice improvers. The second stage of agricultural improvement, the sheep farming introduced after 1782, finally destroyed traditional Highland agriculture and social organization in western Inverness and severely threatened the economic and social position of the clansmen.

The traditional tenant economy in Western Inverness faced considerable stress during the adaptation to a commercial society in the eighteenth century. The basic elements of this subsistence economy as practised in Barisdale are presented in Table 5. The tenants' principal income was derived from the yearly sale of black cattle, usually three to nine animals. With this money, tenants paid their rent and bought oatmeal for family consumption for several months of the year. Five of the thirteen Barisdale farms were reported as not selling dairy products or sheep; presumably the other eight farms continued in some degree the practice observed in 1768 of exporting surplus butter and cheese to Skye in exchange for oatmeal. The

Table 5
Barisdale Tenant Economy, 1771 (in shillings)

| Farms | Tenant income | | Tenant expenses | | | Loss by bone break |
	Sale of cattle	Other sources	Meal	Rent	Servants*	
Muniall	250	no butter, wool, cheese or sheep	48	133	100	75
Li	320	—	48	195	150	—
Riddaroch	336	no butter, cheese or sheep	160	162	180	—
Glaschoille	270	no butter or cheese	96	107	66	—
Miolary	320	no butter or cheese	64	107	50	—
Groab	225	2 boats in herring fishing	80	110	100	140
Reidh a'Ghuail	145	—	64	84	66	84
Braomisaig	270	—	80	181	132	45
Sallachry	120	—	20	110	66	—
Torcruin	120	no butter, milk, cheese or wool	—	82	66	—
Carnoch	768	—	360	385	330	288
Achagline	420	—	160	175	110	84
Sourlies	120	—	40	55	50	—
	166	—	40	55	50	75

*Servants' pay is calculated at the rate of pay stated for Li, Muniall and Carnoch, i.e. 33s. for men and 16s. for women, except for Sourlies where men were paid 20s. and women 10s.
Source: SRO, E741/46.

herring fishing, which furnished a substantial part of the tenants' food supply, must also have added to their cash income since the salt fish sold for 8d. to 4s. a barrel.[21] However, only Groab, which employed two boats in fishing, was likely to have any sizeable income from this activity.

The expenses occurred in operating the Barisdale farms appear in most cases to have been greater than the income received from the sale of cattle. Rent was the largest single expense on all farms except Riddaroch, and on seven farms the rent paid by the tenants equalled more than half the profit from cattle sales. Servants' wages constituted a second major expense, but these were an essential part of the agricultural economy since dairy and arable farming were labour intensive. The Barisdale tenants grew on average one-half to two-thirds of their corn, so that a certain cash expenditure for meal was unavoidable and such costs were, of course, subject to market fluctuations. Undoubtedly the most disheartening expense the tenants incurred was the loss of cattle from broken bones due to falls on the hills. The yearly loss of even a couple of animals was a serious financial drain, although few farms could have matched the experience of Reidh à Ghuail, which lost by fracture a sum equal to the rent.[22] The cash value of the tenants' other economic activities was unlikely to have improved dramatically their financial situation. The income gained from the sale of dairy products, sheep, fish, or horses was small compared to that received from cattle sales.

The Barisdale tenant economy was, therefore, precariously balanced between the consumption of home produce and of purchased foodstuffs barely paid for by the sale of local surpluses. There is no evidence to suggest that the Barisdale tenants substantially failed to meet their expenses, since no heavy arrears of rent were reported for the estate during the Annexed Estates' administration. Yet on most farms there could have been no margin of waste. A poor harvest, the loss of a number of cattle, or the two disasters combined could throw the tenants into debt and extreme hardship.

It is not clear whether this situation was normal for small tenants throughout western Inverness. While the gentry and the larger tacksmen had resources to cope with a changing economy, the small tenants had no financial reserves and were extremely vulnerable to the effects of economic change. On the Lochiel estate, Morison referred to the economic squeeze that had resulted from the "loss sustained by death of Cattle, the high price of Victuall and the Increase of Servants wages of late years."[23] Servants' pay rose steadily through the second half of the eighteenth century. Men's wages rose from 18s. plus keep in 1755 to 33s. in 1771 and from 40s. to 60s. plus keep in 1795. During this period, the wages paid to women remained half that paid to men, but rose at the same rate. The ability of the tenants to pay higher wages depended on an increase in their own incomes. Certainly the price of cattle rose continuously from 20s. in 1740, to 40s. in 1771, and to between 50s and 60s. in 1791, while the price of dairy products also more than doubled between the two later dates. The price of oatmeal, which most tenants had to buy, rose by roughly 40% during the twenty years after 1771.[24] The precise effect of these separate increases probably varied from one tenant to another, depending on additional factors such as population pressures, the impact of improved agriculture, the potato harvest, access to markets and rent increases. Nevertheless, it seems clear that small tenants were forced to balance off a larger income against greater expenses and had very little chance to improve their already marginal economic position.

Of crucial importance to the tenants' economic success was the amount of rent which they paid for their farms.[25] Rents climbed inexorably upwards during the eighteenth century, but the rate of increase varied over time and place. The first significant change in Highland rents was the conversion of services and produce paid to the landlord into a money rent. Before 1750, most tenants paid a proportion of their rent in kind. In Lochiel, for example, the tenants were expected to provide 55 stone of cheese, 55 quarts of butter, 51 wethers, 25 calves, and 26 kids yearly; converted into cash, this payment equalled £58 or 12% of the total Lochiel rents of 1748. Similarly in Barisdale, a set amount of butter, cheese, and sheep was payable with the rent, representing 15% of the total cash rent; services provided by the tenants equalled another 7%. "Casualties" (tenant labour) and hens were paid on the Glengarry estate in 1768 and ranged in value from 12 to 25% of the money rent.[26] The tendency to convert such payments of produce and services into cash grew during the next two decades as landowners spent more time in southern Britain and abroad: their need to live off their estates declined and the desire for a larger cash income correspondingly increased.

On the Forfeited and Annexed Estates, increases of rent were generally linked to agricultural improvement and greater productivity. In Barisdale the rise was particularly modest, a fact which suggests that the rents in Barisdale, as Mungo Campbell suspected, had been high before the estate was forfeited. In 1748, David Bruce established that the Barisdale rents had been set at £83 before 1746 and at £63 after the devastation of that year. However, eight years later Campbell pointed out that the tenants had concealed part of the traditional rent paid to the landlord; incidentals including May Day presents and personal services brought the real rental of the estate to £133. Campbell believed that this figure was much greater than was warranted either by the value of the land or by the tenants' ability to pay.[27] Nevertheless, the Barisdale rent was set at this rate, albeit with minimal increases in succeeding years. The first increase in the Barisdale rents occurred during the 1760s, when nine tenants agreed to build dykes on their farms. The cost of this improvement was borne by the landlord, but the interest on the money expended on each farm was added to its rent. Thus the estate rental was raised by 5% and individual farms paid from 2s. to 20s. more. The tenants accepted a second and more extensive plan of improvement in 1774, when an additional rent of £29 was laid on their farms. All of the rent increases (21% from 1755) were used for the benefit of the tenants and the improvement of the estate. No further rent increases were imposed before 1784, when Barisdale was disannexed and returned to Glengarry.[28]

On the Lochiel estate, rentals followed a pattern of increase similar to that seen in Barisdale. The theoretical rents, estimated in 1748, amounted to £451, but this figure later proved to be inaccurate. In 1752 certain tenants were found to have paid a "superplus" rent to the Lochiel family. Duncan McViccar, collector of customs at Fort William, believed that these payments were possible only because of the inaccuracy of the estimated rent. The 1748 figures were in fact only the "rent which was paid in time of Sir Evan Cameron, Grandfather to the late Lochiel, and Since his death, there was a yearly augmentation of £100 or thereby laid upon the whole estate." The tenants were charged the actual rents paid in 1745 as soon as these were discovered by the factor, although this took until 1756 for several farms.[29] The true rental of Lochiel was finally set at £560, a figure maintained throughout the 1760s.

In 1771 and 1773, the factor of the Forfeited Estates applied additional rents of £9 and £2 to the nine farms on the Lochiel estate that had begun improvements. Then in 1774 Lochiel rents jumped to £863, an increase of £268 or 45%. All of this additional rent was to be spent on the improvement of the estate, in particular on building dykes. The increase was based on the number of cattle each farm could support, and hence was not applied evenly across Lochiel. Farms already stocked to capacity had small rises of perhaps 12%, while the majority of farms had increases of 24 to 50%. This new level of rent in Lochiel roughly equalled £1 for each four soums of cattle, slightly more favourable to the tenant than the Barisdale rate of £1 for each 3.7 soums. Rents were not increased again by the Annexed Estates' commissioners and there is even some evidence to suggest that the full sum was not always collected.[30]

As in Lochiel and Barisdale, rents on the Glengarry estate remained at early eighteenth-century levels until the 1770s. In 1762 Glengarry only collected £300 in rents, while the wadsetters received another £400. Shortly after his marriage in 1772, Duncan McDonell redeemed the wadsetts and raised rents dramatically. In Slishmine, rents were increased by 170% and in Slishgarve by 130%; Knoydart and Abertarff presumably experienced increases of the same order.[31] There is no evidence that McDonell reinvested any of this additional income in improvements to his tenants' farms. The higher rents were merely a financial adjustment in the operation of the estate:

Glengarry increased his income by eliminating the wadsetters and by reaping the benefit of higher cattle prices.

The eighteenth-century trend towards higher prices for cattle allowed both improving and non-improving landlords to increase rents steadily. But the huge market demand for sheep and mutton that developed in the 1780s and 1790s offered even more lucrative prospects to the landowner who owned good grazing land for sheep. The effect first of increased cattle prices then of buoyant sheep prices clearly shows in the movement of rents on Highland estates. On the Glengarry estate, for instance, rents increased by 472%, from £732 in 1768 to £4,184 in 1802. The accelerating rate of increase is particularly evident in the rent of those farms stocked with sheep. Glenquoich and Inchlaggan provided an income of £40 at the midpoint of the eighteenth century under traditional farm organization and production. In the 1770s these farms, with rising cattle prices, paid a rent of £115, an increase of 180%. But by 1802, when sheep farming was well established in this part of the estate, Glenquoich, Inchlaggan, and Kinlochourn paid a rent of £970, a fantastic jump of 740%.[32]

Very large increases of rent were the order of the day on most estates in western Inverness at the end of the eighteenth century. The small estate of McDonell of Scotus, which rented for £56 in 1773, was stocked with sheep in 1785 and yielded an income of £385 by 1795, an increase of 587%. Similarly Barisdale, which had seen very modest rent increases under the Annexed Estates' administration, was rented in 1802 for £906, an increase of 456% from eighteen years earlier. In Lochiel the rate of increase was even more spectacular. From the 1784 total of £971, rents rose by 21% in 1788 and by a further 27% in 1793. In 1804 Glendessary and Locharkaigside were stocked with sheep, and the farms *in this area alone* paid a rent of £2,375, an increase of 873% from 1788.[33]

Farm rents were not raised at the same rate across an estate; the greatest increases were made on farms deemed suitable for sheep. Glenquoich in Glengarry, and Murlaggan and Callich in Lochiel, saw well over sevenfold increases in rent when they were stocked with sheep.[34] In most instances, the old tenants did not have the capital needed to begin large-scale sheep farming and were removed from their farms. A few tacksmen adapted to the new order, but most of the sheep farms were let to incomers from the south, who made substantial profits on their farms, at least during the war years. Particularly in the early years of sheep farming, however, some farms were left in the possession of existing tenants who continued to raise black cattle. On these farms the increase of rent was not as dramatic as on the sheep farms: for instance Braomisaig, Reidh à Ghuail, Groab, and Kylesknoydart paid only £164 to Glengarry in 1802, a mere 250% increase.[35] Nevertheless, the new rents still represented a substantial part of the tenants' earnings, since the price of cattle (their chief source of cash) barely doubled in same forty-year period. As a result, landlords rather than tenants reaped much of the benefit of higher cattle prices at the beginning of the nineteenth century.

The adoption of sheep farming and the high rents that accompanied it did nothing to ameliorate the economic situation of western Inverness tenants. Those who managed to keep their farms were kept at a subsistence level by high rents, and their numbers steadily diminished as more farms were turned over to sheep. Those who lost their farms faced a bleak economic future as day labourers or crofters.

The western Inverness of 1800 could not have been imagined by the men who fought on Culloden Moor. The sixty years following the Jacobite rising saw economic, social, and political change that transformed local society; while part of this change was rooted in the century before 1745, its greatest impact was felt in the succeeding sixty years. For the most part these developments were imposed on Gaelic society from outside or were carried out by local leaders influenced by non-Highland values and objectives. The shift from internally set goals to a dependence on southern ideas and initiatives was an indication of the weakness of the old Gaelic social order compared to the strength of metropolitan British society.

The events of 1745–6 represented the final destruction of Highland political independence. Henceforth the region's political future would be closely bound up with the parliamentary oligarchy of the south. Surviving elements of the ancient Celtic legal tradition were quickly rendered superfluous as southern legal precepts and administration were enforced after 1745. The heritable jurisdictions, which ensured a local, patriarchical form of justice, were abolished in favour of the sheriff court. The accelerated integration of the Highland economy into that of southern Britain had an immediate short-term impact, as well as long-term structural implications. Specialized agricultural production for distant markets and the reorganization both of farming practices and of social structures implied a change in man's attitudes towards the land. Cattle production became more efficient, improved agricultural techniques were made known, and finally highly profitable sheep farming began to replace traditional mixed farming. Although the tenants had relative security of tenure before 1780, the introduction of sheep farming destroyed this security and left the majority of tenants landless or on small crofts, or threatened with such prospects.

The impact of post-1745 economic and political change in western Inverness is evident in the transformation of Highland social structure in this period. While the decay of traditional Gaelic society predated the last Jacobite rebellion, the process was intensified by government policies and economic changes during the second half of the eighteenth century. The paternal leadership of the clan chief was fatally weakened by the loss of heritable jurisdictions and, in some cases, of clan estates. Influence and authority over the lives of the people increasingly shifted away from the chief to government officials, clergymen, teachers, and local community leaders. At different times on various estates the role of the chief changed too, from leading and looking after his people to "improving his estate" – that is, ruthlessly pursuing profit. The tacksmen were squeezed out of their profitable role as middlemen and either became part of the new economic elite or fell into the ranks of the tenants. In their place were the prosperous graziers and traders who now stood between the chief and his clansmen. The tenants no longer had traditional guarantees of land and had lost, or were threatened with the loss of, their share of a farm. By 1800 the traditional social order had been destroyed in western Inverness, and society no longer possessed the wholeness and interdependence that had distinguished traditional Gaelic social life.

The tenants of western Inverness neither wanted nor carried out this transformation, and their immediate reaction to it was to reaffirm traditional values. Many of the early schemes of improvement were only successful insofar as they could be adapted to traditional Gaelic objectives or practices. Gaelic society valued learning and was noted for its religious belief, and so it readily accepted schools and churches. On the other hand, agricultural improvement on the Annexed Estates won acceptance slowly and only if it clearly contributed to keeping people on the land. The deep conservatism and vigorous traditional culture of Gaelic society[36] strictly limited the success of efforts made in the mid-eighteenth century to "civilize" the Highlands.

The sudden large increases of rent and the stocking of sheep farms throughout western Inverness were an immediate and serious attack on traditional life. Rent increases were the spearhead of that attack, and they occurred in two phases. The first large increases, during the 1760s and 1770s, were the result of the landlords' determination to obtain a commercial rent from their estates; the only major estates excluded from such sharp rises were the annexed estates of Barisdale and Lochiel. Even steeper increases in rent followed the conversion of traditional cattle farms to sheep after 1780. Barisdale and Lochiel lost the protection of the Annexed Estates' administration when they were returned to their owners in 1784. After that date, all the estates in western Inverness were vulnerable to the introduction of sheep farms, very large rent increases, and removals. The tenants responded to this devastating change with large-scale emigration to Canada in the closing decades of the eighteenth century.

CHAPTER SIX

The Loyalist Emigrants

The emigration of western Inverness clansmen to Glengarry County occurred during the first cycle of large-scale emigration from Scotland. The half century between 1763 and 1815 represented a turning point in Scottish emigration, from the modest movement of people seen before 1760 to the mass migrations of the nineteenth and twentieth centuries. The story of the Glengarry emigrants – Loyalists included – is part of that greater movement. The experience of the emigrant clansmen during this first cycle of departures provides evidence of a distinct pattern of emigration and documents one of the significant effects of agrarian transformation on the Highlands.

For hundreds of years the wandering Scot had been a familiar figure across Europe: he travelled in search of education, to sell merchandise, to gain employment, or even to satisfy "a mere restlessness which drove ... [him] from place to place."[1] But the Scots had been excluded from the first great migration to North America in the seventeenth century, since some English colonies prohibited foreign settlers and hence were closed to the Scots until the union of the two countries in 1707. Indeed it was only after 1760 that a considerable number of Scots first emigrated to North America, part of the dramatically increased flow of emigrants from Great Britain and Ireland in the fifteen years before the American Revolution. The number of emigrants from the British Isles jumped sharply from an average of 2,000 yearly between 1700 and 1760 to 8,000 yearly between 1760 and 1775. The highest rate of emigration was from Scotland where an average of 2,600 people left annually; 3% of Scotland's population of 1760 emigrated over the subsequent fifteen years. Although the number of Scottish emigrants represented only a fraction of the natural increase in the Scottish population at this time, emigration on such a scale had not been seen before and contemporary observers viewed it with concern.[2]

The clansmen demonstrated a particular interest in emigration during this first cycle of large-scale departures. American historian Ian Graham has suggested that between 1768 and 1775 60% of the Scottish emigrants to America were Highlanders. Between 1776 and 1815, Highlanders continued to emigrate in large numbers as the brief intervals of peace allowed; only their destination altered as Canada and the Maritime colonies almost completely supplanted the now independent United States. J.M. Bumsted estimates that almost 14,000 emigrants left Scotland for British North America in this period, and that 90% of them were Highlanders.[3] Contemporary evidence confirms that the clansmen were eager to cross the Atlantic; tenants from Skye, offered an opportunity to emigrate, "were engaging with ye subscribers as fast as they could wish." The clansmen's interest was always described in hyperbolic terms, such as "the present rage for emigration" in 1771 or the "Buzz of emigration" in 1803.[4]

It appears that patterns of emigration from the Highlands changed in important respects after 1815, and historians have offered various explanations of these trends. J.M. Bumsted claims that during the first cycle of emigration, most departing clansmen left against the wishes of their landlords in order "to avoid modernisation"; their departure was not the result of clearances to create sheep farms, he claims, and the emigrants were able to pay their own passages. After 1815, according to Bumsted, the Highlands were shattered by the postwar economic collapse and by extensive clearances for sheep farms. He argues that emigration in the second cycle occurred because of poverty and overpopulation and was supported, or even forced, by the landlords. Similarly Eric Richards contrasts the "remarkably high level of exodus" from the west Highlands "in the 15 years before the War of Independence, and again at the turn of the century" with the "relatively slow" rate of emigration in the nineteenth century. Richards concludes that "at present there exists no satisfactory explanation for this apparent change in the West Highlander's propensity to emigrate."[5]

The case of the Glengarry County settlers, the great majority of whom emigrated before 1815, confirms certain elements of Bumsted's hypothesis while disproving others. The Glengarry settlers did indeed pay their own fares, with the exception of those who received government assistance in 1815, and they did emigrate in spite of their landlords' wishes to the contrary. A simple rejection of modernization was not, however, the cause of the great exodus from

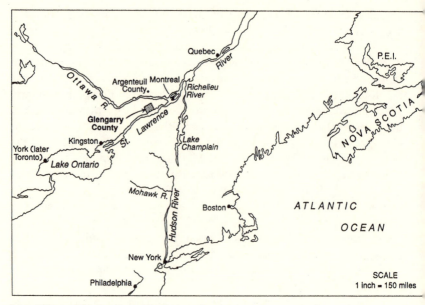

Map 4 Part of Northeastern North America

Sources: Based on a map drawn by John Melish, "Northern Section of the United States, including Canada." in NA, CAAD, negative no. 6761.

the Highlands. The integration of the region into British society and the growth of commercial agriculture did not cause widespread emigration from western Inverness; the clansmen adapted to the new rule of law, and the increase of cattle production for market which began before 1745 accelerated in the second half of the eighteenth century. Only when agrarian change threatened the clansmen's possession of their farms, indirectly through rent increases or directly through clearances to create sheep farms, did farming families emigrate *en masse* to British North America. Those who left were not fleeing from radical social change but from the poor deal which that change offered them. These clansmen were willing and able to look outside Scotland to achieve their central goal: safe tenure of a farm in a Gaelic community.

Much of the character of Highland emigration during this first cycle of departures is hinted at in contemporary comment and in recent historical studies. One obvious characteristic is the departure of locally based groups; thus 100 Lewismen sailed for Philadelphia in 1774, another 200 left Bracadale Parish, Skye in 1788, and 138 travelled together from Strathglass and Glen Urquhart in 1801.[6] A second characteristic of Highland emigration, that of family departures, was identified by customs officials in Fort William in 1773.

One 1775 emigrant group from Killin, Perthshire, consisted of thirty families and included a grandmother of eighty-three as well as a baby of one month.[7] Highland emigration was also known for its concentrated flows to particular destinations in the Carolinas, New York, and Nova Scotia.[8]

A broader context for viewing Highland emigration has recently been provided by Bernard Bailyn in his statistical analysis of the 1774–5 registers of emigrants from England and Scotland. As we have seen, Bailyn found that emigration in these years followed two quite distinct patterns. The first pattern, which he calls the metropolitan stream, consisted of young male craftsmen or tradesmen from the southern half of England. They were not destitute but travelled as indentured servants looking for better prospects in America. The second pattern, which he calls the provincial stream, was composed of rural families from northern England and Scotland who travelled together in vessels hired for the voyage, leaving from small ports near their homes. In particular, Bailyn documents the presence of a substantial number of children among the Scottish emigrants (25%) in contrast to the English voyagers (6%) and an almost equal number of men and women in the Highland departures (six men to each five women from Inverness-shire). Not surprisingly, therefore, he identifies a relatively high percentage of family groups (54% of emigrants from Inverness, Ross, and Argyll and some 80% from Perth, Caithness and Sutherland) among the Highland emigrants. Finally, Bailyn underlines the attraction of particular American destinations for Scottish emigrants; 70% voyaged to New York and North Carolina, while smaller groups were attracted to Pennsylvania and Georgia.[9]

The Glengarry County emigrations offer an opportunity to test Bailyn's model of the provincial emigrant stream. In this case, some 3,000 emigrants travelled to one particular destination over a forty-year period covering most of the first cycle of Scottish emigration. While the movement to Glengarry confirms Bailyn's overall vision of a provincial stream, it throws doubt on certain statistics which he presents for the Highland–Hebrides region (including Inverness-shire). Bailyn's general model of provincial emigration includes substantial family participation (67–80% from rural districts north of the Humber), but his figure of 54% from the Highlands–Hebrides falls significantly below this range. He also contends that a remarkable 57% of those leaving Inverness were labourers, "servants of no particular skill." Bailyn believes that "there are signs of a rural proletariat – of helpless, rootless poor leaving the land in large numbers" in this large contingent of Highland labourers.[10]

The key characteristics of Highland emigration to Glengarry County are summarized and compared to Bailyn's model in Table 6. These statistics make clear the importance of families, and therefore of women and children, in the movement to Glengarry, as in Bailyn's voyages. Similarly, the emigrants from western Inverness, like the provincial emigrants of the 1774–5 period, were carried in vessels hired for the purpose from local ports near their homes. However, in those departures for which information is available, over 90% of the Glengarry County settlers travelled in family groups and over 60% of families were headed by farmers. Overall, the Glengarry County statistics therefore confirm the pattern which Bailyn has identified for the provincial emigrant stream as a whole, although they cast some doubt on his figures for the percentage of families and labourers from the Highland–Hebrides region.

The story of the settlement of Glengarry County also illustrates how the level of emigration rose and fell through three distinct periods within the first cycle of Scottish emigration. The effects both of agrarian transformation and of opportunities abroad exercised a varying effect on the Highlanders' propensity and ability to emigrate throughout this period. Many of the factors that made the Glengarry settlement possible changed after 1815, and the seeming shift in the clansmen's attitude towards emigration is, contrary to Richard's interpretation, not surprising in light of the Glengarry County experience. To view the Highlands in the second half of the eighteenth century as a defeated society with a morbid culture is to miss the social ferment which integration into southern Britain engendered. In emigrating and settling in Canada, the clansmen found a radical, creative solution to the social and economic losses with which they were threatened.

The province of New York was the original destination of most of the first settlers in Glengarry County. Northern New York became attractive to emigrants only after 1763, when the conquest of Canada and its cession to Britain ended the bloody struggle between French and English for the land south of the Great Lakes and the St. Lawrence River. Veterans of the war were offered land in America and many officers and men of Highland regiments accepted that offer. The upper Hudson River Valley was familiar to the Highlanders from the days of war and the area was attractive for settlement when freed from the threat of invasion. Most of the military settlers were enlisted men from Montgomery's Highlanders who took up land near Fort Edward. On a different social scale were lieutenants Hugh Fraser

Table 6
Characteristics of Highland Emigration

Emigrant party	No. of emigrants	% children	% women 14+/1–99	% families	Average size of families	Community of origin	Occupation	Hired own vessel?	Local port
1773	425	47%	44%/—	—	—	Glen Garry Glen Moriston	—	—	Fort William
1785 (partial)	300	23% (age 1–9)	—/50%	97%	4.6	Glen Garry Glen Moriston	principal tenants	—	—
1786	530	—	—	—	—	Knoydart North Morar	better tenants	Yes	Knoydart
1790	87	42% (age 1–12)	—	91%	5.3	Eigg etc.	Agr. 61% Craft 13% Lab. 26%	Yes	Arisaig
1792	150	—	—	—	—	Glen Garry	—	—	Fort William
1793	150	—	—	—	—	Glenelg Glen Moriston	—	Yes	Glenelg
1802 (Neptune)	550	27% (age 1–12)	—	—	—	Knoydart, N. Morar, Kintail Glenelg	—	Yes	Knoydart
1802 (McMillan)	448	32% (age 1–12)	51%/—	91%	5.7	Glen Garry Lochiel Glen Moriston	—	Yes	Fort William
1815	362	49%	48%/—	98%	5.6	Knoydart Glenelg Killin	Agr. 61% Craft 12% Lab. 27%	No	No
Bailyn's Highland region	1,099	25% (of Scottish emigrants)	—/46%	54%	4.5	Inverness Ross/Cromarty	Agr. 30% Craft 10% Lab. 57%	Yes	Yes

and James Macdonald, both of whom acquired large grants of land on which to settle Scottish emigrants.[11] By 1770 such small concentrations of Highlanders were sufficient to make upper New York a new focal point for Highland emigration. Thus at the moment when the agrarian transformation of the Highlands first seriously threatened the clansmen, native Highlanders and other land speculators actively recruited inhabitants for wilderness lands in northwest New York. Among those who responded to their appeal was a party of emigrants some of whom were later to form the nucleus of the first group of clansmen to settle in Glengarry.

In September 1773, 425 clansmen (including 125 men, 100 women, and 200 children) sailed from Fort William on the *Pearl* for the colony of New York. This large emigrant party included a group of some 300 Highlanders, led by gentlemen from the Glengarry estate who were later to form the key element of the first Loyalist settlement in Glengarry County. Three of the gentlemen were brothers – John Macdonell of Leek, Allan of Collachie, and Alexander of Aberchalder – while the fourth was their cousin, Spanish John Macdonell of Scotus. Perhaps fifty of the emigrants led by the Macdonells were members of the gentlemen's immediate families or their servants. The remaining 250 were clansmen drawn from the region about the Great Glen.[12] Close to half of these were Macdonells or associated families – McMillans, McDougalls, McIntoshes, McGillises, or Kennedys – from the Glengarry estate. Another substantial group, including seven Cameron families, five Grants, two Chisholms, and four more Macdonells, came from neighbouring Glen Moriston. Others came from further north and included the Mackay, Rose, Fraser, Sutherland, McLeod, and McLennan families.[13] Although not all of the emigrants came from one estate, many were linked by bonds of kinship. For example, two McMartin brothers, Malcolm and John, and Malcolm's married son sailed together in 1773.

The emigrants led by the Macdonell gentlemen shared a past political commitment and common social origin in the tenant and gentlemen classes of Highland society. Glen Garry and Glen Moriston were solidly Jacobite during the 1745 rebellion, and several of the emigrants were intimately involved with the military campaign and the Prince's escape.[14] While most of the immigrants were not wealthy and did not become so in their new home, neither were they paupers. Only indirect evidence survives to hint at the capital which they brought with them from Scotland; this evidence consists of claims which many emigrants submitted to the British Crown for property lost in New York during the American Revolution. Spanish John, Allan of Collachie, and Alexander of Aberchalder claimed

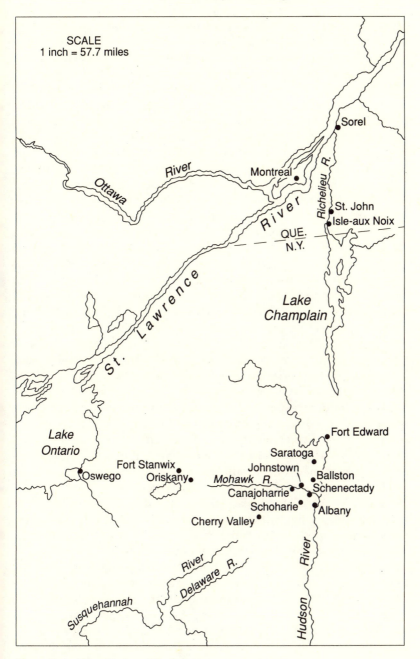

Map 5 Part of New York and Quebec, c. 1775

Sources: Based on a map entitled, "Canada and Nova Scotia," [1821] in NA, CAAD, negative no. 24679.

losses of £909, £543, and £255 respectively;[15] while Spanish John's claim seems unduly large, Aberchalder and Collachie may indeed have left Scotland with resources approaching these claims. Other emigrants submitted claims ranging from £24 to £130.[16] Since these figures included compensation for land (usually rented), improvements and crops, sums brought from Scotland must have been smaller. Nonetheless, even £24 was a substantial amount of capital in the Highlands in 1773, and this did not include the cost of the emigration itself. It seems clear, therefore, that the emigrants had been people of some means and standing in their local communities.

The reason behind this substantial emigration from western Inverness lay in the socioeconomic change that was transforming Glengarry and other estates. On their departure in 1773, some of the *Pearl* emigrants claimed that "the Proprietors ... raised the Lands higher in Rent than they could afford to pay."[17] While increased rents were a hardship which tended to encourage emigration, it was still possible to make a living as a tenant farmer. In 1771 a Glen Moriston farmer named McQueen told Boswell that he would emigrate, but in fact McQueen stayed on his farm and paid the quadrupled rent for ten more years; when he did leave, it was only to a neighbouring farm.[18]

Economic pressure itself did not necessarily result in emigration. It was rather the social effect of and response to economic change that appears to have been the final trigger for this first major emigration from western Inverness. Most immediately affected were the clan gentlemen who, with the chief, had governed the clan in the past. Over five generations, the Glengarry chiefs had provided younger sons with tacks on their estate; these men and their descendants, related to one another in degrees varying from brother to fifth cousin, formed a miniature aristocracy on Glengarry's lands. When Duncan McDonell raised rents and redeemed the gentlemen's wadsetts in 1772, he tightened the economic slack that his predecessors had allowed in the running of the estate and signalled the introduction of commercial rather than paternalistic management, for the chief's personal economic benefit. The gentlemen were faced not merely with the loss of favourable leases but with a new landlord-tenant relationship that ignored their traditional status in the community. In these circumstances, three of the gentlemen tenants of Glen Garry itself, Aberchalder, Collachie, and Leek, chose to lead an emigration of their clansmen to New York. In contrast, the Knoydart gentlemen, with one exception, did not emigrate in 1773 since they had either benefited from the minimal rent increases on the forfeit estate of Barisdale or negotiated new leases with Glengarry on favourable terms several years earlier. Spanish John Mac-donell, who rented the small farm of Croulin in Knoydart, chose to join his cousins in organizing the 1773 departure since his "disposi-tion [was] given rather to roving" and he opted "to leave my native soil and come to this great continent of America."[19]

The clansmen tenants who made up the bulk of the 1773 group also felt threatened by the socioeconomic transformation of their community. In a letter written from Fort William and published in New York on their arrival there, the Macdonell emigrants com-plained that "hardships and oppressions of different kinds, imposed … by the landholders … obliged them to abandon their native country." Indeed the emigrants claimed that if their "farms could but have afforded them bread and water, they would have been satisfied to stay at home."[20] Since Glengarry continued to find tenants for his estate, it is clear that the emigrants' assertion that they faced starvation if they paid the new rents was an exag-geration. Nevertheless, the increased rents took more out of the clansmen's pockets than they had been accustomed to paying, and it is clear from this letter that the emigrants regarded their departure as a choice forced on them by their landlords. Equally important to keep in mind, however, is the fact that the emigrants were described as "free Adventurers going to push their Fortunes abroad."[21] Faced with economic loss and the changed social order that commercial rents implied, some of Glengarry's tenants chose to emigrate as a group in 1773 to North America.

The *Pearl* reached New York on 18 October 1773 after a six-week passage, but the crossing was marred by tragedy, since twenty-five children died of smallpox during the voyage. After ten days in New York, the clansmen boarded a sloop to travel up the Hudson River to Albany. On the vessel the emigrants drank "His Majesty's Health and Prosperity to the Province," a gesture which foretold where their loyalties would likely lie in any struggle between colonists and King. The clansmen must have been well received in New York, since they "expressed the highest sense of Gratitude for the Civilities shewn them by the Inhabitants of [the] … City." Once in Albany, the emigrants sent representatives to look at a number of possible settlement locations.[22] To the west of Albany are the Mohawk River valley and the hilly uplands of the Susquehannah and Delaware rivers. These lands had been purchased from the Indians only in 1768, but the speculators and colonizers who had acquired large grants from the Crown now eagerly sought tenants.

Allan Macdonell of Collachie and his brothers visited Sir William Johnson, the largest proprietor in upper New York, early in November.[23] From the baronet the gentlemen obtained information about the lands available in the district, the quality of the soil, the ease of access and transportation, and the provision for mills. Meanwhile another four emigrants visited the grants of other proprietors in the neighbourhood of the Susquehannah and returned to Albany with the "Most flaterring encouragement."[24]

In the spring of 1774, the great majority of the Macdonell emigrants settled on Sir William Johnson's Kingsborough Patent.[25] This 50,000-acre estate (also known as Johnson's Bush) lay on the north shore of the Mohawk River, above the village of Johnstown. Over fifty Highland families settled there in 1774, renting land from Sir William; the clansmen received 50 or 100 acres, and the gentlemen 200. Until the emigrants established their farms, they were to pay no rent; after that time rent was fixed at £6 per 100 acres. Macdonell of Collachie apparently succeeded in obtaining a year's maintenance and a cow for each family, since Sir William described the settlers as being a considerable burden on him.[26] Such assistance would, however, have to be repaid by the settlers.

Several smaller groups of emigrants took up land in other locations. Most prominent among these was Spanish John Macdonell, who settled with three other Scottish families on a separate property owned by Sir William in the Charlotte River valley, fifty miles south of Johnson's Bush. Spanish John purchased 400 acres and was given another 90, but the men who accompanied him rented adjacent farms from the baronet.[27] Some families may have followed the example of one John Cameron, who leased a farm in Kortwright's Patent and was to buy a further 200 acres on the Delaware River. The neighbouring river valleys of the upper Delaware and the Charlotte, a tributary of the Susquehannah, thus became a second centre of Highland settlement.[28]

The settlement of most of the emigrants in Johnson's Bush in a "compact" body was the result of a conscious effort by both gentlemen and clansmen to keep (as one of them put it) "as close and united as possible."[29] Allan Macdonell told Sir William that he and his brothers had "some influence over people," and clearly the gentlemen expected to occupy positions of prominence as a result of the group settlement. The three brothers balanced self-interest with considerations of status when they gave up the opportunity of buying their own land immediately; instead they took *pro tempore* a small tract of land from Sir John Johnson at a certain Stipulated rate to be annually paid" so as to settle among the clansmen.[30]

Collachie and his brothers did not intend to be tenant farmers for long, however, since he arranged with Sir William that the gentlemen would have the option of selling out and being paid for their improvements. The Macdonell gentlemen may have hoped to gain possession of large tracts of land, like Sir William Johnson, and to convince the clansmen to settle on these lands.

The decision by most of the Macdonell emigrants to settle in Johnson's Bush was likely influenced by the presence there of other Highland families. Seventeen Scottish families had arrived in Albany six months before the *Pearl* emigrants and had taken up farms on Johnson's estate in June of 1773.[31] After the settlement of the Macdonell emigrants, Johnson's Bush had a decidedly Highland character and this made it an attractive destination for future emigrants. At least seven families (three Macdonells, two Grants, a Murcheson, and a McGillis) emigrated in 1774 and settled with the *Pearl* emigrants in Johnson's Bush. The Presbyterian minister of Albany, Harry Munro, also sent one Daniel Urquhart up the Mohawk River to Sir William, since Urquhart "wd fain Settle with his Countrymen, on Your Estate."[32] The establishment of such a distinct Scottish community was an obvious settlement strategy for the Highlanders to adopt in a region where German, Dutch, and English communities already existed. Differences of clan, glen, or religion might lead to the formation of separate settlements, like those on the Charlotte and Delaware rivers, but the communities together formed a small Highland colony in the Mohawk River valley.

The Scottish emigrants who settled in upper New York expected the new Highland community to grow rapidly. The clansmen's letters frequently referred to the willingness of "large Bodies of their Nation … to come over to America." Harry Munro explained that "the lower Class of people are generally discontented, and the Spirit of Emigration prevails greatly." The minister believed that several hundred families would soon follow the Highlanders who settled on Sir William's estate in June 1773.[33] The Macdonell gentlemen also expected to be joined by other Highland emigrants: "It would be agreeable to us that there be room or Scouth in our Vicinity in order that such of our friends & Countrymen as will incline to follow our fate may sit down in our Neighbourhood[;] we have reason to hope that severals of them will appear on this Continent if fortune does not frown upon us & force us to lay an Interdict on their Intentions."[34] This general interest in emigration was the result of the transformation of the Highlands and the clansmen's refusal to accept the losses which that entailed. Building compact settlements in the

New World might satisfy their aspirations for land at a reasonable price and permit the transfer of groups of related families and neighbours. But the events of 1775 *did* lay an interdict on further emigration from Scotland, and the small Highland communities of the Mohawk River soon became one of the most hotly disputed districts of the Revolutionary War.

As the Macdonell emigrants settled into their new homes, relations between the American colonists and the British government deteriorated rapidly. Quarrels over proposals to tax the colonies in the late 1760s had steadily deepened the rift between the British government and the American settlers. Committees of Correspondence sprang up in most Massachusetts towns in 1772 to coordinate and defend the patriots' cause, and this network spread to another twelve of the American colonies in the following year. The celebrated Boston Tea Party of December 1773, a protest against the taxation of tea, provoked stern legislative reaction from the British government in the spring of 1774.[35] In response to these acts of Parliament and to the appointment of General Gage as military governor of Massachusetts, the Committees of Correspondence convened the first Continental Congress in September 1774. Congress was dominated by militants who demanded the repeal of all objectionable legislation passed by Parliament since 1763. Both sides began preparations for war and fighting started at Lexington, Massachusetts, on 19 April 1775.[36]

In the Mohawk Valley, where the Macdonells were concentrated, those loyal to the British government were led by Sir John Johnson. Sir John had inherited Sir William Johnson's property at his father's death early in July 1774. Sir John and his brothers-in-law, Colonel Guy Johnson and Daniel Claus, led the opposition to the measures taken by the patriots and were solidly supported by their tenants and by prominent local landowners, including one John Butler. The Macdonell emigrants had been assisted by the Johnsons, and neither the gentlemen nor the clansmen had much sympathy with the grievances or actions of the patriots. When the revolt broke out, the Highlanders naturally stood together as a community and adopted the cause of King George as a single body. The first large-scale support for the Massachusetts patriots in the Mohawk Valley came at a meeting held in a German settlement west of Johnson's Bush on 27 August 1774.[37] The meeting expressed its allegiance to King George, but decried the recent acts of Parliament and the imposition of unjust taxes. The people of the western Mohawk Valley (or

Palatine district) established a Committee of Correspondence, and other districts in Tryon County, including Canajoharrie, south of the Mohawk River, followed their example. The first battle at Lexington finally split the valley into two warring camps. When patriotic sympathizers attempted to celebrate the victory by raising the first Liberty Pole in the county, they were frustrated by the arrival of the Johnsons, John Butler, Daniel Claus, and "a number of Highlanders" who dispersed the crowd.[38]

The Highlanders, as Alexander of Aberchalder later recalled, "remained peaceably on their Farms without any interruption" until this incident occurred.[39] But by the spring of 1775 those loyal to King George found it necessary to express their opposition to the revolutionary committees active in the Mohawk Valley. The patriots of the Palatine reported bitterly to the Albany committee of the influence and power of the Johnson family in the valley. Various family members were active in opposing the measures advocated by Congress; the District Committee reported that the Johnsons had even appeared at one of their meetings "with all their dependents armed to oppose the people considering of their grievances; their number being so large, and the people unarmed, struck terror into most of them, and they dispersed."[40] The Loyalists of Tryon County were strong enough at this time to sign and circulate a declaration of their opposition to the actions of Congress. In spite of "warm altercations and debates," the loyal statement was signed "by most of the Grand Jury and nearly all the Magistrates" of the county.

The Highland emigrants played an important role in the growing resistance to the revolution in the Mohawk Valley. The number of men available to Sir John had roughly doubled since the arrival of the Scots; their leaders, the Macdonell gentlemen, were seasoned soldiers, accustomed to military command. The Highlanders may actually have had a greater military value than their numbers warranted, since the American patriots seemed to dread the Highland Scots in particular. Their Roman Catholic religion and the fierce martial traditions of the clans clearly intimidated the Palatine District Committee. These German farmers complained that in addition to Guy Johnson's militia regiment, "about 150 Highlanders (Roman Catholics) in and about Johnstown are armed and ready to march."[41] The Highlanders' perspective on the events of 1775 was somewhat different: the clansmen believed that the patriots were jealous of the Highlanders' "attachment to Government, and their connection with Sir John Johnson." As a result, the patriots threatened the clansmen and ultimately came either to imprison them or to make them submit to Congress. In these circumstances, the Highlanders "thought it prudent ... to take up Arms, and put themselves under the Command of Sir John Johnson."[42] At the end of 1775, the political situation in the Mohawk Valley was dead-locked. Though somewhat outnumbered, the Loyalists under Sir John Johnson had managed to maintain both their principles and their property in spite of the threats of their patriotic neighbours.

The freedom of a large body of men hostile to the patriots was an anomaly that Sir John Johnson's family prestige and the military strength of his tenants could preserve only in the short term. On 30 December 1775, Congress ordered General Schuyler to disarm the Loyalists of Tryon County and apprehend their leaders.[43] As Alexander of Aberchalder pointed out, Congress took this action "to oppose a Confederacy which they supposed to be dangerous to their Interests."[44] General Schuyler camped near Johnstown on 16 January 1776 with a force of 3,000 men, including 900 local militia volunteers. Sir John and some of the "Scotch tenants" met with Schuyler and the baronet surrendered certain arms on 20 January. What was more important to the patriots was the arrival at Schuyler's camp on 21 Janaury of between "two and three hundred" Highlanders who "marched to the front and ground their arms which were im-mediately secured." The general still did not rest easy about the Highlanders; he complained the next day "that many of the Scotch had broadswords and dirks which had not been delivered up, either from inattention or wilfull omission." No action, however, seems to have followed this complaint. Schuyler also took hostages for the Loyalists' good behaviour, all of them Highlanders.[45]

In spite of these events and the parole given to Sir John Johnson, relations between Loyalists and patriots remained tense. The Johnson family had long been associated with the Six Nations tribes (the Iroquois confederacy) and since the Indians had allied them-selves with the British and fled to Canada in 1775, Mohawk Valley patriots viewed the arrival of any Indians at Johnstown as warning of an attack on patriot settlements.[46] When the British army evacuated Boston in March 1776, the patriots were encouraged by their victory to take strong measures elsewhere in the colonies. General Schuyler sent troops under Colonel Dayton to Johnstown, ostensibly to remove the Highlanders but in fact with orders to release Sir John from his parole and immediately to arrest him. The general wrote to Sir John of his intention to remove the Scots, claiming that "the elder McDonald [Leek] had desired to have all the clan of his name in County of Tryon removed and subsisted." Johnson consulted the Highlanders and, as they "unanimously resolved not to deliver themselves as prisoners, but to go another way," the baronet decided to accompany them.[47] When Colonel Dayton arrived at Johnstown on 19 May 1776, he found that his quarry had fled. Evidently the patriots were serious in their intention to round up all the Highlanders, for the Albany Committee of Safety remarked after Dayton's abortive sortie: "if the Said male inhabitants have Escaped the Vigilance of Col dayton [sic], ... the Removal of the female old and infirm" was no longer necessary.[48]

The Highlanders who fled north through the wilderness with Sir John Johnson were not the only party of Scottish refugees to reach Canada from the Mohawk Valley. In May 1775, after the battle of Lexington, Guy Johnson had led the Indians of the Six Nations to Canada, accompanied by John Macdonell, eldest son of Aberchalder, and by "thirty armed Highlanders."[49] Sir John Johnson's party of 170 men, roughly half of whom were Scottish, reached the St. Lawrence in June 1776 "almost starved and wore out for want of provisions."[50] A third body of Highlanders arrived in Montreal on 10 May 1777, led by Allan of Collachie and Alexander of Aberchalder. These two gentlemen and the latter's son Hugh had been imprisoned as hostages in Pennsylvania; after their escape in the spring of 1777, they returned to Johnstown where they collected "the scatter'd remains of the Loyalists left after Sir John Johnson's departure which his sudden removal and the shortness of their notice prevented from joining."[51] The party they led included forty-five Highlanders, who offered to serve as soldiers, but only if they would not be separated from their Scottish leaders. Political loyalties notwithstanding, these refugee clansmen would "Serve During the warr But are So Attached to their Chiefs that they Cant Think of Parting with Them."[52] Especially during the hectic days of war, the Highland emigrants made political and military decisions as a community and were determined to follow their traditional leaders.

In Canada, most able-bodied men joined British and Loyalist regiments in compact groups of kin, friends, and refugees. Some of the emigrants from the Mohawk Valley served in the Eighty-fourth or Royal Highland Emigrant Regiment, raised in 1775 by Allan McLean among the Highland settlers of Prince Edward Island, Nova Scotia, and Quebec. John, son of Aberchalder, and Allan of Collachie both held commissions in the Eighty-fourth.[53] Sir John Johnson was authorized to raise a Loyalist corps, the King's Royal Regiment of New York (KRRNY) in June 1776 shortly after his arrival in Montreal, and most of the Mohawk Valley Highlanders who took up arms during the war fought with this regiment. Its officers included Spanish John and his son Miles, Alexander of Aberchalder and his son Hugh, and John of Leek's sons Archibald, Allan, and Ranald. A few Highlanders served in Butler's Rangers, including the Aberchalder brothers Chichester and John (who exchanged from the Eighty-fourth) and Alexander, son of Collachie.[54]

While the Loyalists of Johnson's Bush were forced in 1776 first to give hostages and then to flee, the settlers at the head of the Delaware River, fifty miles to the south, were merely kept under observation that year. Spanish John took an active role in organizing Loyalist resistance and was considered the leader of that "nest of Scottish Toryism" in the Kortwright and Banyar patents. During 1776, the Delaware Valley Loyalists formed a militia company under the direction of Spanish John and convinced those who would not enlist to sign an oath of neutrality.[55] As patriot leader John Harper reported, "the peopell of Harpersfield onfortinately fell into the Hands of McDonald, who amediately Swor them not to take up arms against the King of Britain."[56] By May of 1777, however, the patriots were strong enough to seize the property of prominent Loyalists.[57]

The summer of 1777 brought a two-pronged invasion of New York by the British, intended to cut New York off from the rebellious New England colonies. While Burgoyne marched south *via* Lake Champlain and the Hudson to ultimate surrender at Saratoga, a second force under General St. Leger swung west to Lake Ontario and then south to the Mohawk River. St. Leger commanded 2,000 men, including Sir John Johnson's KRRNY and Joseph Brant and his Mohawk Indians. On 3 August 1777, St. Leger laid siege to Fort Stanwix on the upper Mohawk and three days later ambushed an enemy force sent to lift the siege. Loyalist losses were light, but some 400 patriots were killed at the Battle of Oriskany, "a bloody encounter," fought by brothers and neighbours.[58] A second relief expedition forced St. Leger to abandon the siege on 22 August. In conjunction with the British attack that summer, New York Loyalists were called on to join the flag. Spanish John was one of the prominent Loyalists summoned to Oswego in July to confer with Sir John Johnson before St. Leger's invasion. The old Jacobite then returned to the Delaware settlements where he "accordingly raised, and armed fifty-four men." The company marched north to Schoharie to join forces with other Loyalists, led by the pipes.[59] The patriots sent a company of light horse against the Loyalist force, but these were ambushed and turned back at the battle of The Flockey on 13 August. Macdonell brought some of the victorious Loyalists west to join St. Leger and thence to Canada.[60]

The war fought by Loyalists and patriots in the Mohawk Valley over the next five years was chiefly a guerilla war, characterized by a series of devastating raids. The summer and autumn of 1778 saw the Loyalists destroy seven separate settlements in raids that included the infamous massacres of Wyoming and Cherry Valley. The latter raid was the Indians' incensed response to the destruction of their own town of Oquaga. This pattern of retaliatory raids continued throughout the war years, with buildings burned, cattle and horses driven off, and crops destroyed by both sides. While the military results of this type of warfare are difficult to assess, it seems clear that neither side was able to dominate the Mohawk Valley.[61] Although the Loyalists' families suffered a great deal, so did the patriots'. In April 1780 the entire population of Tryon County was reported to be close to starvation. In October yet another raid by the Loyalists resulted in the destruction of Schoharrie, part of Ballstown, and of farms on both sides of the Mohawk from Fort Hunter to Fort Rensselaer; 150,000 bushels of wheat and proportionate amounts of grain and forage were lost, as well as 200 dwellings. Patriot Governor Clinton admitted that Schenectady (located near the mouth of the Mohawk) "may now be said to have become the limits of our western Frontier."[62]

The Highland Loyalists lived in America only a few years before the outbreak of war, but they showed a predictable aptitude for frontier warfare. In one typical action, twenty-two-year-old Captain John Macdonell took a scouting party of rangers and 100 Indians through the backwoods, gathering information and harassing the rear of an enemy advance.[63] Highland warfare traditionally involved sudden attack, plunder, and retreat over difficult terrain, so the Highlanders, although newcomers, soon became skilled frontier guerillas in the mountainous country north of the Mohawk River. In August 1778 Joseph Newkerk reported a raid by a "Party of the Enemy to the Number of about Twenty Indians and One McDonald, a Tory"; it is by no means certain who Newkerk found more frightening, the Indians or the Highlander.[64]

The families that the Loyalist men left behind when they fled to Canada were vulnerable to Patriotic reprisals for British raids. The confiscation of Loyalist property left both rich and poor dependent on the charity of their enemies. In September 1779 a petition was sent to Governor Clinton by Christine, Ann, Else, and Mary McDonald, Kate McIntosh, and Ann McPherson, explaining that they and many others "are reduced to the greatest distress imagine-able by having their Cattle and Effects sold ... and no way of getting a living whereby they might support themselves."[65] Similarly Spanish John wrote in March 1780 that his wife and children "were both naked and starving" and that "my oldest Girl of about sixteen was oblidged to hire herself to Spinn." The Loyalist men petitioned their commanders and the governor of Quebec for permission and help to bring their families to Canada. Spanish John's plea to Governor Haldimand on the same subject emphasizes the stark desperation felt by lonely husbands and fathers:

If nothing can be done to obtain their speedy delieverance, I beg as the greatest obligation you can lay me under that you apply to his Excellency to send a party of Savages to bring me their six scalps, tho' it may seem unnatural, yet I assure you I would rather see or hear them dead than to linger any longer in misery ... I will most cheerfully head any party he may think proper and make out their number, or perish in the attempt.[66]

The patriots did not immediately expel Loyalist families since they found it useful to keep the women and children hostage for the good behaviour of British troops. Later some Loyalist families were permitted to leave in exchange for Americans taken captive by the Indians. In November 1780 thirty-two Highland families were delivered to Canada in this way.[67] The wives and children of Spanish John and Allan Macdonell of Collachie were not so fortunate; in spite of efforts to organize their exchange, they spent the war years in poverty in New York.[68] Other Loyalist families owed their rescue to British raiding parties, including the one led by Sir John Johnson in May 1780; when the Loyalists retreated they took with them "many Women, Wifes to Persons who ... [had already joined the British in Canada] and their Children."[69]

When peace came to America with the Treaty of Versailles in 1783, the Highland emigrants were scattered across northern New York and the full length of the province of Quebec. Many had fought in and all had suffered from a war that was neither of their making nor to their benefit. The defeat of the British cause meant the final abandonment of lands the emigrants had acquired in New York; in compensation the British government undertook to settle the refugees in the remaining British colonies. In the summer of 1784 the Highland refugees followed the surveyors up the St. Lawrence River and received grants of land from the Crown in the first three townships west of the French seigneuries. The Highland emigrants of 1773 had maintained their sense of community throughout the upheavals of emigration, settlement, and war, and now that peace had come, the same commitment to community directed their actions. Nancy Jean Cameron expressed their hope for their new home when she wrote to friends in Scotland that the "McDonalds ... hope to found in the new land a new Glengarry."[70]

CHAPTER SEVEN

The 1785–1793 Emigrants

When peace returned in 1783, Scottish ports opened again to Highland emigration. The independence of the American colonies, however, substantially reduced Highland interest in emigration to these regions; there was a distinct lull between two active periods in the first cycle of Scottish emigration. Highland communities in Georgia, the Carolinas, and New York were in disarray. The Loyalists, who in some districts formed a large segment of the population, often left to seek new homes under British rule. Of the surviving British North American colonies, Nova Scotia, St. John's Island (now Prince Edward Island), and Quebec held the major concentrations of Highland settlers, and these northern colonies became the primary target of Highland emigration when a new period of departures began.

Emigration from the Highlands in the ten years between the American and French revolutionary wars never reached the levels or intensity that had characterized transatlantic migration between 1763 and 1775. Perhaps some 2,950 emigrants left the north of Scotland between 1783 and 1793,[1] – that is, the yearly emigration averaged less than one-third the annual number in the earlier period. The decline in emigration was in part the result of the political division that resulted from the American Revolution. Clansmen showed a clear preference for emigrating within the British Empire, and some fall in the rate of emigration was to be expected until new colonial destinations could replace the old. Certain Highland districts already had links with the remaining British colonies, and others quickly established such ties with the resettlement of the Loyalist Scots. St. John's Island had small colonies from Uist and Glenfinnan, while Pictou, Nova Scotia, had been settled from Ross-shire. The New York Loyalists from western

Inverness were soon established on Crown lands west of the French seigneuries in Quebec, while veterans of the Eighty-fourth Regiment from the southern American colonies, who had come principally from the Hebrides, settled with their clansmen in Pictou. These settlements were the focal points of the emigration that occurred in the ten years of peace that followed. The second period of emigration witnessed the maturing of these new links between the Highlands and British North America.

During the last two decades of the eighteenth century, emigration gained that crucial acceptance that made it a real option to the clansmen and became the key element of Highland experience which it has long remained. Local clergymen expressed no astonishment at the successive departures of "great Colonies" of Highlanders. "Constant emigrating" and "great preparations for emigrating" became commonplace in many Highland districts and were no longer considered remarkable.[2] The belief that "People in this Age Must move about in quest of Employment & bread" was accepted by gentlemen and clergymen sympathetic to the people and by a large number of clansmen.[3] By end of this period, in 1793, both the practice of emigration and the new Highland settlements in British North America were sufficiently well established to make emigration an obvious option to the clansmen.

During these ten years, emigration was a particularly important choice for the people of a few estates in western Inverness who decided to join their friends in the new Highland settlement in western Quebec. The 1,217 clansmen who reached Glengarry County between 1785 and 1793 formed 40% of the emigrant stream from the Highlands to British North America over these years.[4] Their enthusiastic acceptance of emigration was the result of the growing demographic and economic crisis that threatened the clansmen in the late eighteenth century. Local agriculture had never produced much of a surplus, and the tenants' prosperity was marginal at best. The dramatic rise in population that characterized these years clearly strained agricultural resources, while the famine of 1782–3 hinted at the costs of failing to find a solution to the problem of growing numbers. In 1782, both the grain and potato crops were disastrous, leaving "a great many of the people ... exceedingly ill off for want of means of supporting life." The only way of feeding more mouths, given existing land tenure and usage, was to substitute potatoes (which would feed three or four times as many people per acre) for oats. Without land reform or local industry, only emigration offered an alternative to subsistence based to an ever larger degree on potatoes.[5]

But even as the population grew, changes in landholding and agricultural production tended to diminish the clansmen's resources. The introduction of large-scale sheep farming in the 1780s triggered an economic and social crisis for the tenants of western Inverness. While a few did stock their farms with sheep, most tenants had to pay greatly increased rents from traditional cattle farms. Bishop MacDonald caustically described the situation on the Clanranald estate in 1789:

The Set [rental of the estate] has turned out more favourable to the small tenants than what we were at first given to understand would be the case. Every Body was allowed to overbid each other, notwithstanding the former possessors had preference, & got, some of them, a considerable deduction of the offers made by better Bets than themselves. The rents are however exorbitantly high & great numbers will not be able to make them good for any length of time, unless divine providence will interfer.[6]

Clanranald's tenants emigrated in droves both over the next few years and in subsequent periods.

Even with concessions from their chiefs, the tenants could not long compete with sheep farmers for the possession of their former holdings. The transformation of the economy of western Inverness presented tenants with few choices: loss of status and possible impoverishment, migration south, or emigration. Between 1786 and 1793, more than one-third of the population of Knoydart left Scotland for British North America.[7] Over a thirty-year period beginning in 1785, a majority of the tenants of Knoydart, Glengarry, and Glenelg, as well as a substantial number from Lochiel, did the same. Faced with what they viewed as their chiefs' betrayal, many tenants decided that "the hardships they suffer under their squeezing & unfeeling masters oblige them to look for an asylum in distant Regions." Not all the tenants of western Inverness chose to emigrate at the same time. The first migrations did consist of kin and community-based groups who had experienced or were threatened with the loss of their traditional holdings, but these people "carried with them the means of procuring a comfortable home beyond the Atlantic." Those who stayed "in their much loved native land" faced steady impoverishment, until many of them – now far poorer – also chose to join their friends in Canada.[8] Communities were divided by emigration, but in Upper Canada many of the tenants of western Inverness were able to build their own Highland community.

The second group of emigrants to settle in Glengarry County left Scotland in 1785. The most prominent individual to leave that year was Roderick Macdonell, a Catholic missionary who had worked among the clansmen of Glengarry from 1775 to 1785. Roderick was the son of John Macdonell of Leek, one of the tacksmen leaders of the 1773 emigration; three of Roderick's brothers held commissions in Sir John Johnson's regiment during the Revolutionary War.[9] When his family emigrated in 1773, Roderick was studying for the priesthood in Douai, France, and was unable to accompany them. Upon his return to Scotland, Roderick refused to bind himself to serve the Scottish mission exclusively and instead took the missionary oath "on the express condition of being able to go to America."[10] His reasons for this condition mirrored the concerns of his flock: "as his parents & whole family had already gone to America," Roderick hoped that within a few years "to follow his numerous connections" there.[11] In spite of his vocation Roderick Macdonell shared the clansmen's interest in keeping family and community intact.

Roderick Macdonell's decision to emigrate was not, however, based simply on a desire to be reunited with his family. It also reflected the religious needs of the Highland emigrants settled in Canada. In a petition addressed to the Secretary of State, Lord Sydney, Macdonell explained his reasons: "That Lands have been lately assigned ... [to the Scotch Loyalists] in the higher part of Canada; but being of the Roman Catholic persuasion, they are at a Loss for a clergyman, understanding their Language ... That the Memorialist being known and related to many of them, they have communicated Solicitations to him to go abroad & serve them in that capacity."[12] Bishop Alexander MacDonald was extremely reluctant to give Roderick, whom he considered an excellent missionary, permission to leave Scotland. The scarcity of priests that had troubled the Highlands diocese in the 1760s had lessened somewhat by 1785, but rapid population growth left the clergy barely able to serve their widely scattered congregations; just as Roderick announced his intention of emigrating in 1784, another young priest died suddenly. The Roman Catholic hierarchy was not happy to lose missionaries to Canada, but many priests, like Roderick Macdonell, concluded: "what will the priests do when the people goes [sic] and are we not made for the people more than the place?"[13]

As soon as peace was concluded in America, Roderick Macdonell's family encouraged him to join them in the New World. This pressure mounted when his brother arrived in Scotland early in 1785 and Roderick found that family feeling had not weakened over time. "You may be Sure I was quit [sic] happy to meet a Brother, whom I had not seen for five and twenty years."[14] Both Roderick's brother and his cousin, Captain John Macdonell of Aberchalder, travelled to Britain to present their claims for compensation as Loyalists to the government. It may have been with these claims in mind that Roderick presented a petition of his own to Lord Sydney in June of 1785. His memorial mentioned the poverty of the Roman Catholic Loyalists, and asked for permission to join them, for payment of his travelling expenses to the new settlements, and for an annual pension. After a favourable reception from Lord Sydney, Roderick Macdonell left London on 20 July, boarded the ship *Ranger* at Spithead on 2 August, and reached Quebec after an agreeable voyage on 28 September 1785.[15]

In leaving for Canada, the priest was joining a sizeable portion of his flock. Two hundred clansmen left Glen Garry in 1785, together with 100 emigrants from Glen Moriston. These people were described by their bishop as "the principal tenants" and the "most reputable Catholics" of the two estates.[16] A majority of the emigrants were Macdonalds, but the party also included Frasers, Grants, McIntoshes, Kennedys, McIntyres, McMillans, McTavishes, Chisholms, and a McQueen. A partial list of the 1785 emigrants (151 of a reported 300) shows that most of this group left in family groups; only four adults – two men and two women – were unmarried. The remaining 147 people, or 97% of the 151, travelled with family members. Six couples were childless and the average family with children consisted of 5.6 people.[17]

Their decision to leave the Highlands for America was not taken suddenly. Those who emigrated in 1773 had spoken confidently of other Highlanders following them to New York.[18] Since both the 1773 and 1785 emigrants came chiefly from Glen Garry and Glen Moriston, it seems probable that consideration of a second emigration began almost as soon as the first group left. Although the outbreak of war closed Scottish ports to further departures, the Loyalist emigrants corresponded with their former neighbours, eventually informing them of their move to Canada. As early as 9 June 1784, when the Loyalists were themselves just arriving in Glengarry County and drawing for allotments of land, Father Roderick Macdonell wrote from Inverness-shire: "There is a great emigration from this country to America. 300 Catholics are leaving it to join the 8 or 9 hundred from this and adjacent countries already settled on the Banks of the St. Lawrence."[19] Clearly those who remained in Scotland kept in touch with the Loyalist emigrants, and the moment that political conditions again favoured emigration, clansmen from Glen Garry and Glen Moriston began to plan a second voyage to America.

The general cause for the tenants' departure in 1785 lay in their dissatisfaction with the Glengarry estate and in the attractive prospect of settling as a group with family and friends already in America. The sharp rent increases imposed by Duncan McDonell in 1772 had seriously eroded the economic security of the tenants and the traditional social relationship of chief and clansmen. But in the three years before 1785, the tenants' situation grew steadily worse. In 1782 bad weather destroyed crops across the Highlands. Locally, Glen Quoich, the western half of Glen Garry, had been let as a sheep farm, and the ensuing loss of summer grazing clearly warned the Glengarry tenants of their prospects for the future. Glengarry's attempt to evict the tenants of eleven farms early in 1784 seems to have provided the final impetus to set the emigration in motion. Fifty-five tenants from farms along the north and south shores of the River Garry were ordered to leave by Whitsunday 1784. References to a definite plan of emigration occur at this time, but the tenants did not leave their farms that year, and Glengarry had to obtain a decree and sentence of removal against them from the sheriff-depute of Inverness in April 1785.[20] In addition to the fifty-five tenants ordered to leave, their "Wives, Bairns, Family Tenants, Sub-tenants, Cottars and Dependents" were also cited – a minimum of 100 families or roughly 500 people.

Not all of those evicted from their farms chose to emigrate or could afford to do so. Only 200 people or perhaps forty families left Glengarry in 1785; some 300 people, including the families of at least fifteen tenants, remained in Scotland. A small number of tenants appear to have kept possession of their farms. John Macdonald of Inchlaggan and Donald Kennedy of Auchlouchiach, who were ordered out of their farms in the 1785 decree, were still listed as living there in 1802. Similarly Angus McMillan and his cousins were removed in 1802 from Badenjoig, which Angus and his father and uncle had been warned to leave in 1785.[21] Five other farms, supposedly cleared in 1785, were still inhabited by Glengarry's clansmen in 1802, although by how many and of what status – tenant or crofter – is not known.[22] Possibly a majority of those remaining were unable to pay their passage to Canada, but tenants such as the McMillans of Badenjoig who emigrated in 1802 were not notably poorer than those who emigrated in 1785.

No single list identifies all the emigrants from Glen Garry and

Glen Moriston in 1785. We must instead compare two documents in order to identify the emigrants and to date their arrival in Canada in 1786, after a remarkable journey. The first document is the previously mentioned eviction notice of 1785; the second is a provisioning list dated August 1786. The considerable interval between the two lists is explained in the title of the second: "Victualling list of Emigrants lately Come from Scotland by the way of New York & Albany who meaned to settle in this Province." Similarities between the two lists, and a long oral and written tradition in Glengarry County itself, make a convincing link between the tenants of the Glengarry estate and the "Emigrants by way of New York." The victualling list contains thirty-six names, two-thirds of them Macdonalds. Sixteen of the twenty-four Macdonald names on the victualling list also appear on the 1785 eviction notice. This, of course, proves nothing; any two lists of Macdonalds would overlap, given the prevalence of a few common Christian names like Angus or John. But of the twelve non-Macdonalds on the victualling list, two names definitely suggest a Glen Moriston origin.[23] Another four men can be located on both lists: John McIntosh of Auchlouchiach, Donald McMillan of Badenjoig, Duncan Kennedy of Laggan, and John Kennedy of Laddy.[24] It thus seems probable that some of the evicted tenants were among the 1785 emigrants who reached Canada in 1786.

The story of the 1785 emigration to Canada cannot be established definitely in all its detail, but when documentary and oral sources are put together, a cohesive narrative of the emigrants' journey to Canada emerges. The emigrants left Scotland under the leadership of Allan Macdonell. Later a Justice of the Peace in Glengarry County and described as "Esquire," Macdonell was one of the substantial tenants who dominated this emigration.[25] Macdonell was born at Inchlaggan on the Glengarry estate in 1746. (His younger brother Alexander, later Bishop Macdonell of Kingston, was a commanding figure in Canadian history).[26] On 5 August 1785, the bishop responsible for the Highland diocese reported that the Glen Garry and Glen Moriston tenants had emigrated to America six weeks earlier. In a second letter written in May 1786, the bishop again referred to the emigration that had occurred in 1785, and his letter suggests that these emigrants did not accompany Father Roderick, who sailed in August 1785 from Spithead.[27] Six petitions for land from Highlanders in Glengarry County give the year of the petitioners' emigration from Scotland as 1785.[28] Two of the petitions specifically state that the petitioner was part of a group emigration in that year: "Your Memorialist came to this Country in 1785 with a body of Emigrants from Scotland."[29]

The written record is least forthcoming, however, on the fate of the emigrants between their departure from Scotland late in June of 1785 and their provisioning in Canada in August of 1786. Only Allan Macdonell's obituary and the emigrant victualling list give any account of the emigrants' fortunes between these two dates. Even the obituary is a second-hand report, written by Bishop Macdonell and thus presumably based on his brother's reminiscenes.

After a passage of seventeen weeks they were driven by stress of weather into Philadelphia. Though distant from the place of their destination and assailed by offers which were sufficiently advantageous to induce them to settle in the United States, Mr. M'Donald's [sic] influence over them so prevailed that not an individual remained behind, or departed from his Allegiance. After great privations, and at a considerable expense, the party settled in Glengarry.[30]

The reference in the 1786 victualling list to the arrival of the Highlanders by way of New York and Albany may simply omit the emigrants' port of entry, and it adds weight to the suggestion of a detour through the United States. The assertion in the obituary that all 300 emigrants reached Glengarry County is very definite. It thus seems evident that the 151 people named in the victualling list represented only half the emigrants who reached Glengarry via the United States in 1786.[31]

Although it confuses the date of the 1785 emigrants' sailing, the oral tradition confirms and expands what the documents record of their long journey to Canada. All oral accounts state that two ships left in 1786 (not 1785), and that one group of emigrants arrived a year later by way of New York. One ship *did* leave western Inverness in 1786, carrying a large party of emigrants from Knoydart to Glengarry County but, as we have seen, the ship that failed to reach Canada and whose passengers arrived via the United States sailed in 1785, not 1786. It seems beyond reasonable doubt that the oral tradition of the "delayed" emigrants of 1786 in fact refers to the party led by Allan Macdonell in 1785–6. Exactitude about dates is not, in general, a strong point of oral testimony, and in this instance, tradition has telescoped two events into one year.

The first oral account of the 1785 emigration to be recorded appeared in 1881 in an article published by A.M. Pope.[32] According to Miss Pope, one of two ships that left Scotland in 1786 was forced by bad weather to turn back to Belfast for repairs. Although the ship sailed a second time that year for America, it was prevented from reaching Quebec by the lateness of the season, and instead the emigrants landed at Philadelphia. Lodged for the winter in former British army barracks, the emigrants were the victims of a second disaster when their quarters burned to the ground. Late in the winter of 1787 [sic], the emigrants continued their journey by Lake Champlain to Isle-aux-Noix in Canada, where friends from Glengarry County met them. The source of Pope's account of the 1785 emigration is revealed in George Sandfield Macdonald's oral history collection, preserved in his Glengarry notebooks of 1883–5. Macdonald was clearly intrigued by Pope's tale which he referred to as the "Delaware story." In one of his notebooks, Macdonald quoted material which he described as an "Extract from Miss Pope's Questions." Her source of information was named as "the old man at St. Raphaels."[33] According to the old man, the emigrants "wintered at Philadelphia, lost all by fire and in the spring started for their destination. Were met by their friends at Ile aux Noix."

With his curiosity aroused, Sandfield Macdonald himself attempted to discover more about the reputed 1787 emigrants. His most valuable informant on the subject was Captain Grey (Macdonell), 88 years old in March of 1884. Sandfield concluded that the captain was the source of the Delaware story and recorded his tale in these words: "Says the captain of the ship was Archd. McNeil. Went to New York and then to Albany & stayed that winter & agreed with the quelude [sic] of the states & took up lands in Johnstown. Made an application from Albany to Col. Deschambeau. Left Albany in 87 for Canada in boats to Lake George then by Champlain & river Richelieu to Sorel & to Montreal. They got a years provision."[34] The captain named eighteen of the 1787 [sic] emigrants, as well as the native glens of thirteen: eight from Glen Garry, four from Glen Moriston, and one from Knoydart. John Macdonald agreed with Captain Grey, but another contemporary, James Ranald McGillis, did not believe the Delaware story to be true.[35]

A third version of the 1785 emigration occurs in Carrie Holmes MacGillivray's novel, *The Shadow of Tradition*, first published in 1927. MacGillivray seems to have drawn, if not directly on A.M. Pope, then on the same oral source on which Pope based her article. In the novel two ships leave Scotland in 1786. The first ship is damaged by storms and puts into Belfast for repair. On sailing a second time, it reaches New York, but a lack of accommodation there forces the ship to travel on to Philadelphia. The emigrants are accommodated in empty barracks, which are destroyed by fire on 10 January 1787. The emigrants then travel north to Isle-aux-Noix, where their Glengarry County friends come before the spring thaw to take them to their new home.[36] MacGillivray clearly acknowledged her dependence on the oral tradition in her preface: "Many of the incidents portrayed are based upon the unwritten history. The sufferings of the unfortunate people on the Britannia are not exagerated. The real name of the vessel is uncertain; but the tale of its tragic voyage and the subsequent hardships of the emigrants is tradition known by a few of the present generation, and the truth of which they have no reason to doubt."[37]

The basic story that lies behind all the oral accounts of the 1785 emigration fits well with the few facts we know from the documentary record. Bad weather that delayed the ship and forced it to land in an American port, and the journey via Albany – these appear as common elements in both traditional and written accounts of the journey. Where the oral record gives more detail than the written, that detail is generally neither implausible nor incompatible with the known facts of the migration. The emigrants *did* leave late in June of 1785 and their passage of seventeen weeks is reported to have ended unexpectedly at Philadelphia. The reason for their landing in an American port is not fully explained in the written record, but the refit in Belfast (part of the traditional story), together with a seventeen-week passage, could easily have brought them to North America after the St. Lawrence was closed to navigation by ice. The ship's master, knowing that the river would be closed, may then have made for an American port.[38] Similarly, the destruction of the barracks in which the emigrants were lodged could have been one of the "great privations" referred to in the obituary.

The only part of the oral tradition incompatible with the written one is Captain Grey's account of the emigrants accepting land at Johnstown. This seems improbable if, by his account, the emigrants took only one winter between their arrival in New York and their departure for Canada. The obituary mentions advantageous offers of land to the emigrants in the United States, and perhaps it is to one of these that Captain Grey actually refers. In other respects the captain's narrative rings true. Indeed the man he names as having received the emigrants into Canada, Deschambeau, can be identified in the military records of the time. In 1786 Deschambeau was a lieutenant in the Forty-fourth Regiment, but he later served as a colonel in the Canadian militia. The first battalion of the Forty-fourth was posted at stations near Montreal from late 1781 until the summer of 1786, when it sailed for Britain.[39] While there is no specific proof that Lieutenant Deschambeau helped the 1785 emigrants, the accuracy of the oral record in naming a British officer serving in the border region during the year in question is clearly more than coincidental.

The most striking aspect of the story of the 1785 emigration is its absence from any written history of Glengarry County. Local histories by J.A. Macdonell in 1893 and John Harkness in 1946 mention only the 500 emigrants from Knoydart who left Scotland in 1786.[40] General studies of emigration to Canada also make no reference to the 1785 emigrants.[41] More recently, Ewen Ross and Royce MacGillivray uncovered one of the few documents that mentions the 1785 emigration, but they did not work their material out to its logical conclusion.[42] On the other hand, oral traditions collected from the Glengarry community more than a century after the 1785 emigration continued to report an emigration by way of New York. The combination of two factors – closeness in time of the emigration from Glen Garry and Glen Moriston in 1785 to that from Knoydart in 1786, and the arrival of both groups in Canada in the same year – led over time to a conflating of two emigrations into a single event. Histories of Glengarry County written from documentary sources described only the larger 1786 emigration, while the oral histories preserved the more accurate account of two ships and two emigrations.

The third major emigration to Glengarry County (as mentioned above) originated in Knoydart and North Morar in 1786. Firsthand accounts of the emigrants' departure from Scotland and their arrival in Canada agree that more than 500 people made the passage.[43] Three men, each in a different way a man of standing in the community, figured prominently in the emigration. To the colonial government, Lieutenant Angus McDonell was the leader and spokesman for the emigrants. McDonell (or Sandaig as he was called, after his Knoydart farm) had served in America during the Revolutionary War in the Seventy-first Regiment and returned to Scotland on half-pay in June of 1784.[44] Father Alexander McDonell, a younger son of the Scotus family, was the spiritual leader of the emigrants, and a later generation also remembered him as one of the organizers of the journey. James Ranald McGillis recalled that "the people selected Scotus & Angus Macdonald (Sandeck) to procure a ship to take them over."[45] The third prominent figure among the emigrants was Angus Ban Macdonell, tenant of Muniall on the Barisdale estate. Family tradition, preserved until the present day, names Angus Ban as one of the leaders of the 1786 emigration, and other oral sources confirm his standing in the community. It seems likely that Angus Ban played a pivotal role in the decision to emigrate; as one of the improving farmers on the Barisdale estate and a man of influence in Knoydart, his commitment to emigration would have induced others to leave also.[46]

There is too little information for a statistical analysis of the social and economic position of the 1786 emigrants, but a number of individuals can be identified and a sense of their social status emerges from these references. Several families emigrated from North Morar, but most of the 1786 emigrants left from what had been three estates in Knoydart: Barisdale, Glengarry, and Scotus.[47] From the Glengarry holdings in Knoydart, an unknown number of emigrants left the farms of Inverguseran, Niegart, and Western Croulin. Two of the tenants of the forfeit estate of Barisdale can be identified among the emigrants; one was Angus Ban, who rented Muniall from 1774 and whose father held the same farm twenty years before that, and the other was Samuel Macdonell, the tenant of Sourlies for more than eleven years.[48] Several Scotus tenants were among the 1786 emigrants. Father Alexander McDonell rented part of the farm of Inveriebeg from his nephew Ranald McDonell of Scotus, while James McKay of Glendulochan and Neil Campbell of Scottas farm can be confidently identified with the emigrants of the same names. Two John Macdougalls, one of Scottas farm and the other of Kinlochlochan, are quite possibly the John Macdougalls who emigrated in 1786. John Roy Macdonald, who left Scotland with his pregnant wife and three small children, came from Shenachaidh on the Scotus estate.[49] The emigrants who sailed from Knoydart in 1786 were drawn from all properties on the peninsula, although it is impossible to say in what proportions.

Like the people who left Glen Garry and Glen Moriston a year earlier, the 1786 emigrants were tenants, drawn from the middle stratum of Highland society. What is of particular significance is the fact that, according to contemporary testimony, the 1786 group included a majority of the tenants from Knoydart. On 13 February 1786, McDonell of Scotus pointed out in a letter to his solicitor that "most of the tenants of this country have signed to emigrate to Canada."[50] An entirely separate source confirms Scotus's identification of the emigrants with the tenants of Knoydart. In a letter written just after the emigrants' departure, the Scottish bishops commented: "We could not stop this emigration, but much loss resulted to our missions, which we now see at the lowest point. For those who emigrate are just the people who are a little better off."[51] Each of the emigrants whose identity has been established was a tenant from one of the joint farms that were found throughout the peninsula. The tenants who left Knoydart in 1786 were men of relative substance and the backbone of the community.

These tenants were married men, who emigrated with their own and related families. Angus McDonell (Sandaig) states that he emigrated "with a hundred Families from North Britain in the year 1786."[52] While the number 100 is rather too round to be exact, McDonell does describe the group as consisting of *families*. Another reference to the composition of the emigrant party seemingly describes only part of the group that arrived in Quebec in September 1786. In that month, Commissary General John Craigie warned his agent in Montreal of the imminent arrival of a large number of Highland emigrants. Craigie stated that there were some fifty-two families, including many children, making a total of close to 345 emigrants. If his figures are exact – and this seems unlikely[53] – they give an average family size of 6.6 people and confirm the large number of children in the 1786 group. Part of the difference between Craigie's 345 emigrants and the *Quebec Gazette*'s 530 may lie in the ten cabin passengers, who would not have required his assistance, and a small number of families (McMillans, McGillises, and McPhees) known to have spent a few years in Terrebonne, near Montreal,[54] before joining friends in Glengarry County. Whatever the actual size of families, both sources emphasize the presence of family groupings in the 1786 emigration.

The ties of kinship that characterized the 1786 emigration to Glengarry County were not limited to the parents and children who dominated the passenger list. Many of the families that emigrated in 1786 were related to one another. John and Allan Macdonald were brothers, as were Donald, Archie, and John McDougall.[55] Alexander McMillan, a widower, emigrated with his married children Duncan and Anne and his unmarried son John. John Roy Macdonald of Shenachaidh was accompanied by his brother Angus and family.[56] A niece of Father Alexander McDonell was among the emigrants. Three first cousins, Angus Ban of Muniall, Malcolm Macdougall, and Allan Macdonald, came with their families.[57] Many of the emigrants must also have been related by marriage, as were Angus Ban and his son-in-law Farquhar MacRae. Very few of the roughly 100 families in the 1786 party could have left Scotland without the company of close relatives,[58] and it seems quite likely that each emigrant was bound by family ties to at least half a dozen other emigrant families.

These were by no means the only kinship links at work among the 1786 emigrants; many of them had family members already settled in Glengarry County. John Buie Macdonald was a brother-in-law of Allan Macdonell, leader of the 1785 party. John Roy Macdonald and his brother Angus had first cousins already in Glengarry County, the brothers Alexander and John Macdonald who were Loyalist settlers.[59] Similarly Angus Ban's brother Finan, uncle John, and cousin Duncan were all Loyalists living in Glengarry County. Father Alexander McDonell (Scotus) had extensive family connections in the New World, including his half-nephew Spanish John and distant cousins, the Macdonells of Leek, Collachie, and Aberchalder.[60] These examples show that at least seven of the 1786 emigrant families had relatives already in Canada, but such ties were likely typical of a much larger number of 1786 emigrants.

It was not only the composition of the emigrant groups – their status and their interconnectedness – that the 1785 and 1786 emigrants had in common, but also the cause for their departure. The similarity in their reasons for leaving is not surprising, given McDonell of Glengarry's management of much of the Knoydart district. The scene was set with the disastrous harvest of 1782. When the oat and potato crops failed, many of the inhabitants could not feed either themselves or their animals. Ranald McDonell of Scotus described their plight:

the men of Kyles, & Kyliehorn are ruined by the loss of their cattle, as also the rest of the small tenants of Knoydart, to a few. For they have given their own provisions to their cattle, that are gone, & going fast, & next the poor people have little or nothing for themselves to eat. They made no labouring to speak of, and the miserable, distressed creatures have not seed to sow the little ground they made.[61]

The bad years between 1782 and 1784 impoverished both large and small tenants, but only the more substantial tenants held on to the money needed to pay for their emigration.

The chief impetus to leave Scotland came from the economic upheaval, with its social implications, which followed closely on those years of famine. In 1784 and 1785, Glengarry introduced sheep farming to the Knoydart peninsula and raised rents dramatically.[62] Some of his tenants could not pay the increased rents after the bad years of the early 1780s. Ranald McDonell reported the outcome of their meeting with Glengarry: "I am sorry he did not promise to abate a trifle of the rents to the delegation from the farms of Invergisoren, Nieugart, and Wester Crouline. The consequence is that he had now to look out for tenants as many of those have signed for America; and should the people stay they are but the next thing to beggars."[63] In 1784 Glengarry recovered the forfeited estate of Barisdale and in November 1785 he sent for its tenants. The details of their discussion are not known, but Glengarry was planning to stock the northern part of Knoydart with sheep and to remove tenants from those farms. Before he could do so, however, most of the peninsula's tenants had signed an agreement to emigrate, so that it was not necessary to issue summons of removal.[64]

Also in 1784, Ranald McDonell of Scotus stocked his small estate with sheep and warned twenty-seven tenants to leave the farms of Scottas and Torroray, Inveriebeg, Glendulochan, and North and South Kinlochlochan. In the spring of the following year, however, Scotus found himself fully occupied in stocking the first two farms, so that the tenants of Glendulochan were permitted to remain. At least five of the 1786 emigrants were tenants from the cleared farms, but a sixth, John Roy Macdonald, came from Shenachaidh, which was not cleared.[65] These removals warned both large and small tenants of the insecurity of their tenure and would have forced many of them onto poorer farms. Some of the evicted tenants acquired new holdings, at least temporarily; Father Alexander McDonell of Scotus, for example, moved from Inveriebeg to Sandfield, where he built new "huts," presumably for his sub-tenants, and compensated the former occupants for their improvements.[66]

The complex motivation that lay behind an individual decision to emigrate can be seen in the case of Father Alexander. He was not typical of the emigrants, in that he was an inexpert farmer and manager who left Scotland with his financial affairs in a bad way; his emigration was in part dictated by "the embarrassed situation of his farming," which made the possibility of a government salary in Canada very attractive. But the prospect of settling with old friends in a new Highland community was crucial in convincing the priest to leave Knoydart. In spite of his oath to serve the Scottish mission for life, Father Alexander was "right or wrong determined to accompany" his 500 parishioners to Canada. Father Alexander hoped to obtain a position of authority in the new Highland settlement where, in his own words, he had "a brother, some nephews and nieces, & many scores of old Parishioners & acquaintances."[67]

The organization of the tenants' departure is not well documented, but the few details available underline the tenants' search to find a communal solution to their problem. As early as April 1784, more than sixty of the Knoydart tenants responded to rent increases announced by Glengarry and to McDonell of Scotus's plans for eviction by deciding to emigrate. At a meeting held on 19 April, the clansmen "subscribed articles of mutual engagement to one another … for the purpose of associating for emigration."[68] What is striking about this agreement is its egalitarian tone and, in particular, the communal commitment to emigration. In the face of socially and economically unacceptable losses, the tenants looked *as a group* for a solution to their problems and found it in communal emigration. The tenants' destination at this time was Nova Scotia – not surprising, since the new Glengarry did not yet exist; the 1773 emigrants were then waiting in the Montreal region for ice to clear from the St. Lawrence and for their new lands to be assigned. Information concerning the Loyalists' successful location in the new townships and the departure of other Glengarry tenants for Canada in 1785 likely led the Knoydart emigrants to alter their destination to the new settlement in Canada.

As a large part of the population of Knoydart prepared to leave, the bustle and confusion that prevailed in the spring of 1786 can easily be imagined. McDonell of Scotus's son Charles commented that the district was "all in a ferment with emigration." Some of the emigrants' preparations for departure were spiritual; Bishop MacDonald visited for two weeks and confirmed a large number of men and women in preparation for their arduous future. Sandaig and Father Alexander McDonell of Scotus went south to Greenock to charter a ship for the voyage.[69] The excitement of departure and the hope of a comfortable pension from the government in Canada seem to have led Father Alexander into extravagance during his last months in Scotland. Bishop MacDonald confided to John Geddes that he had been informed that the emigrant priest "had made an elegant appearance there [in Knoydart] in Silks, before he set out for the metropolis[;] so he may while his credit stands but [I] fear that will not be long if he will continue to go on at the rate he does."[70] The bishop's fears were realized since Father Alexander tried to borrow money from him at the moment of departure for Canada.

The ship *McDonald* did not arrive in Knoydart on 23 May, as originally planned; as late as 12 June it had still not been sighted. The result of this delay was to throw all plans into confusion as the emigrants anxiously waited for both the vessel and their spiritual leader Father McDonell, who remained in the lowlands.[71] At length the *McDonald* arrived in Knoydart, the emigrants went aboard, and the ship sailed on 29 June 1786. One of their number, Iain Liath Macdonald, described their departure in verse:

It was on Sunday morning
That we sailed from land
In the big three masted ship
With our parish priest with us.
He made the fervent prayer
To the King of the Elements to protect us
And to the Angel St. Raphael
To bring us safely to land.

Old and new combined as unfamiliar events were given meaning by reference to Gaelic cultural traditions. The seventeen-verse poem written many years later by Iain Liath Macdonald was one such response, preserving in traditional imagery and form the events of departure, and the hopes and sorrows of the emigrants on leaving Knoydart that summer.

As the *McDonald* moved from the harbour, there was no dry eye on board her and a great wailing and lamenting went up from those who remained behind.[73] Yet while the emigration was a heart-wrenching fracture of a deeply loved community, the clansmen carried their language and culture across the Altantic with them. Perhaps the first indication of the ongoing influence of traditional beliefs occurred during the sixty-one-day passage to Quebec. As the *McDonald* entered the Gulf of St. Lawrence

a sea gull perched on the mast. One John McGinnis shot the bird which fell on the deck, the blood shattering about. Shortly after the ship struck upon a sandbar. A council was held ... and they decided that McGinnis must have been guilty of murder in the old country and they would have pitched him overboard but for the intervention of Scotus.[74]

Although an eight-and-one-half-week passage was not long by eighteenth-century standards, the 1786 emigrants arrived in Canada at an inopportune time, on 31 August, shortly before the onslaught of cold weather. Colonial officials in Quebec knew that the emigrants had little money and feared that their friends in the new settlements were too recently established to support the newcomers over the winter. The commander in chief, General Hope, informed Lieutenant Angus McDonell on 25 September of his decision to supply the emigrants with provisions. Hope stated that since the

Loyalists could not assist the new arrivals, "the very destitute and hopeless situation to which these poor misinformed Emigrants are ... reduced is with me a sufficient motive ... to adopt every measure in my power to save them from want ... or from too severe Conditions being exacted by individuals who may contribute to their immediate relief."[75] The emigrants may actually have expected to be given provisions like their Loyalist predecessors, and indeed Hope made special provision to feed them until the 1787 harvest. Rations for adults consisted of a weekly allowance of four and one-half pounds of potatoes, one and one-half pounds of flat fish, three and one-half pounds of flour, and two pounds of beef. The total cost of the provisions was estimated at less than £3 per adult for the whole period, and this sum was to be repaid in two instalments in October 1788 and 1789.

The emigrants left Quebec on 3 September 1786 with a fair wind for Montreal. Oral tradition describes their journey upriver: "The women and children were placed in batteaux and proceeded to make the toilsome journey to Montreal. The men walked. They came up probably on the north shore. Some French Canadians gave them cucumbers – the first time the highlanders saw that vegetable. Afterwards they came across green corn & pumpkins. Eating a large quantity of those they got diarhea & some of them had to be carried."[76] The emigrants expected to meet their friends from the new settlements at Lachine on the west end of Montreal Island, where they had to break their journey to avoid rapids on the St. Lawrence River. Apparently they spent several days here while colonial officials considered what help to give them. Shortly after General Hope wrote to Lieutenant McDonell of his decision to provision them, the Highlanders left Lachine in government bateaux for the last segment of their journey. They finally reached their new home, Glengarry County, early in October 1786.[77]

The 1786 emigration from Knoydart was dramatic; 520 people, perhaps one-quarter of the district's population and one-half of its tenants, left in a single group. These families left not because of the gradual economic and social change that had altered their community over the previous forty years but because of the radical threat to social and economic life that emerged in the few years before 1786. The new sheep farming needed labourers, outside expertise, and capital; it had neither a role nor any use for the traditional tenant farmer. Faced with what they considered betrayal, the tenants of Knoydart had two choices: they could remain as poor farmers in the new commercial society, in which they no longer had any recognized right to the land their fathers had held for generations; or they could emigrate to Canada, where land was available and a new Gaelic community was in the process of forming.

The radical nature of the decision to emigrate must not be overlooked. In a people noted for their intense conservatism and attachment to the land, a mass departure such as occurred from Knoydart in 1786 was clearly a sharp break with the past. But the decision to emigrate represented as well an affirmation of certain key Highland values. If the clansmen had to live with commercial agriculture (and the economic change that had occurred since 1750 showed that they would), they preferred the sure possession of farms in the company of their friends that British North America seemed to offer. Even some of the tenants who remained in possession of their farms chose to give them up, and all the emigrants left in the teeth of their landlords' known wishes – for Glengarry and Scotus opposed the emigration. As the Scottish bishops testified, "all firmly wished to go."[78] Letters and visitors from Canada brought news of land available in the new Glengarry at the same time as agricultural transformation reached a climax in Knoydart.[79] The Knoydart tenants emigrated because they rejected the economic alternatives offered them after the introduction of capital-intensive sheep-farming to the peninsula and because as a group they chose to join kin and friends in the new Gaelic community in Canada.

A fourth group of emigrants left Scotland for Glengarry County in 1790. Unlike earlier parties, which drew predominantly on one or two neighbouring glens, the smaller 1790 group was recruited from eight separate districts across western Inverness-shire. The seemingly miscellaneous origins of this group is in part misleading and in part the result of the vicissitudes which affected a larger group of emigrants that year.[80] In spite of the variety of districts represented, most of the emigrants came from the estates of Macdonald of Clanranald (57%) and McDonell of Glengarry (30%); the two estates meet one another on the west coast at Mallaig. Numerous bonds linked these tenants, including a common religion (Roman Catholicism), former political allegiance (Jacobitism), traditions of the clan Donald, and economic experience.[81] The island of Eigg contributed the largest number of emigrants, thirty of the eighty-seven passengers, while the remaining clansmen came from Glen Garry, North Morar, South Uist, Ardgour, Arisaig, Moidart, and Knoydart. The emigrants from any one district generally left from a single farm.

Most of the 1790 emigrants travelled to Canada in family groups. Only eight passengers were listed individually, four of them servants; it seems probable that three of the four remaining single adults were related to families of the same names and point of origin. Thirteen families on board ship had children twelve years of age and under; another two groups of seven and four emigrants were probably families with children over the age of twelve. Thus seventy-nine of the eighty-seven emigrants, or 91% of the party, came to Canada in family groups, and the average size of a family was 5.3 people. One of the striking characteristics of the 1790 emigration is the large number of young children in the party: thirty-seven of the emigrants, or 42%, were younger than twelve. Indeed, ten were less than two years old, equal to a babe in arms for each young two-parent family. It is particularly revealing to contrast the proportion of children of twelve and under in the emigrant group (42%), to the proportion in the Scottish population as a whole (34%). Families with children were those with most to lose from higher rents and clearances for sheep farms. The very high representation of such families among the 1790 emigrants emphasizes the significance of family emigration in the provincial stream of departures.

While little is known about any kinship links among the 1790 emigrants, rather more information is available about their social status. Given their fairly diverse geographic origins, the 1790 emigrants were unlikely to have many kinsmen among their fellow passengers. Donald McDonald was probably related to the Isabella McDonald whose passage he paid for, while Lachlan and John McKinnon of Eigg were father and son; Donald and Allan McDonald of Eigg were probably relatives, as were Donald and John McAulay of Uist. Similarly, while none of the exact relationships are known, the 1790 emigrants were reported to have both "friends & relatives" in the new settlements.[82] Unlike the 1786 emigrants they could not be described as "chiefly" McDonalds, since thirteen surnames occurred on the 1790 passenger list; nevertheless, one-quarter of this group were named McDonald.[83] Despite their varied points of origin, most of the 1790 emigrants were of roughly equal social status within Highland society. The heads of fifteen families were listed as tenant farmers; two others were smiths and one was a tailor. Craftsmen, especially blacksmiths, shared the same status as tenants, and all these were likely men of standing in their local communities. None of the emigrants, however, possessed much in the way of material resources.[84]

The fundamental reason for the 1790 departures was the increase

of rents and clearances to create sheep farms. Father James Mac-
Donald of Eigg wrote that his people "were obliged for want of
lands" to emigrate, and other observers made the same point.
Bishop MacDonald explained that on the west coast and adjacent
islands "a great number of poor people have no lands at all, and
many of those who possess Lands, their possessions are so triffling
& small, so high rented that they despair of making anything of a
living from them."[85] Not only population pressure contributed to
this land crisis; in particular sheep farming, introduced to western
Inverness after 1780, threatened the economic and social position of
these and other tenants. A colonial committee appointed by the
governor of Quebec, Lord Dorchester, to investigate the 1790
emigration and its Highland causes neatly summed up the tenants'
situation:

They are industrious people & lived on small farms which they rented at
Arasaig and the Island of Egg containing about 50 acres each more or less:
that the proprietors of those lands[,] able to procure higher rents than those
people could afford to pay, found it their interest to throw those small
Farms into grazing grounds [*i.e.*, for sheep], letting a number of them
together to one responsible person from whom he can collect his rent with
ease & certainty.[86]

At the same time as tenants found that they could no longer
count on getting land from their chief, 200-acre land grants were
being given to emigrants settling in Canada. News of the new
Highland community there and of the farms given to the Loyalist,
Glen Garry, and Knoydart emigrants spread throughout western
Inverness. Such reports provided the tenants with an alternative to
the increasing struggle to keep their farms and pay the rent.
"Having heard from their friends & relatives settled in the upper
parts of this Province [Quebec] that upon removing to this Country
they would be able to obtain portions of the waste lands of the
Crown contiguous to them, they were glad to embark for Canada."
The phrase "glad to embark" echoes the words of the parish priest
of Eigg, who reported that the people were "ready to embark with
great che[e]rfulness." Father MacDonald explained that it was "not
that they wanted to leave their native Country for which they have
here (especially the commonality) a blind attachment but they were
overjoyed at the thought that providence would procure for them
in another Corner of the world, that relief and help, that was
refused to them in their own Country."[87]
The small party that arrived in Quebec in 1790 did not include all

those who had intended to leave Eigg that year. Early in March it was reported that eighty-eight people from the island of Eigg had signed to emigrate to America, yet only thirty people from Eigg reached Canada the following October.[88] A dramatic event during the summer months reduced the number of emigrants to British North America. Father James MacDonald gives the bleak details:

at the information of some malicious people, a King's Ship was ordered to the Coast at the time of Emigration to impress everyone fit for service. This frightened the Emigrants so much that few of them went off ... [because they] were afraid of being obliged to part with their families. So that after losing the half of their freight and some of them more, they remained in the Country without Lands, Cattle, Crop, houses, fireing or even work.[89]

Two other ships did sail to the Island of St. John in 1790 with twenty-eight emigrants from Eigg on board,[90] but this leaves the total number of emigrants from the island at sixty, almost one-third less than expected. Father James's account of the naval press gang emphasizes the importance of family participation in emigration and suggests one important reason why relatively few emigrants reached Quebec rather late in 1790.

As with the emigration from Knoydart in 1786, a Highland gentleman made the actual arrangements for the journey of the 1790 emigrants. Miles Macdonell, the son of Spanish John, returned to Scotland and by 5 March 1790 had "opened a subscription lately in the Island of Eigg where 88 subscribed for America; he is to do the same in the different Countries on the west Coast here where ... he shall meet with the like success."[91]

In spite of their fears of the press gang, eighty-seven emigrants boarded the *British Queen* and sailed from Arisaig on 16 August 1790.[92] The ship reached Quebec in mid-October and on the day after its arrival Miles Macdonell petitioned the governor of Quebec on the emigrants' behalf. The petition described the oppression which had driven the clansmen to Canada where they hoped to live "under the British Government." Macdonell explained that a few of the emigrants had no money "after paying their passage and must inevitably Starve this Winter unless some Provision shall be made for them. They wish to go up above Montreal where many of their Countrymen, who arrived here Passengers four years ago, are already settled."[93] The emigrants asked to be granted land on the same terms as the 1786 settlers. On 20 October, before the colonial government could reply to this request, Miles submitted a second petition asking for five or six bateaux and four weeks' provisions for the emigrants to enable them to join their friends in the new settlements. If this assistance was not granted, Macdonell suggested that the emigrants might take up an offer made by P.L. Panet of land on his seigneury in the District of Montreal.[94]

The colonial government was disturbed by this arrival of a second party of distressed Highlanders at Quebec. Settlers were welcome, but emigrants with little cash, such as those on board the *British Queen* (who, the officials estimated, had no more than £200 among them) put a heavy burden on colonial resources. At Lord Dorchester's request, the Quebec Executive Council formed a committee to inquire into the circumstances of the Eigg emigration and the "Course that was to be pursued on the late emigrations from the Highlands of Scotland into this Province and the expenses thereby incurred."[95] The committee believed that emigration was not good for the mother country and that Highland emigration should be discouraged; nevertheless, the committee immediately approved the petition of 20 October requesting transportation upriver for the emigrants. Dorchester accepted his committee's recommendation and ordered that boats be provided for the emigrants. The governor explained this action to the Colonial Secretary by pointing out that the emigrants were in danger of starving over the winter. By sending them to join their countrymen, Dorchester prevented "their becoming a burden to the public, or to the Crown."[96] Neither imperial nor colonial authorities were willing formally to adopt policies favouring emigration; the emigrants of 1786 and 1790 received crucial assistance only because of the lack of government policy on the new issue of the mass emigration of Europeans with limited means.

The precariousness of the clansmen's situation on their arrival in Canada is evident in the case of the 1790 emigrants. When they reached Montreal, the emigrants found it necessary to prepare a petition addressed to the "Charitable and Humane Public," describing their plight. The clansmen had expected to receive provisions for a year, as the 1785 and 1786 emigrants had, but the Eigg emigrants were refused this assistance. As a result their situation was "truly miserable" and they threw themselves on the charity of the public.[97] The response of the Scottish and English mercantile community was immediate, as James Morrison reported three months later. "When the Highlanders arrived from Quebec they was in a distressed Situation Mr. Joseph Howard and myself took upon us at the request of some of our friends to go round and raise a Subscription for them We sent them four Quarters of beef and Seventy odd loaves of bread to Lachine which carried them up to their friends." Only the family of John Ban McGillis stayed in Lower Canada, moving to the Glengarry settlement six years later. The remaining eighty-three emigrants travelled up the St. Lawrence in government bateaux shortly after 6 November. Later that winter, the Montreal merchants gave further aid, forwarding six quarters of beef to be divided among the emigrants according to need.[98] The story of the Eigg emigration was long remembered; in 1884 James Duncan Macdonald, aged 92, recalled that the emigrants of 1790 "endured great hardships," for they "arrived in the autumn late."[99]

At least two other groups of emigrants arrived in Glengarry County from western Inverness in the early 1790s. They were led by Alexander Macdonell of Greenfield and Alexander McMillan of Glenpean in 1792, and by Kenneth McLeod in 1793. Little information survives about these emigrations, but a partial account of the emigrants and their experience can be pieced together. The best known of the 1792 emigrants is Alexander Macdonell of Greenfield, a second cousin of the Glengarry chief and hence a relation as well of the other clan gentlemen. Alexander and his father, Angus Greenfield, were close friends of the post-Culloden Glengarry chiefs, helping in the reorganization of the heavily encumbered Glengarry estate in the 1760s and 1770s.[100] It seems probable that this close relationship (in particular with Duncan McDonell) at first protected the economic and social interests of the Greenfield Macdonells. Unlike most of the other Macdonell gentlemen, whose traditional role and income were seriously eroded after 1745, the Greenfields seem to have had little reason to consider emigration in 1773 or 1785 when large groups left Glen Garry.

By 1792, however, events on the Glengarry estate had altered the Greenfields' previously secure position. Duncan McDonell died in 1788 and, since his heir Alexander was under age, Duncan's widow Margery administered the estate until 1792. Margery Grant was generally disliked by the tenants and showed little attachment to clan tradition.[101] After 1782 sheep farming rapidly transformed the agriculture and society of the Glengarry estate. It is not clear whether Greenfield held on to the farms he had previously rented and, if he did, whether he was forced to pay a rent equivalent to the sums offered by the sheep farmers. It seems quite probable that Greenfield's decision to emigrate was the result of the loss of the chief's favour and a considerable drop in the family's economic and social prospects. The presence of a large number of kinsmen in the new Glengarry in Upper Canada must also have influenced him.

The Scotus family – Spanish John, Miles, and Father Alexander – were his second cousins, and the Aberchalder, Collachie, and Leek families were fifth cousins. Moreover, in 1769 Alexander had married Janet, the eldest daughter of Alexander of Aberchalder. Although his wife died in 1788, Alexander Greenfield brought their nine children to Canada in 1792, joining his prominent in-laws in the Glengarry settlement.[102]

Glengarry tradition indicates that Macdonell of Greenfield was accompanied by some of his clansmen when he emigrated in 1792. A descendant, J.A. Macdonell, stated in his *Sketches of Glengarry in Canada* that Greenfield "brought with him, I believe, a number of the people of his clan."[103] The leader of a later emigration, Alexander McLeod, named Macdonell of Greenfield as one of several men who had led groups of emigrants to Glengarry County.[104] This tradition is confirmed by a contemporary source in Scotland, the Glengarry priest Ranald MacDonald. On 16 July 1792 MacDonald reported that he had gone to Marysburgh (Fort William) "to See Greenfield the last of our Glengarry Gentlemen embark for Canada," taking some of his clansmen with him. The only clue we possess as to the origin of Greenfield's party lies in Father MacDonald's comment that those leaving were "the best part of the dregs that remaind of the Commoners."[105] This brief description of the 1792 emigrants suggests a group slightly lower in status to those who left previously.

A second gentleman was instrumental in organizing an emigration to Glengarry County in 1792. Alexander McMillan was the son of Ewen McMillan who had been tacksman of Glenpean under the Forfeited Estates' administration of Lochiel. The younger McMillan served as a lieutenant in DeLancey's Brigade, a British unit embodied during the American Revolution. In a petition for more land dated 1797, he claimed that he "came to this Province in the Year 1793 [sic] and brought with him a number of Emigrants from Scotland, who, with himself, have become settlers" in Glengarry County.[106] McMillan may indeed have led an emigrant group to Canada, but it is highly unlikely that it was as late as 1793. In meetings held in March and April 1793, the land board of Glengarry and Stormont counties recommended a grant of a 1,000 acres of land to Alexander McMillan, late lieutenant in DeLancey's Brigade. McMillan and the group of Scottish emigrants who received 200-acre grants at the same time could not have obtained these lands unless they were already resident in Upper Canada when the board held its meeting. Most of the clansmen likely reached Glengarry before the close of navigation in the autumn of 1792.[107]

Although the evidence is not as precise as one would wish, it seems probable that these two men, Macdonell of Greenfield and McMillan of Glenpean, organized a single emigration in 1792. Late in September of that year, the *Quebec Gazette* reported the arrival of the ship *Unity* after a nine-week voyage from Greenock with forty families of Highland emigrants bound for Upper Canada.[108] Six weeks later, the chairman of the Eastern District Land Board ordered surveyor Hugh Macdonell to lay out land suitable for settlement for twenty-seven or more families of Highland emigrants. Some thirty-four Highlanders, described as emigrants from Scotland in their application for land in Glengarry County in the spring of 1793, were probably members of the 1792 group.[109] These included seven McDonells, eight McGillises, two McIntoshes, eleven McMillans, one Cameron, and three McPhies. Thus, the little surviving evidence about the 1792 group confirms once again the propensity of clansmen who were a little better off – that is tenants – to emigrate with their families in locally organized groups to a Gaelic community in British North America.

A second emigration from western Inverness followed quickly on the heels of the Macdonell--McMillan party of 1792. Kenneth McLeod, his son Captain Alexander, and Big Norman McLeod organized an emigration of some 150 people in 1793. Kenneth McLeod was a tacksman who had held the farms of Killismore and Upper Maoile in Glenelg. Many of the 1793 emigrants also originated in Glenelg, but other clansmen left from Glen Moriston, Strathglass, and Knoydart.[110] It seems likely that the 1793 emigrants can be identified with most of the thirty-five Highlanders, headed by Norman, Kenneth, and Alexander McLeod, who received land grants in Glengarry County on 25 June 1794. Twelve McLeods are found on this list as well as five McGillivrays, five Macdonells, four Fergusons, two Grants, a McLore, a Murchison, a McPhee, and a McCuaig.[111] Several emigrants' names were omitted from this list, so the names of Kenneth and Alexander McLennan, and Donald Campbell should be added to the McLeod party.[112]

The family of Kenneth McLeod, *Fear na Maoile*, can be traced in some detail to reveal a kinship network embracing both the emigrant party and earlier settlers in Glengarry. On the voyage to Canada, Kenneth McLeod travelled with his adult children, Captain Alexander, Norman, Mary, and Christine; a third generation was also represented by Captain Alexander's three small sons. The McLeods were related to prominent Macdonell families in Glengarry County. The wife of a late seventeenth-century Glengarry chief was a McLeod, and hence Kenneth McLeod was a second cousin of the Macdonell chief and the Greenfield Macdonells. In addition, Captain

Alexander's wife had also been a Macdonell, by tradition a sister of Bishop Macdonell of Kingston and therefore of Allan Macdonell, leader of the 1785 emigration.[113] The other clansmen in the emigrant party may not have had such prominent connections, but most of the 1793 emigrants, especially those from Knoydart and Glen Moriston, probably had friends and relatives already in Glengarry County.

As in the earlier departures, a complex interaction of sheep farming, rent and population increases, and kinship lay behind the McLeod emigration. The parish minister explained this well:

Emigration is thought to be owing in a great measure to the introduction of sheep, as one man often rents a farm where formerly many families lived comfortably; & if the rage for this mode of farming goes on with the same rapidity it has done for some years back, it is to be apprehended emigration will still increase. But this is not solely the cause; the high rents demanded by landlords, the increase of population, & the flattering accounts received from their friends in America, do also contribute to the evil.[114]

Sheep farming had been introduced to one farm in the peninsula of Glenelg by 1795. At this stage of economic development, however, landlords and planners saw no need for tenants to emigrate; they were expected to take up crofts on other parts of the estate and make a living through fishing, kelping, or labouring on the estate. The fact that 130 people chose to leave Glenelg for Canada underlines the tenants' independent assessment of their future prospects. The clansmen felt their economic future threatened by the loss of some land to sheep farmers, particularly since rents had increased and the population was growing fast.[115]

After the decision to leave Scotland was reached, Captain Alexander made two trips to Greenock to charter a ship for the emigrants' use. On 12 June 1793 the vessel arrived at Culreagh in Glenelg, where the passengers had gathered for the departure; both people and baggage were boarded immediately and the group sailed two days later. Unfortunately the emigrants' journey to America was plagued by bad weather. As the ship approached the halfway point in the Atlantic crossing, a terrible storm damaged her and drove her back to Greenock, "rather than run the risk of perishing at sea by prosecuting the voyage." After a fortnight's wait in Greenock, a second vessel was provided for the emigrants by the owners of the damaged ship and they set sail once more. The brig "had not been out more than 4 days when a heavy squall of wind carried away her upper Masts and Sails" and again the emigrants returned to Scotland, this time to Lamlash for three days of repairs. The third time the McLeod emigrants set sail for America they were at last successful, arriving "on the 1st of next November ... during a Severe snow storm and excessively cold weather off Prince Edward Island." Tradition adds that ice lay a foot deep on the ship's deck.[116]

Since the St. Lawrence River was closed to shipping for the winter, Captain Alexander and his party were forced to stay in Prince Edward Island for six months. During that period, McLeod "proceeded to the South side of the island and engaged a large Schooner owned by some Canadians to carry his Settlers early next summer to Quebec."[117] The schooner *Simon Gallon* arrived at Charlottetown late in May and reached Quebec after a ten-day voyage on 3 June 1794. The *Quebec Gazette* announced the arrival of "Mr. M'Cloud & family with 115 men, women and children," and confirmed the story of their long journey and its delays. A week later, a second schooner arrived from Prince Edward Island with forty-two passengers aboard.[118] The Highlanders petitioned the colonial government for assistance to complete their passage to Upper Canada and received fourteen days' provisions by order of Lord Dorchester. They travelled on to Montreal by schooner and then completed the last sixty miles of their voyage by military bateaux to the River Raisin in Glengarry County.[119]

The emigrants who reached Glengarry County between 1786 and 1794 formed a remarkably homogeneous community. They shared the same language, brought the same cultural baggage, and had similar social origins and family links from neighbouring glens in western Inverness. Unlike many parts of Upper Canada, which received mixed proportions of English, Scots, Highland, Irish, German, or American emigrants, Glengarry County had, by 1794, clearly taken on the character of a Highland preserve. Thirty-five years later, the author of a book describing Upper Canada warned prospective emigrants of what was already true in 1794: "Go not to Glengarry, if you be not a Highlandman."[120]

Each of the five emigrant groups to reach Glengarry County between 1785 and 1794 was largely derived from the tenant class, which had constituted between 30% and 50% of the Highland population. The five emigrant parties were dominated by families, many of whom were related to one another. Although the complexity of kinship ties varied among emigrant groups, such relationships always linked certain members of a group with each other, as well as to members of groups already settled in Glengarry County. Similarly, all five groups can in some manner be viewed as community emigrations. Most prominent in this regard is the 1786 party of 500 people predominantly from Knoydart and North Morar, but the 1785, 1790, 1792, and 1793 emigrations were to a lesser extent community migrations from Glen Garry, Eigg, and Glenelg.

One of the striking similarities marking these five emigrations was the organizational leadership provided by clan gentlemen and prominent tenants. Father Alexander McDonell of Scotus, Miles Macdonell, and Greenfield Macdonell were closely related to their clan chief; Lieutenant Angus McDonell was a military officer; and Angus Ban Macdonell, Kenneth McLeod, and Alexander McMillan were members of established tenant families. Less is known about Allan Macdonell, the brother of Bishop Alexander Macdonell of Kingston, but the bishop was reportedly a distant cousin of the Glengarry chief. In serving as leaders of the emigrations, these men shared the tenants' interest in obtaining land of their own, but they could also look forward to a position of leadership in the new Highland community. They possessed the organizational skills and financial expertise useful for planning a community emigration. The pressures in favour of emigration were so great that the small tenants would have emigrated without this assistance, but their departure was eased by the gentlemen's leadership. The emigrants who came to Glengarry County between 1785 and 1794 did so in the company of some of their traditional leaders, thereby reinforcing the conservative, hierarchical quality of the original Loyalist settlement.

For each of the five emigrant groups, the decision to leave stemmed from essentially the same complex balance of social and economic forces. The large rise in population across western Inverness, particularly evident in Knoydart after 1755, strained the traditional Highland economy. While tenants reaped some benefits from the early stages of agrarian transformation in the second half of the eighteenth century, their social and economic position was at first weakened by rising rents and then completely undercut by the introduction of sheep farming after 1780. Historians' persistent belief[121] that the introduction of sheep farming was not a major factor causing emigration prior to 1800 or 1815 is, in the case of the Glengarry emigrants, quite wrong. While not every tenant who emigrated to Glengarry had been evicted from his holding, the clansmen of western Inverness chose emigration in face of the serious threat sheep farming posed to their access to the land. As Lord Selkirk pointed out a decade later, the tenants were not "so blind as to perceive no danger" until they were overwhelmed. "The fate of their friends and neighbours ... [was] a sufficient warning of that which they must sooner or later expect."[122] So sharp was the tenants' reaction to the effects of economic transformation in western Inverness in this period that 40% of all Highland emigration between 1783 and 1794 came from a few estates in western Inverness.

Three factors were primarily responsible for the success of the clansmen's emigration to Upper Canada. First, Highland community leaders provided leadership: priests, clan gentlemen, and major tenants played an important role in organizing all of the emigrations to Glengarry. With the exception of clan chiefs, representatives of all the influential people in local Highland society can be found among the organizers of these emigrations. Second, the clansmen's departure was voluntary and communal. When agrarian transformation severely threatened the clansmen's economic well-being and society, the tenants adopted a communal solution to their dilemma. This mutual dependence is most formally documented in the case of the 1786 Knoydart tenants, who "subscribed articles of mutual engagement,"[123] but joint agreement lay behind all of the group emigrations to Glengarry and was crucial in making emigration an acceptable option. Third, the settlers received support from colonial officials. It is obvious from the plea for public aid made by the 1790 emigrants that many undertook the voyage with very little money. On various occasions government officials provided transportation between Quebec or Montreal and Glengarry County, provisions for the first winter in Canada, and (most important) easy and quick access to land. The combined effect of these factors encouraged the emigration and settlement of Highlanders in Upper Canada. Displaying all the characteristics of Bailyn's provincial emigrant stream, a new flow of people left western Inverness for Glengarry County between 1785 and 1793.

CHAPTER EIGHT

The Peace of Amiens Emigrants

By 1793, agrarian transformation and emigration had altered significantly the society and economy of western Inverness. The demography of the district had begun to change as sheep farms were created and people were moved from their traditional farm holdings; extensive sheep walks were developed on Glengarry's estate and were introduced in Glenelg by this date. Such improvements reduced the land available to joint-tenant farmers, who were squeezed financially as their rents rose faster than the price of cattle. Large groups of tenants emigrated from Glen Garry, Knoydart, Glenelg, and Glen Moriston to Upper Canada and from Arisaig and Moidart to Nova Scotia during the eight years leading up to 1793. Communities were fractured by removals and by emigration, but the bonds of kinship and friendship were strong in the groups that remained and they linked the survivors with those who had left the Highlands for British North America.

The most radical change occurred on the Glengarry estate, where agricultural reform and widespread emigration in the 1780s had transformed McDonell's property. By June 1789, the parish priest Ranald MacDonald spoke with concern of the depopulation of Glen Garry. Father MacDonald pointed out that not one of his flock was "within three miles of me, or the meeting house & they are so scattered & in so precarious a Situation that there is no following them. Where the bulk of them is this year, there will not be one perhaps next year." The priest believed that the "System of Depopulation adopted by the proprietors" was making such progress that most of the clansmen would soon be found in Edinburgh and Glasgow; the landlords' continued "oppression" of the tenants made it unlikely that the latter would be able to afford to emigrate.[1] The reality of Father Ranald's fears could be seen in 1792 when the

Roman Catholic missionary in Arisaig reported that "people goes dalie from these countries" on the west coast "to the Cotton works at Glasgow."[2]

The precarious state of the clansmen still living in the Highlands after the transformation was evident to everyone except the landlords, who were blinded to reality by the higher rents brought by the sheep farmers and the improvements carried out on their estates. Frequent reports were heard of the "reduced situation of the people" and it was agreed that a farm was "no object by the great rise of Rents, but rather threatens ruin." The minister of Glenelg a generation later looked back on this period and pointed out the growing poverty of the parish's inhabitants.[3] Prospects for the clansmen were very bleak indeed, as the destruction of traditional communities seen in western Inverness by 1793 was repeated throughout the west Highlands in the fifty years that followed.

The clansmen's loyalty to their landlord-chiefs remained strong even under the pressure of this radical transformation. Those families who managed to hold on to their joint-tenant farms, and even those who accepted smaller holdings, still looked to their chief with almost filial respect. In February 1793, in a petition asking for Glengarry's support against the encroachments of sheep farmers, the small tenants of Knoydart described themselves as the "antient tenants of Glengarry in the country of Knoydart, and the remains of the former inhabitants." In spite of the evictions and large rent increases that proved the chief's betrayal of traditional ties, the small tenants still believed that generations of support for the Glengarry chiefs entitled them to his favour. With evident emotion the tenants explained that they would not have complained about the sheep farmers as "incomers or intruders, though we were the first servants, and guardians of the family [of Glengarry], if they behave[d] discreetly to any of [us], ... But these grievances are such as scarcely one brother would bear from another."[4] Even after ten years of removals and emigrations, the Glengarry tenants hoped that their faithful adherence to the McDonell family would ensure them their chief's support when incoming graziers threatened them with untraditional attitudes or behaviour. They trusted their clan chief. They were wrong.

The outbreak of war with France in 1793 temporarily slowed the erosion of the traditional landlord-tenant relationship in Knoydart and western Inverness generally. As Lord Selkirk pointed out in 1805, "Many estates which were ripe for the changes that have since been made, and which, if peace had not been interrupted, would have been let to graziers seven or eight years earlier, remained for a time, in the hands of the small tenants."[5] War significantly altered the priorities of Highland landowners, as the need to recruit soldiers led them to see advantages once again in a numerous tenantry. In the past, Highland chiefs had recruited men for military service from their own estates; the introduction of sheep farming threatened this practice, since it reduced the estate population and left those who remained little inclined to risk their lives for farms which might soon be taken from them. In order to aid recruiting, therefore, the removal of tenants to consolidate farms or develop sheep walks slowed radically after 1793. As Lord Selkirk noted, the demand for manpower during the war with revolutionary France gave a real advantage to those landlords "who still had the means of influencing their tenantry."

Highland tenants traditionally paid for their farms with military service to the chief in addition to a modest cash rent. The relatively low rents at the time of the '45 and the many clan regiments deployed then show that this custom survived into the eighteenth century. Although the relationship between chief and clansman generally became commercial rather than paternal over the following fifty years, the tradition of military service under the chief survived. Father Alexander Macdonell explained the practice as it existed in 1794:

the plan of recruiting adopted by men of property in the Highlands is to give a promise of a small pendicle of land for every recruite. Thus when a son, a brother, or a nephew is required to enlist, the father, the Brother or Brothers, & the uncle's family are secured in their small farms during the soldier's absence, & by this means every one that leaves the country secures bread for generally half a dozen in it.[6]

When war was declared in 1793 and recruiting parties were sent out in the Highlands, the clansmen saw an opportunity to provide land for their families in return for their support of the military ambitions of their chiefs.

This factor alone goes far to explaining why emigration to Canada slowed to a trickle during the war years 1793 to 1801, although government restrictions and the demand for manpower also played a role. The recruiting practices of Highland landlords reduced the number of emigrants in two ways. First, when landlords severely curtailed rent increases and the creation of new sheep farms, a large number of tenants, now secure in the possession of their farms, chose not to emigrate. Second, a minority of the dispossessed were offered farms once more if they provided recruits for the landlords' regiments. These clansmen too stayed in Scotland. The enthusiastic competition for men to form Highland regiments had a dramatic impact on the rate of emigration to Canada. The raising of the Glengarry Fencible Regiment provides a good example of the way that traditional loyalties, landlord ambition, and tenant preferences combined to create a military unit and, temporarily, to halt emigration. Fencible regiments were recruited in Scotland for home defence, thereby freeing regiments of the line for overseas duty.[7] On 2 March 1793 orders were issued to raise seven regiments of fencible infantry in Scotland; among these was a Highland regiment to be commanded by Sir James Grant. In October and November of 1794, fear of a French invasion led to the creation of a further twenty battalions of fencible infantry in Scotland, including the Glengarry Fencible Regiment.

The organization of the Glengarry regiment was initiated not by the government but rather by the new Glengarry chief, Alexander McDonell, and his clansmen. In 1793 McDonell was given the command of a company in the newly formed Grant Fencibles; nevertheless, over the following winter the idea of a separate Glengarry regiment gained support. Alexander McDonell turned 21 in 1794 and his ambition of imitating the heroic deeds of his ancestors was given free rein. McDonell knew that his grandfather had brought out two regiments for the Prince. His confidant, Father Alexander Macdonell, pointed out that although five or six strangers now occupied clan lands, "most of their leases will be out in a year or two when GlenG ... might provide lands for every man in the regt., & as soon as he has it in his power he says he'll show to the whole world that he prefers men to sheep."

Father Alexander Macdonell, known as the "chaplain" because of his service in that capacity with the Glengarry regiment, was in fact the animating spirit behind its creation. The priest had no illusions about Highland chiefs: "Our Highland lairds are more, I do believe, than any other set of men upon the face of the earth actuated by self-interest," but he felt that their self-interest could at least temporarily be turned to the tenants' advantage. Since those landlords who wished to recruit a regiment had either to preserve the farms of their small tenants or reintroduce such holdings, the chiefs' military ambition and patriotism were to be encouraged to take this outlet. Father Macdonell also had religious interests in mind when he urged the creation of a Glengarry regiment. Virtually all Glengarry's tenants were Roman Catholics, and their priest hoped that ardent support of the war effort would result in a more favourable relationship between the British government and the Catholic church and its members.[8]

Although posted at the Roman Catholic mission in Glasgow, Father Macdonell visited the Highlands for seven weeks in 1793. It was most likely during this period that the notion of a Glengarry fencible regiment was first given serious consideration. On 26 February 1794, a public meeting held at Fort William unanimously supported the formation of a Roman Catholic fencible regiment under the command of Alexander McDonell. [9] The chaplain and the Glengarry chief proceeded to London in April, where they spent several months lobbying for the regiment. As late as May 1794 Father Macdonell reported that court and political intrigue had created a prejudice against Glengarry's regiment. But by 14 August the urgent need for men overwhelmed political considerations and Alexander McDonell was given a letter of service to raise the Glengarry Fencible Regiment.[10]

If the Glengarry regiment satisfied the martial ambitions of the chief and the pastoral concerns of the chaplain, it also met certain needs and traditional expectations of the tenants. Many of McDonell's clansmen enlisted in Grant's fencibles only to serve in McDonell's company. The Macdonells had not been happy under the leadership of the Grants and had been prominent among mutineers who refused to leave Scotland for England for fear of being sent abroad in March of 1794.[11] When Glengarry was given permission to raise his own fencible regiment, his clansmen exchanged *en masse* to the new unit. The 72 sergeants, corporals, and privates who took advantage of the British government's permission for soldiers to transfer into the new regiments did so because it was their "most earnest desire and ardent wish to follow you [McDonell] to any part of the earth his Majesty may order." These men discounted the bounties and other similar inducements offered by government and emphasized that their traditional loyalty to the chief brought them to enlist. No matter how well treated they were by other officers, the Macdonell clansmen considered that "our minds can never be content separated from you; our foreFathers pertained to your foreFathers and we wish to pertain to you that we may in like manner receive protection from you."[12]

At the same time as the clansmen expressed this fervent loyalty to their chief, they also made clear his responsibility to provide them with land. In February of 1794 when the clansmen were serving under McDonell in Grant's Fencibles, Father Alexander pointed out their expectation of their chief: "All the men that are with him in the

Fencibles rest perfectly satisfied that he'll make good his promise to see them comfortably settled in Glengarry. Their attachment to him is beyond anything you can conceive."[13] The men had enlisted in Grant's Fencibles without making any demands on Glengarry, but when they transferred to their chief's regiment in October 1794, they suggested that McDonell make provision for their families, since he was now of age. The clansmen believed that traditional Highland farm communities could be reinstated: "if we chance to return home ourselves ... we expect to enjoy those possessions which our ancestors so long enjoyed under your ancestors though now in the hands of strangers." In their keen desire to regain their farms in Glengarry, the clansmen promised what most likely they could not fulfill: "we do not wish that you should lose by us we shall give as high Rent as any of your Lowlands shepherds ever give and we shall all become bound for any one whose circumstances may afford you room to mistrust."[14]

Recruiting fencible and regular infantry regiments during the war with revolutionary France offered Highland tenants a unique opportunity to bargain with their landlords for land. The possession of a farm had traditionally been linked in some fashion to military service. The tenants were still familiar with this practice, although it had been considerably eroded in the preceding hundred years. Not all tenants were still willing to follow their chief to war; the small tenants of nine Knoydart farms refused themselves, their sons, or brothers to Alexander McDonell when he came to recruit on that part of his estate. As a result McDonell ordered the tenants (and their many cottars who had also refused to enlist) removed from their farms.[15] In this instance, Alexander's father's behaviour had destroyed the bond of trust and loyalty between clansmen and chief. But other tenants saw the war as an opportunity to restore traditional social and agricultural life; in spite of ten years of removals and emigrations, many of Glengarry's tenants showed deep loyalty to and belief in their chief. The fervour of the clansmen's response perhaps reflected their own vulnerability. That military service to their chief required a *quid pro quo* from him the clansmen made very clear, but even many who had been evicted in favour of sheep farmers grasped eagerly at the chance to renew traditional life brought by the war.

The Peace of Amiens, signed in March 1802, broke the fragile interdependence of chief and clansmen, partially reestablished after

1793 by the exigencies of war. Radical agrarian reform, which had been delayed by Highland recruiting practices, burst forth in the new century as the landlord-chiefs turned their attention again to their own economic aggrandizement. Since the price of agricultural products, especially of wool, had risen substantially during the war years, the profits made by the first sheep farmers were enormous and a further increase was expected. In the islands and on the coast, kelp production offered similar rewards, but it also required a resettlement of the population. On an even wider scale than in the previous century, Highland landlords reorganized their estates and removed the clansmen from their farms. Complaints about this rampant commercialism were heard across the Highlands, as the struggle to compete with sheep farmers for land ruined many tenants. The changes reported on the Duke of Gordon's estate in June of 1803 were typical. All his farms were up for rent in July and "South country farmers" were "offering double, triple and quadriple rents"; "the whole Country" was alarmed. A year earlier Bishop Chisholm had observed that "Our Catholics through the Highlands are in Confusion, on the wing for emigration[;] our Proprietors are extravagent in their demands."[16] Such comments applied equally to Protestant clansmen in the early nineteenth century as landlords in Ardgour, Lochiel, and Skye (to name only a few) reorganized their estates to the detriment of the joint tenants.[17]

The impact of this extensive effort to transform Highland agriculture was dramatic. It resulted in the third burst of departures in the first cycle of emigration from Scotland. Virtually no emigrants left the Highlands between 1794 and 1800. In 1801, 800 people emigrated, a number greater than any year except 1791 since the beginning of the American Revolution. But this was a trickle, compared to the flood that followed; in 1802, 3,300 people left the Highlands for Nova Scotia, Canada, and North Carolina. Over the ensuing winter, talk and interest in emigration was at such a fever pitch in the Highlands that it was widely predicted that 20,000 people would emigrate in the summer of 1803. A more realistic estimate was made by James Grant of Redcastle, who forecast the departure of 5,000 people that year. Such numbers repeated over even a few years represented a considerable depopulation of the Highlands. Grant predicted a total emigration of 25,000 people, one-sixth of the population of the four Highland counties but one-third of the population of the west Highlands and islands, from which most of the emigrants came.[18]

Events in Knoydart, where one-third of the population had already emigrated to Canada, indicate that Grant's prediction was perfectly possible. Emigration was the clansmen's response to the radical agricultural change which denied them their customary lands and community life; the intensified pace of change after 1800 was matched by a correspondingly large increase in emigration. Landlords were horrified; they had expected their former tenants to take advantage of various labouring opportunities available on the estate. But the clansmen preferred to join kin and friends in the British colonies. The emigration of 1802 and the planned departures of 1803 were the beginning of what threatened to become a haemorrhage of emigration from the Highlands.

Among these emigrants were many of Glengarry's tenants. Alexander McDonell's fencible regiment had been disbanded at Ayr in July 1801, and both chief and men had gratefully returned to the Highlands after seven years' military service.[19] A new influence, less favourable to the clansmen's interests than Father Alexander Macdonell's, now came into the chief's life as he arranged to marry the daughter of Sir William Forbes.[20] When McDonell came home and married, he also surveyed his financial situation. Like most Highland proprietors, McDonell found that both his need for income and the market value of his estate had increased substantially. While the Glengarry chief decided to raise rents to reflect current market prices, he intended to offer farms to his clansmen at a discount. "Upon mature reflection & advice, it appeared ... that Ten per Cent was a sacrifice as great as I could afford, and accordingly I made offer to my old tenants of remaining upon their lands at said Ten per Cent below the amount of offers from Strangers ... which the County reported as a handsome sacrifice on my hands, and beyond what it was supposed other proprietors would make."[21]

The real value of McDonell's supposed concession is difficult to assess, but it was clearly not enough for the joint-tenant farmers. They could not afford the higher rents he demanded, even with a 10% discount. Their reaction to Glengarry's "reform" could have been predicted: they left in droves. As Bishop Chisholm testified in April 1802, while Glengarry had a "great Landed Income ... his tenants complain and many of them are to Emigrate this year."[22] Glengarry was shocked when his tenants asked to surrender their leases so as to emigrate to Canada. Both his romanticism and his purse were so disturbed by this development that, on 21 March, he offered the emigrants "Life Rent Tenures of their *old holdings*, and indemnities for all improvements."[23] It did no good; many of his tenants refused and emigrated to Canada over the summer. Clearly the tenants' assessment of social relations on the Glengarry estate had altered dramatically. Only a few years earlier, they would have accepted any offer of life tenure and compensation for improvements with enthusiasm. But by 1802, the Macdonell clansmen had had enough of their chief's promises. For some thirty years they had endured heavy rent increases, removals, and restrictions, all of which benefited only the landlord and sheep farmers; always, it seemed, their interests were sacrificed to the chief's. Possibly what Glengarry asked of them in 1802 was no worse than what they had already endured. But whether the rent increase was really a heavy additional burden or merely the proverbial straw, many clansmen could see no future for themselves on the Glengarry estate and chose instead to join kin and friends in the new Glengarry.

Somewhere in the order of 500 of Glengarry's tenants emigrated in the summer of 1802, in two separate parties. Tenants from the Glen Garry area left from Fort William under the leadership of Archibald McMillan of Murlaggan on the Lochiel estate. This emigration is described in the next section of this chapter. At the same time, the people of Knoydart and North Morar sailed from Loch Nevis, along with tenants from other west-coast estates. Records of this migration are so scanty that it has not been possible to reconstruct it in any detail, but the general circumstances of the voyage can be pieced together to identify some of the emigrants and their experience.

The *Neptune*, a 600-ton vessel, sailed from Loch Nevis under the command of Captain Boyd late in June of 1802. A Scottish customs inspector, most likely from Fort William and hence not on the scene, reported that the *Neptune* carried 550 passengers of whom 400 paid full fare. This account may have slightly underestimated the number of emigrants, since several of them stated on arrival at Quebec that the vessel carried "upwards of six hundred Persons, Men, Women & Children."[24] At least 150 of the emigrants, or 27% of the group, were children, and it seems probable that the additional 50 passengers unknown to the customs officer were mostly children – again, it was a family affair. The actual organizers of the migration have not been identified, but Norman Morrison, Duncan McDonald, and Murdoch McLennan, who served as spokesmen for the group, were likely also men of standing in the community. Three Highland districts provided almost all the emigrants for the *Neptune*: Knoydart and North Morar, Glenelg, and Kintail and Lochalsh.[25] Morrison, McDonald, and McLennan each represented a clan prominent in one of these districts.

It has been possible to identify only twenty-two families or heads of family who sailed on the *Neptune*.[26] Four men were described as natives of Kintail; these include Farquhar McLennan, John and Alick

Macrae, and Murdoch McLennan. John McGillivray (who travelled with his wife and child), Malcolm McCuaig, and Norman Morrison all bear the names of families living in Glenelg and probably came from that peninsula.[27] There is no definite proof that William McPherson was part of this group; he is not, however, named in Archibald McMillan's passenger list, and his arrival in Glengarry in 1802 with a wife and child makes it quite probable that he travelled on the *Neptune*.[28] The remaining fourteen of the twenty-two known families came either from Knoydart or North Morar. Little information other than names survives for John Macdougall, the brothers Hugh and Donald MacDonald, and Roderick, Neil, John, Angus, Hugh, and Allan Ban Macdonald, all natives of Knoydart.[29]

Given the large numbers that had left Knoydart in 1786, the 1802 emigrants from that district were very likely to have kin already settled in Glengarry County. Certainly this was the case for the large Macdonald of Loup family. Alex and John Macdonald were Loyalist settlers in Glengarry County, and their first cousins, Angus and John Rory Macdonald emigrated in 1786.[30] Their brother Lauchlin and a married sister were, with their families, passengers on the *Neptune*, as were their mother, Catherine McGillis Macdonald, and Lauchlin's mother-in-law – clearly age was no barrier to emigration. Moreover, Ewen Roy and John McRory were brothers-in-law of one of Catherine McGillis's daughters, and John at least emigrated on the *Neptune*. Ewen's family had been separated in the departure from Scotland and in 1804 "Caty Eune's Daughter ... [had] not come yet farther than the Nova Schotia."[31] The Macdonalds of Loup may have been exceptional in the degree to which they reconstituted a complex Highland kin group in Glengarry County, but in those few cases for which evidence is available, the *Neptune* emigrants were all rejoining close family members already living in Canada.

Only one of the *Neptune* passengers left an explanation for his departure, in a statement which emphasizes the importance of social considerations in the decision to leave Scotland. Shortly before 1802, Lord Seaforth introduced sheep farming to Kintail and began to evict tenants. Murdoch McLennan, one of the spokesmen for the 1802 party, "gave up a valuable holding on the Seaforth estate, in order to keep with friends and neighbours who were emigrating."[32] By this action McLennan sacrificed a comfortable livelihood in his native glen. Once again not only economic factors but social values of community were responsible for the wave of emigration from northern Scotland. Not many clansmen emigrated against their immediate economic self-interest, as McLennan did, but the passengers of the *Neptune*, like other Highland emigrants during this first cycle of departures, chose emigration not merely as an avenue of escape from the economic consequences of sheep farming but more as the communal solution to the crisis which faced them.

Emigration inevitably broke some family ties, but the pull of kinship remained very strong among Highlanders. Roderick Macdonald, one of the Macdonalds of Loup and a nephew of John Rory, did not accompany his parents and siblings to Glengarry County. In 1804 his cousin Aeneas wrote to him, noting that Roderick's father was surprised that Roderick had not yet come to Canada and that he needed encouragement to do so. The family believed that "the desire of joining ... most of all your nearest relations was enough to induce you to it." Once part of an extended family had settled in Canada, kinship became a magnet, drawing people to the new settlement. In addition, the clansmen saw Canada itself as an attraction. By 1800 so many links joined the Highland communities of Scotland with those of Canada that tenants left in the northern glens must have had a better knowledge of life in Canada than most British subjects, including some in the Colonial Office. At the moment of choice forced on them by the losses caused by agrarian transformation, few in the Highlands could resist a letter from Canada with the plea, "All friends here would wish to see you join them in a Country where reigns peace & plenty."[33]

The *Neptune* arrived at Quebec on 25 August 1802 after a nine-week Atlantic crossing.[34] The communal character of the voyage is reflected in the set of rules and regulations which the emigrants agreed would govern their actions on board ship. When the emigrants reached Quebec after their "tedious" passage, their spokesmen Morrison, McDonald, and McLennan wrote a letter of thanks to Captain Boyd, later published in the *Quebec Gazette*. The three men attributed their arrival in good health to those regulations, "the reverse of which in our crowded state must without your [Boyd's] uncommon care have been the consequence."[35] Few of the *Neptune* emigrants were well-to-do and some had very little money left after paying for the Atlantic crossing. The arrival of this large group of Highlanders created a stir in Quebec and a subscription list was opened for the assistance of indigent passengers from the *Neptune*. Some sixty people contributed a total of £103 10s. 3d.; large donations of £15 and £10 were received from Lieutenant-General Hunter and the owners of the *Neptune* respectively, while Dr. Longmore cared for the sick without charge. On 30 August, six vessels left Quebec carrying the emigrants to Montreal; £97 was spent on fares for the needy, 10s. was used for the purchase of drugs, £1 16s. 3d. for boards for beds, and £2 3s. 7d. was given to the most indigent.[36]

The *Neptune* emigrants had sailed for Quebec hoping "to go on to Upper Canada as they could."[37] Even before leaving Scotland it was evident that limited resources would force some of the party to stop short of their goal. Sir John Johnson, former commander of the KRRNY and owner of a seigneury near Chambly, "induced 25 or 30 families to settle there," but none of these Highlanders remained in Chambly beyond 1815 and many rejoined their friends in Glengarry County.[38] The remaining *Neptune* emigrants reached Glengarry late in September of 1802.[39]

The second major emigration to Glengarry County in 1802 was organized by Archibald McMillan of Murlaggan, who collected fares, made arrangements with the shipping company, and generally organized the departure. Archibald was the son of Alexander McMillan, tacksman of Murlaggan during the Forfeited Estates' administration of Lochiel. Although he trained as a clerk in London in the 1780s, Archibald returned to the Highlands when he succeeded his father in Murlaggan. Another prominent member of the party was his first cousin Allan McMillan of Glenpean, whose brother had led the 1792 emigration. The families of the two men had been Lochiel's principal tenants in Locharkaigside for some 300 years; Archibald was, in addition, a second cousin of the Cameron chief.[40] Eight men in the emigrant party acted as McMillan's lieutenants. These were John Corbet of Ardachy, Alexander McPhee of Aberchalder, and Donald McDonell of Lundy, all from Glengarry; Angus McPhee of Crieff in Lochiel; and Alexander Cameron, John Cameron, Donald McMillan, and Lauchlin McDonell, clansmen from either the Glengarry or the Lochiel estate. Some years after the emigration, McMillan testified that these men had been "useful in forwarding his views [and] in preserving good Order among the people."[41] The eight men represented both the major families and the various districts from which the emigrants came, a fact which points once again to the importance not just of the tacksmen but also of prominent tenants in providing leadership for the clansmen's emigration.

The list that Murlaggan kept of the clansmen enrolled in his party provides a tantalizing glimpse of the family and community structure of this Highland emigrant group.[42] The McMillan party included some 448 clansmen, consisting of about equal numbers of men, women, and children under thirteen. The percentage of young children (32%) fell just shy of that age group's share of the west Highland population. This is not surprising, since earlier Highland emigrant parties to Glengarry were similarly composed. This figure is nevertheless substantially higher than the rate Bailyn identified among emigrants from the Highlands some thirty years earlier.

What was remarkable is the proportion of women over twelve years of age. There actually were four more women than men in McMillan's party (155 to 151), and, while most travelled in family groups as wives, mothers, daughters, or sisters, fifteen women were listed without male companions. Matching of surnames and points of origin suggests that seven of these women likely had relatives in the emigrant party, but the other eight were perhaps travelling without any male relative in the group. The difference between the percentage of women in the McMillan party (51%) and in the Highlands/Hebrides part of Bailyn's provincial group (46%) is not large. However, the contrast with Bailyn's English emigrants, of whom only 16% were female, is dramatic.[43]

Such figures suggest three significant facts about emigration from western Inverness. First, Bailyn's presentation of Highland emigration based on the first years of large-scale departures may not adequately represent the importance of the family emigration that later characterized the movement to Glengarry County. Second, and more importantly, these numbers confirm that Bailyn's general provincial model (amended to allow for a larger number of children) holds for the Glengarry migration and applies to a much longer period than he has dealt with. Third, the large number of women and children in the McMillan party underlines the wholesale transference of large parts of Highland communities to the new Gaelic settlement in Canada. A community which loses its women and children cannot, to the extent that it does so, reproduce itself. Such emigration of entire families was to become a common pattern of departure across Europe in the nineteenth century.

McMillan's list of emigrants is also significant for the family and geographic links it reveals among the members of the emigrant party. Eighty-eight groups of names appear on this list, with each group ruled off from the others by a double stroke of the pen; the groups range in size between one and thirteen people. An analysis of the list makes apparent the variety of relationships among the groups which made up the McMillan party. Six emigrants are listed singly, although even then four of these may have had siblings in the party. Eleven groups consisted of unmarried people above twelve years of age, including four parties of women only and two parties of men only. The vast majority (91%) of the emigrants, however, travelled in one of the remaining seventy-one groups, which included couples and parents and children; the average size of these family groups was 5.7 people. These groups represented the full range of the family life cycle, from husband and wife alone, to couples accompanied by up to six children under thirteen, to a widow travelling with four unmarried adult children and at least one married daughter and her husband. Once again, Bailyn's percentages for family emigration and family size in the Highland departures for 1774–5 seem somewhat low when compared to the McMillan party.[44]

Although Archibald McMillan was a prominent Lochiel tacksman, less than one quarter of the emigrants came from that estate. Like McMillan, however, most of them were from the Locharkaig district of Lochiel. More than half of the 1802 group left from the inland portion of the Glengarry estate, including several McMillan families, who had left Locharkaigside a generation earlier to settle on McDonell lands immediately to the north in Glen Garry. Another one-eighth of the group came from a variety of locations around the Great Glen: Glen Moriston, Glen Urquhart, Strathglass, Glen Spean, and Glen Roy were all represented. Four families joined the emigration to Canada from the Lowlands: the McDonells and McMillans from Paisley and the Camerons and McDonells of Thornhill probably came originally from western Inverness and chose to emigrate with their friends. But the emigrants were not merely from the same estate but often from the same farm as well. This is most obvious in the case of Aberchalder and Inchlaggan in Glen Garry, which sent nine and six families respectively, or fifty-nine and forty-one people.

The McMillan emigrants left in response both to economic transformation and to the ties of kinship linking them to Canada. The 240 emigrants from Glengarry's estate must have been among those who turned down their chief's offer of higher rents (less 10%) in 1802. The eviction of six families from Clunes on the Lochiel estate in 1801 warned other tenants of their own probable fate. After almost thirty years of emigrations to America, family and community ties across the Atlantic also influenced the emigrants' decision to leave. Some from Glen Garry and Glen Moriston left to join relations who had emigrated in 1773, 1785, or 1792. Allan McMillan of Glenpean went to Canada to join his brother Alexander, who had organized the 1792 migration. Other McMillans had close relations in Canada; the six McMillans of Badenjoig had an uncle Donald who had emigrated in 1785 and a second cousin Duncan

Cairibh who had settled in Glengarry County in 1794.[45] The success of the emigration must also be linked to the opportunity of leaving in community groups. The rapid deterioration of the tenants' economic and social situation and the bright prospect of joining a new Highland settlement in the company of kin and friends were critical in ensuring the success of the Murlaggan emigration.

The significant role of gentlemen in making the complex arrangements needed for communal emigration is evident in Archibald McMillan's records. Organizing an emigrant party of 448 people required leadership, months of work, and detailed recordkeeping, as well as a substantial investment of money. McMillan's "considerable trouble and expense" began with a trip to Leith, Glasgow, and Port Glasgow in the spring of 1802 to inquire about shipping. He wrote numerous letters to customs officers, shipowners, and community leaders. He attended meetings with prospective emigrants at Letterfinlay, Gargalt (Glen Garry), and Achnacarry with expenses of 4s. 6d., 7s., and 11s. 6d. respectively. He made a longer trip to "Lochnevishead when going to meet the Cnoydart people" in hope of convincing Glengarry's Knoydart tenants to join his party, but the attempt failed since no one from Knoydart sailed with his group.[46] McMillan's greatest financial task was chartering ships to take the emigrants to Canada; this involved making an accurate estimate of the number of emigrants, determining the size of the vessel required, and collecting fares from would-be passengers. For their trouble in this complex process Highland emigrant leaders made a profit on the fares. Selkirk reported that "a difference of from 10s. to 20s. on each passenger, was not considered as unreasonable."[47] McMillan chartered three vessels for his group, the brigs *Friends* and *Helen* and the ship *Jane*; he agreed to pay the owners of the *Friends* £4 10s. per adult passenger and a similar fare may have been paid on the other vessels as well. The emigrants, however, paid McMillan five guineas in instalments, providing McMillan with an average profit of 15s. per adult fare.[48]

McMillan's final profit from the voyage may not actually have been that large. On 3 July 1802 McMillan paid £545 for the charter of the *Friends*; for the *Jane* and *Helen* he paid £337 and £321 respectively on 8 May and the same sums again on 3 July, for a total of £1861. At five guineas per full passenger, McMillan would have received £1600 10s. for 299 adults and £372 15s. for 144 half fares,[49] or £1979 5s. altogether, leaving a profit of only £118, or a little more than 7s. per adult fare. McMillan may have expected more emigrants to travel in his party – for instance some of the Knoydart tenants – and may therefore have booked more space than needed. Without further evidence, no firm conclusion concerning McMillan's final profits can be drawn, but it seems likely that he received somewhat less than the profit Lord Selkirk believed customary on the transaction.

Conditions on board Murlaggan's three vessels were quite comfortable and underline the advantages of community organization. The agreement McMillan signed with the owners of the *Friends* allowed ten consecutive days for the emigrants to board ship, during which time they were to provide their own rations. McMillan specified that "Divisions made with rough boards for sleeping in six feet by six feet" were to be built for each adult passenger and space proportional to the fare allowed for each child. The emigrants were permitted "room for luggage at the rate of two barrel bulk" for each full fare or equivalent; part of their belongings could be stowed in chests, placed in a row on either side of the ship. Some attention was paid to the passengers' health, since McMillan stipulated that "a companion on the fore hatch" was to be built "for the benefit of conveying air to the hold." On boarding ship the emigrants were to hand over all arms to the captain, who was to act as "judge and umpire" during the voyage but who was to be accountable for his actions afterwards. Cabin passengers on the *Friends* paid an additional £5 and were expected to furnish their own provisions; staterooms were allotted to them at McMillan's discretion. Steerage passengers were supplied with food at no additional cost; children paying one-eighth, one-quarter, one-half, or three-quarters fare were provisioned at the same rate. Each adult of twelve or over was to receive a stone (or seventeen and one-half pounds) of oatmeal and seven gills of molasses weekly, as well as three quarts of water daily. From this ration, the passengers were to be given three and one-half pounds of bread weekly and porridge "cooked by the Brig Company twice a day." It was the shipowners' responsibility to provide the fuel and hearth on which the emigrants' provisions were prepared.[50]

The McMillan party sailed from Fort William on 3 July 1802. The *Jane* and *Helen* reached Quebec on 5 September after a nine-week passage, the *Friends* arrived ten days later.[51] The emigrants immediately went upriver to Montreal in these vessels and were allowed two days on board ship in the harbour to prepare for disembarking. A disagreement over surplus rations with the captains of the *Jane* and *Helen* reveals the emigrants' frugality and the difficulties which the journey could entail. In the belief that they were entitled to any rations not consumed during the voyage, the emigrants had stretched out their rations of meal and molasses with supplies of beef, pork, cheese, and other items purchased for their passage. McMillan brought the case before justices of the peace in Montreal, pointing out "the great want and distress of many of them ... and their Families in a strange country where they are destitute." The judges awarded the emigrants the remainder of eleven weeks' meal ration and eight weeks' molasses, but the case had put the emigrants to an expense and delay for which they were not compensated. While Murlaggan stayed in Montreal to begin business as a merchant, Glenpean and most of the other emigrants continued their journey upriver and reached Glengarry County in October 1802.[52]

Close to 800 Highlanders settled in Glengarry County in 1802, and since the clansmen's interest in emigration was high, many more emigrants were expected in Canada the following year. In June 1803, a Scottish Roman Catholic clergyman observed that "The Spirit of emigration is very great in the western coast – Thousands went away last year, and I am told near 20,000 are ready to emigrate this Summer."[53] Emigration had reached such levels that depopulation was a real possibility; the priest expected that Bishop Chisholm would have few Roman Catholics in his district if the clansmen's enthusiasm for emigration continued much longer. In Canada, the recently arrived Archibald McMillan was so strong a supporter of emigration that he believed that "in a few years this country will contain more Highlanders than the old country." Murlaggan's own enthusiasm had not ended with his arrival in Montreal, and he declared his "Intention of going home to carry more of my Country-men along with me."[54] McMillan's ambition was frustrated at least in part by the reopening of hostilities with France in May 1803, after which emigration from the Highlands slowed again.

Yet the subsequent decline in emigration did not reflect a renewal of the traditional relationship between clansman and chief, as had been the case in 1793. As Lord Selkirk pointed out, by 1804 few parts of the Highlands were untouched by radical change. The experience of the preceding twenty-five years, and particularly of the years after 1793, had destroyed the tenants' trust in their landlords. Thus Selkirk believed that landlords could no longer easily influence their tenants; the latter had "learnt by the experience of their neighbours, that a compliance with the desire of their landlords, may protract the period of their dismissal, but cannot procure them that permanent possession they formerly expected to preserve."[55] Emigration fell dramatically in 1803, not because the tenants had been tempted from that course by the offer of farms in return for military service, but because of the effect of the Passenger Act passed during the same year.

Parliament passed the Passenger Act (which became law in June 1803) in response to the demands of Highland landlords. The loss of tenants resulting from the emigrations of 1801–02 and the more numerous departures feared in 1803 threatened both the social pretensions of landlords and their ability to control a large labour force to develop their estates.[56] The Highland Society, to which most prominent Highlanders belonged (including landlords like McDonell of Glengarry) lobbied government members, claiming that heavy emigration from the Highlands was not in the public interest.[57] The complete depopulation of the Highlands that seemed possible early in 1803 seriously threatened the kelping industry, labour-intensive improvements, and the manning of Highland regiments. Much of the parliamentary discussion of the act focused on the appalling conditions on certain emigrant vessels. But the chief architect of the act, Charles Hope, explained that the legislation was only superficial-ly calculated "to regulate the equipment and victualling of ships carrying Passengers to America." Such humanitarian rhetoric merely veiled the act's real intention: Hope and "other Gentlemen of the Committee" expected "indirectly to prevent ... the rage for emigrat-ing to America."[58] While seemingly concerned with standards of comfort on emigrant vessels, the Passenger Act of 1803 conveniently ensured that emigration was beyond the means of most Highland tenants.

The real purpose of the Passenger Act was widely understood in Scotland. The price of a passage from the west Highlands to Nova Scotia, the cheapest North American destination, rose from £4 to £10 after June 1803; the fare to Canada would have cost somewhat more. One of Lochiel's tenants, Allan Cameron, commented bitterly on the effect of the new act on Highland affairs: "the proprietor encourages extensive grazing which is greatly against the poor tenants who would incline to go to America, but the Government has fallen on a plan to stop their career, as they will not be able to pay freight, as each passenger young or old must take up two tons of the ship, with every other allowance of provisions, surgeons, attendence."[59] Alexander Macdonell, chaplain of the Glengarry Fencibles, was not alone in his opinion that the Passenger Act had been passed only under a "specious pretext of humanity & tender benevolence towards the emigrants."[60] By October 1803 the merchants of Greenock, who considered the act "a severe reflection on their own conduct," were "procuring certificates to disprove the assertions upon which the Emigration Act" was based.[62] The merchants failed in their efforts to ease the restrictions of the act, and emigration from the Highlands fell to a low level. The effectiveness of these fare increases in limiting emigration reflects both the marginal economic resources of prospective emigrants and the knowledge possessed by chiefs and politicians, which enabled them indirectly to set fares at a level that would have the desired effect.

In the first years after the introduction of the Passenger Act, only very small groups of Highlanders reached Glengarry County. Many had already made the decision to emigrate and those people who had more than the pre-1803 price of a passage were able, at the expense of part or all of their capital, to afford the higher fares. One Glengarry inhabitant, James Duncan Macdonald (born in 1792), remembered the arrival of emigrant groups not only in 1802 but also in 1803.[62] Perhaps among the 1803 emigrants were the eight McMillans and Camerons who applied for land in Glengarry as recent emigrants in 1806.[63] Five of these settlers were from Locharkaigside and the others came from Glen Loy, Knoydart, and Glen Garry; four were described as farmers, while the others were listed as a shepherd, yeoman, and labourer.

Among the most celebrated (in Glengarry historiography) but paradoxically the least known of the post-1803 emigrants were the men from the Glengarry Fencible Regiment. After the disbanding of the regiment in 1801, the men returned home to find that their chief planned to increase rents substantially; like Glengarry's other tenants, many of the fencibles chose to emigrate. None of the 1802 emigrants has, however, yet been identified as a veteran of the regiment. One possible reason for their failure to join either of the 1802 migrations to Canada may lie in the activities of their former chaplain. Alexander Macdonell travelled to London in May of 1802 to ask for government assistance for the disbanded fencibles to emigrate to Upper Canada:[64] Macdonell explained to the Secretary of War, Charles York, that the former soldiers were now "intirely secluded from their native soil by the System of Sheep farming newly adopted in the highlands." The men had two options: to accept a humiliating decline in status by becoming day labourers in the Highlands or in the towns or to emigrate to America, where life in the forest was "more congenial to their former habits of life."[65]

Macdonell's efforts on behalf of the Glengarry Fencibles eventually met with success. The Colonial Secretary, Lord Hobart, wrote to the governor of Upper Canada recommending to his care "Highlanders, mostly Macdonalds and partly disbanded soldiers of the late Glengarry Fencible Regiment" and asking that each family be given

200 acres of land "in the usual manner."[66] After the chaplain received notice of Hobart's letter on 1 March 1803, he proceeded to hire shipping for the voyage to Canada; as late as 8 June, one of Macdonell's colleagues mentioned the impending departure of the Glengarry Fencibles. But the planned group emigration never took place.[67] On different occasions Macdonell later gave two distinct reasons for this. In 1806 the chaplain recalled that two months after Hobart's letter was written, "the war broke out & most serious apprehensions of envasion began to pervade all classes .... Your Petitioner when Just on the eve of embarking persuaded his adherents at the earnest request of Government, to delay their departure until those alarms of Invasion had subsided."[68] This explanation appears to be more an attempt by Macdonell to impress government officials with the value of the Highlanders and himself than it is an explanation for the failure of the emigration. But an 1814 letter to the Colonial Secretary, describing the impact of the Passenger Act on departures from Scotland, offers a more concrete reason for the failure of Macdonell's scheme. Macdonell pointed out that the act, by virtue of "many unnecessary restrictions," had amounted "to an actual prohibition" of emigration.[69]

In spite of the increased cost of emigration, twenty-five veterans of the Glengarry Fencibles did eventually reach Glengarry County. Most arrived in the period immediately following their intended 1803 departure.[70] On 16 July 1803 the chaplain reported that "some of the Glengarrymen" were "now resolved to take their passage from Greenoch by the first vessels that sail for Canada," but Macdonell did not expect it to be easy for them to get away that season.[71] Four of the Fencibles, John McMillan, Paul and John Cameron, and Angus McDonald, emigrated in 1803; other emigrants included Angus McLachlan in 1805 and Ewen Kennedy, who left Scotland after 1815. Sergeant Roderick McDonald was still in Knoydart in October 1804, but by 1823 he had joined his relatives in Canada.[72] The chaplain also came to Canada, but when his group emigration scheme collapsed, Macdonell travelled by himself in October 1804.[73]

Father Macdonell shared much of the same background and motivation for emigration as did his flock. Macdonell was born in 1762 and was likely a grandson of Allan Macdonell, tacksman of Kyltrie, and thus a descendant of the seventeenth-century Glengarry chief Donald of Laggan. Through his mother, Nancy Cameron of Clunes, Father Alexander was related to Cameron tacksmen from the Lochiel estate.[74] His branch of the Macdonells was a well-connected, if relatively impoverished, tenant family. Father Alexander was, like the heads of provincial emigrant families, a middle-aged man when he left Scotland. Like them, he tried to organize a group departure for Canada; his solitary voyage can in part be explained by a complex court case which kept him uncertain of when he would be free to sail until just before the last ship left for Quebec in 1804. By that time, changes on the Glengarry estate, a bitter quarrel with its chief, and the death of close friends and relations had cut most of the ties that bound the priest to Scotland.[75] Macdonell had relations already in Glengarry County and their "earnest and incessant entreaty" for him to join them in Canada was a "powerfull inducement" in favour of emigration. But the priest emphasized that a "still stronger motive" was the possibility of "being usefull" to the Highlanders "necessitated to leave their own Country."[76] By July 1804 Father Alexander had received word that the people of Glengarry were eagerly looking for his arrival and had even convinced the Bishop of Quebec to pay his passage.[77]

Father Alexander Macdonell found that ties of family and community pulled him across the Atlantic to the new Highland settlement in Glengarry County. Other clansmen from western Inverness still hoped to make the same passage, but communal emigration slowed dramatically after 1803 and the third phase of the first cycle of Highland emigration sputtered to an end.

The sudden decline in Highland emigration after 1803 has traditionally been associated with the resumption of hostilities by Britain and France in May of that year. The evidence presented above emphasizes the role of the Passenger Act in June of 1803 as more directly responsible for the sudden reduction in the flow of emigrants. Whichever factor was more significant, the result is clear: emigration remained at a very low ebb until the new social and economic climate following the end of the war in 1814 began a second cycle in emigration from Great Britain. Between 1803 and 1814 Highlanders were still anxious to emigrate to America and were prevented from doing so primarily by the cost of passage. Some emigrants did reach Glengarry during these years, but many others who wished to leave the Highlands for Canada were unable to make that journey. The pathetic tale of the Canadian Fencible Regiment documents the lengths to which some clansmen went (in this case unsuccessfully) to emigrate to Canada.

The need for a defensive military force in Canada, and a desire to assist Highlanders stranded in Scottish ports by the enforcement of the new Passenger Act, led the Secretary at War and for the

Colonies to authorize the raising of the Canadian Fencible Regiment in August 1803.[78] Recruiting was not limited to those clansmen already committed to emigration but soon extended throughout northern Scotland. Men flocked eagerly to enlist when recruiters promised land and a free passage to Canada for women and children. Charles Hope complained that "it was in vain for any other Officer to offer his paltry [financial] bounty, in Competition with the paradise of America." Some of these recruits were drawn from the districts which had peopled Glengarry County; the sixty people who left the parish of Glenelg to follow the regiment in 1804 may have had either MacLeod or Macdonell kinsmen in the Canadian county.[79] One Alexander McDonald, who had served as sergeant of the grenadier company of the Glengarry Fencible Regiment, enlisted in the Canadian Fencibles so as to emigrate to America with his wife Ann. Mrs. McDonald explained that her husband intended to serve "as Sergt. for a year or two Merely to get his passage to ... [Canada] for it is very Ill to get over to America this critical time."[80]

Government officials were overwhelmed by the large number of dependents with the Canadian Fencibles: 683 privates were accompanied by 432 wives and 1,069 children, all of whom expected to receive passage to Canada. Highland landlords, through their spokesman Charles Hope, strongly condemned the formation of the regiment, complaining that it was rekindling the fever of emigration that had just begun to die down in the Highlands after the Passenger Act.[81] Mishandling of the regiment by both its officers and the government provoked a mutiny in August 1804, when the men took their orders to march from Glasgow to the Isle of Wight as a first step not to Canada but to the East Indies. The mutineers were lightly punished, but the government decided that it had no use for such a heavily encumbered regiment. The Canadian Fencibles were disbanded at the end of the year and the fate of the would-be emigrants is unknown. A few may have been able to raise the price of a fare to Canada, but the choices facing the vast majority lay between enlistment in a regiment of the line and casual employment in the new industrial cities of the Clyde.[82]

Highland emigration in general, and emigration to Glengarry County in particular, reached new heights during the Peace of Amiens. By 1800 traditional society in western Inverness had fractured under the impact both of the landlords' demand for high rents (which took no account of the tenants' right to land) and, in particular, the introduction of sheep farms. The resulting demographic upheaval was most obvious on the Glengarry estate, where many tenants were removed from their farms. The clansmen who were able to do so responded to this crisis with communal emigration.[83] That the emigrants took their families with them testifies to the clansmen's abandonment of western Inverness in favour of a new Highland community in Canada. Had emigration gone on unchecked for even three or five more years, western Inverness would indeed have been substantially depopulated. Such large-scale departures seemed to threaten the economic security of Highland landlords, who quickly made use of their wealth and political power to protect their position by virtually prohibiting emigration from the Highlands. This measure could not, however, surpress the desire of many clansmen to obtain land and to join their kin and friends in the new Highland communities of British North America.

CHAPTER NINE

The Post-1815 Emigrants

When the Napoleonic Wars ended, emigration fever rose once again in the Highlands. The landlords' opposition to emigration remained, but their resistance to the movement cooled in the twelve years after 1803 as they encountered some difficulties in finding employment for their clansmen in the new Highland economy. The consolidation of holdings to create large-scale sheep farms, significant on certain estates before 1803, intensified after 1815 and extended into remoter Highland districts. The economic depression of the postwar years was to make apparent the incongruity of landlords' attempts to create sheep farms and at the same time maintain large populations on their estates.

By 1815, certain Highland gentlemen had even reached the conclusion that emigration might benefit both landlords and clansmen. One such convert was John Campbell, law agent for Lord Macdonald, the Earl of Breadalbane, and other proprietors.[1] Campbell rejected the eighteenth-century belief that emigration caused depopulation, arguing instead that the Highlands possessed a surplus population that could best be provided for by emigration to Canada. The military qualities of the Highlanders would be an asset to the colony, and their desire to join relatives already resident in Canada would motivate the movement. The difference between Campbell's beliefs and those held by most of the gentry before 1815 was nowhere more apparent than in his favourable comments about Lord Selkirk's enthusiasm for emigration. Selkirk's book, he claimed, had been "received at the time with some prejudice & considerable opposition. But it has been found that it contains much of truth in it."[2] Such support for Lord Selkirk, whose arguments had seemed heretical to most clan chiefs, marked the beginning of a radical shift in upper-class opinion. The collapse of both agricultural prices and the wartime market for kelp, as well as continued population growth, ultimately led most landlords to adopt Campbell's view. Their determined opposition to emigration soon turned into support for the departure of their now surplus tenants.

If landlords changed their attitude towards emigration after 1815, many of the clansmen did not. But the financial barrier to their emigration created by the Passenger Act was heightened by the general economic depression following the Napoleonic War and still more extensive evictions. In addition to such financial difficulties, the would-be emigrant also faced the social consequences of agrarian transformation: less frequently were large groups of clansmen able to emigrate together, and most of the gentlemen who had played a role in organizing such parties in the past had already gone. Nevertheless, people from western Inverness continued to arrive in Glengarry County for another forty years, and the manner in which this emigration occurred offers insight into the factors governing the movement from the Highlands after 1815. Only one large-scale emigration to Glengarry occurred between 1815 and 1855, and it was a government-sponsored experiment in colonization at the war's end. More typical of this period were the families that emigrated singly or in small groups. They came from the same or adjacent districts of western Inverness and were very often related to those who had emigrated to Glengarry before them. This prolonged, if uneven, trickle of emigrants was the result of the dense kinship and community links which joined the people of western Inverness and Glengarry County; it also hints at the considerable continuity visible over time in the movement of people from the Highlands.

Government ministers and official policies reflected, if they did not actually lead, the shift in elite opinion from opposition to support for emigration. As early as October 1813, the Colonial Secretary, Lord Bathurst, concluded that emigration could not be prevented and should therefore be directed towards the British colonies.[3] The War of 1812 between the United States and Great Britain seriously threatened Britain's hold on Upper Canada, and loyal Highlanders settled in Canada would strengthen the colony's defences. Lord Bathurst, therefore, proposed giving assistance to Highland emigrants for military purposes. In the summer of 1814, the colony's acting governor, Sir Gordon Drummond, responded enthusiastically to the prospect of increased Highland emigration and urged that the clansmen be sent out immediately.[4]

The Colonial Office began its first programme of assisted emigration with the publication in Glasgow of an offer to would-be emigrants on 22 February 1815. Notices were subsequently sent to other Scottish newspapers, and a handbill, made available throughout Scotland, was distributed most heavily in Argyll, Perth, and Inverness. The scheme offered 2,000 free passages to Canada with bedding and rations included, with sailings from the Clyde planned for April. The government scheme was not intended to promote emigration but rather to divert those who had decided to emigrate to America to the Canadian colonies. To guarantee that this objective was met, the government demanded a £16 deposit from each adult male and a two-guinea deposit from each adult woman.[5] When settlement duties were fulfilled, these sums would be returned to the emigrants.

The government offer of an assisted passage to Canada was made across Scotland, but the response from the Highlands greatly exceeded government expectations. There was actually little need to introduce such a scheme since the clansmen had already shown a clear preference for settling in British North America. The government offer led to a flood of applications from those who had already decided to emigrate and from some who had been deterred by the cost of a passage. The deposit required of the emigrants, however, was a substantial sum – in certain cases equal to the commercial cost of a family passage. For many clansmen, whose ability to raise money had been seriously eroded by economic change and wartime inflation, the gap between awakened expectations and financial resources was very large.

Some hoped that the government might be induced to reduce the required deposit. Among these were twenty-nine subscribers to a memorial prepared by Allan McDonell at Fort Augustus early in March 1815. The would-be emigrants assembled with the intention of "Embrasing this precious encouragement offered by our Gracious Sovereign and Government to such as will Emigrate which we are most eager to grasp at so favourable an opportunity, but we are in dread our Sincere attention will prove frustraneous."[6] The memorial expressed two reasonable objections to the government proposal. First, the advertised departure in the month of April left too little time for Highland families to dispose of their possessions and reach the embarkation point on the Clyde. McDonell suggested that sailing be delayed until 16 June. Second, the required deposits were beyond the means of most of the petitioners. Many of the would-be emigrants were discharged soldiers, who were at present supporting their families by wage labour. With the "exhorbitant" cost of living during the war years, these former soldiers had been unable to put money aside and they, unlike tenant farmers, had no stock to sell to raise the cost of the deposit. McDonell's petition proposed that the deposit be waived on condition that each man swear before a magistrate, and find security for his promise, that he would remain on his Canadian grant till the end of his life unless called away to fight for the king.

The twenty-nine subscribers to McDonell's memorial shared the same social characteristics as the successful emigrants to Glengarry County, with one notable difference. With the exception of one John Hall, the memorialists came from the same western Inverness clans as were found in Glengarry County; half of the subscribers were Macdonells. The remaining petitioners included three Kennedys, three Frasers, and one McPhee, MacKay, Robertson, McMillan, McKinnon, Gillis, Ferguson, and Cameron. The great majority of the petitioners (90%) were heads of family, few of them newlyweds since each family included on average 3.7 children. Only in occupation did the twenty-seven male subscribers to the memorial differ significantly from the Glengarry settlers. Not one described himself as a farmer. One man was a student and six were listed only as former soldiers. The remaining 20 men were described either as labourers (nine) or as skilled workers (eleven), and half of these had also served in the army. The skills of a traditional economy were well represented (with three shoemakers, two tailors, one weaver, and a mason), but the three shepherds and one gardener were more likely to find employment in improved agriculture.[7]

This absence of farmers among the twenty-nine petitioners illustrates the effect which agricultural transformation had on the population of western Inverness and the shift in occupation that it produced. Twenty-five or forty years earlier it would have been difficult to find a group of potential migrants of this size that did *not* include a substantial number of tenant and subtenant farmers. The subsequent change in occupation and decline in economic status made it even more difficult for the clansmen to emigrate. Only a few of the petitioners were able to pay the £16 deposit, and hence very few could afford a passage without substantial help. Yet some of the twenty-nine subscribers must have been the children of tenants, whose small stock might well have provided the price of a fare a generation earlier. Others may have been the children of poorer tenants or cottars, who even then might have found it difficult to raise such a sum. The twenty-nine clansmen from Fort Augustus were not alone in lacking the necessary deposit; McDonell commented that many others would have signed the memorial had more time been available.[8] As appealling as the government offer was, it was very difficult for landless Highlanders, now a large part of the population, to meet the attached conditions.

Plans for an April sailing of the assisted emigrants were soon discarded, at first because of the distance many emigrants had to travel and later because shipping was not available.[9] Nonetheless, the emigrants began trickling into Glasgow early in April, afraid that if they waited for notice of the sailing to appear in the newspapers, they would be unable to reach the Clyde in time. On 29 April, Campbell informed Bathurst of their arrival and asked for directions as to how to treat the emigrants; Campbell feared that a long delay might "create grudges & discontent among ignorant country people."[10] By 26 May, the emigrants were waiting less patiently on the Clyde and one of their number, Alexander McNabb of Glasgow, petitioned Lord Bathurst on their behalf. The emigrants felt abandoned by government and requested compensation for their expenses in Glasgow, as well as for the time lost in Canada by the delay.[11] Upon receipt of Campbell's third request for help for the emigrants, Bathurst ordered they be paid a daily allowance from the date of their arrival in Glasgow.[12]

The four ships provided for the emigrants finally arrived in the Clyde early in June, but embarkation and then departure were delayed, in part by the loss of eight sailors to the press gang. Even by early June not all the emigrants had reached the Clyde; fifty families made their deposits after 12 June, and several families from Inverness-shire arrived in Glasgow only on 11 July.[13] While life on board ship awaiting departure must have been cramped and anxious, at least some of the settlers enjoyed long, convivial nights with Peter Stewart, Campbell's Gaelic-speaking clerk.[14] The experience of emigration with its long delays could not stop the usual progression of life; several children were born while the party waited at Greenock, and Colin McPherson, aged four, and Janet McDonell, aged six, died there. In mid-July three ships finally sailed for Canada: the *Atlas* on 11 July with 242 settlers, the *Dorothy* on the following day with 194, and the *Baltic Merchant* on 14 July with 140. A fourth vessel, the *Eliza* sailed three weeks later on 3 August with the remaining 123 emigrants.[15]

This government-assisted emigration to Canada was neither planned nor advertised as an emigration to Glengarry County; indeed the official destination of the emigrants was ultimately set as the Bathurst district of Upper Canada, some eighty miles west of the Highland county. But many of the 1815 emigrants must have left Scotland with a keen interest in settling in Glengarry County, and more than half of the 699 emigrants ultimately ended up there.[16] Of the 362 assisted emigrants who settled in Glengarry County, 85%, or 291, originated in the Scottish Highlands, and 95% of these came from just five parishes.[17] Half of them came from the parish of Glenelg in western Inverness and another 25% came from the neighbouring parishes of Killin and Kenmore in Perthshire. In the years before 1815, the parish of Glenelg (including the districts of Glenelg, Knoydart, and North Morar) sent 1,000 people to Glengarry County,[18] and the other two parishes also had ties to the Canadian settlement. Moreover, almost no other Highland parishes were represented among the 1815 settlers in Glengarry County or among the assisted emigrants.[19] Other parts of Inverness, Argyll, Ross and Cromarty, and Sutherland had experienced substantial emigration over the previous fifty years, but their people went to Nova Scotia, Prince Edward Island, and the former American colonies, not to the colony of Canada. The government-sponsored emigration attracted significant participation only among clansmen whose friends and relations were already settled in Canada, the advertised destination of the voyage.

The desire of 291 clansmen from five Highland parishes to settle in Glengarry County gave a particular character to the Scottish response to the assisted emigration programme. With their participation, 52% of the 668 Scottish emigrants were drawn from the Highlands; since this region possessed approximately one-quarter of the Scottish population, the Highlanders' rate of participation in the government scheme was twice that which might have been expected. On the other hand, had the link between Glengarry and these five parishes not existed, it is quite likely that most of the 291 emigrants would have ignored the government programme, as did the clansmen in most other Highland parishes. The assisted emigration would then have been much smaller in size, with the overwhelming majority of its participants drawn from lowland Scotland. A narrowly recruited group of Highlanders overcame barriers of time, geography and culture and dominated the assisted emigration to Canada because of their ties with Glengarry County.

In addition to sharing the same geographic origins as earlier Glengarry settlers, the 1815 emigration to the county was, like its predecessors, composed almost entirely of families. Of the 362 emigrants who settled in Glengarry in 1815, only eight were single men; the remaining 98% travelled in family groups. Each family included an average of 5.6 people, or about the same number as in the families of the Eigg and the McMillan emigrations. What is remarkable is the fact that 30% of the families from the parish of Glenelg were headed by men fifty years of age or older. These were men who had, quite literally, missed the boat, since they had been of age when large bodies of emigrants left Knoydart or Glenelg in 1786, 1793, and 1802. Their decision to take advantage of the government offer is indicative of the bonds joining Highland communities on both sides of the Atlantic, and of the continuity of the emigration experience in western Inverness. The percentage of women over twelve among the 1815 Glengarry settlers was only slightly smaller than in the McMillan party, 48% rather than 51%. However, the percentage of children among the 1815 settlers was very high: 49% were under thirteen compared to 42% in 1790 and 32% in 1802.

The overwhelming predominance of families among the assisted emigrants and the large number of women and children is largely explained by the terms of the government offer. No adult woman was permitted to enroll in the scheme unless accompanied by a husband, father, or brother. Each male over the age of seventeen was required to pay a deposit of £16 and every female of similar age two guineas, sums that were to be returned to the emigrants upon fulfilment of settlement duties. Since a passage to Canada cost £5 before 1803 and rose to over £10 after that date, the government programme cost a single man 50% more than a commercial voyage and offered little savings to a childless couple. In contrast, for a family with a number of children under eighteen, the £18 2s. deposit for husband and wife was substantially cheaper than the cost of private emigration. Such bargain-basement prices for family emigration would have had little effect, however, if families were not strongly interested in emigration before the scheme was announced. What the government program did was to make it possible for families who could just afford commercial fares, or who were marginally unable to pay them, to emigrate to Canada. The effect of the fare structure on the assisted emigration was to minimalize the participation of single adults and thereby to accentuate the existing bias of Highland and Lowland Scots to emigrate in family parties.

The effect of such extensive family emigration from only a few parishes was to transfer to Canada some of the complex kin groupings characteristic of Highland society. Among the eleven families from Killin, for instance, were eight in which husband or wife bore the name McLaren; there were also two McPhersons and two McDiarmids. While possession of the same surname does not prove close kinship in a Highland community, it does seem likely that some of these clansmen, drawn from relatively small parishes, were cousins, if not siblings. The same conclusion could also be drawn about the probability of kinship among the twenty-five families from the peninsula of Glenelg, which included twelve McRaes, three McCuaigs, and five McCrimmons who were either heads of household or their wives, and the twelve families from Knoydart, which included six McDonells and five McDougalls. The passenger list for the voyage proves this assumption in a number of cases. John McRae is listed as a son of Roderick McRae, Farquhar McCrimmon as a son of John McCrimmon, and James McDougall as a son of Donald McDougall. In other instances, a common name and place of origin, as well as age range, make kinship between emigrants seem highly probable. The John McCrimmon named above was the father not only of Farquhar, aged twenty-eight, but likely also of Donald, twenty-four, and of Duncan, twenty-two, since his dependent children ranged in age from three to seventeen.[20] Knoydart and Glenelg had a population of some 2,500 people; the emigration of 7% of its inhabitants in 1815 inevitably resulted in the departure of clusters of related families.

The 1815 assisted emigration was designed to attract to Canada not the poorest members of the community but men of modest means. The scheme's success in doing so is evident from an analysis of the occupations followed by the great majority of the participating heads of household. Of the forty-one men from Glenelg, Knoydart, Fort Augustus, and Glenshiel, 80% were farmers – that is men with cattle to sell to pay the deposit. The remaining 20% were labourers drawn from two groups. One group consisted of young men in their twenties, mostly unmarried, whose status as labourers was likely the result of their age and hence, quite possibly, temporary. The second group of labourers consisted of three married men in their thirties; these men were among the twenty-nine labourers and craftsmen who signed Allan McDonell's petition asking for the waiver of the assisted emigration deposit. When that request was denied, only these few families were able to participate in the government scheme. Similarly, 80% of the emigrants from Killin and Kenmore were craftsmen or farmers, while the remainder were labourers. The occupational status of the heads of household in the 1815 emigrant party, particularly compared to that of the unsuccessful emigrants who signed Allan McDonell's memorial, underlines the need for, at least some financial resources in making emigration possible. Farmers could often afford passage; labourers most often could not.

The assisted emigrants who settled in Glengarry were remarkably similar to the emigrants who had arrived over the preceding forty years in privately organized groups. The three factors examined above – geographic origin, predominance of families, and respectable, if modest status – are evident in public as well as private emigration to Glengarry County. The one obvious difference – government sponsorship – is more apparent than real; earlier groups had, after all, also received government aid, albeit after they arrived in Canada. Families of similar status also dominated the other half of the assisted emigrant party, which settled eighty miles west of Glengarry. But this group of 337 emigrants was drawn from forty-six different parishes; with the exceptions of Edinburgh and Glasgow, there were only a few instances of families from the same parish jointly participating in the government scheme. The assisted emigrants who settled in Glengarry in 1815 shared the characteristics of the provincial emigration model with the exception of government sponsorship. In addition, both families and farmers were more important in the 1815 movement from Scotland than Bailyn's model would predict.

The 1815 emigration was the last large-scale movement of people from the Scottish Highlands to Glengarry County. Assisted emigration offered a new way for clansmen to emigrate in community groups to Canada, but the British government refused to repeat the experiment, in spite of numerous requests to do so from western Inverness and other Highland districts.[21] Two factors militated against the continuation of privately organized large-scale emigrations to Glengarry. First, Glengarry County no longer had large blocks of ungranted crown lands; group settlement therefore became increasingly difficult.[22] Vast tracts of land were available further up the Ottawa Valley, in the western districts of Upper Canada, or in the cheaper, more accessible destinations of Nova Scotia and Cape Breton. Large bodies of Highland emigrants were drawn to these locations in the forty years following the end of the Napoleonic Wars. Second, after 1803 the clansmen were, as a group, increasingly unlikely to be able to raise the price of a passage to Canada. Higher fares, economic depression, and smaller land holdings resulting from population growth and agricultural transformation made it much more difficult for tenants to organize a communal emigration.

Nevertheless, the clansmen continued to emigrate from western Inverness to Glengarry in a steady stream of single families and smaller groups for more than forty years after 1815. Once in Canada these later emigrants rented or purchased the scattered lots of land that remained in the county. Although this movement is poorly documented, the ongoing flow of emigrants is evidence of the existence of a community that reached across the Atlantic Ocean but whose core was now in the New World.

Not surprisingly most of the emigrants who reached Glengarry during this period came from the same Highland districts that had provided earlier generations of settlers. In 1819, four-year-old Marcella Macdonald came with her family from Knoydart to Glengarry, where they joined an extensive kin group. The new arrivals were closely related to the brothers Ranald, Rory Og, and Alexander Macdonell, each of whom had large and (by then) adult families.[23] In 1822 Angus and Flora McDonell also emigrated with their three children from Knoydart to settle among relatives in Glengarry.[24] In 1827 twenty-year-old Ranald D. McDonell came to the county from Inverness-shire with his parents and most likely his siblings.[25] Similarly, at least one family left Morar for Glengarry; Archibald McGillis, his wife, and daughter emigrated on the ship *Morningfield* in the summer of 1816.[26] The communities of Glenelg and Kintail also continued to send a steady trickle of emigrants to Glengarry County. Norman McLeod, his wife, and their newborn son left Swordland, Glenelg, in July 1816; two years later Patrick McCuaig followed with his wife and seven children. In 1832 several Glenelg families, including Angus Campbell's, accompanied a large emigrant party from Skye to Glengarry.[27] Glenelg continued to send its families: Angus and Janet McCuaig with seven children in 1842; Duncan and Sally Campbell with three children in 1843; Donald McLeod in 1849, with his wife, a niece, six unmarried children, a married daughter, son-in-law, and two grandchildren.[28] From neighbouring Kintail came Ann and George McRae with two children in 1847.[29] These west-coast families were part of the small but continual stream of emigration to Glengarry County after 1815.

Inevitably families were divided by the decision to leave the Highlands, but this break was often mended by subsequent emigrations. The history of the MacIssac Macdonalds of Knoydart is a case in point.[30] Ranald MacIssac's second son, Jock, left Scotland with his wife and two small children for Canada in 1831. The young family sailed on the *Tamerlane*, accompanied by a close friend, Big Jim MacDonald. The elderly Ranald MacIssac and his wife Janet Cameron followed Jock to Glengarry a few years later in 1837 with their remaining five children. Only the eldest son, Donald, who had emigrated to Australia sometime before 1830, failed to join the family. Ranald's decision to follow Jock to Canada, instead of joining

Donald in Australia, may have been based on the comparative cheapness of the fare, but it seems likely that kinship ties with earlier Glengarry settlers may also have had an influence. The family of Angus Ban Macdonald, leader of the 1786 emigration, was nicknamed McKiasaig (or MacIssac) and Jack's companion, Big Jim, was Angus's son. In coming to Canada in the 1830s, the MacIssac Macdonalds may well have reunited a kin group divided by emigration fifty years earlier.

Like the Knoydart and Glenelg settlers, the 1815 emigrants from Loch Tay also attracted other Perthshire clansmen to their Canadian destination. Most emigration from Perthshire to Glengarry County occurred in the five years after 1815, when the assisted emigrants had only just reached their new homes; at least twenty-three families, described as both large and helpless, arrived in the county during this period.[31] The clansmen left Scotland because of religious differences with their landlords – many of the tenants had recently become Congregationalists – and because of the pressure put on agricultural resources by a rapidly growing population and the amalgamation of tenant farms into sheep farms.[32]

Finlay Sinclair, who arrived in Canada in 1816, headed one of the first families to leave Loch Tay for Glengarry County after the assisted emigration. The next year a larger group of families followed him to Glengarry. Among these were Donald McDougall, his wife, and five children, his sister Janet, her husband Malcolm Fisher, and their family.[33] The McDougalls and the Fishers shared the same farm, Callelochan, on Loch Tay and were accompanied or followed by other neighbours and relations. Hugh McEwen, who married a McDougall, emigrated in 1819 and his brother John left the next year.[34] James Anderson and Duncan and John Kippen also came to Glengarry during this period, but at least one family, that of Robert Kippen from Croftmartaig, left Perthshire considerably later in 1833.[35] The Tayside emigrants were the only major group of settlers in Glengarry County not to come from western Inverness. Like their northern compartriots, however, the Perthshire emigrants came to the county in successive waves of families, drawn by ties of kinship and the availability of land.

Glengarry County also attracted emigrants from Skye, although few (if any) arrived before 1816. The people of Skye had first established settlements in the old British colonies of Georgia and Carolina in the early years of Highland emigration. After the American Revolution, many Skye emigrants went to Prince Edward Island and Nova Scotia, destinations that drew emigrants from across the Hebrides. The Skye emigrants who came to Glengarry

County were likely following in the footsteps of the large number of Glenelg emigrants to the county, since both Scottish districts were part of MacLeod of Dunvegan's estate. Knowledge of the opportunities that Glengarry County offered must have travelled from one part of the estate to another,.as tenants from Skye and Glenelg often journeyed together to the county.

The first Skye emigrants to settle in Glengarry were part of a group of seventeen families that left Duirinish in the summer of 1816. These families found themselves unable to pay their rent because of the fall in cattle prices and other agricultural products; they therefore "resolved to emigrate" under the leadership of Norman Stewart rather than endure further distress.[36] When the sailing of the brig *John and Samuel* was delayed until late in August, Norman Stewart (doubtlessly with the 1815 experiment in mind) petitioned the Colonial Secretary for provisions to see the emigrants through the winter and for a grant of land. Bathurst did not have the funds to provide rations for the emigrants, but he did write to the Commander in Chief in Quebec on their behalf, recommending that Sherbrooke give them aid to survive the winter.[37] Most of the emigrants reached Glengarry in October of 1816 and at least one family stayed in the county:[38] Isabelle McLeod, the widow of Ranald Stewart of Big Carbost, settled in Glengarry with her ten children, aged three to twenty-six. Twelve years later in 1828, Murdoch Stewart also left the same district in Skye for Glengarry; Stewart was accompanied by his wife Ann Macdonald and seven children.[39]

It was primarily Skye and Glenelg that, in 1832, provided the last large group of clansmen to emigrate together to Glengarry. Declining economic conditions left many tenants unable to pay for an Atlantic crossing, but by the 1830s Highland landlords had completely abandoned their former opposition to emigration and some began to help their tenants pay for passage to Canada.[40] In Bracadale and Duirinish in western Skye, evictions were widespread in this period, and many of MacLeod's dispossessed tenants applied for assistance to emigrate to Canada. Yet according to one strongly held Glengarry tradition, the group of emigrants who left Greenock on the *Fanny* on 28 August 1832 both paid their own fares and bought provisions for the voyage. Although the emigrants reached Canada with few worldly possessions, their ability to finance their own Atlantic crossing suggests that they belonged to the same group of tenants that had dominated earlier migrations to Canada.[41]

At least forty settlers in Glengarry can be identified as passengers on the *Fanny*, including a number of young adult men and women, some newly married and others shortly to be so, as well as families with children. Like earlier arrivals, ties of kin and community bound many of the emigrants to one another and (in a few cases) to other emigrant parties. One such group of related families were the Macdonalds, Stewarts, and McPhees of Bracadale, Skye. Norman Macdonald and his wife Margaret arrived in Canada with three adult daughters, Mary, Catherine, and Anne. John McPhee, who married Catherine, was accompanied by his two sisters, while John Cameron (whose wife Anne became) travelled with his brother Angus and nephew Norman. Mary Macdonald left with her husband Murdoch McRae, his brother Kenneth, and her own young family. The Macdonalds and the Stewarts were related through the marriage of Norman Macdonald's sister Anne to Murdoch Stewart many years before their emigration to Glengarry in 1828. Mary Stewart, their daughter, married another of the *Fanny*'s passengers, Alexander Stewart, himself a cousin of the 1816 Stewart emigrants. A tangled web of kinship born of marriage and sibling relationships was part of the baggage which the Bracadale emigrants brought to Glengarry.[42]

Other emigrants on the *Fanny* travelled in similar social groups and a few were related to the Skye families. For example, four Campbell brothers, one of whom married a Stewart, were among the migrants. From Glenelg came Malcolm McLeod, a widower, and his son and daughter, as well as Donald Dewar and his wife Jessie McLeod.[43] Alexander Grant left Ardersier in eastern Inverness-shire with his wife and child, while John McLeod was accompanied by his family of four and David Urquhart by his young wife. Some of those left behind by the departure of the *Fanny* joined their friends in Glengarry in later years. Norman Cameron went back to Scotland to bring his father to Canada. Donald Cameron, his wife, and six children reached Glengarry sometime after 1835, accompanied by another six families. The migration of Jessie's brother Donald McLeod and his family occurred in 1849.[44] A very complex series of kin and community ties joined the 1832 emigrants and those who followed them to Canada in later years. Agricultural transformation and the resulting loss of tenant lands to sheep farms came later in certain districts in Skye than in mainland western Inverness, but like their neighbours, the Skye emigrants were then attracted to the economic opportunities offered in the new Highland community of Glengarry County.

Not all those who settled in Glengarry went directly there from Scotland, but the pull which the new Highland community could exert on the clansmen is evident in the numerous secondary migrations which carried people from districts across British North

America to the county. Among these were the families from the 1786, 1790, and 1802 emigrations who stayed varying lengths of time in Lower Canada before proceeding to Glengarry. This experience was more common after 1800, when land became less available in the county and the acquisition of a Crown grant no longer followed automatically on arrival. In some instances, emigrants who intended to settle in the new Highland community were forced to take up land on its fringes. At least five of the seventeen families who left Duirinish in 1816 fell into this group. In November of 1818, their spokesman Norman McDonell petitioned the Lower Canadian government for land in Godmanchester, across the St. Lawrence from Glengarry's Lancaster township. McDonell explained that the emigrants had arrived in the eastern district of Upper Canada in October of 1816, but "the situation of such land as they could then obtain from the Government in upper Canada ... being very inconvenient," they waited for more land to be surveyed. Finally in May of 1818 they decided to lease land near Godmanchester.[45] Only emigrants determined to settle in a Highland district would have endured such delays and inconvenience when land remained cheap and plentiful in the western regions of the province. Some of those who settled in Godmanchester later acquired land in Glengarry County. For example, Neil McGillis and family arrived in the Lower Canadian township between 1827 and 1831 but moved into Glengarry shortly after 1845.[46]

A number of Highland emigrants came to Glengarry County after some years in Nova Scotia, 800 miles to the east. In 1797, for instance, "many years after leaving Scotland," the families of Donald, Angus, and John McDonald and of John McLellan left Nova Scotia for Glengarry. The land which these men were granted had "proved so barren as hardly to afford subsistence to their numerous families." The emigrants received letters from their friends in Upper Canada inviting them to go there, where the soil was more fertile and the climate milder. Despairing of success at Pictou, the four families accepted the invitation and "disposed of their little all" in order to pay their passage to Quebec. With their funds exhausted, they petitioned Governor Robert Prescott for help to complete the journey; their request was granted and a bateau was provided to take them upriver, doubtlessly to Glengarry County. Families and friends, separated by emigration to different destinations, did sometimes keep in touch and could be reunited.[47]

The poor quality of land in Nova Scotia, as well as family ties to Glengarry County, may also have brought another eight families to the county from the Maritime province by 1851. Some of these emigrants stayed only a few years in Nova Scotia before moving on to Glengarry. Angus McGillis and his eldest son were both born in Scotland before 1834, while the younger children were born in Cape Breton between 1837 and 1841. Similarly Duncan and Sally McGillis were natives of Scotland, their three older children were born in Cape Breton between 1844 and 1848, while the youngest, Ewen, was born in Canada in 1849.[48] Other families seem to have spent several decades in the Maritimes before leaving for Glengarry. Donald McDonald was born in Scotland in 1788, but his wife Elizabeth was born in Nova Scotia in 1795. After spending much of their married life in Nova Scotia, the McDonalds travelled to Glengarry between 1847 and 1850.[49] Movement between Glengarry County and Nova Scotia seems likely to have encouraged a sense of a larger Highland community in Canada.

One of the striking features of the post-1815 emigration to Glengarry County is the long period over which emigrants continued to arrive in the county. Years after Crown land ceased to be readily available in Glengarry County, Highland emigrants, in small but still significant numbers, chose that county or its vicinity as their new home. In the decade or two following the great group emigrations of 1786 to 1815, it is not surprising that Highlanders continued to join friends and relatives settled in the county. That such emigration should persist into the 1840s and 1850s points to a powerful bond uniting the people of Glengarry County and western Inverness. Several of these later emigrants have already been identified, as they were part of the continuing emigration from particular west Highland districts to Glengarry County.[50] In addition, another forty-odd Scottish-born families were resident in the county in 1861, with surnames which suggest that these clansmen too came from western Inverness.[51] Twelve Roman Catholic families reached Glengarry County in the early 1850s and these may have been among the crofters cleared from Knoydart and given an assisted passage to Canada by Lady Glengarry.[52] The attraction of Glengarry's Gaelic community, with its network of related Highland families, far outweighed the disadvantage of its lack of cheap land. Emigration had divided the clansmen, but the ties which linked western Inverness and Glengarry County remained strong for a very long time indeed.

Until the Passenger Act put the cost of a passage beyond the reach of many Highland tenant families, west-coast emigrants were able to leave Scotland in the large community emigrations that they preferred. By virtue of the British government's extraordinary support, the 1815 emigrants were also able to travel in the company of family and friends. After 1815, however, the choices open to the clansmen narrowed as the loss of land that began in the late eighteenth century became a common experience in the nineteenth.

The reaction of several hundred people from Glenelg, Kintail, Glenshiel, Lochalsh, Locheanan, and Strath to the government's refusal to repeat the assisted emigration of 1815 underlines the clansmen's growing poverty, as well as their continuing interest in emigration. High rents, severe weather in 1816, and plummeting cattle prices led these clansmen to despair "of being able any longer to live in comfort in the land which has produced the *Killed Heroes of Waterloo*." Rather than accept indigence, the tenants preferred to go "with the wreck of their property to America where many of their relatives have been comfortably settled for several years."[53] The clansmen could afford only £4 or £5 for the voyage, not the £7 minimum that an Atlantic passage then cost. The clansmen's petition for emigration assistance points out that more people could be provided with crofts if sheep farming were less prevalent, and by implication suggests that some of them would accept crofting with its minimal economic benefits. Nevertheless, when the clansmen could not "enjoy the comforts or possess even the necessaries of life," most of those who had a choice preferred to emigrate to Canada where they could settle with "those relatives who have gone before them."[54]

The poverty described by these west coast clansmen became endemic in the northwest Highlands in the nineteenth century and made group emigration less common unless it was assisted. Those who did manage to leave most often travelled in single-family groups or to the cheaper destination of Nova Scotia. During the first cycle of Scottish emigration, emigrants to North America chose to obtain land in the company of kinsmen, whereas emigrants of later years more often had to leave Scotland to save their families from bare subsistence or even starvation. At the same time, Glengarry County ceased to be the most appropriate destination even for Highland emigrants. Land in Glengarry was mostly occupied by this time and relatively expensive, compared to land in newer Highland communities such as those in Ontario, Grey, and Bruce counties, on the edge of settlement in Upper Canada.

Even so, emigrants continued to come to Glengarry County in the nineteenth century. Fifty years after the line of settlement moved north or far to the west of Glengarry, strong ties of kinship led Highland emigrants to the Upper Canadian county and to cousins they might never before have seen. In 1850 John McKinnon, aged 60 and accompanied by his wife and nine children, arrived in Glengarry from Scotland. The McKinnons were related to Angus McDonald, who was born in Glengarry County some fifty years earlier, and the emigrants stayed for a time with the McDonald family.[55] On other occasions, the chain of emigration had several links and continued over many years. Thus Coll and Samuel McDonell came to Canada in 1815; Angus and Flora McDonell, one a sibling and the other his or her spouse, followed in 1822;[56] and Flora, Angus, and Mary McDonald, "nearest friends," joined them in 1850.[57]

While the circumstances and manner of their departure had changed substantially, the identity of the emigrants of the earlier and later periods remained remarkably similar. The same names were found in the lists of emigrants after 1815 as before – Macdonalds, McPhees, McKinnons, McLeods. The same Highland districts were given as their homes – Glen Garry, Knoydart, Glenelg. The same family groupings seem to dominate the lists of settlers. The people who emigrated to Glengarry County from western Inverness after 1815 were drawn there by family and community bonds, and they continued an emigration tradition that was as old as the county itself. After 1784, many western Inverness communities were divided between settlements in Scotland and those in Canada, but if those communities still existed in the mid-nineteenth century, it was in Glengarry County, Upper Canada.

CHAPTER TEN

Settlement, 1784–1797

Emigration is completed only when the emigrant has chosen a place to live and established his or her new home there. All emigrants exchange life in one particular city, village, or rural community for life not just in another country but in another community. For this reason the process and meaning of emigration can only be understood by looking at both the departure of the emigrants and the choices they made when they reached the new land.

The clansmen from western Inverness examined in this study generally chose to settle in the single geographic district centered on Glengarry County and extending over its boundaries into adjacent counties. Those who arrived before 1797 easily acquired grants of land from the Crown, while later arrivals bought farms or (more frequently) first rented and then purchased land. By their emigration and settlement, these people from western Inverness created in Upper Canada a community that was Gaelic in culture, populated by a complex network of related families. In Glengarry County, the clansmen themselves owned land which they expected would provide for the support of their families. What agricultural transformation had threatened in Scotland – economic prosperity and the survival of their communities – the emigrants achieved through their settlement in Glengarry.

The following two chapters examine the clansmen's experience in settling Glengarry County and the effect that changing government policies and conditions of land acquisition had on the building of the new Highland community. But first we should look at Glengarry County itself, as well as at imperial and colonial actions that set the stage onto which the emigrants stepped when they sought land for a new community in Canada.

The bountiful resources and easily available land of American had long stirred imaginations in Europe. Yet during the years of incessant war between English and French colonists in America, no major settlement was organized in the vulnerable upper St. Lawrence and lower Great Lakes region. After the defeat of the French in 1763, the region was set aside as a reserve for the Indian allies of the British Crown. Only twenty years later, when Britain lost control of thirteen of its American colonies, was western Quebec opened to European settlement. Government surveyors laid out two ranges of townships along the St. Lawrence and Lake Ontario for the Loyalist refugees.[1] Several years later, the colony of Quebec was divided into the two colonies of Upper and Lower Canada, and the two most easterly of the fourteen Loyalist townships were united in the county of Glengarry.

The government surveyor, Patrick McNiff, provided the first assessment of the Glengarry townships. Lancaster (originally Lake) Township was next to the French settlements of Lower Canada: "The land in front of the township is generally low and Wet and will require a number of small drains cut thro. it to make it fit for Culture[;] the land five and six Concessions back is much better being high and dry Interspersed with Wild Meadows." The land in the front of the more westerly township, Charlottenburgh, was also "flat, but very Rich," while a few miles inland it became "high and stoney."[2] Like the rest of Upper Canada, the Glengarry townships were of course covered with "great virgin forests" that were a formidable obstacle to cultivation.[3] Thus, the southern third of Glengarry County was poorly drained and would require much labour to be brought into production. But the soil, once cleared of its covering of American elm, white ash and red maple, was deep and black. In contrast, the northern two-thirds of the county was rolling, with a series of ridges roughly parallel to the St Lawrence River. The hollows between these ridges were often swampy, and the clay soil was less fertile and harder to cultivate. In the northern part of the county, the land was stony, even in the valleys, while the ridges were strewn with boulders, a product, according to geologists, of the ancient Champlain Sea.[4]

Land was the colony's most significant resource, and policies concerning its use were therefore of great importance both to government and to settlers. Under the direction of imperial authorities, the Governor and Executive Council of the colony, not the local assembly, regulated the Crown lands of Upper Canada.[5] During the first forty years of Upper Canadian history, Crown land was available to settlers, in theory as a free grant; only in 1826, long after the major emigrations to Glengarry County, was a policy of land sales introduced. In the first years of settlement, the imperial government compensated Loyalists, incoming settlers, and public officials with grants of land, often without survey or patent fees. Gradually, however, imperial and colonial governments shifted towards a policy which used unoccupied land as a source of revenue for the Crown. In 1796, London suggested that the expenses of land granting be borne by its recipients, and the Upper Canadian administration imposed survey and patent fees on new grants. The cost of the two fees on a standard 200 acre lot rose from £4 16s. 2d. in 1796 to £8 4s. 1d. in 1804. Other changes made in the procedure for acquiring a grant in this period added to the difficulties new settlers faced in obtaining land.[6]

The major emigrations to Glengarry County straddled a period when Upper Canada was moving towards a more restrictive land policy. This first chapter analysing settlement in Glengarry discusses the years between 1784 and 1797, when land was easily available; the following chapter explores the effect of rising land costs on the settlement of Glengarry County during the early years of the nineteenth century.

Between 1784 and 1786 some 1,300 people arrived in Glengarry County and government officials and settlers together established the basic pattern of settlement in the new county. The first surveys of the land, begun in 1783 and completed in the following summer, gave the county the grid layout which formed the basis for settlement. The county was originally divided into two townships, Lancaster and Charlottenburgh, each about nine and one-quarter miles east to west and twenty-seven miles south to north. As surveyors laid out the townships, they divided them into concessions, running east to west and parallel to the St. Lawrence and marching northwards; these were numbered 1 to 18 from south to north. Each concession was then divided into lots, numbered 1 to 37 from east to west. In the Glengarry townships, the original concessions were a mile and one-quarter deep and the lots were one-quarter of a mile wide; each lot, therefore, took in 200 acres. Property was (and still is) identified by concession and lot number – for example, concession 3, lot 16, or concession 5, lot 6 – or, more colloquially, 16 in the 3rd and 6 in the fifth.

The system is usually straightforward enough, but in Charlottenburgh things went a little differently. The original survey adjusted the standard grid to take advantage of the transport and communication route provided by the River Raisin.[7] The river flows

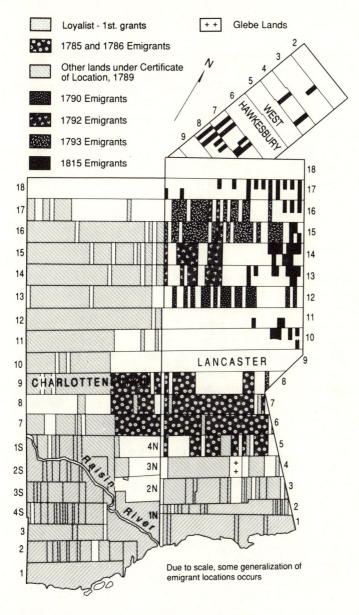

Legend:

- Loyalist - 1st. grants
- + + Glebe Lands
- 1785 and 1786 Emigrants
- Other lands under Certificate of Location, 1789
- 1790 Emigrants
- 1792 Emigrants
- 1793 Emigrants
- 1815 Emigrants

N

WEST HAWKESBURY

LANCASTER

CHARLOTTEN[BURGH]

Raisin River

Due to scale, some generalization of emigrant locations occurs

Map 6 Selected allocations of land in Glengarry County

Sources: Ontario, Department of Lands and Forests, Plan of Charlottenburgh [1784]; *ibid*, James McDonell, Plan of Lancaster; NA, CAAD, 13193 (1786); NA, RG19, vol. 4447, Sundry Persons List; NA, RG1 L4, vol. 12, Charlottenburgh and Lancaster; NA, MG11, CO42/71, f. 82 (reel B-48); NA, RG1 L3 UCLP C2(1796–7) no. 2 (reel C-1647); NA, UCLP M Misc. (1792–1816) no. 21 (reel C-2189); AO, RG1 C-1-4, vol. 9, Return ... Glengarry, 10 Oct. 1794; AO, Locations in the Eastern District, 1793; AO, RG1 A-1-1, vol. 49, 327; AO, RG1 C-1-3, vol. 96, Fiats of Military Emigrants and vol. 101, Return of Locations, March 1816, Lancaster.

diagonally from the western edge of the township southeast to the St. Lawrence. Two concessions, each running either north or south of the river, were laid diagonally across the township, producing a staggered line in their neighbouring concessions. Only concession 1 on the St. Lawrence River and concessions 7 to 9 north of the Raisin run straight east and west; all the others are skewed, and a single line of lots may contain parts of several concessions.[8] Not surprisingly, this unusual layout created a considerable amount of confusion later, and even today, Charlottenburgh Township is a surveyor's nightmare.

The Loyalists were the first Europeans to settle in Glengarry, but they enjoyed substantial government support as they began the task of building homes in the wilderness. The imperial government was faithful to its promise to reward its American supporters for their loyalty, and the governor of Quebec, Sir Frederick Haldimand, was extremely sympathetic to their needs. In June 1784 government bateaux carried the Loyalists from refugee camps in the settled part of Quebec to the new townships, where they received land in the best locations and provisions for over two years. In addition, Loyalist families were given assorted clothing, household goods, and farm tools, and a share in some livestock.[9]

The government had decided to settle the Loyalists together in their military units, and the King's Royal Regiment of New York was assigned the first five townships west of the French seigneuries. The Scottish Roman Catholic and Presbyterian soldiers of the regiment were placed chiefly in the first two townships, whereas most of the German and English members of the regiment settled in the next three townships to the west. Highlanders who had served in other units (principally the Eighty-fourth Regiment and Butler's Rangers) joined their countrymen in Lancaster and Charlottenburgh townships and spilled over into nearby Cornwall. Sir John Johnson's decision to put the Scottish members of his regiment in the two most easterly townships may have been designed to settle the Roman Catholic men of his unit near their coreligionists in the French settlements. Aside from this consideration, it was chance which assigned this location in Upper Canada to the founders of the new Highland community.

The royal instructions of July 1783 set out the amount of land Loyalists were to receive and promised such grants free of either survey or patent fees. The heads of Loyalist families and discharged privates were to receive 100 acres of land for themselves and 50 acres for each additional family member. Single men were also allocated 50 acres, while noncommissioned officers were promised

200 acres. The grants to higher ranks were of course much larger; 500 acres for subalterns, and staff and warrant officers; 700 acres for captains; and 1,000 acres for field officers. Haldimand suggested that the officers receive only a single 200-acre lot at first and, like their men, draw for the available land.[10] The Loyalist officers were unwilling to accept this rather egalitarian plan, and Sir John Johnson, by virtue of his position as superintendent of the new settlements, was able to change it in their favour.[11] At first glance, the land in Lancaster township, because of its low, wet situation, looked "unfit for settlement" and most of the Loyalists preferred to take up land in Charlottenburgh. However, Lieutenant Walter Sutherland of the KRRNY found the township sufficiently attractive that he offered to settle there, albeit on special terms: Sutherland asked that settlers in Lancaster be given double the acreage they were entitled to. Government officials accepted this proposal, since they considered a line of continuous settlement along the St. Lawrence essential to maintain communication between the upper and lower regions of the province.[12]

By 1786, a total of 785 Loyalists had obtained land in Glengarry County.[13] In spite of Sutherland's incentive to settle in Lancaster, less than one-quarter of the Glengarry Loyalists chose to do so, and only one-third of these were Highlanders. All of the Lancaster families received some land in the convenient first concession, which borders the St. Lawrence, and a minority actually received a full 200-acre lot there. Most of the Glengarry Loyalists, however, preferred to avoid the low land of Lancaster and settled in Charlottenburgh. Here also were the larger number of Highlanders; 449 people, or three-quarters, of the Charlottenburgh Loyalists had Highland surnames. In the first hurried year of settlement, 100 acres was the standard grant in Charlottenburgh; later, additional grants made up the difference between the original grant and the amount of land to which a family was entitled. Only the officers received more than this minimum in 1784, and even they did not immediately receive all their lands.[14] The officers were also given preferential treatment in their access to lots in the first concession; six of them received twelve and one-half lots along the St. Lawrence in Charlottenburgh. With thirty-seven lots in a concession and some 184 families requiring land in Charlottenburgh, only forty-six families could be given land in the first concession, generally with two families on each 200-acre lot.[15]

The majority of the Charlottenburgh Loyalists therefore settled on the Raisin River. Excluding the ten lots that fronted on both the St. Lawrence and the Raisin, 100 families received grants on the north or south bank of the Raisin. The remaining forty families settled on the concessions lying between the two rivers. Close to twenty of these families were placed in the second concession north of the St. Lawrence River, while others were scattered in the second and third concessions south of the River Raisin (SRR).[16] The actual lots received by the settlers were chosen in a draw, but some trading must have taken place to accommodate friends or kinsmen who wished to settle beside one another.[17] In this way, Angus Grant was able to settle with his son Duncan on lot 24, first concession SRR, while brothers Alexander and John McDonell shared lot 14 in the third concession SRR.[18] A fairly compact community, formed rather in the shape of the letter V lying on its side, grew along the two rivers. Along the two arms of the letter was a continuous line of settlement, while the territory between was more sparsely filled.

The 1773 emigrants led to New York by the Macdonell gentlemen formed the heart of the Loyalist settlement in Charlottenburgh.[19] The few Lowland Scots, English, and Irish Loyalists who settled amongst the Highlanders in the township were fellow soldiers from the KRRNY or neighbours from the Mohawk Valley. Other Highlanders, who had settled in Johnson's Bush before the revolution and had subsequently served either in Johnson's or the Eighty-fourth Regiment, also joined the 1773 emigrants in Charlottenburgh.[20] A small number of the Highland Loyalists also settled in Cornwall Township, just west of Charlottenburgh, where perhaps one-third of the community was Scottish.[21] Alexander of Aberchalder and his sons John and Hugh all received land in Charlottenburgh, while Spanish John and his son Miles settled in Cornwall township.[22]

The other Macdonell gentlemen found their leadership wanted elsewhere in the new colony and rose to prominence as members of the Tory elite. John of Leek died before 1784, but his sons Archibald and Allan took up land in Osnabruck Township, Stormont County, and in Matilda Township, Dundas County, respectively. Allan of Collachie received land 200 miles farther west in the Home District (centred on York, later Toronto), where his son Alexander rose to a position of prominence.[23] In spite of the upheaval of war, a substantial part of the 1773 emigrant group obtained land together in Charlottenburgh. The Macdonell party became the core community that drew in other Loyalist and emigrant Highlanders.

The Loyalists were barely settled on their new lands when two large groups of Highland emigrants arrived in Canada, the first of the flood of clansmen who were to give Glengarry County (and, it sometimes seemed, Canada itself) its strikingly Highland flavour.[24] In 1785, 300 emigrants left western Inverness, arriving in Canada only in the summer of 1786 (see chapter 7), while in October of 1786 another 500 Highlanders arrived in Canada. Before the arrival of the two groups from Scotland, Highlanders formed roughly two-thirds of the population of Lancaster and Charlottenburg. The settlement of most of the 1785 and 1786 emigrants in Glengarry and its vicinity ensured the dominance of Highlanders in the new community.[25]

In early 1786, the new Glengarry settlements only included some 785 souls. The 300 emigrants in the 1785 group were accommodated, apparently within existing administrative arrangements, but the potential influx of another 500 in October 1786 posed a considerable challenge to colonial officals. No one in the province of Quebec was prepared for "so great an accession of Numbers" as the second group of Highlanders represented. The first problem was how and where the impoverished emigrants would pass the winter. The governor's secretary, John Craigie, wrote that it was "of utmost concern that more of these people should not proceed to the Settlements than there are means of maintaining during the Winter." Craigie called on the Inspector of Loyalists "to exert your advice both with these New comers and with their Friends, who may come down to La Chine to meet them, in order to prevent the distress which may ensue to all, if the matter is not thoroughly considered and means devised amongst them to avert it."[26] Some of the 1786 emigrants were likely persuaded to spend their first winter not in Glengarry but in the vicinity of Montreal, so as not to overtax the resources of the new settlement. The government came to the rescue of both Loyalists and emigrants by providing them with rations for the next twelve months.[27]

The arrival of a large number of emigrants in the autumn of 1786 caught the colonial government by surprise; until that time land west of the French seigneuries had been granted almost exclusively to Loyalist refugees. The approach of winter enabled the government to delay a decision on the emigrants' request for land for a few months, and they were simply helped to join their friends in Glengarry County. Then, on 2 June 1787, Governor Dorchester brought the question of land grants to emigrants before the Executive Council. While the Crown officers agreed that the emigrants ought to be given land, not quite enough surveyed lots were then available in the concessions settled by the Loyalists (first to third concession of Lancaster and up to the first concession NRR in Charlottenburgh) to accommodate them. Rather than separate the 1786 group, placing some in the Loyalist concessions and others farther north, Dorchester ordered that "parcels of the ungranted Lands of the Crown" be surveyed and "subdivided into small farms [of] two hundred acres" for each emigrant family.[28] A great majority of the 1786 and some of the 1785 emigrants settled on these parcels of land, which were north of and entirely outside the original Loyalist concessions. Dorchester's decision to settle the 1786 emigrants as a group initiated a pattern of settlement that was repeated with the 1790, 1792, and 1793 emigrants to Glengarry.

The substantial role which the Glengarry gentlemen played in establishing the new Highland community is evident in the settling of the 1786 group. The task of surveying land for the emigrants was given to one of the Glengarry gentlemen, James McDonell, the son of Allan McDonell of Collachie. In 1787, the Surveyor General's department was both new to the job of laying out townships and very busy; as surveyor William Chewett commented fourteen years later, "the Office then had very little form." James McDonell was therefore left to his own devices as to the ordering of the land he was to survey, and he numbered the lots which he marked out in an unconventional fashion. When the Deputy Surveyor General saw what McDonell had done, he corrected the numbers to conform to the usual practice. William Chewett was ordered to give the emigrants new certificates for their lots with the corrected numbers, but he found that the clansmen were reluctant to apply to the survey office for the corrected forms. Like other Canadian officials, Chewett found it necessary to use one of the Highland leaders, Lieutenant Angus McDonell, as an intermediary through which official documents might be distributed.[29]

Late in the spring of 1787, James McDonell surveyed four concessions in Lancaster and three in Charlottenburgh for the emigrants. At least two clansmen, William McQueen and Roderick McDonell, were employed to help McDonell with his work.[30] In Lancaster, the fourth concession was left empty for the Loyalists, while in Charlottenburgh the second, third, and fourth concessions NRR were similarly reserved. Most of the 1786 and some of the 1785 emigrants drew lots for land in the fifth to eighth concessions of Lancaster and the adjacent seventh to ninth concessions of Charlottenburgh. The new community, referred to by government officials as the "Highland settlement," was compact, roughly eleven miles long and five miles wide.[31] Within this rectangle, the clansmen occupied 114 out of the 162 lots available. The settlement was 44 lots wide, stretching from lot 8 on the eastern side of Lancaster to lot 14 in Charlottenburgh. Fifteen lots were occupied in the fifth concession of Lancaster; 41 lots fell in the concession line formed by concession 6 of Lancaster and concession 7 of Charlottenburgh; 35 lots were in Lancaster concession 7 and Charlottenburg concession 8; and 23 lots were occupied in the line of Lancaster concession 8 and Charlottenburgh concession 9.[32]

Since no more than 30 of the 114 lots were occupied by 1785 emigrants (see below), the remaining 85 lots must have accommodated the great majority of the 1786 party. One of their leaders, Lieutenant Angus McDonell of Sandaig, settled with the group in the eighth concession of Charlottenburgh. However, at least one 1786 emigrant, Angus Ban Macdonell of Muniall, settled in the Loyalist third concession SRR, five miles south of the main body of emigrants in Charlottenburgh. Angus Ban may have received land in the "Highland settlement"; if so, his choice of the third concession SRR may well have been dictated by family ties since, according to tradition, Angus Ban joined his Loyalist brother and uncle in Canada.[33] Other trading of lots took place as a few emigrants moved into Cornwall Township,[34] and others exchanged land within Charlottenburgh and Lancaster. Local historian George Sandfield Macdonald gives some indication that fathers and sons, as well as brothers, tended to settle, if not on the same or adjacent lots, then within a mile or so of one another.[35] Since land was drawn for by lot, exchanges were most likely necessary to produce such family-based settlement.

The Highland settlement laid out by James McDonell accommodated most of the 1786 emigrants and, it appears, a number of the 1785 emigrants. It is now very difficult to distinguish between the two groups, particularly since Macdonalds with a handful of Christian names formed about 70% of each party.[36] However, the less common surnames found in the list of 1785 emigrants, as well as a few individuals named by Sandfield as arriving in "1787," together show that some of the 1785 emigrants did settle with the larger 1786 party. Four non-Macdonald names from the 1785 departure appear on the list of persons given land by James McDonell.[37] These are Colin Fraser of lot 29 and William McQueen of lot 18, both in Lancaster concession 6; Donald McMillan of lot 24 in Lancaster concession 7; and Duncan Kennedy of lot 7 in Charlottenburgh concession 9. Of the Macdonalds who emigrated in 1785, Squire Allan Macdonell and Archie Roy Macdonald received land in Charlottenburgh, while the Squire's brother-in-law John Buie Macdonell settled in Lancaster, all within the Highland settlement.[38] But at least six people with less common surnames, known to have emigrated in 1785 (John McIntyre, Alexander Fraser, John McIntosh, Henny Macdonald, Eva McTavish, and Annie McIntosh) cannot be found among the families of the "Highland settlement." It seems probable that not all the Macdonalds who emigrated in 1785 were placed here either; perhaps fewer than half of the 1785 emigrants received land in the "Highland settlement."

The whereabouts of the other 1785 emigrants can be pieced together from evidence concerning the settlement of some of them. A small number of the 1785 emigrants took up land outside the "Highland settlement" in other parts of Glengarry. Thus one Angus Macdonell settled in the ninth concession of Lancaster, just a mile to the north of the settlement, while Archibald Grant, Alexander Roy and Kenneth and Alexander Macdonell settled amongst the Loyalists along the St. Lawrence front in Charlottenburgh.[39] James Duncan Macdonald's father was another of the 1785 emigrants, and he settled "in the south Branch [of the River Raisin], where there are still descendants."[40] There is also considerable evidence to show that some of the 1785 emigrants settled in Cornwall Township. Nine emigrants with less common surnames can be identified among those who received land in the eighth concession of Cornwall, and another ten Macdonalds, some of whom may have emigrated in 1785, are found in the same concession.[41]

According to tradition, the 1785 emigrants reached Canada in the spring of the following year, via the United States. It seems plausible to hypothesize that these emigrants, coming by way of New York City and Albany and given a land grant immediately north of the Loyalist concessions in Cornwall Township, were merely treated as a sort of "late" Loyalist.[42] Confirmation of this hypothesis is provided in the land petitions of John and Ranald Macdonell, both of whom claimed to be "Emigrant Loyalists," resident in Cornwall since their emigration from Scotland in 1785.[43] The idea of an emigrant Loyalist is unusual, since even the 1773 emigrants, who lived in America only for a year or two before taking up arms for the King, were referred to simply as Loyalists. At least some of the 1785 emigrants seem, therefore, to have been considered a type of Loyalist and were given land in July of 1786, three months before the 1786 emigrants reached Glengarry.[44] There was of course no way in which the 1786 emigrants could be portrayed as Loyalists; they came straight to Quebec from Scotland, without ever entering the new United States. That direct emigration, along with their substantial numbers, forced Lord Dorchester to provide separately for them and resulted in the survey of the "Highland settlement."

The 1785 and 1786 emigrants were located in the Glengarry area as the result both of their own wishes and of government decision. Faced with an influx of Gaelic-speaking Scots, government officials found it convenient to place them near their Loyalist compatriots. The arrival of the large 1786 contingent forced the colonial government to make separate provision for the growing number of Highland migrants. The 1785 emigrants could be treated like Loyalists, but the size of the 1786 emigration convinced the government to settle the new group, as well as some 1785 emigrants, in newly surveyed land in Glengarry County and to approve a policy granting 200 acres to emigrants from Great Britain.

Settlement in Glengarry was shaped by the colonial government's need to balance the claims both of Loyalists and of emigrants from Britain, and Lord Dorchester made certain that the Loyalists received more land than the latter arrivals. Pressures of time and manpower limited the grants first made to ordinary Loyalists to 50 acres, but by the autumn of 1786 private soldiers from all Loyalist units were demanding the same grant of 200 acres promised to the men of the Eighty-fourth Regiment.[45] On 2 June 1787, the same day on which Dorchester ordered the survey of the "Highland setttlement," he also granted each Loyalist head of household an additional 200 acres, later known as Lord Dorchester's bounty. Some two years after this order, Dorchester extended the grant of 200 acres to the children of Loyalists – to their sons at 21 and to their daughters at marriage.[46] The effect of these additional grants to the Loyalists was to more than double the number of assigned lots in Glengarry County without a proportionate increase in population.

Map 6 gives a general sense of the extent of settlement in Glengarry in 1789 after the Loyalists, the 1785, and the 1786 emigrants had received most of their lands. Of 643 lots in concessions 1 to 17 of Charlottenburgh, 77% (499) were assigned and 144 lots were left unallocated. Less land had been assigned in Lancaster, where concessions 12–18 remained completely empty. In concessions 1–11 of Lancaster, 68% (252 lots) had been granted and 118 remained in the Crown's possession.[47]

Loyalists received their additional lands in the same township in which their first lot was located, but not usually in one consolidated holding.[48] It was expected that the Loyalists would rent, sell, or provide for their children with these additional parcels of land. Thus in 1784 Alex Macdonell of the Eighty-fourth Regiment received 100 acres in the west half of lot 55, first concession NRR in Charlottenburgh, but his additional lands included 150 acres in the ninth concession and 200 acres in the fourteenth concession. Similarly Donald Ban Macdonell, a corporal in the KRRNY, first obtained 100 acres in lot 19, second concession SRR in Charlottenburgh. He was later given a second 100 acres in the seventh concession, 200 acres in the tenth concession, and another 200 acres in the thirteenth concession.[49] On the other hand the Lancaster Loyalists, who were considerably fewer in number, managed to obtain much of their additional land in Lancaster concessions 2–4. Alex Grant acquired half of lot 27 in both the first and second concessions, and all of lot 27 in the fourth. Grant also received all of lot 33 in the third concession and half of the same lot in the fourth. However, some of the Lancaster Loyalists also received land in the northern part of the township, particularly in the ninth concession.[50]

By the end of the 1780s, the new settlements along the St. Lawrence began to take on a cultivated appearance. The population of what was to become the colony of Upper Canada approached 10,000 people,[51] of whom some 13% (1,285) had settled in Charlottenburgh and Lancaster townships. Perhaps 1,000 of these, or 10% of the colony's entire population, were Highlanders.[52] Land that had been virgin forest in the early spring of 1784 was now, for eleven miles inland, sprinkled with tiny clearings and small log buildings. More than 95% of the future county was, of course, still covered with trees, although only one concession in Charlottenburgh and seven in Lancaster remained completely unallocated. Even the concessions which had been allocated, however, were not necessarily occupied. The additional lots received by the Loyalists awaited either settlement by a second generation or sale to emigrants of later years. An impressive start had been made on the settlement of Glengarry County, but land was still easily available.

As the first hectic years of settlement ended, the need for local access to government programs, as well as for a separate colonial administration, became apparent. New settlers, particularly in the western reaches of Lake Ontario, faced a long wait before obtaining land when their applications had to be approved by the Executive Council, 500 miles away in Quebec City. The first administrative change occurred in July 1788 when Lord Dorchester divided the Loyalist settlements into four districts: the Glengarry settlement was included in the Lunenburg district, which stretched from the French seigneuries west almost to Kingston and north to the Ottawa River. Several months later, Land Boards were appointed in each of the four districts with the power to grant each new settler a single 200-acre lot. The Land Boards survived until November 1794 and hence were the agency through which the 1790, 1792, and 1793 emigrants received land in Glengarry.[53]

A second, more fundamental change occurred in 1791, when

Quebec was divided into the two colonies of Upper and Lower Canada. The movement of the Loyalists into the western regions of Quebec posed a serious problem for the imperial government. Since 1763, the need to gain support from the native French population had shaped British policy in Quebec. Although the imperial government had introduced English criminal law to the province, French civil law and the seigneurial system of landholding had been left intact.[54] Land grants to the Loyalists and other early settlers along the upper St. Lawrence River and Lake Ontario were made under seigneurial tenure: the Crown, as seigneur, was entitled to an annual quit-rent after the first ten years. Quebec Loyalists unanimously demanded that they receive land in free and common soccage, as was the case in the larger Loyalist settlements of the Maritimes. In order to satisfy this demand, and also to recognize the distinct societies represented by the new settlement and the French seigneuries, the imperial parliament passed the Constitutional Act in May 1791, authorizing the division of the province of Quebec into Upper and Lower Canada.[55]

One of the most contentious provisions of the Constitutional Act related to the establishment of clergy reserves. Crown land equal to one-seventh of all lands granted in the colony was reserved for the support of clergy of the established Protestant church. The imperial government also issued a separate instruction in September 1791, ordering that an equal amount of land be set aside as a Crown reserve.[56] The latter reserve was intended to provide the colony with a source of revenue separate from imperial grants or local taxes. The amount of land set aside for Crown and clergy reserves considerably restricted the quantity of free land available to emigrants and, in most parts of the province, tended to make consolidated settlement difficult.

It is not clear when these reserves were laid out in Glengarry County, but the Land Committee of Quebec's Executive Council considered the question of where to locate the reserves as early as February of 1791. Deputy Surveyor General Collins pointed out the difficulty of reserving land in Charlottenburgh township, where so many lots were already allocated under government certificates. These certificates had been issued in response to the demand for "land in the said Townships to satisfy the numerous settlers who then applied for Farms in that quarter."[57] The Land Committee decided to locate the reserves in the back concessions of Charlottenburgh and Lancaster townships where land, even if granted, was not yet cultivated. Nevertheless, the surveyors evidently had trouble finding enough ungranted land in Glengarry County. While almost all the necessary Crown and clergy reserves were set aside in Lancaster (172 lots out of 179), fewer than half the required number were found in Charlottenburgh (76.5 lots out of 196).[58] Even this total reserve of 248.5 lots, however, represented a substantial amount of land which subsequently could not be granted to new settlers.

Just before the government adopted the policy of creating reserves, the 1790 emigrants arrived in Canada from the island of Eigg and adjacent districts. These emigrants reached the Glengarry settlement some time early in November 1790. Within a month, on 7 December, the Land Board for the counties of Stormont and Glengarry had granted land to some sixteen of the twenty-three heads of household in the party.[59] In April of 1791, the Eigg families, along with "many others," drew for lots at a meeting in Lancaster and received their new lot numbers from Land Board member John Macdonell of Aberchalder.[60] Five of the remaining seven heads of households were unlikely to receive a lot; three of them were servants[61] and two were women unaccompanied by an adult male. one emigrant received land at a subsequent meeting of the land board, while the last emigrant has not been located. At least 80% of the 1790 emigrants settled in the twelfth concession of Lancaster (later known as the third concession Lochiel). James McDonell's plan of the township shows the random distribution of the sixteen lots first occupied by the Eigg emigrants, as well as the relative isolation of the inhabitants of the twelfth concession.[62] During the early 1790s, the Land Board granted a little more than a third of the lots in the tenth and eleventh concession, but most of these were unoccupied additional Loyalist grants. Another eleven lots in the twelfth concession were allocated during this period, and at least three of these were given to members of the 1790 emigrant party, while the remainder were acquired by Loyalists and other emigrants from Scotland.[63] Only two heads of families from the 1790 group settled outside the twelfth concession, but their reason for doing so is unknown: one was Lauchlin Campbell who received lot 25 in the eighth concession of Lancaster in 1793, and the other was Duncan McCraw, who settled on lot 22 of the sixteenth concession of Lancaster in the same year.[64]

A compact community emerged in the lands settled by the 1790 emigrants, centred on what is today still called the Eigg road. Like their predecessors, the Eigg emigrants received what must have been crucial assistance in their first months of settlement. While the colonial government provided transportation by bateau from Quebec to Glengarry, the poverty of the 1790 emigrants awoke the charitable instincts of Scottish and English merchants in Montreal. The money raised by men such as James McGill and Thomas Forsyth not only furnished the emigrants with beef and bread for the trip inland but also paid for the 726 pounds of beef sent up to Glengarry in February of 1791 for the "twenty-one or twenty-two families that arrived last fall."[65] The Eigg emigrants were not necessarily satisfied with the lots they had drawn by chance; when Dougal McMillan found lot 21 in the twelfth concession of Lancaster unfit for cultivation, he took Colonel John Macdonell's advice and settled instead on lot 29.[66] Angus and John Gillis both abandoned their lots in the eastern end of the same concession to settle in the tenth concession of Lancaster and in northern Charlottenburgh respectively. John gave no reason for his move, but Angus explained that he "would have lived on the [first] Lot himself but that it was so remote from neighbours when he located it that he was induced to purchase that on which he now resides." Nonetheless, a community soon took shape in the twelfth concession of Lancaster, and empty lots were often filled by members of the 1790 group or their kinsmen.[67]

The speed with which the 1790 emigrants were granted land was repeated two years later in the case of the thirty families from Glen Garry and its vicinity, led by Macdonell of Greenfield and Lieutenant Alexander McMillan. A few of the migrants may have taken up land in the southern part of the county, as did one of their leaders (Macdonell settled in the ninth concession of Charlottenburgh) but the great majority appear to have settled in northern Lancaster.[68] On 6 November 1792, Richard Duncan, then chairman of the Eastern District Land Board, ordered surveyor Hugh Macdonell "to set out as soon as possible for the purpose of exploring and ascertaining a situation suitable for the accommodation of a number of Highland emigrants." Duncan noted that this group of at least twenty-seven families were "exposed to great expense and inconveniency and therefore anxious to Set themselves down on Land belonging to the Crown."[69] The 1792 party arrived in Quebec late in September; from Duncan's comment it seems likely that they reached Glengarry in October and most were eager to settle on Crown land. Hugh Macdonell surveyed part of northern Lancaster, laying out twenty lots in concessions 13 and 14 (the last three lots were in impenetrable cedar swamp) and another seventeen lots in concessions 15 and 16. With the survey complete, most of the 1792 emigrants received their land at the Land Board meeting held on 25 March 1793.[70]

There is only indirect evidence that people who received land in concessions 13–16 of Lancaster in March of 1793 were members of the Macdonell–McMillan party. However, since the Land Board had settled the 1790 emigrants within a few months of their arrival and its chairman had ordered the survey of 13–16 concessions so as to provide land for recently arrived emigrants, a very strong presumption exists that many of those settled in these concessions in 1793 were members of the 1792 emigrant group. Two lists survive describing those who received land in March of 1793. The first names the applicants and classifies them as Loyalists, kinsmen of Loyalists, or emigrants from Scotland or from elsewhere;[71] the second is a return of settlers and their land locations in Lancaster in 1793.[72] A comparison of the two lists makes it possible to identify most of the 1793 settlers in concessions 13–16 of Lancaster as the 1792 emigrants. The settlers included four of unknown origin, one Loyalist, one 1790 emigrant, and twenty-one families from Scotland.[73] This total does not include four Scottish emigrants who also settled there in the same year but whose lot locations were given in a later Land Board report.[74] Thus no fewer than twenty-five Highland emigrants settled in these four concessions of Lancaster, most likely all members of the Macdonell–McMillan party.

The twenty-one families from the 1792 emigration who obtained land in concessions 13 and 14 settled in a double-fronted line.[75] Unlike the twelfth concession of Lancaster, where a road led through the interior of the concession, surveyor Hugh Macdonell opened a road on the boundary line between the thirteenth and fourteenth concessions and laid out lots north and south of that line. Settlers were then expected to cluster along the road dividing the two concessions, an arrangement designed to lessen the isolation of a pioneer community. None of the 1793 lot locations was east of lot 22, so twenty-one out of thirty-two lots were occupied on either side of the boundary road for a distance of four miles. The two emigrants who obtained lots 22 and 23 in the fifteenth concession, as well as the two who received lots 22 and 25 in the sixteenth, were also no more than four miles away from their eight fellow emigrants who settled on lots 22 to 25 in concessions 13 and 14. Certain patterns are evident in the distribution of emigrant families which suggest that the settling of lots in 1793 was influenced by the emigrants themselves. In the fourteenth concession, lots 22 to 25 were all occupied by McMillans, while lots 30 and 31 in concessions 13 and 14 were each settled by a McGillis family. Like earlier groups of emigrants to reach Glengarry county, the 1792 emigrants were given land during their first winter in Canada and a majority of them settled as a group in adjacent sections of a previously unoccupied district.[76]

Some 140 emigrants, mostly from Glenelg and led by Kenneth McLeod, were the next to reach Glengarry County. The emigrants arrived in mid-June 1794 after shipping mishaps forced a winter stopover in Prince Edward Island. Because the McLeod emigrants reached Canada in spring rather than autumn, they received land within a few weeks of their arrival in Glengarry. The surveyor's correspondence suggests that certain formalities were waived in order to place the emigrants on their land before the summer ended. Hugh McDonell wrote to the Surveyor General in October 1794 explaining that he had given location tickets to "some of the late Emigrants ... to enable them to settle and improve lots, to obviate a tedious and grievous delay." McDonell's efforts to organize a Land Board meeting had met with excuses of sickness, absence, distance, or private business, but he expected his locations to be ratified by the board at their next meeting.[77] The lots allocated to thirty-five Highlanders in Lancaster on 25 June 1794 were confirmed by the Land Board three and one-half months later.[78] These thirty-five lots,[79] as well as another five lots which the surveyor failed to register,[80] ran the length of concessions 15 and 16, with three exceptions.[81] Twenty-one emigrants received land in the fifteenth concession between lots 6 and 37, including Alexander McLeod, one of the leaders of the emigrant party, who settled on lot 18. Another fifteen clansmen were placed in the sixteenth concession on lot 9 and between lots 15 and 35. The western two-thirds of concessions 15 and 16 were thus substantially filled by the 1793 emigrants, most of whom settled in this one district.

Settlement in Glengarry was so rapid (it extended to the sixteenth concession of Charlottenburgh in 1789 and reached the same point of Lancaster in 1793) that government surveyors had trouble creating Crown and clergy reserves in the county. More than half of the seventeenth and eighteenth concessions in both Lancaster and Charlottenburgh were reserved some time after 1794,[82] as were scattered lots in the recently settled tenth to sixteenth concessions. Unfortunately, somewhere between the Land Board and the Surveyor General's office, information concerning at least six of the lots assigned to the emigrants of 1793 and 1794 was lost, and these lots were mistakenly set aside as Crown and clergy reserves. Most of the double allocations occurred in concession 15 where Archibald McGilvray's lot 27 and Donald McDonell's lot 35 were made Crown reserves, while Alexander McLennan's lot 14, Kenneth McLennan's lot 29, and (probably) Donald Campbell's lot 37 were made clergy reserves. The only 1792 emigrant affected was Lieutenant Alexander McMillan; two of his lots in both the thirteenth and the fourteenth concessions of Lancaster were reserved.[83]

In order to clear their title to the land, the occupants of the disputed lots found it necessary to petition the Executive Council of Upper Canada for redress. One memorial, submitted by Kenneth McLennan, explained the mistake that had been made in omitting his name from the surveyor's plan in 1794 and noted the subsequent setting aside of his lot as a clergy reserve. McLennan asked for the "right of Soil in the Said lot," a request which echoes the Highland belief that the men who farm the land have a right to own it.[84] The Executive Council was prepared to acknowledge the emigrants' claims and ultimately ordered the land under Crown reserve to be transferred back to its occupants, McDonell, McGilvray, and McMillan. The process was more difficult in the case of the clergy reserves: Lieutenant McMillan traded his reserved lots for other lands, while Alexander McLennan and Donald Campbell seem to have chosen to rent the lots that were originally to have been granted to them.[85] Administrative errors such as these created difficulties which took ordinary emigrants years to resolve. McDonell and McGilvray petitioned twice, first in 1796 and then in 1809, and Alexander McLennan submitted memorials in 1796 and 1817. On the other hand, a gentleman emigrant was more likely to know the correct procedures and to have the official contacts to resolve such a mishap quickly: Lieutenant McMillan's petition was granted at once in 1797.

By the end of the eighteenth century, the steady granting of lots and the establishment of reserves had alienated much of Glengarry's land from the possession of the Crown. While individual lots were still available, no large block of ungranted land remained and emigrants could no longer expect to settle with large groups of their fellow voyagers. The first half of the 1790s saw continuous emigration into Glengarry and the settlement of much of Lancaster concessions 12–16; between 1793 and 1797 grants were also made in the seventeenth and eighteenth concessions of the township.[86] Lots left vacant during the first opening of a concession were often occupied a few years later. In southern Lancaster, thirteen new grants were made in the fifth and eighth concessions between 1789 and 1792, and an additional twelve lots in concessions 13–16 were granted shortly after the settlement of the 1792 and 1793 emigrants.[87] The steady granting of land also continued in Charlottenburgh township during the same period.[88]

No more than 138 lots were still available as Crown grants to settlers in Glengarry in 1797. But if no more than 11% of the lots in the county remained unallocated after thirteen years of settlement, this did not actually represent the true amount of vacant land there. For those willing to forego a free grant, land could be acquired in a number of ways. As late as 1812 Colonel (formerly Lieutenant) Alexander McMillan commented that the population of the county was much scattered because the Loyalists held "several Concessions in different Townships without being inhabited."[89] Officers, gentlemen emigrants, and even private Loyalists had all received more land than they could cultivate themselves and unimproved "farms" could be bought or rented from these men. In addition, the Crown and clergy reserves, which were intended to produce income, were available shortly after 1800 at a moderate rent. Finally, a few of the Charlottenburgh Loyalists (likely English or Irish) proved either bad farmers or poor patriots and abandoned their farms for the United States. Their land reverted to the Crown and might be granted to settlers again.[90] In 1797, therefore, the possibility of group settlement was sharply reduced by a lack of unallocated Crown lots, but land for individual families remained plentiful and relatively easy to obtain in Glengarry County.

Neither the Land Board nor government surveyors left any formal policy statement concerning the settlement of emigrants in Glengarry, but an analysis of the actual peopling of the country reveals the importance of settlement by emigrant groups. One of the striking facts of settlement in Glengarry County is that no attempt was made to settle emigrants on single unassigned lots scattered among earlier settlers. The clansmen who arrived in the 1786, 1790, 1792, and 1793 were located in groups in newly surveyed concessions north of previous settlers. The predominant factor in the settlement of Glengarry County during this period was therefore the group with which the emigrant travelled. The importance of the emigrant group in settlement was enhanced when vacant lots in their assigned concession(s) were acquired by the adult sons of the emigrants. Although bonds of kinship joined members of several different emigrant groups, relatively few emigrants seem to have chosen their place of settlement on the basis of kin links with other groups. Ties of blood and community existed *within* emigrant parties, and it was through these ties that both kinship and the emigrant groups shaped the settlement of Glengarry County.

CHAPTER ELEVEN

Settlement, 1797–1816

The clansmen who arrived in Glengarry after 1797 faced greater difficulties in obtaining land together in the new Highland community than had their predecessors. The frontier had retreated beyond the county boundaries and new policies directed the administration of colonial lands. In spite of these difficulties and in spite of the availability of large quantities of good land elsewhere in Upper Canada, emigrants continued to settle in or near Glengarry County – evidence of the importance of the Gaelic community in their movement to Canada. Once settled, the clansmen made determined efforts to acquire land in the county by purchase, grant, or lease, a fact that underlines their resolve to establish their economic independence in the new world.

Members of the first six emigrant groups received land in the spring following their arrival in Canada, and every family wanting land was accommodated. The Executive Council of Quebec, under Lord Dorchester's direction, had immediately provided for the 1785 and 1786 emigrants, no doubt in order to strengthen the Loyalist settlements. The Eastern District Land Board[1] and its surveyors were equally prompt in responding to the demand for land from the 1790, 1792, and 1793 emigrants. Perhaps too, an element of concern for fellow clansmen led gentlemen such as the Aberchalders, sitting on the Land Board, or surveyors such as James and Hugh McDonell, to settle the land-hungry emigrants as expeditiously as possible. Although the Land Boards were abolished in November 1794, their concern for and efficiency in settling emigrants was not initially lost; local magistrates, many of them former members of the boards, were given the power to grant emigrants 200-acre lots.[2] However, in 1796 not only was this degree of local autonomy in land granting lost but the Executive Council of Upper Canada also introduced what later proved to be an escalating scale of fees on grants of Crown land. On 1 July, the council ordered that settlers be required to petition the Lieutenant Governor in Council for land and adopted a table of fees for land grants, set at £2 18s. 8d. for the patent deed and £1 7s. 6d. for the survey. The same motivations lay behind first the introduction and later the increase in these fees: the need to obtain more revenue for the colony, to differentiate later settlers from the deserving Loyalists and (in the interest of large property owners) to increase the value of land.[3] Thus two years later, the patent fee was raised to 6d. per acre, bringing the total cost of survey and patent for a 200-acre lot to £6 7s. 6d. In 1804 these fees were increased again to £8 4s .1d.[4]

Other Executive Council regulations similarly made the process of land acquisition more cumbersome and ultimately more expensive. In 1798, the council ordered that settlers whose petitions for land were approved would have to obtain a location from the Surveyor General within one month and pay the survey and half the patent fees within the same period. In 1802 this regulation was made more restrictive; settlers were then required to pay the entire survey and patent fee within three days of the approval of their land petition. The council gave the screw another twist when it decided, in June 1803, that "all future applicants for land must present themselves in person." A journey to York was time consuming and expensive, especially from Glengarry, the easternmost county, which was 275 miles from that centre. The regulation might almost seem to have been passed either to limit the granting of land to people who had other business in the capital or to encourage settlement in the districts near to or west of York. Lillian Gates has commented on the effect that changes in land regulations between 1799 and 1804 had across the province: "The new settler was disappointed in his hopes of receiving a free grant, the old settler found himself harried into paying his fees, and even the loyalist or military claimant found that his privileges had been restricted."[5]

In Glengarry County, the loss of local control of land granting, the imposition of escalating fees, and the scarcity of Crown land presented major obstacles to the Highland emigrant who hoped to obtain a grant. Nevertheless, most clansmen who arrived in Glengarry between 1800 and 1820 did manage to obtain land in the county or its vicinity. This achievement reflected the value placed by the emigrants on settling in the new Highland community, as well as their willingness to sacrifice the opportunity to obtain Crown land quickly elsewhere in the Canadas.

No major emigrant group came to Glengarry between June 1794, when the McLeod party finally reached Upper Canada, and the late summer of 1802, when the McMillan and *Neptune* parties arrived there. Unlike their predecessors, the 1802 emigrants found a Crown grant difficult to get; in some cases several decades went by before they acquired title to a farm. Before 1796 the clansmen applied to local officials, often Highlanders, for a grant of land; after 1803 the emigrants faced a considerable geographic and cultural distance from the bureaucratic elite now assigned that responsibility in York. At least two of the 1802 emigrants, John McGillivray and Malcolm McCuaig, later pointed out that they were "ignorant [of] how to obtain land as was then given to emigrants," and they therefore chose to rent land in Glengarry.[6] In the final reckoning, however, the 1802 emigrants successfully settled in the Highland community in Glengarry.

One factor which limited the clansmen's knowledge of the local land granting system was the linguistic barrier between Gaelic-speaking emigrants and English officials. Many were in the same unfortunate position as Angus McDonald of the Glengarry Fencible Regiment, who failed to apply for land, at least in part, because of his "ignorance of the English language."[7] Many emigrants found it difficult to raise the £6 or £8 needed to pay land fees, as the case of Alexander McPherson illustrates. Although a Crown lot was available when he reached Lancaster in 1801, McPherson found that he "was unable to advance the fees required on the Grant ... owing to the weak and helpless condition of his Family and having no other means for their support than his daily labour."[8] Father Alexander Macdonell argued in 1819 that "great numbers" of the Glengarry settlers had not acquired Crown land "owing to the distance between this [county] and York preventing them from applying personally, their want of means to defray the expenses of so long a journey, their ignorance of the English language and &c."[9] Being local in orientation, the district Land Boards had obviated some of these difficulties. The boards were reestablished in 1815, but this was long after the last Crown lands had been assigned in Glengarry County and too late to be of use to the 1802 emigrants in obtaining land.

Various proposals were made for the accommodation of the 1802 emigrants, but none met with any substantial success, principally because the emigrants refused to be separated from their friends in Glengarry. In 1803, Lieutenant Governor Hunter suggested that the emigrants settle near York, where Crown grants could be made to them, but the emigrants wished to stay with their friends in

Glengarry and "would not agree to go so far out of the world." One year later, Lord Selkirk travelled through the county and observed the unsettled (in both senses) state of the recent emigrants. His hope to recruit three or four emigrant families for his colony at Baldoon, 200 miles west of York, was similarly frustrated.[10] Somewhat more attractive was Father Alexander Macdonell's scheme to open Prescott County, north of Glengarry on the Ottawa River, for settlement by the 1802 emigrants. In May 1806 after considerable prodding from the priest, the government finally ordered the survey of Caledonia township in Prescott County immediately north of the eighteenth concession of Charlottenburgh.[11] Macdonell claimed that Governor Hunter had intended the township "for the exclusive use of Highlanders," but for some undetermined reason, the proposed settlement failed to materialize and the lots in Caledonia remained ungranted in 1817.[12]

The importance of community in determining the location in which the 1802 emigrants settled is evident in the attempt made by Archibald McMillan of Murlaggan to create a new Highland settlement north of Glengarry in Lower Canada (now Quebec). McMillan did not arrive in Canada with any intention of organizing the settlement of his fellow travellers, and his responsibility for them ended when the emigrant ships reached Montreal. The clansmen expected to obtain land for themselves in Glengarry County. However, the difficulties that many of the McMillan and *Neptune* emigrants experienced in obtaining land of their own tempted Murlaggan to organize a new settlement and thereby fulfill his personal ambition of becoming a laird.[13] Since McMillan became a resident of Montreal on his arrival in Canada in 1802, he was unable to apply for land in Upper Canada. Instead, encouraged by the much different land-granting policies of the lower province, McMillan applied for land there in August of 1804 on behalf of some of the 1802 emigrants and other Glengarry settlers.[14] The new Highland community was to occupy three townships in the county of Argenteuil along the northern shore of the Ottawa River, sixty miles west of Montreal and thirty-five miles north of the nearest point in Glengarry (see Map 4, page 80).

McMillan's proposal achieved a considerable initial success because of the possibility it seemed to offer for community set-tlement. In August of 1804, McMillan petitioned the Governor of Lower Canada for land and submitted the names of 209 heads of household who wished to settle with him.[15] While 25% of these first applicants later decided against participating in the scheme, in 1806 McMillan forwarded a second list of another seventy-five people who wanted land in his proposed settlement. The people whose names appeared on these two lists were drawn not just from the group that McMillan brought to Canada but also from the emigrants who arrived on the *Neptune* in the same year and Highlanders already resident in Glengarry.[16] Such interest in the creation of a second Highland community is not surprising in light of the relative lack of land available from the Crown in Glengarry and the complexity of the application process. Not only the 1802 emigrants, but also the adult sons of earlier emigrants must have welcomed the opportunity to settle in the community that McMillan's scheme seemed likely to create. The difficulties of meeting the conditions set for a group settlement resulted, however, in considerable delay, and the government's final decision did not meet the approval of many of the clansmen named on either of McMillan's two lists.

Relatively few of those clansmen who applied for land with McMillan appear actually to have settled in Argenteuil County. Two specific causes can be identified for the failure of the scheme. According to some emigrants, McMillan's demand for £4 in fees after patents for land in Argenteuil were issued in March 1807 was quite "unexpected" and they were not then able to advance the necessary sum. As a result, at least seventy-three of the clansmen signed over their rights to their 200-acre grants, not to the government (as they believed at the time) but to Murlaggan himself.[17] Equally significant, however, in discouraging the clansmen from settling in Argenteuil was the government's decision to treat differently applicants on McMillan's first and second lists. The settlers on the first list were to receive patents to their land immediately, while those on the second list had first to clear three acres of land and put up log houses. McMillan reported that the applicants on the second list "were quite disatisfied at any distinction having been made" since they considered themselves "countrymen & conexions & consequently intitled to the same" as the first group. Not only did applicants on the second list withdraw from the proposed settlement but their relations whose names appeared on the first list threatened to do the same.[18]

McMillan's own analysis of the reasons for the failure of his countrymen to move to Argenteuil points out the significance of community to the settlement of the Highland emigrants, particularly when faced with bureaucratic land-granting procedures. McMillan believed that the emigrants' desire to "live among their friends" and their consequent "aversion to going on new land" was the major factor in influencing their choice of settlement location. Since the post-1800 emigrants had trouble obtaining land of their own, they helped the friends on whose farms they settled to clear the land. The earlier settlers thus had a considerable incentive to encourage the 1802 emigrants to stay in Glengarry County, and McMillan noted the active influence of these settlers in discouraging movement out of Glengarry. Moreover, resettlement also went against the economic interests of numerous Glengarry gentlemen, who urged the emigrants to remain in the county. The gentlemen had acquired large property holdings which they hoped to rent to their country-men; as McMillan pointed out, "the more population the more will their lands become valuable." Finally, McMillan emphasized the bureaucratic procedures and physical remoteness of the colonial government's land-granting system, a complaint echoed by the emigrants themselves. Although McMillan believed that many of the would-be settlers were "wrong headed," he felt that "their unsteadi-ness was much augmented by their delays, the Formality and Suspicious conduct of Govern't." All of these factors served to weaken fatally the interest of a majority of the 1802 emigrants in forming a new Highland settlement in Argenteuil County.[19] The incident underlines the importance of community ties (emotional and economic) among the emigrants and the need for group support of a settlement scheme.

Fifteen months after the arrival of the 1802 emigrants in Canada, it was clear that their settlement pattern would differ substantially from that of earlier settlers. While earlier groups had received land grants in the spring following their arrival in Canada, the great majority of the McMillan and *Neptune* emigrants were not living on land of their own by January of 1804. Instead of establishing homesteads of their own, the emigrants were, according to Lord Selkirk, "received into the houses of the old Settlers – those who had money for pay – the poor gratuitously."[20] Over the longer term, families found individual solutions to the lack of land grants, solutions which enabled them to become permanent members of the Glengarry community. We can trace the experience of a substantial minority of the 1802 emigrants, and the variety of options they followed indicates both how difficult and how important the acquisition of land in the Highland settlement was for the post-1802 emigrants to Glengarry County.

For various lengths of time, the emigrants' families lived as tenants or cottars, cultivating pieces of land on the farms of earlier settlers. It took time to amass the price of a farm, particularly for recent Scottish emigrants, who lacked the skills needed in the forests of North America.[21] A large proportion of the 1802 emigrants were able to stay with kin already settled in Glengarry; some forty emigrants who could not immediately afford the fees for land grants testified that for some years they were obliged "to Shelter themselves among their relations in the county of Glengarry."[22] John McRory is known to have stayed with his brother Eune until he could get land of his own. Other emigrants lived with those friends who needed help on their farms.[23] Renting a farm was another immediate course of action for some of the poorer 1802 emigrants; one older emigrant was reported in 1804 to have settled "on another's lands where he ... raised crops enough" for his large family, and kept five milk cows.[24]

Crown and clergy reserves, the various additional grants to Loyalists, and the extensive land grants made to gentlemen, all created a pool of land potentially available to rent in Glengarry County.[25] A number of the Glengarry gentlemen took advantage of the reserves to establish themselves as landlords, expecting both financial and social rewards for their effort. Alexander McMillan, leader of the 1792 emigration, rented two reserved lots in 1802 "with a view of having some Lands in readiness for a number of Emigrants then expected in the Province from Scotland."[26] Among the other gentlemen who leased reserve lands were Father Alexander Macdonell (the chaplain), Alexander MacDonell of Greenfield, and Norman McLeod. Some emigrants rented directly from the Crown, as did Malcolm McCuaig of lot 37 in concession 16 of Lancaster, but a majority of the emigrants seemingly obtained their leases through the agency of the gentlemen. Father Alexander Macdonell settled "a number of widows & poor people, who would wish to live near their families and friends" on the eleven reserve lots that he rented.[27] The reasons for the emigrants' willingness to rent land in Glengarry were mixed, but both financial and social considerations played a large part in it. John McGillivray testified to the significance of the latter, commenting that he had "purchased a lease of lot 19 in concession 15 of Lancaster being a Crown reserve from Norman McLeod" because of his ignorance of land-granting procedures.[28] Here again is an example of how the Highland gentlemen with their knowledge of both Gaelic and colonial society, served as mediators, generally at a profit, between the clansmen and the larger society of Upper Canada.

Many of the 1802 emigrants seem eventually to have became landowners in Glengarry and district. A fortunate minority were able to buy farms shortly after their arrival. One such man was Lauchlan Macdonald, who bought a farm fronting on the St. Lawrence in Lancaster township for £150, while Duncan McGillis purchased land in the fifth concession of Lancaster "from a Negro [Loyalist] residing in Lower Canada."[29] Another thirty-eight emigrants had money available in 1804 to pay the fees required for a Crown grant in Finch Township in Stormont County, fifteen miles west of northern Charlottenburgh. Here, too, kinship played a significant role in the settlement of the clansmen. Most of the 1802 emigrants who settled in the township came from the Lochiel estate, with smaller groups coming from Glen Garry, Kintail, Glenelg, and other parts of the Highlands.[30] The 1802 emigrants from Knoydart and Morar, who had the densest network of kin ties to Glengarry County, were *not* among the Finch settlers, of whom only one was a McDonald and one a McDonell. In contrast, Donald McMillan and Duncan McMillan, who were sons of earlier emigrants, asked for land grants in Finch so that they might settle "among their Relations lately arrived from Scotland."[31] But many emigrants waited a much longer time before they could buy land. The case of Duncan McLean was probably typical. In 1824 he acquired lot 19 in concession 15 of Charlottenburgh from its Loyalist owner, Thomas Munro, and some sixteen years later he purchased the neighbouring lot 20, a clergy reserve.[32]

Although the 1802 emigrants could not settle in one or two large groups like their predecessors, small clusters of settlers from the *Neptune* and McMillan parties ultimately formed across Glengarry County. One group settled on swampy land, previously unclaimed, in the first concession of Lancaster, while eight families obtained land in the ninth concession of the same township.[33] Another ten families from Knoydart, Glen Garry, and Kintail settled together in the third-concession Indian lands on the western edge of Charlottenburgh township.[34] Northern Lancaster and Charlottenburgh, both of which contained large Crown and clergy reserves, were peppered with 1802 emigrants.[35] The rest of the 1802 emigrants seem to have scattered across the county. For instance, Duncan McGillis located in the fifth concession of Lancaster, while in Charlottenburgh Alex McNaughton settled in the fourth concession NRR, Alex McLennan in the tenth, and Donald the War McMillan and Ludovic Morrison in the seventeenth.[36]

With the settlement of the 1802 emigrants, the boundaries of the Highland community extended well beyond those of Glengarry County itself. From 1784 on, the Highland community had spread over the county boundary into Stormont County, first into Cornwall Township, then into Finch. It had also crossed the provincial boundary into parts of Soulanges County, Lower Canada.[37] "Glengarry County" as a community was larger than the geographical unit of that name.

In the years before and after the large 1802 emigrations, a number of small parties of Highlanders also arrived in Glengarry County. Those families that have been identified obtained land in the same fashion as the 1802 emigrants. For instance, Duncan McDiarmid who emigrated in 1801 settled in the Indian lands,[38] while eight Cameron and McMillan families who reached Canada in 1803 or 1804 paid fees and obtained Crown grants in Stormont.[39] Although Lord Hobart promised Crown grants in Canada to the men of the Glengarry Fencible Regiment in 1803, they faced the same experience as other emigrants during these years. With Crown land scarce in Glengarry County and fees for grants high, most chose to rent and ultimately to purchase lots in the county.[40]

The Highland community of Glengarry County was given its final, pervasively Gaelic character with the settlement of the 1802 emigrants on much of the remaining vacant land. No evidence can be found for the settlement of a large number of the McMillan or *Neptune* emigrants outside Glengarry and the surrounding districts. The only serious attempt to do so – Archibald McMillan's scheme to settle the 1802 emigrants in Argenteuil County – was not generally a success. A single motif runs through the efforts of the 1802 emigrants, and earlier groups as well: they wanted land in or near Glengarry County. Community, kin and friends, were crucial in motivating their actions. The acquisition of land was important, but this had to take place in the company of friends and relations. By 1812, when war broke out between Great Britain and the United States and the fiery cross called the men of Glengarry to defend their new home, the settlement of the southern two-thirds of the county was complete and the new Highland community was well established in Glengarry.[41]

In 1815, shortly after peace returned to Upper Canada, the first assisted emigration to the colony brought 362 settlers (principally from Glenelg, Knoydart, and the district around Loch Tay in Perthshire) to settle in Glengarry County. Government officials were persuaded to settle these assisted emigrants in Glengarry by the identity and wishes of the emigrants themselves, even though the original impetus behind the emigration scheme lay in British military interests in Canada.

The war of 1812 between Britain and the United States was fought primarily across the Canadian frontier and it made clear the crucial importance of control of the St. Lawrence River between Montreal and Kingston if Britain were to maintain possession of Upper Canada. The region between Cornwall and Kingston was particularly vulnerable to an American attack, since only the width of the river separates the two countries over that ninety-mile distance. In the twenty-eight years between the settling of the Loyalists along the St. Lawrence and the outbreak of war in 1812, American citizens had crossed the border in considerable numbers and taken up residence on the Canadian side of the river. In these circumstances, British officials feared that Upper Canada might become "a compleat American Colony." Had it not been for the "counterpoise afforded by the Loyal Scotch Settlers of that place Stormont and Glengarry," Upper Canada might have been lost to the British."[42] The Colonial Secretary, Lord Bathurst, was thus induced to adopt a scheme of assisted emigration to provide additional settlers of proven loyalty for eastern Upper Canada.

Although the administration of the scheme was under the control of the military, civilian officials (in particular the Surveyor General of Upper Canada) had to work with the military authorities to arrange for the settlement of the assisted emigrants. As soon as it became apparent that most of the emigrants would come from Scotland, Canadian officials suggested that they be settled in Glengarry. In April 1815, the administrator of Upper Canada, Sir George Murray, commented that "It would appear sensible, if possible, to place the Settlers from Scotland in the vicinity of the Glengarry Settlement." Three months later, Murray's successor Sir Frederick Robinson also urged that the assisted emigrants be settled in Glengarry where they would "be more comfortable and ... prosper more rapidly under the friendly assistance and Local knowledge of their Countrymen."[43] In order to accommodate the 1815 emigrants, Crown reserves in Glengarry, Stormont, and Dundas were specially opened for their settlement, and the Surveyor General prepared a report detailing the vacant lots available in these three counties. But these lots were scattered – an arrangement that failed to appeal to the British commander in Canada, Sir Gordon Drummond. Thus in February 1816, after much wrangling and delay, the Lieutenant Governor of Upper Canada set aside five unsettled townships north of the Rideau River for the accommodation of the assisted emigrants.[44]

The fact that slightly more than half of the assisted emigrants settled in Glengarry, in spite of the official decision to locate the party some eighty miles farther west, underlines once again the importance of community in determining the destination of the emigrants from western Inverness. The 699 people in the assisted emigrant party left their homes in the spring of 1815 without knowing where they would settle; the government advertisement promised a grant of land in Canada, but made no mention of a specific location. On their arrival in the colony, an official responsible for settling the emigrants proposed to have "a full conversation with them and ascertain where they wish[ed] to settle." Slightly more than half the emigrants, including *all* of those from western Inverness, asked for land in Glengarry County.[45] In February 1816, Drummond made the decision to settle the assisted emigrants in the Rideau Valley townships, except for those who had been "promised the Indulgence of Settling among their Countrymen" in Glengarry County.[46] The assisted emigrant party was thus divided into two major groups: those with family or community ties to Glengarry, as well as those who preferred a Highland district, settled in the now well-established Highland county. The others went to the Rideau Valley. While considerations of colonial defense had prompted the organization of the assisted emigration, it was the support of officials in Canada and the choice made by more than sixty emigrant families that resulted in the settlement of a ninth emigrant group in Glengarry.

As was the case for earlier groups reaching Glengarry, much of the administration of the settlement of the 1815 emigrants was handled by Highland gentlemen. Thus in June 1815, when Thomas Ridout discovered that the emigrants were being recruited only in Scotland, he selected Duncan McDonell to survey lots in the Eastern District for their use. McDonell, a younger son of the leader of the 1792 emigration, was appointed by Ridout because he spoke "the Erse Language," an essential qualification for dealing with the emigrants.[47] One month later, Alexander McDonell was named superintendant of the assisted emigrants. The son of one of the Loyalist gentlemen, Allan of Collachie, McDonell had himself served as member of the Legislative Assembly for Glengarry County.[48] Angus McDonell, nephew of the chaplain and a lieutenant in the Glengarry Light Infantry Regiment, acted as Alexander McDonell's assistant, with responsibility for the emigrant depot at Cornwall.[49] When the assisted emigrants reached Canada in September, those from western Inverness discovered that the men in charge of the settlement not only spoke the same language but were also sons of their traditional leaders.

Because the 1815 emigrants arrived in Canada in the autumn, they were forced, like their predecessors, to wait until spring to receive land of their own. Some 350 of the assisted emigrants who settled in Glengarry spent the winter in barracks in Cornwall and Lancaster. Only a few could do as McDonell wished and stay "for the winter in the neighbourhood of Glengarry, where they may be accomodated with quarters by mixing them with their Countrymen already settled there."[50] The failure of the inhabitants of Glengarry to take the emigrants into their homes resulted from the crop failure of 1815.[51] In the barracks along the St. Lawrence, the emigrants were at least assured of army rations lasting the winter. The haste with which the assisted emigration had been organized, however, meant that the accommodation provided in the barracks was not always satisfactory. In November of 1815, the Quartermaster General, Sir Sidney Beckwith, reported that the fifty settlers in the "small Barrack at the River Raisin" were "comfortably lodged." But in Cornwall Beckwith found 300 people "without adequate accommodation." Sir Sidney ordered that three buildings (previously rejected as barracks because of their bad condition) be repaired; windows were to be replaced, berths improved, stoves acquired, and a "moderate issue of fuel" supplied.[52] After several months in Glasgow, two more on board ship, and six months in quarters such as these in Cornwall, the emigrants must have been grateful indeed to settle on land of their own.

At the same time as the imperial authorities experimented with assisted emigration, they also tried to bolster Upper Canada's military strength by offering land to military veterans willing to settle in the colony. Both regular British infantry units, which had served in Canada during the War of 1812, and regiments which had been locally recruited to defend the province were eligible for land grants. Even as the Quartermaster General's department administered the settlement of the assisted emigrants under the direction of Alexander McDonell, it was also granting land to veterans. Like the emigrants, the former soldiers had a choice of settling in Glengarry or in the Rideau Valley townships. Here again ties of community prevailed over other considerations. Many of those who chose Glengarry did so because they preferred to be "Located near their friends."[53] Of the forty-six soldiers who received land in Glengarry County, forty had served in the Glengarry Light Infantry Regiment, a fencible unit partially recruited in the county in 1812. Only sixteen of the military settlers from the Glengarry Regiment were Highlanders; most of these men had likely been residents of the county or its vicinity before the war.[54] The remaining twenty-four Fencible veterans were a mixed group of Scottish, Irish, and English soldiers who decided to settle in Glengarry where some of their comrades had close ties.

The discharged soldiers were already in Canada and were released from military service by the early summer of 1815. Since Duncan McDonell had not then completed his survey of the Lancaster

Crown reserves, the veterans had to wait for land to be assigned them. The delay was partly the result of the low wages offered to men employed on the survey; on 1 August 1815 Superintendent McDonell had to order soldiers of the Glengarry Light Infantry to join the surveyor's crew.[55] By late July 1815, seventy-six veterans had reported to the settling depot, where forty-three of them drew rations. McDonell sent another thirty-three men to "their relations & friends in the immediate neighbourhood ... [where they could] be collected at a short notice."[56] On 3 August 1815, the military settlers were to draw for their lots in Lancaster, but it is not clear if the men occupied them immediately.[57] Although the noncommissioned officers and men of the Glengarry Light Infantry had been promised 200 acres of land each when they enlisted, they actually received only 100 acres.[58] In arranging the release of Crown reserves, the Upper Canadian Surveyor General argued that 100 acres located amidst the older settlements or near water transport was equivalent in value to 200 acres on the fringe of settlement.[59] The standard grant made to both the military settlers and the assisted emigrants was thus half the size received by earlier arrivals in the county.

The assisted emigrants and military veterans who settled in Glengarry received their 100-acre grants in the northeastern quarter and across the seventeenth concession of Lancaster township on 29 February 1816.[60] The Lancaster settlers included fifty-two assisted emigrants, forty-nine of whom can be identified from the 1815 passenger list, and forty veterans of the Glengarry Light Infantry.[61] The surveyor had divided each 200-acre lot in half so that the settlers received either a south (front) section or a north (rear) section. The distribution of settlers on these lots was not random. Emigrants linked by family or neighbourhood settled together in identifiable clusters.[62] Even the few lowland families – no doubt somewhat adrift in a Gaelic sea – tended to settle together, in spite of their more heterogeneous origins. Of thirteen Lowland families, six settled in the fourteenth concession and three in the seventeenth concession of Lancaster. An ostensibly Lowland couple, Donald McPherson and Margaret McDonald, accepted a lot in the tenth concession amidst several McDonald families. Some of the men of the Glengarry Light Infantry and other regiments settled in a cluster in the southeast corner of the township, occupying seventeen out of twenty-four lots within a radius of a mile and a quarter.

This pattern of settlement by community of origin is even more significant in the case of the emigrants from Perthshire and western Inverness. *All* of the emigrants from Killin and Kenmore ultimately settled in the sixteenth and seventeenth concessions of Lancaster;

the two families that were first given land in the thirteenth concession soon exchanged lots. Archibald McLaren explained that he did
so because he was "desirous to Settle near his friends & Country
men."[63] Forty-one families from the parish of Glenelg formed several
clusters in Lancaster and the adjacent township of West Hawkesbury. Families from Knoydart, the southern half of Glenelg parish,
settled together in the tenth, eleventh, and fifteenth concessions of
Lancaster. A small group of emigrants from the peninsula of Glenelg
acquired land in the thirteenth concession of Lancaster, but another
nineteen families settled in West Hawkesbury Township. Most of
those who settled in West Hawkesbury occupied land in the seventh
and eighth concessions, while a smaller group was located in the
third and fourth concessions.

Within these community groupings, the importance of family ties
is evident from the distribution of land to the assisted emigrants.
Donald McDougall and his sons James and Alexander settled on
three adjacent 100-acre lots in the fifteenth concession of Lancaster,
while Duncan McDougall and his son Donald, also from Knoydart,
occupied neighbouring lots.[64] The only three McCuaigs in the
emigrant party (probably a father and two adult sons from Glenelg)
settled in the thirteenth concession between lots 6 and 13. Similarly,
the only two McLeoirs, perhaps a brother and sister, settled two lots
apart in the eighth concession of West Hawkesbury. In some cases,
the value placed on settling in the immediate vicinity of kin was so
high that emigrants were led to accept land of inferior quality. Thus
when Duncan McDonell of Knoydart turned down the rear half of
lot 2 in the thirteenth concession because it was bad land, the same
lot was accepted by John McRae from Glenelg. McRae explained that
he had made this choice "as no other vacant Lot was to be had in
settlement & ... [he was] anxious to be settled along with his
Brothers & names sakes who were located on adjoining lots."[65] Such
family ties were a significant factor in shaping both the emigration
and the new community which the assisted emigrants joined in
Glengarry County.

This examination of the emigrants' experience in settling Glengarry
County reveals the interplay of two factors influencing the settlement process. The first was the availability of land; the second
was the bond of kinship and community that joined emigrants with
members both of their own group and of other emigrant groups.

Of critical importance in the settlement of the county was the
availability of land on which the emigrants might settle. Between

1784 and 1796 government policy encouraged rapid allocation of land and settlement. As each group arrived in Glengarry, its members were quickly assigned land in a body across one or more concessions. A majority of the emigrants settled with other members of their own party, some of whom were close relations, and may have accepted a separation of ten or fifteen miles from other kinsmen already living in the county. As in Scotland, the clansmen did not live next door to all their kindred. After 1796, government policy made the acquisition of a Crown grant increasingly difficult for poor emigrants and Crown land virtually disappeared in Glengarry County. In these circumstances, western Inverness emigrants more often preferred to rent or purchase in reasonable proximity to their kin rather than to receive a Crown grant in a quite distant township. The 1802 emigrants, and others of this period, settled wherever they could find land that they could afford and as near as possible to kinsmen already resident in the county. In 1815 the assisted emigrants settled on the lots made available for them. The west Highlanders in the party unanimously chose Glengarry, where kin and neighbours were already located, rather than the Rideau townships. Related families or friends formed small clusters within the larger settlements. The peopling of Glengarry occurred under the limits set by the interaction of these two factors, the availability of land and the importance of community.

The reason behind the overwhelming importance of these two factors lay in the nature of the emigration from the Highlands to Glengarry County. The chief attraction of Upper Canada for the emigrants was its abundant land. In the late eighteenth and early nineteenth centuries, profit-oriented landlords had threatened or denied the Highland tenants' right to land. In response, many tenants left western Inverness for Glengarry where they could obtain land of their own. Their departure was, however, predicated on a belief that they would be able to settle in a community of family and friends. Thus, close-knit individual emigrant groups accepted Crown grants in a body within the same county as kinsmen who had arrived before them. When Crown land became available to western Inverness emigrants only at some distance from Glengarry, the emigrants chose the seemingly more costly route of renting and purchasing land in the vicinity of their friends.

Also evident in the settlement of Glengarry County is the pivotal role played by certain traditional leaders; this in turn underlines the conservative nature of the community which emerged there. Given that emigrants to Glengarry dealt almost exclusively with Highland gentlemen during the process of settlement, they might easily have believed that, in a social sense at least, they had not left western Inverness at all.

Leaders such Miles Macdonell played a critical role in acting for their fellow clansmen at three points during the settlement period. The first occurred as the various emigrant groups arrived in Canada eager to acquire land. Colonial officials, themselves often Scottish, depended on the traditional leaders within each group to mediate between clansmen and government. This relationship was evident in the case of Lieutenant Angus McDonell and the 1786 emigrants, but all of the emigrant parties between 1784 and 1815 had a prominent member of the group to act as their spokesman. The second role for the gentlemen was in the county itself. Far more often than not, the local official engaged in some aspect of land granting – as a Land Board member, surveyor, magistrate, or receiving officer – was a Highlander, related to one of the leading families in western Inverness. The third role for traditional Highland leaders lay in working out the fine print of settlement arrangements. Problems invariably arose over the emigrants' land holdings, particularly in the case of the 1802 emigrants, who did not immediately receive Crown grants but were forced to acquire land on their own. Highland gentlemen served as intermediaries in these cases, advising what action to take, providing recommendations, and acting as agents for the clansmen. The chaplain, Father Alexander Macdonell, was especially active in this regard, but so were members of the Legislative Assembly such as Lieutenant Angus McDonell and (later) Duncan Cameron.[66]

In some instances, however, the gentlemen's economic interests clearly conflicted with the emigrants' own best interests. The Glengarry leaders encouraged population growth in the county so as to profit from the subletting of leases on reserved lots and from the sale of additional lands they had acquired. The social elite throughout Upper Canada operated in much the same fashion but, unlike the Glengarry gentlemen, the elite of other Canadian counties rarely came from the same district in Europe as ordinary settlers. Because of the dense pattern of emigration to Glengarry, not only was the local elite from the same Highland districts as the great majority of the population, but that elite was also related by blood to the clan leaders who for generations had led their forebears.

The emigrant party and the kin group were two overlapping bodies of fundamental importance in the settlement of Glengarry County. Of course, not all members of an extended family settled next door to each other. But most managed to settle in the county or its immediate vicinity, and each nuclear family was likely very near other related families. The Loyalists and the emigrants of 1785–6, 1790, 1792, 1793, and 1815 were placed in six geographically distinct parts of Glengarry. Even the 1802 parties, while scattered across the county, partially conformed to the pattern of group settlement, since they formed small clusters within the districts allocated to earlier groups. Part of what gave the emigrant party its cohesion was the bond of kinship which linked many of its members. Yet the shared experience of a heart-wrenching emigration and of group settlement made the emigrant party perhaps as important as the kin group. The emigrant party and the kin group each reinforced the tight web of social relationships that bound Highland families to one another. Together the emigrant party and the kin group formed the warp and the woof of the Highland community of Glengarry County.

CHAPTER TWELVE

Conclusion

The story of the Glengarry settlers reveals how and why economic transformation resulted in emigration, and it points to the significance of local cultures and events in shaping the pattern of emigration to and settlement in America. The clansmen's emigration from western Inverness to Glengarry County represents one stream among the flood of people who left Europe after 1600. The detailed examination of the Glengarry emigrations presented here underlines the relationship between European economic transformation and this movement of people.

In the case of western Inverness, economic transformation followed on the heels of the final military defeat of the Highland clans during the Jacobite Rebellion of 1745. Within a short time, the social elite, most particularly the clan chiefs, adopted the radically different perspective of the capitalist economy, including the key concept that land was a commodity to be put to the most profitable use. Highland society was transformed. The clansmen who lived through this period were a people in transition. They could not adapt to commercial society in the same manner as their landlords, since the benefits brought by the new order were largely unavailable to the joint tenants and cottars who constituted over 90% of the community. The commercialization of land tenure threatened the clansmen's possession of the land and broke traditional social organization across economic lines.

Economic transformation led to a second transition for some of the clansmen, as they emigrated from western Inverness to British North America in two stages. Between 1760 and 1780, rents rose sharply to reflect new commercial land values and an expanding economy. Where such increases swallowed up too large a percentage of the clansmen's rising incomes, they emigrated to

America. In western Inverness, the administration of the Forfeited Estates was notable in limiting rent increases to a share of the increased productivity resulting from improved agriculture. On the Glengarry estate, where this was not the case, the first group of clansmen left in 1773 to settle in North America, ultimately in Glengarry County, Upper Canada. Beginning in the 1780s, economic transformation in western Inverness took a new course, that of large-scale sheep farming, and this new direction threatened more directly the clansmen's access to the land. In the years of peace between 1783 and 1815, many tenants were evicted to create sheep farms, and many more lived under the fear of clearances. A large number of clansmen accordingly emigrated from western Inverness to Canada. These included the 1785 party from Glen Garry and Glen Moriston, the 1786 party from Knoydart, the 1790 group from Eigg and the west coast, the 1792 party from Glen Garry and Locharkaigside, the 1793 party from Glenelg, and the 1802 parties from Knoydart, Glenelg, Lochiel, and Glen Garry.

In arguing that economic transformation was the key underlying cause of emigration from western Inverness in this period, I am quite aware of conflicting interpretations. Scholars such as Flinn and Richards have emphasized the growth of population as the fundamental cause of emigration, and the role of the clearances in producing the transatlantic movement is controversial. The population of western Inverness may well have grown by 40% over the thirty years prior to 1794.[1] Yet the tenants who left western Inverness before 1803 complained not of overpopulation but rather of losing their land to incomers, any one of whom might occupy several farms. It is clear from the evidence of the nine emigrations to Glengarry County that the clansmen left western Inverness when and as they did specifically as a result of the rent increases and clearances for sheep that were the manifestations of economic transformation in the Highlands. A growing population would eventually exert substantial pressure on Highland resources, but in the case of western Inverness, economic transformation brought the clansmen's fortunes to a crisis before population pressure could do serious harm.

The Glengarry emigrations illustrate the crucial role which clearances for sheep played in the departures from western Inverness in this period. The introduction of sheep farming in Glen Garry, Knoydart, and Glenelg set in motion the 1785, 1786, 1793, and 1802 emigrations. But removals also affected people who still farmed traditional holdings. Some tenants chose emigration after their neighbours lost their farms, as did John Roy Macdonald, a 1786 emigrant from Shenachaidh in Knoydart, and Murdoch McLennan, an 1802 emigrant from the Seaforth estate in Kintail.

Margaret Adams and Eric Richards are representatives of a long tradition which has denied the significance of the clearances as a cause of emigration from the Highlands before 1815. Recently J.M. Bumsted has taken this tradition to its logical conclusion when he argued that guilt-ridden, self-critical Highland emigrants *invented* clearances for sheep as the cause of their emigration in this period.[2] But the evidence provided by a detailed analysis of certain estates in western Inverness indicates that this viewpoint cannot be defended. Clearances for sheep substantially accelerated the movement of people from western Inverness, but emigration was part of the clansmen's ongoing response to those aspects of economic transformation which threatened their possession of the land. Whether the experience of tenants in western Inverness was substantially different from that of other Highland districts has yet to be determined. Nevertheless, the emigrations from western Inverness suggest that the clearances often had an important role in causing Highland emigration – a role that can only be assessed by an examination of local conditions behind the departures.

Emigration was not the automatic result of economic transformation in the Highlands. The clansmen faced a variety of options: wage labour; the adoption of new agricultural activities or of new occupations such as crofting and fishing; or more drastically, migration to southern cities. Their preference was to stay on their traditional holdings, but after 1770 this option was steadily withdrawn from them. Many of the tenants of western Inverness – the people able to raise the money needed for emigration – chose, in these circumstances, to leave with their friends for Glengarry County.

The experience of the Glengarry emigrants underlines the double-edged nature of this choice. On the one hand, the emigrants believed that landlords had forced them to leave; the movement from Glenelg was, as one participant described, "of necessity and not by choice," while landlords were reported to have "obliged ... [the 1773 emigrants] to abandon their native country."[3] On the other hand, the determination of the clansmen to emigrate and the extent of their efforts to achieve that goal can be seen in the evidence of the nine group emigrations which ended in Glengarry County. The clansmen regarded their departure as a forced choice, made necessary by the actual or threatened loss of their farms. In this sense the emigrants would never accept one author's interpretation of the departures as "the people's clearance."[4] Clearance and emigration were not synonymous. In fact, between 1770 and 1815, so far from forcing the clansmen to leave Scotland, landlords discouraged and obstructed the clansmen's determined efforts to emigrate to British North America.

In spite of Eric Richards' assertion to the contrary, it is clear that before 1815 emigration from western Inverness was a protest against the course which economic transformation took there.[5] The emigrants were not refusing to participate in a commercial economy; they had increasingly done so in the eighteenth century and would, of course, do so again in Canada. What they objected to was the role which landlords assigned to them in the new order, as payers of rapidly escalating rents, or as crofters and labourers with little or no land to farm. The clansmen rightly assessed their situation as one of declining status and comfort and knew that the prospects of resistance were nil. Rather than be exploited, they left – the action of a proud and self-reliant people. The most effective and telling critique of the place offered the joint tenants in the transformed Highland economy lies in their mass emigration to North America. Even when (for example) Glengarry offered a 10% rent reduction to his old followers, the clansmen of western Inverness chose to leave. The hostility which these departures raised among the landlords and gentry, culminating in their attempt to stifle emigration with the passage of the Emigration Act in 1803, is proof of the fact that the clansmen were still wanted as a labour force. The clansmen rejected this role. Their emigration registered a radical protest against the impact of economic transformation in the Highlands.

We have seen a pattern in the social characteristics of those who chose to emigrate to Glengarry County and in their experience of emigration. They went almost entirely in family groups; in those departures for which statistical evidence is available, over 90% of the emigrants travelled with family members. The large number of women and children included in these groups in part reflects the importance of family emigration to the county. In the three parties for which evidence is available, women formed between 44 and 51% of the adults in the group, while children under 13 years formed at least 27% and up to 49% of the passengers in five sailings to Canada. Because children were numerous, the average size of each family was relatively high, ranging from 4.6 to 5.7 people.

The Glengarry settlers came principally from contiguous districts in western Inverness, each of which sent successive groups of settlers to the county – five departures from Glen Garry, two from Lochiel, five from Knoydart, and three from Glenelg. In addition, districts near this core area (Glen Moriston, Eigg, North Morar, Kintail, and Lochalsh) joined their neighbours for the voyage to Upper Canada. Surviving passenger lists do not document adult sibling or extended kin relationships, but genealogical evidence suggests that the family and community basis of the nine emigrant parties created an intensive network of kin relations linking all the settlers in Glengarry. This family and community emigration from western Inverness testifies to the emigrants' total rejection of the place offered them in the transformed Highlands.

Most of the emigrants fit a similar socioeconomic profile and followed a common pattern of departure. In the two voyages for which statistical evidence is available, three out of five emigrants were farmers, one out of eight was a craftsman, and one out of four was a labourer or servant. In other departures for which documents survive, the emigrants are described as "the principal tenants," the better-off tenants, or (later) "the best part of the dregs ... of the commoners." Clansmen of middling status and resources – tenants and craftsmen – therefore dominated the emigrant parties, but some poorer members of the community also left for Glengarry County. With the exception of the 1815 emigration, in which the clansmen took advantage of a government program to accomplish their own ends, the Glengarry settlers themselves organized their departure for Upper Canada. The seven voyages for which the port of embarkation is given all began in small western Inverness communities: three in Fort William, two in Knoydart, and one each in Arisaig and Glenelg. The clansmen are known to have hired a vessel in five of these cases, but it seems probable that all sailings from western Inverness (which had no normal passenger traffic or ongoing trade with North America) were on vessels chartered for the purpose. The clansmen who settled in Glengarry between 1784 and 1815 shared a common background and displayed remarkable initiative and control in organizing their emigration to Canada.

Four factors are easily identifiable as crucial to successful emigration in these years. First, families emigrated together to Canada: their response to the impact of economic transformation in western Inverness was communal. There is little evidence to suggest that individual or single-family emigration played a significant role in populating the county before 1815. The clansmen chose to emigrate because it was an option which offered them land *and* which they could undertake together. Economic transformation might destroy traditional relationships, but out of their ruin the clansmen sought to preserve life as a community.

Second, the clansmen succeeded in community emigration because a substantial number of people were able to raise the money necessary for the voyage. The second half of the eighteenth century, and in particular the years of war with revolutionary and Napoleonic France, saw rising prices as well as rising rents. As long as the tenants kept their traditional holdings, their cattle could serve as walking capital to underwrite the voyage to Canada. The cost of an Atlantic passage, at least before the adoption of the Emigration Act, was within the means of many clansmen.

Third, the clansmen found leaders for this radical undertaking within their own communities. Some of these leaders emerged from the traditional clan leadership, including gentlemen closely related to the chief, such as the Macdonells of Leek, Aberchalder, Collachie, and Greenfield. Others were clergymen such as Alexander McDonell of Scotus, former soldiers such as Lieutenant Alexander McMillan of Glenpean, or prominent tenants such as Angus Ban Macdonell of Muniall, Kenneth McLeod of Glenelg, or Murdoch McLennan of Kintail. While the nature of the role played by these men is not uniformly documented and probably varied somewhat, their status and resources must have aided the effective organization of the emigrations.

Fourth, the aid that the clansmen received on their arrival in Canada was a final factor in their successful emigration. Government officials provided five of the emigrant groups with free transportation for at least part of the journey inland. Six groups received provisions for varying periods, and seven were allowed to settle in their first summer on Crown land in Glengarry County. When government assistance was either inadequate or not available, the 1790 emigrants threw themselves on the generosity of the people of Montreal, while the impoverished state of some of the *Neptune* emigrants in 1802 led to a public subscription on their behalf. In addition, the major role which Highland gentlemen played in imperial, military, and colonial administrations ensured that the clansmen who arrived to settle in Glengarry often dealt with men who were Highlanders, some even of the same clan.

These factors, which ensured the success of the clansmen's emigration to Glengarry, also provide an explanation for the puzzling decline, which Eric Richards has noted, in the Highlanders' propensity to emigrate after 1815.[6] In spite of the overwhelming enthusiasm for emigration in the Highlands in the late eighteenth century, the clansmen's circumstances were, in fact, so marginal that only a modest decline in their net income could prevent large numbers of them from leaving. After the Napoleonic Wars, economic change seriously curtailed the clansmen's ability to finance their departure. The postwar economic collapse dramatically lowered the amount of cash that tenants might expect to earn from cattle sales, while clearances for sheep limited still more severely the number of people able to maintain their cattle stocks. This major decrease in the number of people able to pay for their passage abroad in turn substantially reduced the possibility of communal emigrations, which had been the second factor in the success of the Glengarry settlement. In addition, the gentlemen and many of the principal tenants, who in the eighteenth century had organized the departures for Canada, had now disappeared both as individuals and as a class from the Highlands. Nor could the clansmen any longer expect the help from colonial officials that their predecessors had enjoyed. British emigration to Canada grew exponentially after 1815, and Highlanders were no longer the only large groups of marginal emigrants arriving in Quebec.

Individual families and groups of emigrants continued to arrive in Glengarry, as well as in British North America as a whole, but the seeming shift in the clansmen's attitude towards emigration was quite rational, given the change in their circumstances. When landlords offered to fill the gap by subsidizing group emigrations, the clansmen's response depended on their own interest in emigration. Where the clansmen wished to remain on their holdings and the landlords wished to evict them, unwilling or forced emigration could be the result. Where the clansmen wished to leave Scotland, subsidized fares might provide a new means of emigrating to British North America.

The pattern of participation and organization observed in the Glengarry emigrations generally fits the model of Bernard Bailyn's "provincial" emigrant stream – in fact, it is more like the model than the model itself (see Table 6). Like Bailyn's Highland emigrants, the Glengarry settlers were almost equally divided between men and women; there was, however, a much larger percentage of families and children in the Canadian group, as well as a larger average family size, than in Bailyn's model. The emigrants to Glengarry were predominantly farmers, but unlike Bailyn's Highland emigrants (only 30% of whom named agriculture as their occupation), over 60% of the western Inverness heads of families did so. Finally, as in the "provincial" stream, the Glengarry settlers sailed from local ports in large, organized groups on vessels hired for the purpose.[7]

Two aspects of the case of the Glengarry emigrants suggest that Bailyn's "provincial" model can be further elaborated. First, the Glengarry settlers left Scotland because of the loss of land, status, or income that they experienced or expected as a result of economic transformation. It is not yet clear whether middling tenants' rejection of the place allowed them in the new agrarian order was generally significant in shaping "provincial" emigration from other European communities. I would, however, suggest that such emigration was often linked to economic transformation, including the case of Bailyn's Highlanders and Yorkshiremen. Second, the evidence of the Glengarry emigrations points to the importance of group and chain emigration as a significant aspect of provincial emigration. Bailyn's analysis is limited by the evidence available in the 1774–5 emigration registers, which document less than two years' departures and which list only the emigrants' county of origin. The local chartering of vessels for large numbers of people does hint at group departures among the 1774–5 emigrants, but Bailyn claims that extended families scarcely existed in the emigrant parties. Further investigation of the degree to which related families emigrated and settled together in North America might reveal that such emigration is an important feature of the "provincial" stream and that the case of the Glengarry settlers should be taken as a model for such departures.[8]

What effect did the Glengarry emigrations have on the history of the land in which they settled? The pattern of departures from western Inverness between 1773 and 1815 created a new Highland community in Upper Canada's easternmost county. The arrival of whole families and parts of Highland communities, chiefly during the seventeen years in the midst of this period, ensured a remarkable degree of cultural transfer and continuity. The clansmen were not blind traditionalists seeking to reestablish feudal life in the new world, as their acceptance of Upper Canada's dispersed pattern of settlement reveals. The clansmen took advantage of the land available in the new Glengarry to become not joint tenants but individual owners of 100 acres or more; thus they ensured the survival of their community in a commercial world. They did not treat their own land as a commodity but were adept and energetic enough to retain ownership of it through several generations. The traditional characteristics of a Highland community – loyalty, defense of local interests, and conservatism – were notable in the history of Glengarry County and of Upper Canada too.

The story of the Glengarry settlement is evidence of the substantial degree of cultural transfer resulting from the "provincial" emigrant stream. How significant the "provincial" model was in the settlement of British North America has yet to be determined. Certainly other Highland communities in Ontario, Nova Scotia, and Prince Edward Island were settled by the same family and kin-based emigration which peopled Glengarry. Studies of the Welsh emigrants who arrived in New Brunswick in 1819 and of the North Tipperary Protestant Irish who settled in Ontario between 1818 and 1855 show a similar pattern of related families of modest resources settling together in North America. Perhaps more surprising are the similarities between the experience of the English Puritans who settled in New England in the seventeenth century and that of the clansmen who came to Glengarry County.[9] Late nineteenth- and twentieth-century emigration from eastern and southern Europe also appears frequently to have followed the "provincial" model.

Canadian historians have done relatively little comparative analysis of the social characteristics and experience of the emigrants who settled in Canada or the communities that they created there. The concept of a "provincial" stream of emigration offers a useful analytical tool with which to examine this movement of people. Emigrants who travelled and settled in groups of related families from the same European districts could reproduce their culture and community in Canada. Canadian society may be seen as a product of the synthesis of the elite culture and values of British officials, of the melting pot produced by metropolitan emigration, and of the many traditional cultures recreated in Canada by groups of "provincial" emigrants, including the clansmen who settled in Glengarry County, Upper Canada.

The clansmen of western Inverness created a new Highland community in Glengarry County. Emigration from the western Highlands and islands was, in fact, so extensive that Glengarry County was only one of a series of Gaelic communities which emerged in Upper and Lower Canada, Nova Scotia, and Prince Edward Island. The seventy-five years of departures from western Inverness to Glengarry is one proof that Highland communities were at first divided, not broken, by emigration to Canada. Ties of kinship remained important and the Atlantic was not necessarily a barrier to the inheritance of land.[10] The long-term emigration of substantial segments of the Highland population had, however, a not surprising effect; by 1841 a Scottish clergyman believed that the clansmen who remained in Scotland were now disposed "to view Canada and Nova Scotia as their own country ... by reason of the numbers who have gone out."[11]

The continuing stream of emigration to Glengarry County reflected the enthusiastic reaction to Upper Canada of the first generation of clansmen to settle there. A man of education such as

Father Alexander Macdonell, later bishop of Kingston, saw the potential of British North America in sophisticated terms: "The govrts of the continent of Europe seem like old crazy machines which age & abuse are hurrying fast into decay, & whose constituent parts appear almost beyond repair. That the new world will have its own time of power, of civilization, & Religion requires no reflection to see."[12] The great appeal that Glengarry County had for the clansmen lay in its virtual freedom from the control of landlords; Iain Liath Macdonald now felt "lively with no harassment under the sun," while Anna McGillis believed that Father Alexander McDonell Scotus had, like Moses, led his people to freedom. Even more tempting to some was the opportunity "to kill a Deer sooner than ... in Guisich without fear or controul from any superior power." McGillis was overwhelmed by the fertility and richness of the land in Glengarry; the familiar image of America as a land of plenty is visible in her description of its wheat, sugar maples, grapes, and wine. But what guaranteed the emigrants' freedom from want and oppression was the land which they could acquire in Upper Canada. The emigrants "obtained townships for themselves" in Glengarry and, as McGillis emphasized, in Canada the clansmen had "firm title from the king" for their farms.[13]

Under such circumstances it is not surprising that the population of Glengarry County grew quickly. As Father Alexander Macdonell pointed out to a Scottish colleague, "all the young people remain always in the Country & Marry as soon as they become of age. There [sic] constant endeavours to get settled as near as to their friends as possible make lands in this district very scarce and valuable." By the end of the Napoleonic Wars, the "Glengarry Scotch" had populated the Glengarry townships, as well as nearby parts of Hawkesbury, Cornwall, Finch, and Roxborough townships. In 1816 Father Alexander Macdonell asked colonial officials to reserve another seven townships north and west of Glengarry for future Highland emigrants and for the children of present Scottish settlers. The chaplain predicted that the Highland "settlement would in a few years join that forming now on the River Rideau & in the course of a few years would extend to the Rice Lakes and from thence to Lake Simcoe." In the second decade of the nineteenth century, it was possible for the clansmen to dream of an eastern Upper Canada populated chiefly by Highland settlers.[14]

While this vision was not realized, the 3,300 clansmen who arrived in Glengarry in the nine group emigrations described in this volume dominated the new Highland county and adjacent townships.[15] By 1832 the population of the county had topped 8,500, and twenty years later it had doubled again to 17,596. Of this number, over three-quarters of Glengarry's inhabitants in 1852 were Scottish clansmen or their descendents. The west Highland origin of the original emigrants was reflected in a roll call of the clans prepared from the 1852 census. One person in six in the county was named McDonald or Macdonell, but there were also about 500 each of the McMillans, McDougalls, and McRaes, about 400 McLeods, Grants, and Camerons, some 330 McGillis, Kennedys, McLennans, and Campbells, and 250-odd McIntoshes, McGillivrays, and McKinnons.[16] Altogether 45% of the population bore one of these fifteen Highland names. The overwhelming predominance of these clansmen from western Inverness and vicinity gave Glengarry County its strong Highland identity in the nineteenth century.

The clansmen's emigration to Glengarry County successfully met their principal goal of obtaining land together and left them free to establish the economic and cultural life of the new community according to their own priorities. Life in the Highland settlement was shaped both by the Canadian environment and by Gaelic culture, as a glimpse at basic economic activities such as agriculture shows. Outside observers were always critical of Glengarry agriculture, and even their pastor Father Macdonell pointed out in 1808 that "owing to the advanced prices of Lumber & potash which now employs not only the young people but almost every young & old who are able to work at all, ... agriculture & the raising of grain is entirely neglected & their lands converted to grassing farms & the breeding of Cattle, the mode of life in which they have been brought up from their Infancy & the most congenial to the nature of a Highlander."[17] This charge was not totally accurate, since the clansmen travelled every year to Montreal to trade their produce for farming utensils and other necessities.[18] But the people of Glengarry evidently saw economic opportunities more attractive than the colonial norm of commercial wheat production. Only over the long term would the new geographic environment of Upper Canada and the social institutions of an English colony such as schools and elected governments change the expectations and practices of the Glengarry settlers.

An oral account of the first election for an Upper Canadian assembly in 1792 reveals the ways in which traditional ways of life were superimposed on British North American institutions. Most heads of family in the county met the property qualification for the franchise. The candidates (who were Highland gentlemen) thought it appropriate to deal with this alien institution, an election, by addressing the crowd, which was mostly unilingual Gaelic-speaking, in English. Donald Sutherland testified that "the candidates couldn't speak english very well & their efforts at speachifying were comical."[19] The emigrants turned the election into a Highland social gathering, quite unlike the rough, male-only elections that became typical of Upper Canada. While two men were elected to represent Glengarry County, their position as leaders of the community did not depend on poll books; Captain John and Lieutenant Hugh Macdonell were sons of Alexander of Aberchalder, one of the leaders of the 1773 emigration. The clansmen accepted the political institutions of their new country, but in the early years of the settlement, they saw them through the prism of traditional Highland values and concerns.

Although the people of Glengarry shared a common Gaelic culture, there were nevertheless separate loyalties within the groups that populated the county. One nineteenth-century resident observed that "there was a feeling between the Knoydart and Glengarry people which continued to a certain extent in the colony."[20] If tensions between Macdonalds survived the Atlantic crossing, clan and religious differences dividing (for instance) Macdonalds, McMillans, and McLeods were also easily carried to Upper Canada. Given the significance of settlement by emigrant group, and hence by community, these differences were readily perpetuated in the new county. Even today, local people refer to the quite distinct characteristics of Maxville, Dunvegan, Kirkhill, Lochiel, and St. Raphaels. Each of these communities was settled by a separate group of emigrants: the 1817–20 Congregationalists, the Glenelg and Skye emigrants, the 1793 party, the 1792 group, and the 1785–6 emigrants respectively. It is not implausible to suggest that the varied personalities of today's communities reflect, in part, the slightly different backgrounds of the emigrant groups of 150 to 200 years ago.

But apart from these very local distinctions, the transition from Europe to North America produced a new dual identity which grew up as the settlement matured. The people of Glengarry came to view themselves not only as Highlanders but also as Canadians. Their continuing sense of a Scottish identity did not prevent the emergence of an equally deep commitment to Canada. At the same time, the people of Knoydart, Lochiel, Glen Garry, Morar, Glenelg, Kintail, Bracadale, and Loch Tay were knit into a new Glengarry community, its ties of kinship and neighbourhood as dense as those of any Highland parish in the eighteenth century. In Scotland, the Grants may "belong to" Glen Moriston or Strathspey, whereas Glen Garry is Macdonell territory. But a dozen clans coexist in Glengarry

County, each contributing its special characteristics to the community, and each as fiercely loyal to the place as a Scots McLeod is to Skye or Glenelg or a McNeill is to Barra.

The clansmen of western Inverness were pleased with what they found in Upper Canada. Whether they saw their new home, in McGillis's words, as bringing "land, liberty and happiness," or in Aeneas Macdonald's phrase, as "a Country where reigns peace & plenty," the people of Glengarry expressed their pride in it loudly and for all to hear. That pride resounds in the stories of Ralph Connor, where Highland lumbermen rally with the cry "Glengarry," and the long tall tales of the county that led a stranger to ask its native sons, "is Glengarry in Canada or Canada in Glengarry?"[21]

Notes

SRO	Scottish Record Office
SRR	South of the River Raisin
TGSI	Transactions of the Gaelic Society of Inverness
UCLP	Upper Canada Land Petitions
UCS	Upper Canada Sundries

CHAPTER ONE

1 Immigration, as the movement across the Atlantic is called when seen from the American shore, has long attracted scholarly attention. In the United States, immigration studies have ranged from accounts of particular ethnic groups, such as Thomas and Znaniecki's *Polish Peasant* or Blegen's *Norwegian Migration*, to the general overview of the movement found in Hansen's *Atlantic Migration*. More recently, Bernard Bailyn has presented a new analysis of emigration from Britain to the American colonies in the years just before the Revolution, in his two volumes *Peopling of British North America* and *Voyagers to the West*. While authors such as Cowan (*British Emigration to British North America*), and Carrothers (*Emigration from the British Isles*), explored the parameters of nineteenth-century British immigration to Canada, only in the past twenty years has serious attention been given to a detailed analysis of the immigrant experience. Robert Harney and others have examined twentieth-century immigrant groups. More recently Akenson's *Irish in Ontario* and Elliot's *Irish Migrants in the Canadas* have raised interest in the experience of nineteenth-century immigrants.

2 Ralph Connor's Glengarry novels, *The Man from Glengarry* and *Glengarry School Days*, were bestsellers throughout the Englishspeaking world. The notion that Glengarry is a special place recurs constantly in conversation and in print. I have heard the Montreal-born grandson of a Glengarrian explain to a South American that Glengarry was a special place, and MacGillivray and Ross make the same point in *History of Glengarry*, 646.

3 While Bumsted concludes that the clansmen emigrated so as "to be left alone to continue their old pastoral way of life," he also, quite rightly, emphasizes the extent to which the Highlanders were "makers and masters of their own destiny in the New World"; Bumsted, *People's Clearance*, xvi, 221.

4 Bailyn, *Voyagers to the West*, especially pages 89–239. The case of the Glengarry emigrants generally conforms to the pattern which Bailyn describes for Scottish emigration in the 1770s; any discrepancies that the Glengarry experience reveals tend only to bolster his larger argument.

5 See Gray, *Highland Economy*, for an excellent overview of economic development in the Highlands in the century of agrarian transformation. Hunter's *Making of the Crofting Community* is a complete contrast in approach and commitment. Making good use of newspaper reports, oral history, and Gaelic poetry, Hunter documents sympathetically the emergence of the crofting community and its struggle to obtain recognition of certain traditional rights. In two massive volumes entitled *A History of the Highland Clearances*, Eric Richards explores the context and events of the clearances, their interpretation, and the reaction of the clansmen.

6 For Knoydart in 1755, see *Statistics of the Annexed Estates* (1973); thirty-eight tenants shared sixteen farms totalling more than 13,000 acres. For the same area in 1857, see Hunter, *Making of the Crofting Community*, 85.

7 This view is expressed most forcefully in Flinn, "Malthus, Emigration and Potatoes," 47–64. Richards supports this interpretation; see *Highland Clearances* II, 272–5.

8 For Selkirk, see Selkirk *Collected Writings*, 116–24. For changed attitude of Highland landlords, see Hunter, *Making of the Crofting Community*, 41–2, 73–4.

9 For Flinn, see "Malthus, Emigration and Potatoes." Hunter quotes several crofters on this point, one of whom commented: "I have never seen that emigration gave more room to people, though it did to sheep," (*Making of the Crofting Community*, 80).

10 Richards, *Highland Clearances*, II, 184–5.

11 Gray, *Highland Economy*, 102; Richards, *Highland Clearances*, II, 279.

12 For demographic causes, see Flinn, "Malthus, Emigration and Potatoes," especially 51, and Richards, *Highland Clearances*, II, 272–5. For the effect of sheep farming, see Richards, II 195–6; 216–17 and Bumsted, *People's Clearance*, xi, 29. For the argument that the clansmen wished to avoid change, see Bumsted, *People's Clearance*, 68–70.

13 Malcolm Gray made this point in "Scottish Emigration," 95–6.

14 Hunter, *Making of the Crofting Community*, 84, 95–6.

15 Anna McGillis's poem "Canada Ard," describing her reaction to conditions in Upper Canada, is found in A.M. Sinclair, *Gaelic Bards*, 7–8.

16 Future research might well focus on the peninsula of Glenelg, which was one of the major points of origin of the Glengarry emigrants. Various collections relating to Glenelg, most particularly the MacLeod of Dunvegan papers, might yield useful information about the emigrants to Glengarry County.

17 For a more detailed listing of the relevant sources for this study, see the accompanying bibliography.

18 See Cressy, *Coming Over*, especially 286–91.

19 Dumbrille, *Braggart in My Step*, 72–3.

CHAPTER TWO

1 For more detailed information, see Darling, *Highlands and Islands*, 1–21; and Johnstone, *Western Highlands*, 11–22.

2 Fraser-Mackintosh, *Antiquarian Notes*, 124. The Duke of Gordon showed an interest in purchasing Abertarff, which lay adjacent to his estate.

3 The wadsett was, very loosely, a form of mortgage common in the Highlands and used to raise money. In return for the loan of a certain sum, a landowner would allow the lender the use of particular farms. These farms were usually rented out by the lender and the income thus produced served as interest on the loan. The wadsett could be redeemed by the landowner only at a stated time upon repayment of the loan, whereupon the land came under his control again.

4 Unlike many Highland chiefs, the pre-1745 Cameron chiefs had been good financial managers who left the estate "in very good Circumstance" with little debt on it. See SRO, E768/29/1, Memorial of William Alston. Large debts were chronic on Highland estates throughout the eighteenth century.

5 SRO, RH2/8/24, 107–8, Blackadder's survey, 1799.

6 For example, only three of Cameron of Lochiel's farms, (Ballachulish, Onich, and Moy) produced enough corn to sell the surplus.

7 For *cas-chrom*, see SRO, E741/46, 1. The mill at Achnacarry on the Lochiel estate was destroyed by Cumberland's troops in 1746, but was eventually rebuilt in 1759. For mills, see SRO, E768/32/2 and SRO, E741/38/2. For housing, see SRO, E768/36/4, memorial of Henry Butter.

8 Gray, *Highland Economy*, 35.

9 See Thomson's excellent *Introduction of Gaelic Poetry*.

10 Other inhabitants of western Inverness also suffered, including McDonell of Glengarry, who had not personally participated in the rebellion. His estate was laid waste, his tenants' houses were burnt, and the family papers and charters were carried away.

11 SRO, E768/41, list of losses; for McPhie, see SRO, E768/41/3, and for Cameron, see SRO, E768/41/23.

12 The Duke of Argyll held a subject superiority over part of Cameron of Lochiel's estate. SRO, E768/11/3, Donald Campbell to John Cameron of Fassifern, 28 Dec. 1747.

13 SRO, E768/12/6/1, George Douglas to D. Moncrieff, 8 Feb. 1753.

14 Willis, *Reports*, introduction.

15 Other annexed estates on the southern fringe of western Inverness were Callart, Ardsheall, and Kinlochmoydart, none of which sent

more than a few emigrants to Glengarry County. Strictly speaking, the Crown could not legally annex Barisdale since Macdonell only held it on a wadsett from Glengarry. However, the Glengarry chief failed to put forward his claim during the allotted time and Barisdale was annexed with the other Highland estates in 1752. The feudal superiorities that the Dukes of Argyll and Gordon held over Lochiel prevented the annexation of that estate until the Crown purchased these rights in 1770.

16 SRO, E786/5/2, Mungo Campbell to D. Moncrieff, 12 June 1753.

17 The appointment in 1757 of a new minister for the parish of Kilmallie (which was almost contiguous with the Lochiel estate) was the subject of an acrimonious dispute between Jacobites and government officials in the area. See SRO, E768/13/10, D. McViccar and M. Campbell to D. Moncrieff, 15 July 1757.

18 Smout, *History of the Scottish People*, 314.

CHAPTER THREE

1 SRO, E741/30/1, Petition read by Board on 15 Dec. 1763; SRO, E741/23/7, Butter to Board, 28 May 1764; and SRO, E741/15/1, 4, memorial for Archibald McDonell of Barisdale, 1784.

2 Smout, *History of the Scottish People*, 322–4. The roots of this change can, of course, be found in the first half of the eighteenth century and, to a lesser extent, in the seventeenth century.

3 SRO, E741/46, description of the Barisdale farms, 33–4.

4 For the population of Knoydart in 1764, see R. Macdonald, "Highland District in 1764," 150. The number of people on the Barisdale farms is unknown, but Glengarry and Scotus's properties in Knoydart were together slightly bigger in area and probably therefore in population.

5 The factor, Mungo Campbell, visited Knoydart and interviewed most of the tenants in order to obtain accurate information for his report. See *Statistics of the Annexed Estates*, 4–5.

6 Flinn, *Scottish Population History*, 257.

7 This figure could seriously underrepresent the number of cottars, etc., in Barisdale, if my estimate that Barisdale held some 40% of Knoydart's population is wrong. Nonetheless, even if Barisdale held 50% of Knoydart's population (480 people), tenants would still outnumber the others 249 to 231. For the two references to servants or cottars in Barisdale which I have located, see SRO, E741/38/2, Butter to Commissioners, read 21 Feb. 1763; also Willis, *Reports*, 51.

8 SRO, E741/20/1, "Judicial Rental of Barisdale," taken by Mungo Campbell, 1755; and SRO, E741/43, "Plan Settled by Henry Butter," 1767.

9 Willis, *Reports*, 49, 52.

10 Ibid., 50. The Macdonell gentlemen resident in Knoydart included Scotus and Barisdale, cousins of Glengarry, James McDonell, brother to Glengarry, and Dr. John McDonell, uncle to the same.

11 *Statistics of the Annexed Estates*, 4–5.

12 SRO, E741/46, "Report of the Contents, Measures, & Estimate Rents of Barisdale," William Morison, 1771.

13 The soum was the number of stock any particular farm was considered capable of supporting; the basic unit of the soum was the cow, and other livestock were rated proportionally.

14 Willis, *Reports*, 50.

15 Ibid., 51.

16 Ibid., 100.

17 SRO, E741/38/2, Butter to Board, read 21 Feb. 1763.

18 Ibid.

19 SRO, E786/37/2, memorial by Henry Butter, 3 March 1764.

20 SRO, E741/43, "Plan Settled by Henry Butter," 1767.

21 For MacLeod's petition, see SRO, E741/31/2/1; for Butter's response, see SRO, E741/31/2/2; for the Commissioners' refusal, see SRO, E721/17, minutes, 20 Jan. 1770.

22 SRO, E741/38/2, Butter to Board, 21 Feb. 1763.

23 SRO, E741/20/7, rental of Barisdale. Torcruin, Glaschoille, Groab, and Riddaroch were leased in 1776, Sallachry, Braomisaig, Reidh à Ghuail and Muniall in 1777. See also Willis, *Reports*, 101.

24 For Morison, see SRO, E741/46, 2; for Butter, see SRO, E741/27/11, Butter to Commissioners, read 24 March 1766.

25 For Lieutenant Macdonell, see SRO, E741/46, description of the Barisdale farms, 1771, 29–30. Duncan McDonald gave up one-sixth of Inverie because he had lost most of his stock (SRO, E741/43, 3, plan of 1767). Butter recommended that Alexander McIntosh be removed from Inverie because of bad farming (SRO, E741/31/3/2). The commissioners ordered John Gillis to leave Sourlies unless he paid two years' arrears (SRO, E721/17, minutes, 26 Feb. 1770). Butter recommended to Barclay that quarrelling tenants in Li be separated (SRO, E741/23/11).

26 See the rentals, etc., of Barisdale in the SRO: for 1755, E741/20/1; for 1767, E741/43; for 1771, E741/46; for 1774, E741/20/6; and for 1784, E741/20/8.

27 Youngson, *After the Forty-Five*, 35–6.

28 The disbanded men were all from the West Highlands, including two from Knoydart; see SRO, E741/23/8. For displaced tenants, see SRO, E741/27/9, March 1765; for failure of John Macdonald, see SRO, E741/39; for unused bounty and nets, see SRO, E741/23/13.

29 SRO, E741/27/11 and E741/46, description of Barisdale, 1771, 19–20.

30 SRO, RHP 112; also E741/46, Coalisbeg, 8–9.

31 SRO, E741/23/16, Butter to Barclay, 8 July 1769; SRO, E786/37/9, Feb. 1771.

32 For Scotus's mill, see SRO, E741/38/2, Feb. 1763. For bridges, see SRO, E786/33/1, report by Henry Butter, and E741/41/2. For roads, see SRO, E786/37/2, March 1764; SRO, E741/27/11; and SRO, E786/33/1.

33 SRO, E786/37/1, memorial from Butter, June 1760; SRO, E741/23/3, Butter, 16 Aug. 1762; SRO, E741/27/6, 7 March 1763; and E786/33/1.

34 For language of the community, and ability to read and write in 1755, see Willis, *Reports*, 49. For petition, see SRO, E741/31/5.

35 SRO, E721/19, minutes, 8 March 1779.

CHAPTER FOUR

1 Johnstone, Western Highlands, 50, 59–60.

2 Sinclair, *Statistical Account* (known as *Old Statistical Account*; hereafter cited as *OSA*), VIII, Kilmallie (1793), 432.

3 For the mid-eighteenth century, see Kyd, *Scottish Population Statistics*, 59. For 1793, see *OSA*, VIII, Kilmallie (1793), 434. For the 1801 census, see Register House (Edinburgh), Parochial Register, Kilmallie, 520/1.

4 In 1801 the Lochiel estate included the following census district: Mamore, Lochielside, Strath Lochy, Loch Arkaig and Fassfern.

5 SRO, E768/1, abstract rental, 1748/9; SRO, E768/7/1, valuation of Lochiel, 1762, 62–5; SRO, RH2/8/26, survey of Lochiel by William Morison, 1772, Clunes, 35–6, and Invermallie, 44–6.

6 SRO, E768/1, abstract rental, 1748–9. The wadsetters were: Dougal Cameron, Inverskilavulin; Alexander Cameron, Muirshearlich; Evan Cameron, Drimnasallie; Alexander Cameron, Stronlia; John Cameron, Fassfern; Donald Cameron, Clunes; Alexander McPhee, Glendessary; Donald Cameron, Crieff; Donald Cameron, Glenpeanbeg and Lagganfern; Ewen Cameron, Errocht; Alexander McLachlan, Cornranan; Allan Cameron, Lundavra; and John Cameron, Culchenna.

7 SRO, E768/41/1–43. It is not clear if these claims were expressed in pounds sterling or Scots.

8 SRO, E768/7/1, 66–75.

9 These farms were Corryshenrachan, Achintore, Kilmallie and Achnacarry, Kenmore, Murlaggan, Invermallie, Kiliross, Barr, Strone, Achdalieu, and Corribeg.

10 Tenants paying less than £2 consisted of six of the eight tenants of Annat, three from Banavie, and three from Inverarkaig, twelve from Moy and four from both Onich and Ballachulish. See SRO, RH2/8/26, 151–3.

11 SRO, E768/7/1, valuation, 1762, 62–5.

12 SRO, RH2/8/26, survey, 1772, 35–8, 44–6, 56–60, 82–4.

13 SRO, RHP 11608, RHP 3424–76.

14 SRO, RH2/8/26, 15–17, 26–34, 44–6; SRO, RHP 11608, plan of road from Loch Nevish Head to Loch Lochy, surveyed in 1796 by George Brown.

15 See SRO, RH2/8/26, 56–60. The farm of Errocht had five shielings in Glen Mallie, two of which were permanently inhabited. Straden and Innisdarroch are probably the houses noted by Brown on either side of the river Mallie at the Alt a' Cham Dhoire. See SRO RHP 11608.

16 SRO, RHP 11606; SRO, RH2/8/26.

17 SRO, E768/7/1, valuation; SRO, RH2/8/26, survey.

18 For the size of the estate, see SRO, E768/56/4; for purchase of meal, see SRO, RH2/8/26.

19 Butter was factor not only of Lochiel and Barisdale but also of three other annexed and forfeited estates in the area.

20 SRO, E768/36/4, memorial of Henry Butter, 1763.

21 SRO, E786/13/13, "Memorial and plan of Improvement...."

22 SRO, RH2/8/26. Stone houses were built in Murlaggan, Achnasaul, Glenpeanbeg, Kinlocharkaig, Invermallie and Ardnosh, Barr, Easter Moy, Muirshearlich, Culchenna and Ballachulish.

23 SRO, RH2/8/26, 3.

24 Ibid., 15–16, 32–3, 61–2.

25 Ibid., 15–17, 18–20, 29–30, 35–6, 44–6, 54–5.

26 SRO, E768/32/2, "Memorial of Mungo Campbell to clear his Accts. for 1755"; SRO, E786/13/1, 14 Aug. 1759; SRO, E786/13/12, 19 Feb. 1765.

27 SRO, E786/33/1, 2, reports by Henry Butter, 1761, 1767; SRO, E786/33/7, 12 Feb. 1774.

28 SRO, E786/33/1, 2.

29 SRO, E723/2, "Answer to the Lords of Treasury," 14 Dec. 1765, 103–6.

30 SRO, E786/13/9, 21 Dec. 1761; also SRO, E786/33/6, 7 Aug. 1773.

31 SRO, E786/33/1, report, Oct. 1761; also SRO, E786/37/2, annotation.

32 SRO, E768/58/5 (2), certificate for Alexander McIntosh.

33 Darling, *Highlands and Islands*, 53, 66–7, 70–1. Youngson, *After the Forty-Five*, 30, 175.

34 The prominent men included Sheriff-substitute George Douglas, Cameron of Fassifern, Cameron of Corryshenrachan, Cameron of Glenpean; and James Glass (advocate), William Stewart, and William McIntosh, all of Fort William; see SRO, E768/13/5/1, 2, McViccar to Alston, 8 Feb. 1753. For destruction by Cameron of Drimnasallie, see SRO, E768/12/8; for appointment of woodkeepers, see SRO, E786/5/3.

35 SRO, E768/35/1–2; SRO, E786/13/13, 2.

36 SRO, E786/11/8, memorial of Mungo Campbell, 1755.

37 SRO, E786/32/7, Campbell to Barons, 26 Dec. 1755.

38 For Lord George Beauclerk, see SRO, E768/17/2 (3), 21 Nov. 1758. For factor, see SRO, E768/16/10, Campbell to Moncrieff, 3 Dec. 1758.

39 SRO, E768/7/1, valuation of Lochiel, 1762.

40 SRO, E768/23/38; SRO, E768/61/2, memorial from Henry Butter, 2 March 1772.

41 SRO, E768/23/14, 7 April 1763; SRO, E768/23/13, 26 March 1763; SRO, E768/-23/12, petition of the tenants of Banavie.

42 For the destruction, see SRO, E768/23/36, 1767; for Butter's report, see SRO, E768/19/8, Butter to Moncrieff, 11 June 1768.

43 SRO, E768/23/19, petition of John Cameron. For Butter's response and Dugal Cameron, see SRO, E768/10/1–2.

CHAPTER FIVE

1 SRO, E741/14/1, memorial of Duncan McDonell, 1783.

2 For population, see Macdonald, "Highland District in 1764," 148–50. For schools, see *OSA*, XVII, Kilmonivaig (1796), 545. Glen Garry forms close to half the parish of Kilmonivaig.

3 SRO, GD44/25/28, undated, unsigned letter quoting McDonell of Greenfield; ibid., estimate of Glengarry's estate (hereafter cited as Estimate). The fact that many of the tenants were McDonells and that only a few Christian names were used makes it impossible to establish definitely the number of tenants. Only in a few instances do the rentals indicate that the tenant of one farm also has another farm.

4 SRO, GD44/25/28, estimate; also ibid., assessment for the Duke of Gordon of the five parts of the Glengarry estate (hereafter cited as Assessment).

5 SRO, GD44/25/28, Estimate; ibid., Assessment.

6 SRO, GD44/25/29, division and arrangement of Knoydart.

7 SRO, GD44/25/28, Assessment.

8 Fraser-Mackintosh, *Antiquarian Notes*, 125.

9 SRO, GD44/25/28, copy of letter from Andrew MacPherson of Benchar to Charles Gordon, Writer to the Signet, 29 Nov. 1768.

10 SRO, GD44/25/29, A. MacPherson to C. Gordon, 23 June 1769.

11 SRO, GD44/25/28, Assessment.

12 Fraser-Mackintosh, *Antiquarian Notes*, 124–6.

13 Cameron of Fassifern, appendix 1 in Robson, *General View of Agriculture*, 53–4.

14 Hunter, *Making of the Crofting Community*, 15.

15 For Butter's recommendation, see SRO, E741/27/11, Butter to Board, 24 March 1766. For results, see SRO, RH2/8/26, "Report of the contents … of Lochiel."

16 *OSA*, VIII, Kilmallie (1793), 427.

17 A discussion of the impact of sheep farming on western Inverness rents is part of the general analysis of rents in the following section of this chapter.

18 For removals, see Fraser-Mackintosh, *Antiquarian Notes*, 127–8; see also SRO, GD128/65/12, "Precept of Removing," 1 April 1785. *OSA*, XVII, Kilmonivaig (1796), 544.

19 SRO, GD128/8/2/80, answers for R. MacDonell, 17 Nov. 1786; SRO, GD128/8/2/38, list of tenants, 1784; and SRO, GD128/7/1/29, letter from R. MacDonell, 30 April 1785. SRO, GD128/7/1/41, letter from R. MacDonell, 30 Nov. 1785; also SRO, GD128/7/2/8, letter from E. MacDonell, 29 June 1788; and *OSA*, XVI Glenelg (1795), 269.

20 Fraser-Mackintosh, *Antiquarian Notes*, 210–11; also *OSA*, VIII, Kilmallie (1793) 424–7. MacMillan, *Bygone Lochaber*, 174–5.

21 SRO, E741/46, 3.

22 Ibid., 21–2.

23 SRO, RH2/8/26, 2.

24 For 1755 wages, see Willis, *Reports*, 51. For 1771 wages, see SRO, E741/46, 10–11. For 1795 wages, see *OSA*, XVI, Glenelg (1795), 273–4. For meal and cattle prices, see Gray, *Highland Economy*, 142, and *OSA*, VIII, Kilmallie (1793), 435.

25 The rent paid by Highland tenants in the first half of the eighteenth century and earlier included a variety of cash payments and services to the landlord. Thus statements of rent vary considerably, depending on whether or not services were converted to cash and then added to the cash rental for a seemingly higher payment.

26 For Lochiel see SRO, E768/1, abstract rental, 1748–9. For Barisdale see SRO, E741/19, rental of Barisdale, crop 1755. For Glengarry see SRO, GD44/25/28, estimate, 1768.

27 SRO, E741/1/1, judicial rental, 1748; SRO, E741/25/1, memorial of Mungo Campbell, 15 March 1756; SRO, E741/19, rental of the estate of Barisdale, crop 1755.

28 SRO, E741/20/4, rental of the annexed estate of Barisdale; SRO, E741/20/6, rental of Barisdale, 1774; and E741/20/8, rental of Barisdale, 1784–5.

29 SRO, E768/1, abstract rental of Lochiel, 1748–9; SRO, E768/13/1, letter from D. McViccar, 23 June 1752; SRO, E786/11/13, memorial of Mungo Campbell, read 20 Feb. 1756.

30 SRO, E768/56/1, rental of Lochiel, 1770; SRO, E768/56/2 (1); SRO, E768/56/4. For failure to collect full rent, see SRO, E723/3.

31 Fraser-Mackintosh, *Antiquarian Notes*, 120–4; SRO, GD44/25/30, rental of Glengarry's Estate, 1779.

32 Fraser-Mackintosh, *Antiquarian Notes*, 120–32; SRO, GD44/25/28, estimate, 1768, and GD44/25/30, rental, 1779.

33 For Scotus see Fraser-Mackintosh, "Macdonells of Scotos," 88. For Barisdale and Lochiel, see Fraser-Mackintosh, *Antiquarian Notes*, 131–2; 208–11. For Lochiel, see Cameron of Lochiel Papers, copy of a letter from D. Cameron to A. McMillan, 23 March 1804.

34 The exact increase of rents is difficult to establish since several old farms were often combined to make the new sheep farms under one of the previous names. The comparative boundaries of old and new farms could not be established from the written record.

35 Fraser-Mackintosh, *Antiquarian Notes*, 131–2.

36 See Thomson, *Introduction to Gaelic Poetry*, 156–7.

CHAPTER SIX

1 Donaldson, *Scots Overseas*, 23.

2 These figures are drawn from the statistics presented in Bailyn's *Voyagers to the West*, 25–6. Since I am only considering emigration from Great Britain and Ireland, I have taken Bailyn's total of 700,000 emigrants between 1600 and 1760 and subtracted the 75,000 German emigrants and 175,000 black slaves from that figure to get a total of 450,000 emigrants from Great Britain and Ireland in that period. Since 210,000 of these emigrants left between 1630 and 1660 alone, the years 1605–30 and 1660–1760 saw an average of some 2,000 emigrants arriving yearly in the first British North America. Bailyn states that 55,000 Irish, 40,000 Scots, and 30,000 English arrived in the fifteen years between 1760 and 1775. This number of Scottish emigrants is somewhat higher than that given either by Flinn (*Scottish Population History*, 443), who believes that emigration rarely averaged much more than 2,000 departures annually, or by Graham (*Colonists from Scotland*, 188), who states that some 20,000 people emigrated from Scotland between 1768 and 1775. Graham's figures cover only half of the period that Bailyn discusses, but those years saw by far the heaviest emigration. Flinn's figures likely underestimate the volume of emigration, since they are drawn principally from official records of departures which seriously underregistered the number of people leaving. For the fears aroused by this level of emigration, see Flinn, *Scottish Population History*, 92, 443.

3 For 1768 to 1775, see Graham, *Colonists from Scotland*, 188. See also Bumsted, *People's Clearance*, 218 and appendix A, Table 2.

4 Rage for emigration seen in Boswell, *Journal of a Tour to the Hebrides*, 132, and the buzz of emigration is quoted in Richards, *Highland Clearances*, II, 206.

5 Bumsted, *People's Clearance*, xv–xvi, 46, 216–20; Richards, *Highland Clearances*, II, 200.

6 See Graham, *Colonists from Scotland*, 70–7, 95; *OSA*, III, Bracadale, quoted in Flinn, *Scottish Population History*, 445; Bumsted, *People's Clearance*, passenger list for the *Sarah*, 250–9.

7 PRO, T1/499, Colin Campbell and Duncan McPhaill to William Nelthorpe, 13 Dec. 1773; Graham, *Colonists from Scotland*, 70–7, 95.

8 Graham gives examples of pre-1775 emigrant streams in *Colonists from Scotland*, 50, 106.

9 Bailyn, *Voyagers to the West*, 103, 119, 127, 133, 140, 206.

10 Ibid., 140, 163, 165–6.

11 Graham, *Colonists from Scotland*, 47–9.

12 There were eight in Aberchalder's family, seven in Collachie's, ten in Leek's, and six in Scotus's. Collachie had seven indentured servants and Aberchalder five. See NA, MG14 AO13/81, 226–7, 289–90.

13 See NA, MG14 AO12/28–31, Highland claimants from New York settled in New Johnston or near the River Raisin. Their claim identifies them as settling in Johnstown in 1773.

14 Grant, *Story of Martintown*, 8–9, 122. Spanish John carried gold from Europe to Scotland to bankroll the Jacobite army. After the money was stolen, he was captured and imprisoned for nine months. Alexander of Aberchalder was an aide-de-camp to Prince Charles. The father of the two Chisholm emigrants was among the Seven Good Men of Glenmoriston who aided Prince Charles in his wanderings across the Highlands after Culloden. Big John Grant, who emigrated with his son Angus in 1773, had served fourteen years in Barbados for his part in the 1745 uprising.

15 NA, MG14 AO12/27, 270–2, Spanish John; ibid., AO13/81, 226–7, Collachie; ibid., 289–90, Aberchalder. John of Leek died c. 1782 and no claim on his behalf was found.

16 NA, MG14 AO12/29, 101–2; ibid., AO12/27, 209–10.

17 PRO, T1/499, 13 Dec. 1773.

18 Boswell, *Journal of a Tour to the Hebrides*, 104.

19 *Canadian Magazine and Literary Repository* 4 (1825): 399.

20 *New York Journal or General Advertiser*, 28 Oct. 1773, extract of a letter from Fort William, Scotland, 20 Aug. 1773, quoted in Bailyn, *Voyagers to the West*, 584.

21 PRO, T1/499, 13 Dec. 1773.

22 Mathews, *Mark of Honour*, 5; *New York Journal or General Advertiser*, 21 Oct. 1773 and *New York Gazette and Weekly Mercury*, 1 Nov. 1773, both quoted in Bailyn, *Voyagers to the West*, 584.

23 Despite a thorough investigation, the reason for the emigrants' choice of New York and in particular of Johnson's lands has not been discovered. Popular tradition suggests that Sir William asked the Macdonells to settle on his estate, but does not explain why this was the case; no documentary evidence has been found to back up this belief. It is possible that the link with Johnson was forged during the New York campaign of the Seven Years' War. Many Highlanders, including perhaps a Macdonell, served as officers, and a knowledge both of the country and of Sir William gained then may have later influenced their choice of destination.

24 Johnson, *Sir William Johnson Papers*, VIII, 916–17.

25 Fraser, "Sir John Johnson's Rent Roll," 181–2, 187. Most of the 1773 emigrants settled on Johnson's land in Kingsborough. A rent roll of this property listing the names of those who received land includes, in a consecutive listing, first the gentlemen who led the 1773 emigration and then another fifty-nine men, all but three having Highland names; all sixty-two men were to begin paying rent on the same day and year, suggesting that they had settled together. Bailyn argues that the largest group of the 1773 emigrants settled further to the south between the Delaware and Susquehanna rivers, but does not discuss the Kingsborough rent roll whose evidence would seem to be conclusive (*Voyagers to the West*, 582–6).

26 Johnson, *Sir William Johnson Papers*, XII, 1111–12.

27 NA, MG14 AO12/27, 270–2. See also Johnson, *Sir William Johnson Papers*, XII, 1111–12. For those who accompanied Spanish John, see Mathews, *Mark of Honour*, appendix A, Roderick Macdonell; also NA, MG14 AO13/14, Alexander Macdonell's claim, 91.

28 NA, MG14 AO12/27, 209–10. A few emigrants reportedly went to St. John, Quebec; see Johnson, *Sir William Johnson Papers*, XII, 1111–12. The identity of these emigrants is unknown, but they were likely drawn from the segment of the 1773 emigrants not led by the Macdonell gentlemen.

29 NA, MG14 AO13/81, 226–7.

30 Ibid. Sir John was Sir William's eldest son and heir, and was named here in mistake for his father.

31 Johnson, *Sir William Johnson Papers*, XII, 1023–4; ibid., VIII, 816.

32 The 1774 emigrants are mentioned in NA, MG14 AO12/28, Roderick Macdonell, 403–4; ibid., AO12/27, John McDonell, 206–7; ibid., AO12/29, John McDonell, 238–9; ibid., Archibald Grant, 77; ibid., Peter Grant, 96; ibid., Donald McGillis, 90; ibid., Duncan Murcheson, 65–6. For Urquhart, see Johnson, *Sir William Johnson Papers*, VII, 1026.

33 Johnson, *Sir William Johnson Papers*, XII, 1023–4; NA, MG11 CO5/1078, fols. 15–16, 2 Nov. 1773, letter from Governor Tryon to Lord Dartmouth (reel B-3808)

34 Johnson, *Sir William Johnson Papers*, VIII, 977.

35 Harkness, *Stormont, Dundas and Glengarry*, 25–31.

36 *Encyclopedia Americana*, I, 25–31.

37 W. Campbell, *Annals of Tryon County*, 30.

38 Mathews, *Mark of Honour*, 32–3.

39 NA, MG14 AO13/81, 289–90, memorial of Alexander McDonell, 14 May 1788.

40 W. Campbell, *Annals of Tryon County*, 33–5.

41 Ibid., 35.

42 NA, MG14 AO13/81, 289–90.

43 Jones, *History of New York*, I, 578.

44 NA, MG14 AO13/81, 289–90.

45 Jones, *History of New York*, I, 580–2. Highland practices of hiding weapons when asked to surrender them easily crossed the Atlantic. The hostages were Allan of Collachie, his brother Alexander of Aberchalder, and four of the former's nephews. See NA, MG14 AO13/81, 226–7, memorial of Allan McDonell, 13 March 1786.

46 Sir William Johnson was superintendent of Indian Affairs from 1755 until his death in 1774; he was succeeded by his nephew, Guy Johnson.

47 Jones, *History of New York*, I, 585–7.

48 Sullivan, *Minutes of the Albany Committee of Correspondence*, I, 410. Clearly the Americans at least contemplated placing the Highlanders and their dependents in concentration camps.

49 NA, MG21 B213, 47–50, memorial of John Macdonell, 14 Dec. 1779.

50 Mathews, *Mark of Honour*, 38.

51 NA, MG14 AO13/81, 289–90.

52 NA, MG21 B158, 34, letter from Major Grey to Carleton, 12 May 1777.

53 John was an ensign and lieutenant in the First Battalion, while Allan served as a captain in the Second Battalion.

54 NA, MG21 B105A, 394, officers, 30 Nov. 1783.

55 Mathews, *Mark of Honour*, 39.

56 Clinton, *Public Papers of George Clinton*, II, 328.

57 Mathews, *Mark of Honour*, 40.

58 Ibid., 42–4.

59 NA, MG21 B162, 135–6, Capt. John McDonell to Major Mathews, 12 Dec. 1783.

60 Mathews, *Mark of Honour*, 42–4.

61 Ibid., 51, 57, 59.

62 Clinton, *Public Papers of George Clinton*, V, 628–32; ibid., VI, 346, letter from Clinton to James Duane, 29 Oct. 1780.

63 Captain John Macdonell was the son of Alexander of Aberchalder. See NA, MG21 B100, 210–1, John McDonell to Major Butler, 24 July 1779.

64 Clinton, *Public Papers of George Clinton*, III, 678, 21 Aug. 1778.

65 Clinton, *Public Papers of George Clinton*, V, 297.

66 For Spanish John, see NA, MG21 B73, 54, John McDonell, 20 March 1780. For petitions from other Loyalists see NA, MG21 B158, 351, memorial of John and Alexander McDonell; ibid., 352, petition of sundry soldiers of KRRNY; NA, MG21 B215, 253–4, petition of Martin Walker, Murdoch McLean, Duncan Murchison, etc.

67 Clinton, *Public Papers of George Clinton*, VI, 452.

68 Mathews, *Mark of Honour*, 98.

69 Clinton, *Public Papers of George Clinton*, V, 769–70.

70 Cameron of Lochiel Papers, Achnacary, Inverness-shire, Scotland, copy of letter from Nancy Jean Cameron to Mrs. Kenneth McPherson, 12 May 1785, Breadalbane, NY.

CHAPTER SEVEN

1 Bumsted, *People's Clearance*, appendix A, tables 2, 3. To Bumsted's figures of 689 + 350 + 1771 Highland emigrants between 1783 and 1793 should be added the 150 people who reached Glengarry in 1792. Thus some 2,951 clansmen emigrated in this eleven-year period. The reader should approach Bumsted's tables with caution since they unfortunately contain typographical and mathematical errors. Two hundred and sixty emigrants did *not* reach Red River between 1776 and 1789 as stated; this figure belongs in the column listing the number of emigrants to reach Nova Scotia, while the 830 emigrants listed as arriving in Nova Scotia actually reached Upper Canada (as Bumsted himself indicates in Table 1, 224). Similarly, the 1,080 clansmen who reached British North America between 1776 and 1789 in Table 3 are likely the (830 plus 260 = 1,090) emigrants who reached Canada and Nova Scotia between the same dates in Table 2.

2 SCA, Blairs Papers, Bishop A. MacDonald, 22 May 1786; ibid., Austin McDonald, 24 April 1786; ibid., James McDonald, 24 June 1785.

3 Ibid., Capt. John McDonald (Glenaladale), 8 Jan. 1785.

4 See Table 6 for the number of emigrants to reach Glengarry between 1785 and 1794; see also Bumsted's *People's Clearance*, appendix A, Table 2.

5 See SCA, Blairs Papers, Bishop A. MacDonald, 4 June 1786, and Flinn, *Scottish Population History*, 428–9. Flinn makes the point that the adoption of the potato imposed a check on emigration. I would argue instead that potato subsistence was sometimes chosen as an alternative to emigration, but that more often it was the recourse of tenants or cottars who were unable to emigrate.

6 SCA, Blairs Papers, Bishop A. MacDonald, 20 April 1789.

7 OSA, XVI, Glenelg (1793) 267 estimates that Knoydart's population in 1793 was 1,000 people. Some 600 people had emigrated from the district between 1785 and 1793, or 38% of the total population.

8 For hardships, see SCA, Blairs Papers, Bishop A. MacDonald, 22 May 1786. For the better circumstances of earlier emigrants (reportedly the case of tenants in Glenelg and Knoydart, but likely true for western Inverness generally), see NSA, IX, Glenelg, 135.

9 *Fighting Men of a ... Jacobite Clan*. Archibald was a captain in the First Battalion of the KRRNY. Allan was a captain-lieutenant in the same unit, and Ranald was a lieutenant in the Second Battalion.

10 AO, Father Ewen J. Macdonald Papers, B-7, box 8, letter from Bishops Hay, MacDonald, and Geddes to Propaganda Fide, 8 Aug. 1785. The original reads: "Questo sacredote avena fatto il giuramento delle Missioni coll' espressa condizione poter andare all' America ...."

11 SCA, Blairs Papers, Bishop A. MacDonald, 10 Aug. 1784.

12 NA, MG11 CO42 Q 24, part. 2, 280.

13 SCA, Blairs Papers, Bishop A. MacDonald, 10 Aug. 1784; ibid., Alexander Macdonald, Sr., Keppoch, 20 April 1784; ibid., Austin McDonald, 24 April 1786.

14 Ibid. Bishop A. MacDonald to John Geddes, 1784 and to Roderick Macdonell, 10 March 1785.

15 NA, MG14 AO13/81, 289–90, memorial of Alexander McDonell. NA, MG11 CO42 Q 24, pt. 2, 280. SCA, Blairs Papers, Roderick Macdonell, 10 Nov. 1785.

16 SCA, Blairs Papers, Roderick Macdonell, 9 June 1784; Bishop A. MacDonald, 5 Aug. 1785.

17 NA, RG19, vol. 4447, parcel 2, no. 7, "Victualling list of emigrants lately Come from scotland by the way of New York and Albany who meaned to settle in this Province[;] Commencing 25th and ending 31 Aug. 1786 Inclusive," hereafter cited as "Emigrants by way of Albany." This list only names 151 emigrants and not the 300 described by Bishop MacDonald. On the other hand Bishop MacDonald's figures for the 1786 emigration are confirmed by the *Quebec Gazette*. It remains uncertain whether the emigrant group never consisted of more than 151 people, whether some emigrants – possibly as many as 149 – failed to receive victuals with their companions, having perhaps left the group at some time during their extended voyage, or whether another list exists to document the missing 149. See note 31, below, for further discussion of this issue of the number of the 1785 emigrants.

18 See chapter 6.

19 SCA, Blairs Papers, Roderick Macdonell, 9 June 1784. The word "country" is used in the sense of district.

20 SRO, GD128/65/12, "Precept of Removing," 1 April 1785.

21 Ibid. See also MacMillan, *Bygone Lochaber*, 89, 236–9.

22 Crofters are, of course, tenants, but this distinct social and economic grouping only emerges in the Highlands after agricultural transformation.

23 NA, RG19, vol. 4447, parcel 2, no. 7, "Emigrants by way of Albany." Grant and McQueen are Glenmoriston names; McIntyre, Fraser, Chisholm, and McTavish are names common in neighbouring Inverness-shire glens. Annie McIntosh could be the widow of Angus McIntosh of Auchlouchiach or another Glengarry tenant.

24 The names of the first two men appear only once on both lists. Two Duncan Kennedys and two John Kennedys are found on the removal decree, but one Duncan and one John Kennedy were again ordered to leave in 1786, so these two were not the emigrants of 1785. Fraser-Mackintosh, *Antiquarian Notes*, 128.

25 NA, RG5 D1, *Upper Canada Gazette*, 20 Jan. 1827, obituary of Allan M'Donald, Esq. The year of M'Donald's emigration is inaccurately given as 1784, but a petition by his son Angus Macdonell of 9 Dec. 1835 refers to this obituary and corrects the date to 1785. MacGillivray 2nd Ross were the first to locate this information in *History of Glengarry*, 10–11. No evidence has been found to show whether Allan held a tenancy before leaving Scotland. Only one Macdonell (John) is listed as a tenant of Inchlaggan in 1785; since a John Macdonell emigrated in 1802, age makes it possible, but not probable, that Allan was his son. Alternatively, Allan may have been a subtenant in Inchlaggan or on some other farm, or one of the 1785 tenants of Laggan or Auchlouchiach may have been named Allan Macdonell.

26 NA, MG9/D7/6 microfilm reel C-3029, parish register of St. Raphael's, 15 Dec. 1826, 520. This identification of Bishop Alexander Macdonell of Kingston as the brother of Allan Macdonell, leader of the 1785 party, is based on notes in George Sandfield Macdonald's oral history of Glengarry. Sandfield Macdonald names Squire Allan Macdonell as one of the 1787 emigrants by way of Albany (NA, MG29 C29, notebook with first page blank, interview with Captain Grey). The date (1787) is an error for 1785, as will be shown in the following pages. George Sandfield Macdonald also refers to Squire Allan as the bishop's brother (ibid., notebook, Family II). The obituary of Squire Allan Macdonell that appears in the *Upper Canada Gazette* names Allan as leader of the 1785 emigration (see note 24, above) and was written by Bishop Macdonell (MacGillivray and Ross, *History of Glengarry*, 10).

27 SCA, Blairs Papers, Bishop A. MacDonald, 5 Aug. 1785, 22 May 1786.

28 NA, RG1 L3, Upper Canada Land Petitions (UCLP), M4 (1789–99), no. 118, John McDonell, and no. 211, Alexander MacDonald (reel C-2193); ibid., M5 (1800–01), no. 100 Ranald McDonell (reel C-2194); ibid., Mc. Misc. (1788–95), no. 41d, Alexander McDonell (reel C-2188) ibid., M11 (1812–18), no. 176, Lt. Angus McDonell (reel C-2199); ibid., Mc Misc. (1788–95), no. 88, Alexander McIntosh (reel C-2189). It is not at all clear that the 1785 or 1786 emigrants ever petitioned the governor for land, and thus it is not surprising that the few petitions found for the 1785 emigrants postdate the first acquisition of land. All the petitions referred to here are requests for land between 1790 and 1817, some years after emigration. Three petitioners specifically describe themselves as sons of 1785 emigrants.

29 The quote is taken from Alexander McDonell's petition, no. 41d (see note 28, above). The other petition (no. 176) mentioning a group emigration was that of Lt. Angus McDonell, son of the leader Allan Macdonell; see note 28.

30 NA, RG5 D1, *Upper Canada Gazette*, 20 Jan. 1827.

31 It seems implausible that Bishop Macdonell would claim that not a single person remained in the United States but rather that all settled in Glengarry, if as many as 150 people had separated from the group that did reach Glengarry. It is possible that some emigrants stayed in the United States and that others sought work in Montreal rather than overwhelm the resources of the Loyalist community, which was barely two years old. George Sandfield Macdonald's list of emigrants indicates that a certain number lived elsewhere before rejoining the Highland community in Glengarry. Bruce Elliot has also noticed a tendency for emigrant groups to fracture under the stresses of the journey; see his *Irish Migrants in the Canadas*, 66.

32 Pope, "Scotch catholic settlement in Canada," 73–4. Pope gives no reference for her material. There is no suggestion that she has family connections in Glengarry, but there is an indication that she visited the county.

33 NA, MG29 C29, notebook, Family I, "Interview with Misses Lachlan McD.," Jan. 1884. St. Raphael's is the oldest Roman Catholic parish in Glengarry County located in the centre of the 1785–6 emigrants' settlement. "The old man" must have been a resident of the village about the church or in the general neighbourhood.

34 Ibid., Family II, interview with Captain Grey; ibid., notebook with blank first page, interview with Captain Grey.

35 Ibid., Family II, "John Macdonald, 71 in March 1884": "Miss Pope's account of the 2 ships in 86 is correct." Ibid., notebook with list beginning "Donald Sutherland," interview with J.R. McGillis.

36 MacGillivray, *Shadow of Tradition*, 19–25, 65–6, 81–2, 92–6, 98–104.

37 Ibid., author's preface.

38 There are three possible reasons: (1) they had intended to land in an American port; (2) bad weather forced them so far south that it seemed sensible to land at an American port; or (3) bad weather forced a refit at Belfast or another British port, which, when added to a seventeen-week passage, brought them across the Atlantic after the St. Lawrence was closed by ice in late November. Of these the first seems unlikely just after the war's end and the second is not quite convincing since seventeen weeks, without a refit, would have them on the western side of the Atlantic by mid-October, before the St. Lawrence's closing.

39 Great Britain. War Office. *A List of Officers of the Army* (hereafter cited

as *Army List*) (1786), 107, Lt. F. DeChambault, 27 May 1783; Stewart, *The Service of British Regiments*, 208; NA, MG21 B76, 180.

40 Macdonell, *Sketches ... of Glengarry in Canada*, 127; Harkness, *Stormont, Dundas and Glengarry*, 50.

41 Cowan, *British Emigration to British North America*, 16–18. Cowan refers to the 1790 emigrants joining kinsmen who had settled in Canada in 1785 and 1786. Her source is not evident in NA, MG11 CO42/82 council minutes, 11 Jan. 1791. Cowan discusses the 1786 emigration in some detail but names no other emigration in the 1780's, so it seems unlikely that she realized there was a separate migration in 1785.

42 MacGillivray and Ross, *History of Glengarry*, 10–11.

43 Bishop MacDonald reported on 22 May 1786 that there was "a numerous emigration ready to take shipping in Knoydart of upwards of 500 souls, all Catholics"; see SCA, Blairs Papers. The *Quebec Gazette* announced the arrival of the *McDonald* with 10 cabin passengers and 520 steerage passengers; see NA, RG4 D1, *Quebec Gazette*, 7 Sept. 1786.

44 NA, RG4 A1, 9909–15, copy of letter from Brig. Gen. Hope to Lt. Angus McDonell, 25 Sept. 1786 (reel C-3001). Hope dealt with McDonell regarding the provisioning of the 1786 emigrants and expected McDonell and two others to take responsibility for repayment. See also NA, RG1 L3, UCLP, Mc Misc. (1788–95) no. 44 (reel C-2188).

45 NA, MG29 C29, notebook beginning Donald Sutherland, interview with J.R. McGillis, question 2.

46 On 14 April 1786, Ranald McDonell of Scotus wrote that Angus Ban was going to Canada; see SRO, GD128/8/1/5. This naming of Angus Ban is suggestive of his prominence in Knoydart. The factor of the Annexed Estates had earlier identified Angus Ban as an improving farmer; see SRO E741/31/2/2, report by Henry Butter. Angus Ban's great-great-granddaughter, Mrs. Florence Macdonell, confirmed his leadership of the 1786 emigrants in an interview in Sept. 1977. One of the Sandfield Macdonald notebooks states that "Col. James' father was a leading man." Colonel James was the youngest son of Angus Ban of Muniall; see NA, MG29 C29, notebook, Family I, from R.S., question 2.

47 The estates of Barisdale and Glengarry were reunited in 1784 when the forfeiture to the Crown was lifted from Barisdale and it was returned to Glengarry and not to its wadsetter, Barisdale. But the two estates are considered separately in this section since they are geographically separate districts and their divergent administration between 1748 and 1784 may have affected later development.

48 SRO, GD128/7/1/14, letter from Ranald McDonell, 1 May 1784; SRO, E741/20/8, rental of Barisdale 1784–85; ibid., rental of Barisdale 1774; NA, RG19, vol. 4447, "List of sundry persons as Emigrants from North

Britain who were located by Mr. James McDonell in the township of Lancaster & Charlottenburgh in the years 1786 & 1787" (hereafter referred to as "Sundry Persons"). See also NA, MG29 C29, Sandfield Macdonald's list of 1786 emigrants, Samuel Macdonell.

49 For a list of Scotus's tenants, see SRO, GD128/8/2/38. For the 1786 emigrants, see NA, RG19, vol. 4447, "Sundry Persons." John Roy is named as an emigrant from Shenachadh in AO, Father Ewen J. Macdonald Collection, B-1-14, box 6, envelope 2, and C-1-2, box 8, History of St. Raphaels, 17.

50 SRO, GD128/7/1/45, R. McDonell to A. Macdonald, 13 Feb. 1786.

51 The original reads: "Has quidem emigrationes nos impedire non possumus, sed multum damni Missionibus nostris allaturas, imo jam attulisse, videmus. Nam, qui emigrant illi plerumque sunt qui paulo erant locupletiores, et apud quos Missionarri in Apostolicis suis itineribus poterant hospitari ...." See AO, Father Ewen J. Macdonald Collection, B-7, box 8, two extracts from an apostolic letter of Bishops Hay, MacDonald, and Geddes, 28 July 1786.

52 NA, RG1 L3, UCLP, M5 (1800–01), no. 81 (reel C-2194). McDonell was applying for more land on the basis of being a reduced lieutenant, and not on the number of families he had brought to Canada.

53 NA, RG4 A1, 9909–15, copy of letter from John Craigie to Stephen Delancey, 4 Sept. 1786 (reel C-3001). 52 families seems much too low when compared to Sandaig's figure of 100.

54 Duncan McMillan, Corriebuie, comments in his land petition of 1817 that he came to Canada in 1786 but lived in Terrebonne for several years before coming to Glengarry, c. 1792. See NA, RG1 L3, UCLP, M11 1811–9), no. 302 (reel C-2200). In George S. Macdonald's list of 1786, Duncan McMillan and his father Alexander are said to have gone first to Terrebonne, as had John McGillis, Donald McGillis and John McPhee; see NA, MG29 C29, list. Both Duncan McMillan and his wife and his sister Anne and her husband had children in Terrebonne; see Masson, *Genealogie des familles de Terrebonne*, III, 1740.

55 NA, MG29 C29, list of emigrants.

56 Information regarding the McMillans was obtained from Mary Beaton of Ottawa, genealogist and descendant of Alexander McMillan. Information concerning John Roy was provided by Alexander Fraser, president of the Glengarry Genealogical Society. He possesses a chart of the family tree of the Macdonalds of Loup to which John and Angus belonged.

57 SCA, Blairs Papers, Alexander McDonell, 21 Nov. 1785; NA, MG29 C29, notebook with first page blank, 92, interview with James Duncan Macdonald.

58 An interview with Mrs. Florence Macdonell (Sept. 1977) provided

information concerning Angus Ban. Personal family genealogies were well known in Highland society and relationships as distant as fourth cousin were recognized as close family ties. Unfortunately the surviving records rarely make use of the patronymics that would enable us to reconstruct the dense kinship pattern, which characterized western Inverness communities and, therefore, the emigrant parties.

59 NA, MG29 C29, list. In the 1786 list John Buie Macdonald was described as married to Bishop Macdonell's sister and hence was brother-in-law to Allan. Information on the Roy Macdonalds comes from an interview with Alexander Fraser, Charlottenburgh Township, Glengarry County.

60 Interview with Mrs. Florence Macdonell; SCA, Blairs Papers, Alexander McDonell, Sandfield, 21 Nov. 1785.

61 SRO, GD128/7/1/14, R. McDonell, 1 May 1784.

62 See chapter 5.

63 SRO, GD128/7/1/14, R. McDonell, 1 May 1784.

64 SRO, GD128/7/1/39, R. McDonell, 26 Nov. 1785; GD128/7/1/41, R. McDonell, 30 Nov. 1785; GD128/7/1/45, R. McDonell, 13 Feb. 1786.

65 SRO, GD128/8/2/38, list of tenants to be removed, 1784; GD128/7/1/29, R. McDonell, 30 April 1785. The emigrants were Father Alexander McDonell (Inveriebeg), John Macdougall and Neil Campbell (Scothouse), James McKay (Glendulochan), and John Macdougall, piper (North Kinlochlochan).

66 SCA, Blairs Papers, A. Macdonell, 14 July 1785 and A. Macdonell, 6 Oct. 1785.

67 Ibid., Bishop MacDonald, 22 May 1786, and A. Macdonell, 21 Nov. 1785.

68 SCA, Blairs Papers, Alexander McDonell, Scothouse, 19 April 1784.

69 SRO, GD128/8/1/3, Charles McDonell, 1 April 1786; SRO, GD128/8/1/4, R. Macdonell, 1 April 1786; SCA, Blairs Papers, Bishop A. MacDonald, 12 June 1786; NA, MG29 C29, "Notebook ... Donald Sutherland," J.R. McGillis, 2.

70 SCA, Blairs Papers, Bishop A. MacDonald, 12 June 1786.

71 Ibid. See also ibid., Alex. MacDonald, Keppoch, 23 May 1786.

72 "Oran" of Iain MacDhomhnuil, printed copy from scrapbook owned by John J. McLeod, Glen Nevis, Glengarry County. The original reads *"Sann air maduin Didomhnich/Rinn sinn seladh bho thir/Air long mhor nan tri chranac/S'air sagairt pareisde linn/Rinn e fhein an ard-urnuigh/Ri Righ nan Dal ga air dian/S'ris an aingeal Rafael/Air eur sabhailt gu tir."* This text contains errors of spelling and grammar which indicate that the scribe was not a master of written Gaelic.

73 Ibid., The original reads: *"Nuair a ghluais sinn bho challa/Bha moran gal ann s'caoidh/...Nuair chuir i cul ris a'n fhearan/S'na suil gheala ri crainn."*

74 NA, MG29 C29, notebook, Family I, R. S. (Ranald Sandfield, uncle to the author of the notebook), no. 2. In MacGillivray's *Shadow of Tradition*, the chief characters, the Kennedys, are dogged by bad luck because of the curse of "am Fitheach Dubh." There is no indication if this element of the story is derived from oral tradition, perhaps from the story of John McGinnis or a similar tale of the voyage.

75 NA, RG4 A1, 9909–15, Hope to Lt. McDonell, 25 Sept. 1786, and Craigie to Delancey, 4 Sept. 1786 (reel C-3001).

76 NA, MG29 C29, notebook, Family I, R.S., no. 2.

77 AO, Father Ewen J. Macdonald, C-1-2, box 8, History of St. Raphaels, 17, Father John's family history.

78 AO, Father Ewen J. Macdonald, B-7, box 8. The original reads: "... Ferme omnes exituri erant." Taken from one of two extracts from the bishops' letter of 28 July 1786.

79 The emigrants informed the colonial authorities that they had come to Canada on the invitation of their friends; see NA, RG4 A1, 9909–15, letter of 4 Sept. 1786 (reel C-3001). Lt. Angus McDonell, Sandaig, Capt. John Macdonell, Aberchalder, and his cousin Macdonell of Leek all visited the Highlands after 1783.

80 Information concerning the 1790 passengers is, unless otherwise stated, taken from the passenger list of the *British Queen*, the only pre-1800 passenger list to survive for the Glengarry County settlers. It is found in NA, MG11 CO42/71, 82 (reel B-48). For the vicissitudes affecting the 1790 emigrants, see the account of the migration itself which follows an analysis of the composition of the emigrant party.

81 Clanranald's estate included South Uist (nine emigrants), Eigg (thirty-two), Arisaig (five), and Moidart (four), while Glengarry's included Glen Garry (eleven), Knoydart (four), and (before 1768) North Morar (eleven). Like Glengarry, Clanranald had raised rents (see SCA, Blairs Papers, Norman Macdonald, 23 April 1791) and introduced some sheep farming (see SCA, Blairs Papers, James McDonald, 27 April 1791).

82 NA, RG4 A1, 15916–8, "Report to Lord Dorchester of the Committee appointed to look into the Emigrants lately arrived from Scotland," 31 Oct. 1790 (reel C-3006).

83 Ibid., 9909–15, letter from Craigie (reel C-3001). The other twelve surnames of the seventeen families were McAulay, McKinnon, McMillan, Gilles, McCormick, McKay, Fraser, Campbell, McCraw, McDougall, McLellan, and Henderson.

84 Ibid., 15916–8, report to Dorchester (reel C-3006). The report states that all the emigrants were tenants except four men: two smiths, a taylor, and a joiner. The passenger list for the *British Queen* (see NA, MG11 CO42/71, 82) lists only the first three of these; perhaps the joiner

was principally a farmer. Servants were generally people of lower social and economic status in Highland society; however, the children of tenants sometimes worked as servants, usually in the houses of the gentry, where a wider experience might be gained.

85 SCA, Blairs Papers, James MacDonald, 12 Oct. 1790, and Bishop A. MacDonald, 5 March 1790.

86 NA, RG4 A1, 15917, report to Dorchester (reel C-3006).

87 SCA, Blairs Papers, James MacDonald, 12 Oct. 1790.

88 Ibid., Bishop A. MacDonald, 5 March 1790.

89 There is no indication of who the "malicious people" that gave information were; one wonders if some landlord, sorely threatened by an overly large loss of tenants and labour, was responsible. See ibid., James MacDonald, 12 Oct. 1790.

90 Bumsted, *People's Clearance*, 238–41, passenger lists for the *Jane* and *Lucy*.

91 SCA, Blairs Papers, Bishop A. MacDonald, 5 March 1790.

92 NA, MG11 CO42/71, 82, list of passengers per *British Queen* (reel B-48).

93 Ibid. 83–4, first petition of Miles Macdonell.

94 Ibid., 84–5 second petition of Miles Macdonell, 20 Oct. 1790.

95 NA, RG4 A1, 15916–8, report to Dorchester (reel C-3006).

96 NA, MG11 CO42/72, 57–8, Dorchester to Grenville, 10 Nov. 1790 (reel B-48).

97 NA, MG23 GIII 5, vol. 1, 269–72, petition, Montreal, 6 Nov 1790.

98 For John Ban McGillis, see NA, RG1 L3, UCLP, M13 (1816–22), no. 131 (reel C-2203). For Morrison's report and later aid, see NA, MG23 GIII 5, vol. 2, 576–7.

99 NA, MG29 C29, notebook with blank first page, James Duncan Macdonald.

100 SRO, GD44/25/28, "Estimate of Glengarry's Estate made out by Mr. MacDonald Younger of Greenfield in December 1768."

101 Fraser-Mackintosh, *Antiquarian Notes*, 124–5.

102 NA, MG30 C22, address by A. McLean Macdonell to UEL Association, 14 Feb. 1924: Family history of Col. John Macdonell, Greenfield. In 1792 Alexander Greenfield's brother-in-law, John Macdonell of Aberchalder, had just been elected Member of the Legislative Assembly and Speaker of the first House of Assembly in the new Province of Upper Canada.

103 Macdonell, *Sketches ... of Glengarry in Canada*, 131.

104 Clan MacLeod, *MacLeods of Glengarry*, 59.

105 SCA, Blairs Papers, Ranald MacDonald, 16 July 1792.

106 MacMillan, *Bygone Lochaber*, 72–3. See also NA, RG1 L3, UCLP, M4 (1793–9), no. 200 (reel C-2193).

107 NA, RG1 L4, vol.15, 6 (reel C-14028). A comparison of the dates of land

grants and of the arrival of emigrants reveals that those who arrived in the autumn of one year generally received land that winter or the following spring. Thus the names of the 1790 emigrants appear in a December 1790 list of applicants who were granted land; see NA, RG1 L4, vol.10, 107a.

108   AO, Father Ewen J. Macdonald Collection, A-3-2, genealogical notes; these state that Greenfield and Glenpean emigrated together. While the ship *Unity* is the only vessel reportedly carrying Highland emigrants (*Quebec Gazette*, 27 Sept. 1792), the brig *Jane* did arrive from Fort William, the emigrants' reported port of departure, a week after the *Unity* (*Quebec Gazette*, 4 Oct. 1792). It seems unlikely that a vessel from Fort William would come to Canada without emigrants; it is possible that Glenpean and Greenfield chartered two vessels.

109   For the chairman's order, see AO, RG1 A-1-1, vol. 49, 88, Richard Duncan, 6 Nov. 1792. For the list of applicants, see NA, RG1 L4, vol.15, 1–6 (reel C-14028); the 36 consecutive emigrants from Scotland listed on pp. 1 and 2 are likely members of the 1792 party, with the exception of the non-Highlander Edward Williams (no. 36) and Lauchlin Campbell (no. 2); the latter had emigrated in 1790. See NA, MG11 CO42/71, 82, list of emigrants (reel B-48).

110   Clan MacLeod, *MacLeods of Glengarry*, 29, 35–6, 58. In 1837, Alexander McLeod (son of Kenneth) claimed that he had brought 150 emigrants from Glenelg, Glenmoriston, Strathglass, and Knoydart; his son John McLeod told J.A. Macdonell that there were forty families in the party. See Macdonell, *Sketches ... of Glengarry in Canada*, 133.

111   AO, Crown Land Department, Locations in the Eastern District, 1794, C-1-4, vol. 9. Of the two other clansmen to receive land on this date, Neil McKinnon was a son of Lauchlin McKinnon from the 1790 group (interview with L.R. McLean), while Donald McDougall may have been part of the 1793 group or the younger son of a 1786 emigrant.

112   See NA, RG1 L3, UCLP, C2 (1796–7), no. 2, Donald Campbell (reel C-1647); ibid., M Misc. (1792–1816), no. 21, Kenneth McLennan (reel C-2189); ibid., M11 (1808–17), no. 80, Alexander McLennan (reel C-2199); ibid., C2 (1796–7) no. 2, (reel C-1647).

113   Clan MacLeod, *MacLeods of Glengarry*, 37, 63–4, 66.

114   *OSA*, XVI, Glenelg, 265–74.

115   Ibid., *NSA*, IX, Glenelg, 135–6.

116   NA, RG1 L3, UCLP, Mc21 (1837–39), no. 46 (reel C-2139), (quoted in Clan MacLeod, *MacLeods of Glengarry*, 58–60.)

117   Clan MacLeod, *MacLeods of Glengarry*, 27, 37–8, 58–9.

118   For the *Simon Gallon*, see *Quebec Gazette*, 5 June 1794. One week later

the *Quebec Gazette* reported that a second schooner from Prince Edward Island had landed with forty-two passengers, probably the remainder of the McLeod party. This conclusion is contrary to McLeod's statement more than forty years later that only one schooner was hired and carried "all" his emigrants to Quebec; see NA, RG1 L3, UCLP, Mc21 (1837–39), no. 46 (reel C-2139). Since McLeod himself claimed to have brought 150 emigrants to Canada, the 115 and 42 passengers in the two schooners were all likely members of his party. An unidentified source in Clan MacLeod, *MacLeods of Glengarry* (37–8) states that two vessels were hired in Prince Edward Island.

119 NA, RG4 A3, vol. 3, no. 19. Kenneth McLeod (Capt. Alexander's father) petitioned on behalf of his own family and 93 other individuals. This is less than the 115 named by the *Quebec Gazette* or the 150 stated in the petition of 1837. See also Clan MacLeod, *MacLeods of Glengarry*, 59.

120 MacTaggart, *Three Years in Canada*, I, 193.

121 This claim goes back to Margaret Adams's argument in "The Causes of Highland Emigration, 1783–1803" (p. 83) that sheep farming was of minimal importance in causing emigration in this period. Eric Richards also downplays sheep farming as a cause of emigration (*Highland Clearances*, II, 195–6, 217), while J.M. Bumsted argues that emigrants of this period falsely blamed their emigration on clearances for sheep as a psychological balm for their guilt in leaving the Highlands (*People's Clearance*, 220).

122 Selkirk, *Observations*, 52.

123 SCA, Blairs Papers, Alexander McDonell, 19 April 1784.

CHAPTER EIGHT

1 SCA, Blairs Papers, Ranald McDonald, 23 June 1789.

2 Ibid., Alexander Macdonald, Sr., 8 May 1792.

3 Ibid., Archibald McRa, 4 March 1794; *NSA*, IX, Glenelg, 136.

4 Fraser-Mackintosh, *Antiquarian Notes*, 134–5.

5 Selkirk, *Observations*, 71.

6 SCA, Blairs Papers, Alexander McDonell, 12 Feb. 1794. The author later served as chaplain to the Glengarry Fencible Regiment, emigrated to Canada, and became the first Bishop of Kingston.

7 The declaration of war in 1793 caught Britain desperately short of trained soldiers; fencible regiments, which were created in the place of militia in Scotland, helped solve this problem. See Fortescue, *History of the British Army*, IV, part 1, 83.

8 SCA, Blairs Papers, Alexander McDonell, 12 Feb. 1794. Such words seem typical of the man Walter Scott dramatized as Fergus MacIvor, the Jacobite hero of his novel *Waverley*.

9 MacWilliam, "The Glasgow Mission, 1792–1799," 87–8.

10 SCA, Blairs Papers, Alexander McDonell, 12 May 1794. See also Fortescue, *History of the British Army*, V, 943.

11 Prebble, *Mutiny*, 303–13.

12 SRO, GD51/1/844/3, copy of a letter to Colonel MacDonell, 27 Oct. 1794.

13 SCA, Blairs Papers, Alexander McDonell, 12 Feb. 1794.

14 SRO, GD51/1/844/3, copy of a letter of Colonel MacDonell, 27 Oct. 1794.

15 Fraser-Mackintosh, *Letters of Two Centuries*, 327–8.

16 SCA, Blairs Papers, Charles Maxwell, 10 June 1803; ibid., Bishop Chisholm, 1 Aug. 1802.

17 Hunter, *Making of the Crofting Community*, 19, 22.

18 Great Britain. Parliament. House of Commons. *Parliamentary Papers* (hereafter cited as *Parliamentary Papers*), 1802–3, V, appendix A, 40, emigrant vessels reported by a customs collector in North Scotland, 1801; ibid., 38, 28 March 1803, statement of committee set up to consider emigration by the Highland Society; ibid., 39, extract from evidence of James Grant; SCA, Blairs Papers, Charles Maxwell, 8 June 1803.

19 Cowan, *British Emigration to British North America*, 29.

20 SCA, Blairs Papers, Bishop Chisholm, 25 Jan. 1802.

21 SRO, RH2/4/87, fol. 151, letter from A. Macdonell, 21 March 1802.

22 SCA, Blairs Papers, Chisholm, 3 April 1802.

23 SRO, RH2/4/87, fol. 151, 21 March 1802.

24 *Parliamentary Papers*, 1802–3, IV, appendix A, 41. See also *Quebec Gazette*, 16 Sept. 1802, letter of thanks given to Captain Boyd by his passengers, Quebec, 29 Aug. 1802.

25 *Parliamentary Papers*, 1802–3, IV, appendix A, 41. See also SRO census of Inverness-shire (1811), Answers to questions with the Census; 300 people were reported to have left Glenelg parish (Knoydart, North Morar, and Glenelg) in 1802 for America.

26 I have concluded that virtually all emigrants to Glengarry County from the west coast of the Highlands in 1802 came on board the *Neptune*. The passenger list for the three vessels chartered by McMillan gives no west coast points of origin for his emigrants.

27 NA, MG29 C29, notebook, Family II, list, 1–26, "Interview with Alick Allan Ban in the Glen, Mch. 84," list of 1802 settlers. Ibid., "Interview with John Macdonald, 71, Mch. 84," no. 2. See also McLennan, "Early Settlement of Glengarry," 113–21. McGillivray, Morrison, and McCuaig are all names common in Glenelg; McGillivray rented land

from Norman McLeod, a prominent 1793 Glenelg emigrant. See NA, RG1 L3, UCLP, M13 (1821), nos. 12 and 13 (reel C-2203).

28 NA, RG1 L3, UCLP, M9 (1804–11), no. 122 (reel C-2196).

29 NA, MG29 C29, notebook, Family II, list 1–26, interviews with Alick Allan Ban and John Macdonald.

30 See chapter 7.

31 AO, Father Ewen John Macdonald, C-1-2, box 8, typescript, copy of letter from Angus McDonald to Roderick McDonald, 14 Oct. 1804. The author was John Rory's son.

32 McLennan, " Early Settlement of Glengarry." 118–19.

33 AO, Father Ewen J. Macdonald, C-1-2, box 8, letter dated 14 Oct. 1804. The recipient could not resist the plea, and he too emigrated to Glengarry County some time before 1823.

34 *Quebec Gazette*, 25 Aug. 1802.

35 Ibid., 16 Sept. 1802, quoting letter of 29 Aug. 1802.

36 Ibid., 30 Sept. 1802.

37 *Parliamentary Papers*, 1802–3, IV, 41.

38 Selkirk, *Diary*, 220. In his *History of Huntingdon, Chateauguay and Beauharnois*, 48–9, Robert Sellar mentions these families who settled on Johnson's land in Chambly.

39 Selkirk, *Diary*, 199. Selkirk refers to the arrival of 170 families in 1802; these included the McMillan emigrants as well.

40 MacMillan, *Bygone Lochaber*, 66–79.

41 NA, RG1 L3L, Lower Canada Land Petitions (LCLP), 66478, petition of Archibald McMillan, 6 Aug. 1804 (reel C-2545).

42 Manuscript list found in NA, MG24 I183, 7–9. I have added to the list the families of the leaders of the voyage. Allan McMillan of Glenpean and Archibald McMillan of Murlaggan.

43 Bailyn, *Voyagers to the West*, 127–33.

44 Ibid., 140–5. The McMillan emigration most closely resembles Bailyn's Perthshire emigrants, 78% of whom travelled in families, which averaged 6.0 people. In contrast, 54% of his Highlands–Hebrides contingent was composed of families, which averaged 4.6 people.

45 MacMillan, *Bygone Lochaber*, 176–7, 73–5, 86–9.

46 NA, MG24 I183, Account Book, Voyage to America, 44–5; see also RG1 L3L, LCLP, 66477, petition of Archibald McMillan, 6 Aug. 1804 (reel C-2545).

47 Selkirk, *Observations*, 144.

48 NA, MG24 I183, 34, 73; also "List of emigrants with the Amount of their Bills," 11.

49 NA, MG24 I183, 35, 73.Children's fares were proportional to age. Two- to four-year-olds travelled for one-eighth of a full fare; four- to six-year-olds for one-quarter; six- to eight-year-olds for one-half; and eight- to

twelve-year-olds for three-quarters. For the purpose of a rough estimate, I have assumed that this worked out to the equivalent of a one-half fare for all children.

50 Ibid., typescript of an agreement between the owners of the *Friends* and Archibald McMillan, 34.

51 *Quebec Gazette*, 5 and 15 Sept. 1802.

52 NA, MG24 I183, 34; ibid., case in Montreal, 23 Sept. 1802, 36–8; ibid., letterbook, Archibald McMillan to Duncan Cameron, 30 September 1803. See also Selkirk, *Diary*, 199.

53 SCA, Blairs Papers, Charles Maxwell, 8 June 1803.

54 NA, MG24 I183, letterbook, McMillan to Duncan Cameron, 30 Sept. 1803.

55 Selkirk, *Observations*, 72.

56 Hunter in his *Making of the Crofting Community*, 24–5, made the very convincing connection between landlord self-interest and the Passenger Act of 1803.

57 *Parliamentary Papers*, 1802–3, IV, appendix A, 35–8; SRO, RH2/4/87, fols. 151–2, letter from A. Macdonell, 21 March 1802.

58 SRO, RH2/4/89, fols. 140–3, letter from Charles Hope, 3 Sept. 1804.

59 Hunter, *Making of the Crofting Community*, 25; MacMillan, *Bygone Lochaber*, 181, letter from Allan Cameron, 1 July 1803.

60 NA, MG24 J13, Rt. Rev. Alexander Macdonell, Bishop of Kingston, "The Glengarry Highlanders," 28.

61 SCA, Blairs Papers, Alexander MacDonell, 24 Oct. 1803.

62 NA, MG29 C29, notebook, Family II, list 1–26, interview with James Duncan Macdonald, 2.

63 NA, RG1 L3, UCLP, C8 (1806–8), no. 5 (reel C-1650). They are not found on Murlaggan's list of 1802 emigrants.

64 NA, MG24 J13, letters of Rev. Alexander MacDonell, 8. See also SCA, Blairs Papers, Bishop Chisholm, 29 April 1802.

65 NA, RG5 A1, Upper Canada Sundries (UCS), 9050, Macdonell to Bathurst, 20 Dec. 1814 (reel C-4544).

66 NA, RG7 G1 vol. 54, 93–4, Hobart to Hunter, 1 March 1803.

67 NA, RG1 L3, UCLP, M8 (1806–7), no. 14, Rev. Alexander McDonell; (reel C-2195); SCA, Blairs Papers, Charles Maxwell, 8 June 1803.

68 NA, RG1 L3, UCLP, M8 (1806–7), no. 14, Rev. Alexander McDonell (reel C-2195).

69 NA, RG5 A1, UCS, 9052, Macdonell to Bathurst, 20 Dec. 1814 (reel C-4544).

70 The chaplain is very evasive on the question of how many of the Glengarry Fencibles came to Canada; see MacGillivray and Ross, *History of Glengarry*, 15. Harkness in his county history (p. 522) reports that the men all emigrated in 1802–03. MacGillivray and Ross correctly point out that only a minority of the fencibles actually came to

Canada, but they err in assuming that almost none of these did settle in Glengarry and vicinity. See AO, Township Papers for concessions 7–9 of Charlottenburgh, as well as the Indians Lands (lot 14 of concession 11 and lot 13 of concession 7).

71 SCA, Blairs Papers, Alexander MacDonell, 16 July 1803; NA, RG1 L3, UCLP, C8 (1806–08), no. 5. (reel C-1650).

72 NA, RG1 L1, Land Book L (1821–24) vol. 30, 9 July 1823, petition of the reduced soldiers of the First Glengarry Fencibles. For Angus McDonald, see NA, RG1 L3, UCLP, M13 (1816–24), no. 275 (reel C-2204); for Angus McLachlan, see ibid., M10 (1807–11), no. 30 (reel C-2197); for Ewen Kennedy, see NA, RG5 A1, UCS, 6490–3 (reel C-4508). Kennedy was one of twenty-nine petitioners who asked, unsuccessfully, for special assistance to emigrate in 1815 when the Colonial Office gave some help to emigrants going to Canada. His departure must therefore have been after that date; see NA, MG11 CO42 Q135, part 2, 355A, list of would-be emigrants). For Sergeant Roderick McDonald, see AO, Father Ewen John Macdonald, C-1-2, box 8, Angus McDonald to Roderick McDonald, 14 Oct. 1804, and NA, RG1 L1, Land Book L (1821–24) vol. 30, 9 July 1823, petition of Glengarry Fencibles (reel C-103).

73 In letters written to Bishop Cameron immediately before his departure the chaplain mentions no travelling companions, and it is clear that his sailing on 23 August was based on a last-minute arrangement – hardly possible if he were leading a group. See SCA, Blairs Papers, Alexander MacDonell, 15 Aug., 22 Aug. and 3 Sept. 1804.

74 Interview with Alex Fraser, August 1977; see also Forbes and Anderson, "Clergy Lists of the Highland District," 160, and Macdonell, *Sketches ... of Glengarry in Canada*, 322.

75 For the last ship, see SCA, PL2/31/16, Alexander Macdonell to Margaret Fraser, 30 Aug. 1804. For "Scotland has few claims to my regards or attachment now," see SCA, PL2/29/9, Alexander Macdonell to Mrs. MacDonell Scothouse, 9 Dec. 1803 and SCA, PL2/29/6, Alexander Macdonell to Miss Fraser Culbokie, 26 Aug. 1803.

76 SCA, PL2/29/6, Alexander Macdonell to Miss Fraser Culbokie, 26 Aug. 1803.

77 SCA, PL2/31/15, Alexander Macdonell to Mrs. MacDonell Scothouse, 16 July 1804.

78 Prebble, *Mutiny*, 445.

79 SRO, RH2/4/89 fols. 140–3, Home Office Correspondence, Scotland, Hope to Lord Advocate, 3 Sept. 1803. For Glenelg recruits, see SRO, census, Inverness-shire: answers to questions with the census, 1811, Glenelg.

80 SCA, Blairs Papers, Ann McDonald, 13 Aug. 1804.

81 SRO, RH2/4/89 fols. 140–3, Hope to Lord Advocate, 3 Sept. 1804.

82 Prebble, *Mutiny*, 445–74, 485–6, 488–9.
83 Father Alexander Macdonell seems to be the only emigrant to whom relatives in Canada sent money. Possibly a few other passages were financed in this way, but I have found no evidence to this effect. Because Highland emigration was communal, Glengarry County settlers did not need to send money home to pay for relatives' passages, as the Irish often did. Moreover, the overwhelming preference for family emigration would have made the practice of remitting a fare relatively expensive, since an average of five people emigrated at one time.

CHAPTER NINE

1 NA, MG11 CO42/165, 83–4, Colquhoun to Bathurst, 15 Feb. 1815 (reel B-134).
2 Ibid., 180–5, Campbell to Bathurst, 14 Oct. 1815 (reel B-134).
3 NA, MG11 CO43/23, Bathurst to Prevost, 29 Oct. 1813 (reel B-841).
4 NA, MG11 CO42/335, Drummond to Prevost, 12 July 1814 (reel B-296).
5 NA, MG11 CO42/165, Campbell to Bathurst, 12 Feb. 1814 (reel B-134); ibid., *Caledonian Mercury*, 27 March 1815.
6 NA, MG11 CO42 Q135, part 2, 354–5A, memorial of Allan McDonell, etc., Fort Augustus, March 1815.
7 Ibid.
8 Ibid., Allan McDonell to John Campbell, 11 March 1815.
9 NA, MG11 CO42/165, Colquhoun to Bathurst, 22 Feb. 1815 (reel B-134).
10 Ibid., Campbell to Bathurst, 29 April and 6 May 1815 (reel B-134).
11 Ibid., 147–8, petition of Alexander McNab, 26 May 1815 (reel B-134).
12 The daily rate was 9d. per man 6d. per woman. See ibid., Campbell to Bathurst, 24 May 1815 (reel B-134).
13 Ibid., 159–60, 164–5, Campbell to Bathurst, 20 June and 11 July 1815. For dates of deposits, see NA, MG11 CO385/2, "General List of Settlers Inrolled for Canada under the Government Regulations at Edinburgh, 1815" (hereafter cited as "list").
14 NA, MG11 CO42/165, 1779, Campbell to Gouldburn, 29 Sept. 1815 (reel B-134).
15 NA, MG11 CO385/2. Births and deaths are reported near the names of emigrants, while sailings are found at the end of the volume.
16 Unless otherwise stated, the following analysis of the 1815 emigrants is based on the list found in NA, MG11 CO385/2. The Glengarry settlers have been identified by matching the names in the Edinburgh list with the names of the assisted emigrants from Glengarry found in AO, RG1 C-1-3, vol. 101, "Return of Locations," March 1816.
17 Of the 307 Highlanders who settled in Glengarry, 189 came from the

parish of Glenelg (including both Glenelg and Knoydart), 64 from Killin, 18 from Kenmore, 14 from Fort Augustus, and 6 from Glenshiel.

18 Emigration from Glenelg parish has been described in the preceding chapters; people from Fort Augustus were associated with the Glengarry estate and emigrations, and those from Glenshiel with the 1802 departure via the *Neptune*. Emigrations from Killin and Kenmore to Glengarry had not involved large groups before this time, but were rather small groups of one to three families. One 1784 settler originated in Kenmore (NA, MG24 I3, vol. 2, 972) and another two Kenmore families had reached Glengarry, one in 1800 and another in 1801. At least seven McDiarmids arrived in Glengarry from Killin in 1799 and 1800 (Campbell and McDermid, *Glengarry-Stormont Pioneers*, 266, 363–4, 378–9, 421). Kinship linked at least one of the 1815 emigrants from Killin, John McLaurin, to earlier Killin settlers in Glengarry; see *Glengarry News*, 26 Sept. 1902, obituary.

19 The assisted emigration attracted one family of eight from Argyll and one from Ross and Cromarty (Glenshiel, which was on the periphery of the Glengarry County recruiting area), but none from Sutherland or the Hebrides. Another forty-one assisted emigrants originated in Perthshire parishes other than Killin and Kenmore.

20 Other probably related families among the Glenelg emigrants were the McCuaigs. Malcolm, aged fifty, had dependent children aged between nine and twenty-three, so it is probable that John (twenty-five) and Duncan (twenty-six) were also his children. Among the Knoydart emigrants, the Donald McDougall (fifty-two), named in the text, may have been the brother of Duncan (fifty) while Mary McDougall (twenty-five) and Jean McDougall (twenty-four) may have been daughters of these two men. Other examples could be drawn of possible kinship links among the emigrants, based on surname, age, and point of origin.

21 NA, MG11 CO42/165, Campbell to Bathurst, 14 Oct. 1815 (reel B-134).

22 See the following two chapters for a description of the progress of settlement up to 1815. Not all the assisted emigrants could be accommodated in Glengarry; some were settled farther north in the adjacent township of West Hawkesbury. The land in Glengarry for the 1815 emigrants was made available by lifting the Crown reserve on certain lots.

23 *Glengarry News*, 14 July and 11 Aug. 1905, obituary of Mrs. Ranald McDonald. See also AO, Father Ewen John Macdonald Collection, A-3-2, genealogy of Rory Og.

24 NA, RG31, 1851 Manuscript Census, Glengarry County, Lancaster, Personal Census, 121. Also *Glengarry News*, 9 Feb. 1906, obituary of William McDonell.

25 *Glengarry News*, 3 Oct. 1902, obituary of Ranald D. McDonald.

26 NA, RG1 L3, UCLP, M leases, (1809–19), no. 196, Archibald McGillis (reel C-2235).

27 Clan MacLeod, *MacLeods of Glengarry*, 285, 291; also interview with Mrs. Sybil McPhee, 1977.

28 For McCuaig, see *Glengarry News*, 9 March 1906, obituary of Donald McCuaig, and NA, RG31, 1851 Manuscript Census, Glengarry County, Lochiel, Personal Census, 103. For Campbell, see *Glengarry News*, 19 Dec. 1902, obituary of Donald Campbell. For McLeod, see Clan MacLeod, *MacLeods of Glengarry*, 317–8.

29 *Glengarry News*, 23 Feb. 1906, obituary of Mrs. George McRae.

30 Guldan, *MacIssac MacDonald Story*. For the relationship between Angus Ban and the MacIssacs, see SRO, E741/43, 1767 Plan, Muniall. In the plan of improvement for Barisdale, Angus Ban's father, Donald Ban Macdonell, is described as "alias McKiasaig". There also appears to be a second McKiasaig family on the neighbouring farm of Li; see SRO, E741/31/2/2, Butter's report on Lt. R. MacLeod's application for the farm of Li.

31 NA, RG5 A1, UCS, 25342–4, petition to Sir P. Maitland, dated Indian Lands, 13 Feb. 1821 (reel C-4606). Twenty-three of the thirty-two petitioners have names that are most likely of a Perthshire origin. Certain families have definitely been identified as natives of Loch Tay. Local tradition states that most of the families came from the same general area, with the exception of one Kippen family.

32 Michael Vance's forthcoming doctoral dissertation for the University of Guelph will examine the circumstances behind emigration from Perthshire in the period.

33 *Glengarry News*, 16 March 1906, obituary of Donald Sinclair; also interview with Mrs. Sybil McPhee, 1977. Local tradition emphasizes that the emigrants were rejoining friends from the 1815 group.

34 AO, Mss. Glengarry Collection, Kippen etc. families, letter from Hugh McEwen; see also *Glengarry News*, 10 Oct. 1902, obituary of Janet McEwen; also interview with Mrs. Sybil McPhee, 1977.

35 NA, RG5 A1, UCS, 25342–4, petition to Sir P. Maitland, 13 Feb. 1821 (reel C-4606); see also AO, Mss. Glengarry Collection, Kippen etc. families.

36 NA, MG11 CO42 Q321, 128, memorial of Norman Stewart, 27 Aug. 1816.

37 NA, RG8 C622, 148–9, Bathurst to Sherbrooke, Oct. 1816, no. 40 (reel C-3158).

38 At least five other Duirinish families arrived in Glengarry at the same time as the one family that stayed, but the difficulty they had in acquiring a Crown grant led them to settle across Lake St. Francis from Glengarry in Godmanchester, Lower Canada, in May 1818. It seems probable that most of the remaining eleven families took up land either

in Glengarry or its vicinity. See NA, RG1 L3L, LCLP, vol. 131, 64296–8, petition of Norman McDonell, etc., 12 Nov. 1818 (reel C-2543).

39 Glengarry Historical Society, *Glengarry Life*, 1980, 17. *Glengarry News*, 21 April 1905, obituary of Lachlan Stewart, son of Murdoch who emigrated to Glengarry in 1828; also interviews with Mrs. Sybil McPhee, and Mrs. Harriet McKinnon, 1977.

40 Hunter, *Making of the Crofting Community*, 40–8.

41 *Quebec Gazette*, 3 Oct. 1832. Also interview with Mrs. Sybil McPhee. A few of the 1832 emigrants may, like the Stewarts of Carbost, have had quite substantial holdings in Scotland.

42 Interviews with Mrs. Sybil McPhee and Mrs. Harriet McKinnon.

43 Clan MacLeod, *MacLeods of Glengarry*, 291, 317.

44 Interview with Mrs. Sybil McPhee; also NA, RG31 1851 Manuscript Census, Glengarry County, Kenyon, Personal Census, 127, Donald Cameron; see also Clan MacLeod, *MacLeods of Glengarry*, 317.

45 NA, RG1 L3L, LCLP vol. 131, 64296–8, petition of Norman McDonell, etc., 12 Nov. 1818 (reel C-2543).

46 NA, RG31, 1851 Manuscript Census, Glengarry County, Lancaster, Personal Census, Neil McGillis, 15.

47 NA, RG8 C505, 38–40a, petition to His Excellency Robert Prescott, dated Quebec, 1 August 1797 (reel C-3043).

48 NA, RG31, 1851 Manuscript Census, Glengarry County, Lancaster, Personal Census, Angus McGillis, 51; ibid., Charlottenburgh, Personal Census, Duncan McGillis, 214–5.

49 Ibid., Lochiel, Personal Census, Donald McDonald, 53; ibid., Kenyon, Personal Census, Hugh McDonald, 21–3. Hugh McDonald and his family also fit this description.

50 The families of George McRae in 1847 and Donald McLeod in 1849.

51 Only families with children twenty and under born in Scotland were included in this estimate, taken from the NA, RG31, 1861 Manuscript Census, Glengarry County, Personal Census; such families obviously emigrated some time after 1840. Other Scottish-born residents were not counted. Most of these would have emigrated in the earlier part of the century, but a few, particularly young adults, were possibly recent emigrants. NA, RG31, 1861 Manuscript Census, Glengarry County, Lancaster, Personal Census, 9, 11, 22, 33, 37, 63, 81, 85, 90, 93, 100; Lochiel, Personal Census, 1, 2, 7, 13, 14, 19, 21, 40, 41, 44, 45, 71, 111; Charlottenburgh, Personal Census, 36, 37, 85, 119, 124, 125, 133; Kenyon, Personal Census, 7, 20, 23, 30, 54, 63, 71, 82, 85, 91, 93, 106.

52 Hunter, *Making of the Crofting Community*, 85; also Macdonell, *Sketches ... of Glengarry in Canada*, 152. Macdonell mentions that an area of Glengarry County is referred to as Little Knoydart, after the Scottish home of its 1852 settlers.

53 NA, MG11 CO42/170, memorial of D. McCrummen, 20 Nov. 1816 (reel B-137). The petition mentions recent emigrants' loyalty in the late war, which is probably a reference to the *Neptune* emigrants who left this area in 1802, settled in Glengarry Country, and fought against the Americans in the War of 1812.

54 Ibid.

55 NA, RG31, 1851 Manuscript Census, Glengarry County, Lancaster, Personal Census, 109–11, family of John McKinnon and of Angus McDonald, Concession 9, Lot 31 W. In the 1861 census, John McKinnon and family lived in Lochiel; see ibid., 1861 Manuscript Census, Glengarry County, Lochiel, Personal Census, 40.

56 *Glengarry News*, 9 Feb. 1906, obituary of William McDonell. Coll and Samuel are likely sons of Alexander McDonell, one of the assisted emigrants from Knoydart; see NA, MG11 CO385/2, no. 121.

57 "Nearest friends" was often used as a synonym for kinsmen by Highlanders. See NA, RG31, 1851 Manuscript Census, Glengarry County, Lancaster, Personal Census, 121.

CHAPTER TEN

1 Other Loyalists settled in the Niagara Peninsula, the British territory most convenient to their former homes in New York and Pennsylvania.

2 NA, Cartographic and Architectural Archives Division (hereafter cited as CAAD), Patrick McNiff, "A Plan of the New Settlements, " 1 Nov. 1786.

3 Craig, *Upper Canada*, 7.

4 Chapman and Putman, *The Physiography of Southern Ontario*, 247–9, 252.

5 Gates, *Land Policies*, 303.

6 Ibid., 24, 30, 45–8, 69–70.

7 NA, CAAD, F 430, Charlottenburgh Township, 1953.

8 For instance the straight line of lots that begins with lots L and K and 60 to 50 of concession 1, North Side of the River Raisin (NRR) continues with lots 5 to 9 of concession 2, South Side of the River Raisin (SRR), then with lots 10 to the eastern half of lot 24 of concession 3, SRR, and from the western half of lot 24 to lot 26 of concession 4, SRR. This immensely complicated survey, combined with the repetitive character of Highland surnames, created great difficulty in the Land Registry Office.

9 Craig, *Upper Canada*, 7–8; NA, RG4 A1, 10772, "Account of donations ..." (reel C-3002).

10 Gates, *Land Policies*, 15–6.

11 NA, MG21 B64, 53, Haldimand to Johnson, 15 July 1784.

12 AO, RG1 A-1-1 vol. 19, William Chewett to D. Smith, 26 April 1797.

13 To identify the loyalist settlers and their place of settlement, see NA, RG19 vol. 4447, parcel 2, no. 6, "Provisions for Lake Township ... 1786"; and ibid., no. 1, "List of Loyalists, Township no. 1." See also Ontario, Department of Lands and Forests, plan of Lancaster by Lt. James McDonell, Cornwall, 2 Feb. 1791.

14 Ontario, Department of Lands and Forests, plan of Charlottenburgh (1784). Mr. Delancey, a Loyalist officer administering the new settlements for the government, also acquired a lot in the first concession. For a list of the KRRNY officers, see Pringle, *Lunenburgh*, 366–8.

15 NA, RG19 vol. 4447, parcel 2, no. 1, Township no. 1. A total of 190 families is given, but six of these (nos. 149, 163, 165, 173, 177 and 180) have no one listed under the family name. See also Ontario, Department of Lands and Forests, plan of Charlottenburgh (1784).

16 NA, RG1 L4 vol. 12, Charlottenburgh Township, "Locations in the 1st concession north of the River Raisin and the 1st concession south of the River Raisin and locations in the 2nd and 3rd concession south of the River Raisin." See also Ontario, Department of Lands and Forests, plan of Charlottenburgh, 1784. These two sources do not correspond exactly, but the differences between them are not surprising, since they were compiled five years apart during a time when settlers exchanged or received additional lands.

17 Pringle, *Lunenburgh*, 34.

18 For the Grants, see R. Grant, *Story of Martintown*, 19. For the McDonells, see NA, RG1 L4 vol. 12, Charlottenburgh, concession 3, SRR, lot 14. Also interview with Mrs. Florence McDonell, 1977.

19 All citations in notes 19–21 are from NA, MG14, AO12; for the reader's convenience, only volume and page numbers are given. The 1773 emigrants (not necessarily only from the McDonell party) who settled in Glengarry County included John Cameron (27/209); William Chisholm (29/204); Peter Ferguson (29/206); Angus Cameron (29/210); Widow McGruer (29/122); Donald Grant (31/33); Donald Grant, Sr. (31/37); Alexander Chisholm (27/141); Duncan McDonell (31/147); Alexander Kennedy (29/105); Donald McGillis (29/109); Donald McDonald (29/74); Hugh McDonell (29/103); Alexander McDonell (29/101); Kenneth McDonnell (28/370); John Macdonell Sr. (28/384); Murdoch McLean, Donald McLeod, William Rose, and John McKay (29).

20 Most of the Highland emigrants also came to Johnstown during the 1770's, but a few had come to America during the Seven Years War. These include Duncan McIntyre (29/130); John McDonell (27/206); Roderick Macdonell (28/403); John McDonell (29/238); Roderick Macdonell (28/390); Alexander MacDonell (28/388); John Fraser (27);

Duncan Murchison (29/65–6); Archibald and Peter Grant (29/77, 96); William McKay (29/93).

21 The Cornwall settlers included Alexander Cameron (29/202); Duncan Grant (29/208); John Macdonell (29/236); Allen Grant (31/17); Angus McDonell (31/183); Alexander McDonell (31/192); John Macdonell (28/401).

22 Alexander and Hugh have both been reported as receiving land in concession 1, while Harkness (*Stormont, Dundas and Glengarry*, 66) reports that John received land in Charlottenburgh as well. For Spanish John, see *ibid.*, 80, 119.

23 John of Leek's widow petitioned for assistance on 30 Nov. 1782; see NA, MG21 B214, 365. For Archibald, see Harkness, *Stormont, Dundas and Glengarry* 62; for Allan, see ibid., 49. For Allan of Collachie, see Pringle, *Lunenburgh*, 386. For Alexander of Collachie, see Macdonell, *Sketches ... of Glengarry in Canada*, 116.

24 Parliamentary Papers, 1841 (182) VI, evidence of T. Rolph, answers 1593 and 1594, and Thomas Knox, answer 2325: "If they went to Canada they would find plenty there who can talk Gaelic."

25 NA, RG19 vol. 4447, parcel 2, no. 1 (Township 1) and no. 6 (Lake Township), Aug. 1786. The 1785 emigrants are named in ibid., no. 7, "Emigrants lately Come ... by way of Albany," 31 Aug. 1786. For the 1786 emigrants, see NA, RG4 A1, 9909–15, Craigie to Delancey, 4 Sept. 1786 (reel C-3001).

26 NA, RG4 A1, 9909–15 Craigie to Delancey, 4 Sept. 1786.

27 Ibid., Hope to McDonell, 25 Sept. 1786; see also NA, MG11 CO42/82, 39. In 1787, Dorchester refused further rations to both emigrants and loyalists.

28 AO, RG1 C-1-2, vol. 8, Orders in Council, extract of minutes, 2 June 1787.

29 AO, RG1 A-1-1, vol. 15, William Chewett to D. Smith, 26 Feb. 1801.

30 NA, RG1 L3, UCLP, M2 (1795–6), no. 268 (reel C-2192).

31 AO, RG1 A-1-1, vol. 15, William Chewett to D. Smith, 26 Feb. 1801. Reference is made to the emigrants drawing for lots in Angus McGillivray's petition; see NA, RG1 L3, UCLP, M2 (1795–6), no. 271 (reel C-2192).

32 NA, RG19 vol. 4447, parcel 3, no. 7, "Sundry persons ... located by Mr. James McDonell ..." (hereafter cited as "Sundry Persons"). This list, prepared in 1804, was based on the township plan of Lancaster and Charlottenburgh drawn up by James McDonell and on a 1790 list of locations in Glengarry, from which the names of the 1785 and 1786 emigrants were extracted.

33 NA, RG1 L3, UCLP, M9 (1808–10), no. 79 (reel C-2196); also interview with Florence Macdonell, 1977. Angus Ban purchased the western half of lot 12 from its Loyalist occupant, Duncan Macdonell, sometime before the latter's death in 1791.

34 NA, RG1 L3, UCLP, M9 (1808–10), no. 91 (reel C-2196). Ranald McGillis was given lot 36 in the Lancaster concession 5, but he exchanged it for the west half of lot 37 in Cornwall concession 4.

35 NA, MG29 C29, List. Sandfield lists 90 of the 1785 and 1786 settlers, including points of origin and some family relationships; however, only 33 of his names and locations are confirmed by the Sundry Persons list. Sandfield may be more accurate than this correlation suggests, since it is possible that men traded lots to be closer to other family members. Because of its date (1804) Sundry Persons may have been prepared before such movement.

36 Twenty-six of the thirty-six families named in the 1785 list were Macdonalds (67%); see NA, RG19 vol. 4447, parcel 2, no. 7. Eighty-one of the 114 families reported in the Highland settlement were Macdonalds (71%). See ibid., parcel 3 no. 7.

37 The 1785 list is found in ibid., parcel 2, no. 7.

38 NA, MG29 C29, List. The Sundry Persons list confirms that an Archibald Macdonald occupied this lot.

39 NA, MG29 C29, notebook 4 with first page blank, Captain Grey, [age] 93.

40 Ibid., notebook 3, Family II, list 1 to 26, "James Duncan Macdonald, [age] 92, March' [18]84."

41 For locations in Cornwall concession 8, see NA, RG1 L4 vol. 13, 143–4. John McIntyre, Duncan Kennedy, and Donald McMillan did not receive land in Cornwall; the latter two did obtain land in Lancaster or Charlottenburgh. William McQueen, Colin Fraser, and Finlay (Phillip) Macdonald were granted land both in Cornwall and in the "Highland settlement."

42 A considerable number of late loyalists entered Upper Canada from the United States after 1784. Some of these were in fact political refugees, whereas others merely followed the opening of a new frontier into Canada. The 1785 emigrants, by virtue of their entry into Canada via the United States, must have seemed to fit into this category and hence could be treated in a manner similar to their Loyalist relations.

43 NA, RG1 L3, UCLP, M5 (1800–01), no. 100, Ranald McDonell (reel C-2194); ibid., M4 (1797–8), no. 118, John Macdonell (reel C-2193).

44 Other Loyalist grants in that concession were made in July 1786; see NA, RG1 L3, UCLP, M9 (1808–10), no. 92 (reel C-2196).

45 NA, RG4 A1, 10073–4, S. Delancey to William Falkner et al., 24 Dec. 1786 (reel C–3001).

46 Craig, *Upper Canada*, 12. A deadline for application for bounty lands was suggested in July 1790 and finally set on 1 August 1797; see Gates, *Land Policies*, 17, 21.

47 NA, RG1 L4 vol. 12, "List of locations." See also MacGillivray and Ross,

History of Glengarry, 676–9 for the total number of lots in the townships. I have omitted lot 38 in all concessions from my calculations since it is not marked on the early plans. Locations in Lancaster concessions 9–11 are taken from James McDonell's plan of Lancaster, 1791 (Ontario, Department of Lands and Forests).

48 The officers were the notable exception to this rule. For instance, Spanish John Macdonell, as a captain in the KRRNY, received lots 33 to 37 in Lancaster concessions 10 and 11, a single block of 2000 acres.

49 For Alexander, see NA, RG1 L3, UCLP, M11 (1811–19), no. 345 (reel C-2200); for Donald, see ibid., M12 (1815–20), no. 528 (reel C-2201).

50 Ontario, Department of Lands and Forests, Plan of Lancaster by Lieutenant James McDonell, 1791.

51 Gates, *Land Policies*, 22.

52 Of the Loyalists, 515 were Highlanders, and a minimum of 500 Highlanders entered Glengarry in the 1785–6 groups.

53 Craig, *Upper Canada*, 12; Gates, *Land Policies*, 19, 29. The land boards could also recommend to the Executive Council individuals to whom more extensive grants should be made.

54 Land obtained from the seigneur was subject to an annual rent (cens et ventes), but the tenant or censitaire had security of tenure and disposition of the farm.

55 Craig, *Upper Canada*, 9–18.

56 Exactly who were the clergy referred to in the Act was the subject of political controversy in Canada for more than a generation. A narrow interpretation limited support to the Church of England; more broadly it might include the Presbyterian church, as the established church of Scotland. See also Gates, *Land Policies*, 29.

57 NA, RG1 L4 vol. 10, Land Board meeting, 22 Feb. 1791.

58 MacGillivray and Ross, *History of Glengarry*, 676–9. In Lancaster, there were the correct number of Clergy reserves (89 out of 89.5); in Charlottenburgh no Crown reserves were established, and there were 76.5 rather than 96.5 Clergy reserves.

59 The report to Dorchester on the Eigg emigrants commented that they applied for transportation to New Johnstown on 20 October and that this petition was granted; see NA, RG4 A1, 15916–18 (reel C-3006). For the list of emigrants, see NA, MG11 CO42/71, 82 (reel B-48). For land board applicants, see NA, RG1 L4 vol. 10, 107a.

60 This is borne out in the land petitions of two of the 1790 emigrants, Angus and John Gillis; see NA, RG1 L3, UCLP, MC22 (1839–40), no. 74 (reel C–2140) and ibid., MC22 (1840), no. 142 (reel C-2141). Aberchalder was known as Colonel John because of his militia rank.

61 One of the two male servants did get land two years later on 25 March 1793. Duncan McCraw obtained lot 22 in Lancaster concession

16; see AO, RG1 A-1-1 vol. 49, 327. Lauchlan Campbell received land on 25 March 1793. No grant in Glengarry to Donald Fraser, blacksmith, has been found.

62 This estimate is based on a comparison of Dorchester's list of the 1790 emigrants (NA, MG11 CO42/71, 82 [reel B-48]) and James McDonell's plan of Lancaster (Ontario, Department of Lands and Forests). The lots occupied in 1790 were 2, 4, 13–15, 17, 20–22, 24, 26–27, 30, 32, and 35. The names given for thirteen of the occupants of these lots correspond to Dorchester's list. The two Donald McCormicks on Dorchester's list have been identified with Donald McCormick of lot 17 and Roderick McCormick of lot 24. McCormick is an extremely uncommon name in Glengarry, and it seems likely that the list is inaccurate as to one man's Christian name. Similarly, I have identified Dorchester's John McAulay as James McDonell's James McAulay of lot 15. Ewen McMillan in Dorchester's list is likely the Hugh McMillan who received lot 30.

63 John and Donald McKinnon, sons of Lauchlan McKinnon, obtained lots 16 and 36 in 1791 and 1796 respectively (personal communication, L.R. McLean of Ottawa, Ontario). Angus Gillis emigrated in 1790, according to his land petition, and received lot 10 in April 1791; see NA, RG1 L3, UCLP, MC22, (1840), no. 142, reel C-2141. McGillis is not named in Dorchester's list, but it seems likely that he is one of the seven people over the age of twelve who accompanied Duncan McGillis. I have not been able to determine whether any kin or community relationships existed between the Eigg emigrants and the other eight occupants of concession 12.

64 AO, RG1 A-1-1 vol. 49, 327.

65 NA, MG23 G III 5, vol. 1, 269–72, petition for the Highlanders; ibid., vol. 2, 576–7, James Morrison to James Gray, 4 Feb. 1791.

66 NA, RG1 L3, UCLP, M10 (1811–6), no. 307 (reel C-2198).

67 NA, RG1 L3, UCLP, MC22 (1840), no. 142, Angus McGillis (reel C-2141). Ibid., (1839–40), no. 74, John McGillis (reel C-2140). Aulay, who was probably a kinsman of 1790 emigrant Donald McAulay, received lot 25 in concession 12 in August 1792; see AO, RG1 A-1-1 vol. 49, 327. Alexander Macdonell of Eigg was granted lot 29 in the adjacent concession 11 in 1796; see AO, RG1 A-1-1, box 5, "Return of Locations in E.D. 24 July 1796 to 31 January 1797".

68 NA, MG29 C29, List. Sandfield names Greenfield as one of the settlers in Charlottenburgh concession 9. The McLennans of lot 25 in Lancaster concession 3 and the McIntoshes of lot 4 in Charlottenburgh concession 4 may also have been 1792 emigrants. See NA, RG1 L3, UCLP, M9 (1804–11), nos. 189, 190 (reel C-2197).

69 AO, RG1 A-1-1 vol. 49, 88, Richard Duncan, 6 Nov. 1792.

70 Ibid., vol. 48, 88, Hugh McDonell; ibid., 327, "Return of Sundry Persons."

71 NA, RG1 L4 vol. 15, list of applicants 18 and 26 March, 1 and 16 April 1793 (reel C-14028). "Emigrant from Scotland," of course, does not necessarily mean a 1792 emigrant.

72 AO, RG1 A-1-1 vol. 49, 327.

73 The Loyalist was Allan Cameron, identified on the list of applicants for land as a Loyalist who settled lot 26 in concession 14. Duncan McCraw was named in Dorchester's list of 1790 emigrants, and he settled lot 22 in concession 16.

74 AO, RG1 C-1-4 vol. 9, locations in the Eastern District, 1793.

75 Unless otherwise stated, the following paragraph is based on the list of emigrants in AO, RG1 A-1-1 vol. 49, 327, and ibid., C-1-4 vol. 9, "Return ... Glengarry," 10 Oct. 1794. The emigrants occupied lots 22–26, 29–31, 33, and 37 in concession 13 and lots 22–25, 29–34 and 37 in concession 14.

76 Since the 1792 group, with the exception of Greenfield McDonell, has only been identified in terms of those who settled in northern Lancaster, it is quite probable that some 1792 emigrants have escaped notice. A few Macdonells from Glen Garry may have chosen to settle with kinsmen in the southern part of the county.

77 AO, RG1 A-1-1 vol. 5, Hugh McDonell to D. Smith, 10 Oct. 1794.

78 Ibid., C-1-4 vol. 9, "Return ... Glengarry," 10 Oct. 1794.

79 The 1793-4 emigrants are popularly held to have settled in concessions 15 and 16; Clan MacLeod, *The MacLeods of Glengarry* locates many of them in these concessions. There is no specific tradition linking the four Ferguson and two Grant families with the McLeod emigrants, but until evidence to the contrary is found, it is possible that they too were recruited by McLeod, possibly from Glen Moriston.

80 The five unregistered lots caused problems for their occupants, who petitioned the Executive Council for redress. See NA, RG1 L3, UCLP, C2 (1796–7), no. 2, petition of Donald Campbell, Alexander McLennan, Donald McDonell and Archibald McGilvray (reel C-1647); see also ibid., M Misc. (1792–1816), no. 21, Kenneth McLennan (reel C-2189). The township papers in the Archives of Ontario confirm that these men had difficulty getting patents for their reported lots.

81 Three men were granted land outside concessions 15 and 16 on 25 June 1794. Of these, John McCuaig, who settled in Lancaster concession 8, was a member of the McLeod party; see Clan MacLeod, *MacLeods of Glengarry*, 42–3. Neil McKinnon was the son of Lachlan McKinnon, a 1790 emigrant, and Donald McDougald was probably one of the Knoydart McDougalds and hence one of the 1786 emigrants.

82 The precise date on which the reserves were set aside in Glengarry is not known, but it was after June 1794 and before May 1797; see NA, RG1 L3, UCLP, M Misc. (1792–1816), no. 21, Kenneth McLennan (reel C-2189).

83 For Campbell, McDonell, and McGilvray see NA, RG1 L3, UCLP, C2 (1796–7), no. 2 (reel C-1647); for the last two, see also NA, RG5 A1, UCS, report from Chewett and Ridout, 8 July 1809 (reel C-4504). For Kenneth McLennan, see NA, RG1 L3, UCLP, M Misc. (1792–1816), no. 21 (reel C-2189). For Alexander McLennan, see ibid., M11 (1808–17), no. 80 (reel C-2199) and ibid., C2 (1796–7), no. 2 (reel C-1647). For Lt. McMillan, see ibid., M4 (1793–9), no. 200 (reel C-2193).

84 Ibid., M Misc. (1792–1816), no. 21, 17 May 1797 (reel C-2189).

85 See petitions cited above. The township papers in the Archives of Ontario (Lochiel Township, concession 6) report a John Campbell leasing lot 37 in Lancaster concession 15 before 1809.

86 John McGillis of lot 37 in concession 18 and Angus McGillis of lot 36 in concession 17 Lancaster received their locations in March 1793 (AO, RG1 C-1-4 vol. 9, return, Glengarry, 10 Oct. 1794). Between August 1796 and January 1797, seven lots were located in concession 17 and four in concession 18 of Lancaster (ibid., A-1-7 box 5, returns, Eastern District, 31 Jan. 1797).

87 Compare the 1789 list (see NA, RG1 L4 vol. 12, Lancaster) with the plan of Lancaster by Lt. James McDonell. (Ontario, Department of Lands and Forests).

88 Compare McNiff's map of *Charlottenburgh Township* in 1796 (NA, reel M-308, 756) to the 1789 list. Lots were, for instance, granted to Duncan McIntyre (lot 2, concession 10), Alexander McDonell (lot 25, concession 14), and to Finlay Ross (lot 37, concession 13) of Charlottenburgh. See AO, RG1 A-1-1 vol. 49, 327, returns, 10 April 1793.

89 NA, RG9 I B1 vol. 2, McMillan to Shaw, 7 April 1812.

90 NA, MG11 CO42 Q 46, part 2, 14 May 1790, minutes of council on the waste lands of the Crown.

CHAPTER ELEVEN

1 In 1792, Lunenburgh District was renamed the Eastern District.

2 Gates, *Land Policies*, 29.

3 Ibid., 47.

4 Ibid., 48, 70. Another increase of 1s. 9d. occurred in 1803 when payment was demanded in sterling and not the previously acceptable Halifax currency.

5 Ibid., 69–70.

6 NA, RG1 L3, UCLP, M13 (1821), nos. 12 and 13 (reel C-2203).

7 Ibid., M13 (1816–24), no. 275 (reel C-2204).

8 Ibid., M14 (1821–6), no. 479 (reel C-2207).

9 NA, RG5 A1, UCS,21343–4, Macdonell to Hillier, 16 June 1819 (reel C-4603).

10 Selkirk, *Diary*, 200, 342. See also MacKenzie, *Baldoon*, 36. MacKenzie points out that Selkirk recruited three young men from Glengarry for Baldoon, but these were probably not recent arrivals, since Selkirk only considered recruiting the 1802 emigrants three months later.

11 NA, RG5 A1, UCS, 1714, letter dated 20 March 1806 (reel C-4503).

12 NA, RG5 A1 UCS, 2872–5, Macdonell to Halton, 31 Jan. 1808 (reel C-4504). Governor Hunter had come into contact with the men of the Glengarry Fencibles in Ireland as a military officer, and he was favourably inclined towards the Glengarrians as a result. See NA, RG1 L3, UCLP, M12 (1819), no. 193, Donald McLeod (reel C-2201).

13 NA, MG24 I 183, file 7, letterbook, McMillan to Duncan Cameron, 30 Sept. 1803 and 8 Jan. 1807.

14 NA, RG1 L3L, LCLP, 66477–8, Archibald McMillan, 6 Aug. 1804 (reel C-2545).

15 Ibid.; 66562–6, first list of names (reel C-2545).

16 For second list, see ibid., 66691–2. For 25% of the first applicants withdrawing, see NA, MG24 I 183, letterbook, 235–6, 12 July 1806, where McMillan discusses people "relinquishing lands." While he is not specific as to the total number who withdrew their application, the figure can be calculated by comparing the various lists submitted by McMillan. An endorsement to the second list (NA, RG1 L3L, LCLP, 66693 [reel C-2545]) states that the seventy-five new names on the second list had all been included in a third "List of Emigrants presented by Mr. Archibald McMillan who ... [had] taken the Oaths" (ibid., 66605–10 [reel C-2545]. If all of the 209 applicants on the first list had remained interested in acquiring land with McMillan, the third list should have numbered 284 (209 + 75). The third list, however, only names 233 people; 51 emigrants, or almost 25% of the people named on the first list had therefore dropped out of the scheme.

17 For the emigrants' surprise at McMillan's request for £4 and for a list of names, see NA, RG5 A1, 44934–5, petition of John Corbet, 10 March 1827 (reel C-6863). For some additional names of those who gave up their land to McMillan, see NA, MG24 I 183, file entitled, "Lochaber, Templeton and Grenville Townships, 1804–07."

18 For government decision, see NA, RG1 L1 vol. 14, 59 Report of Committee of Council, 21 Oct. 1806 (reel C-96). For clansmen's reaction, see McMillan's letter to John Munro, 15 Dec. 1806 in NA, MG24 I 183, 247–8.

19 NA, MG24 I 183, letterbook, McMillan to Ewen Cameron, 20 Oct. 1805.

20 Selkirk, *Diary*, 200.

21 Ibid.; on p. 342 Selkirk refers to Knoydart and North Morar emigrants.

22 NA, RG5 A1, UCS, 44934–5, petition of John Corbet and others, 10 March 1827 (reel C-6863).

23 For John McRory, see AO, Father Ewen John Macdonald, C-1-2, box 8, typescript book, Angus McDonald to Sergeant Roderick McDonald, Oct. 1804. Duncan McLean stayed with the McDonalds of lot 25 in Lancaster concession 16, Duncan McKinnon with the McLeods of lot 18 in concession 15, and Malcolm McCuaig with the McLeods of lot 31 in the same concession. See NA, MG24 I, 183, Lochaber, Templeton and Grenville Township, 1804–07, list of those who assigned their rights to the lands in Suffolk, Templeton, Grenville, etc.

24 AO, Father Ewen J. Macdonald, C-1-2, box 8, Angus McDonald to Sergeant Roderick McDonald, Oct. 1804.

25 Crown and Clergy reserves were first made available for rent by the Executive Council in 1801. The lots were granted on a seven-year lease, twice renewable; rents were set at 10s (or three bushels of wheat) for the first seven years, 20s (or six bushels of wheat) for the second year, and 30s (or nine bushels of wheat) for the third seven; see Gates, *Land Policies*, 164–5, 198.

26 NA, RG1 L3, UCLP, M12 (1819), no. 180 (reel C-2201). Unfortunately the lots (numbers 16 and 22 in Lancaster concession 18) were "so bad in quality of Soil & Situation that no Person could settle upon them."

27 For gentlemen with leases, see NA, RG1 L3, UCLP, vol. 379 nos. 18, 58, 91, and 92 (reels C-2234 and C-2235). For Malcolm McCuaig, see NA, RG1 L3, UCLP, M13 (1821), no. 13 (reel C-2203). For Father Macdonell, see NA, MG11 CO42/360, fol. 195, Alexander McDonell to Lord Bathurst, 7 July 1817 (reel B-299).

28 NA, RG1 L3, UCLP, M13 (1821), no. 12, John McGillivray (reel C-2203).

29 For Macdonald, see AO, Father Ewen John Macdonald, C-1-2, box 8, Angus McDonald to Sergeant Roderick McDonald. For McGillis, see NA, RG1 L3, UCLP, M11 (1811–19), no. 375 (reel C-2200).

30 For Finch Settlers, see NA, RG1 L3, UCLP, M6 (1803–04), no. 80, Allan McMillan (reel C-2194).

31 For Donald and Duncan McMillan's petition, see ibid., no. 81 (reel C-2194).

32 Interview with L.R. McLean of Ottawa, Ontario.

33 For concession 1, see Selkirk, *Diary*, 198. For concession 9, see NA, MG29 C29, notebook 3, Family II, list 1–26, John Macdonald, age 71, March 1884.

34 NA, MG29 C29, notebook with first page blank, Uncle Donald, "In 1802 came..."; this interpretation was confirmed in my interview with Mrs. Florence Macdonell. The Indian Lands are a strip of land, three miles wide from east to west and 25 miles from south to north. The strip runs from the St. Lawrence between the original boundaries of Glen-

garry and Stormont and was reserved for the St. Regis Indians in 1784. In 1847 the land was surrendered to the Crown and those holding leases from the Indians, including many 1802 emigrants, were able to purchase the farms which they then occupied.

35 See for instance the list of settlers and their locations in northern Lancaster in NA, MG29 C29, George Sandfield Macdonald papers.

36 NA, RG1 L3, UCLP, M11 (1811–19), no. 375, Duncan McGillis. For Mac-Naughton, see Dumbrille, *Braggart in My Step*, 169; and *Belden's Illustrated Historical Atlas of Stormont, Dundas & Glengarry*, 48 (Charlottenburgh Township, Concession 4 NRR, lot 7). For Alexander McLennan, see Dumbrille, *Up and Down*, 180. For McMillan, see family tree of the McMillans, copy held by Hugh McDougald, concession 4, Kenyon. For Morrison, see Thomas, *History of Argenteuill, Que., and Prescott, Ont.*, 628.

37 NA, MG24 I 183, Lochaber, Templeton etc., 1804–7, list of those who assigned their rights to the land. Donald McDonell, Malcolm McCuaig, and Peter McCuaig were in Côte St George, next to Lancaster concession 7. Murdoch McLennan also settled in Soulanges County; see Dumbrille, *Up and Down*, 35. Hugh McDonell's parents settled in Cornwall Township in Stormont County on lot 10 of concession 9; see NA, RG1 L3, UCLP, M11 (1811–19), no. 316 (reel C-2200).

38 NA, RG1 L3, UCLP, M10 (1809–16), no. 223 (reel C-2198).

39 Ibid., C8 (1806–8), no. 5 (reel C-1650). Six of these emigrants were from Lochiel, one from Glengarry and one from Knoydart.

40 For the poverty of the Glengarry Fencible soldiers and their failure to receive Crown grants, see NA, RG1 L1, Land Book L (1821–4) vol. 30, 9 July 1823 (reel C-103). Most of the fencibles who did come to Canada settled in Glengarry; see NA, RG1 L3, UCLP, M10 (1807–11), no. 30, Angus McLachlan (reel C-2197). See also AO, Township Papers, Charlottenburgh for the following: Sergeant Donald McDonald, lot 31, concession 9; James McDonell, lot 8, concession 8; Angus McInnis lot 13, concession 8; Finlay McRae, lot 10, concession 7; in the Indian Lands, Roderick McDonald, lot 13, concession 7, and Ranald McDonald, lot 14, concession 11.

41 Macdonell, *Sketches ... of Glengarry in Canada*, 180.

42 NA, RG5 A1, UCS,8495–506, Edward Baynes, 18 June 1814 (reel C-4544).

43 For Murray, see ibid., 9789, Murray to Ridout, 29 April 1815 (reel C-4544). For Robinson, see NA, MG11 CO42/356, 70–1, Robinson to Bathurst, 29 July 1815 (reel B-296).

44 AO, RG1 A-1-2 vol. 22, 113–14, Ridout to McDonell, 4 June 1815; NA, MG11 CO42/357, Drummond to Gore, 25 Nov. 1815 and Gore to Bathurst, 23 Feb. 1816 (reel B-297). The land on which these townships was located had not yet been purchased from the Indians.

45 NA, RG4 A1 vol. 147 fol. 36, Beckwith to McDonell, 7 Sept. 1815.

46 NA, RG5 A1, UCS, 12279–82, Drummond to Gore, 15 March 1816 (reel C-4546).

47 AO, RG1 A-1-2 vol. 22, Ridout to Murray, 4 June 1815.

48 NA, RG5 A1, UCS, 9999–10006, Loring to Robinson, 17 June 1815 (reel C-4545); see also Macdonell, *Sketches ... of Glengarry in Canada*, 114–7.

49 NA, RG8 C621, Robinson to Drummond, 4 Oct. 1815 (reel C-3158).

50 Two principal "barracks" were opened to accommodate the emigrants over the winter of 1815–16, one in Cornwall, near Glengarry, and the other in Prescott, 40 miles farther up the St. Lawrence. Those who wished to settle in Glengarry chose to stay at Cornwall. See NA, RG8 C621, 67–73, Robinson to Drummond, 25 Sept. 1815 (reel C-3158); see also NA, RG5 A1, UCS, 10501–4, McDonell to Gibson, 23 Sept. 1815 (reel C-4545).

51 NA, RG5 A1, UCS, 13699–702, petition, 1 Oct. 1816 (reel C-4547).

52 NA, RG8 C621, 103–9, report by Sir Sidney Beckwith to Drummond, 21 Nov. 1815 (reel C-3158).

53 NA, RG7 G16C vol. 7, letter to Surveyor General, 26 Oct. 1815.

54 AO, RG1 C-1-3 vol. 101, return of locations, March 1816, Township of Lancaster. There is a suggestion in Macdonell's *Sketches ... of Glengarry in Canada*, 180–4, that the Glengarry Light Infantry Regiment was recruited primarily in Glengarry County. This does not appear to be the case, since only a minority of the rank and file bore Highland names.

55 AO, RG1 A-1-7, box 10, envelope 2 , McDonell to McDonell, 11 May 1816; NA, RG5 A1, UCS, 10283–5, McDonell to Robinson, 1 Aug. 1815 (reel C-4545).

56 NA, RG5 A1, UCS, 10202-6, McDonell to Robinson, 28 July 1815 (reel C-4545); see also ibid., 10214–6, lists.

57 Ibid., 10283–5 McDonell to Robinson, 1 Aug. 1815 (reel C-4545).

58 NA, RG8 C622, 38–56 petition (reel C-3158).

59 AO, RG1 A-1-2 vol. 22, Ridout to Murray, 4 June 1815.

60 NA, RG1 L3, UCLP, M13 (1818–23), no. 180, Archibald McLaren (reel C-2203).

61 NA, RG5 A1, UCS, 12906, abstract of locations (reel C-4547).

62 The following analysis of the emigrants' locations is based on AO, RG1 C-1-3 vol. 101, return of locations, March 1816, Lancaster, and ibid., vol. 96, "Fiats of Military Emigrants."

63 NA, RG1 L3, UCLP, M13 (1818–23), no. 180, Archibald McLaren (reel C-2203).

64 Ibid. For names and family relationships, see NA, MG11 CO385, vol. 2, "List of settlers ... 1815," nos. 129, 130, 131, and 164.

65 NA, RG1 L3, UCLP, M14 (1821–6), no. 540, Duncan McDonell. Such re-

arrangements of lot locations to bring kin and friends together were made possible, at least in part, by the lack of interest that some military settlers showed in occupying their grants. Duncan McDonell was able to find a lot more to his liking in Lancaster because William Barret of the Fifth Regiment had left the rear half of lot 1 in concession 10 for Charlottenburgh township. Similarly, Alexander and John Macdonell were granted lot 2 in concession 10 and lot 38 in concession 15 respectively after these lots were abandoned by their military occupants. See NA, RG1 L3, UCLP, M13 (1816–24), no. 283, Alexander McDonell (reel C-2204) and ibid., M14 (1821–5),no. 234, John Macdonell (reel C-2203).

66 AO, Father Ewen John Macdonald Collection, B-4-2, box 8, Bishop Macdonell Papers, "The Address of Bishop Macdonell to the Catholic and Protestant Freeholders," [1836]. Bishop Macdonell emphasized how many people he had helped to get land.

CHAPTER TWELVE

1 In 1764 Knoydart had 960 inhabitants (see Macdonald, "Highland District in 1764," 148); by 1793 some 600 clansmen had emigrated from Knoydart, while an estimated 1,000 people remained; see *OSA* XVI, 267.

2 Adams, "Causes of the Highland Emigrations of 1783–1803," 73–89; Richards, *Highland Clearances* II, 195–6, 216–17; Bumsted, *People's Clearance xi*, 29, 220. The oral tradition that Bumsted decries can be an important source of information.

3 *NSA*, IX, Glenelg, 135–6 describes the Glenelg emigrants as leaving of necessity, not by choice. The same is said of the 1773 emigrants in a letter written in Fort Williams, Scotland, and published in the *New York Journal or the General Advertiser*, 21 Oct. 1773.

4 Eric Richards has suggested that the clansmen would have regarded their emigration as a forced choice (*Highland Clearances*, II, 196) and the evidence from the Glengarry emigrations makes it clear that this was the case. Bumsted, in describing emigration before 1815 as "the people's clearance," does not use the word "clearance" in its usual sense of removal from a farm, croft, or estate.

5 Eric Richards does not accept my analysis that the Glengarry emigrations should be seen as an act of social protest (*Highland Clearances*, II, 199), since he believes that emigration was too widespread a phenomenon in Britain for the departures to be categorized that way. Richards's argument does not hold water. Emigration was, of course, a mass British and European experience, but that does not prevent it from having a particular meaning in certain times and places. Emigra-

tion from the Scottish Highlands between 1770 and 1815 should generally be seen as a radical protest against the effect of economic transformation on the clansmen there. It is also quite possible that emigration should be regarded as a protest in other times and places as well.

6 Richards, *Highland Clearances*, II, 200. This discrepancy in the clansmen's interest in emigration before and after the first decade of the nineteenth century is a key to understanding the nature and meaning of emigration from the Highlands.

7 Bailyn, *Voyagers to the West*; for gender, see 133; for children, see 127; for families, see 140–5; for occupation, see 163; for groups, see 103; and for sailing, see 119–25.

8 Bailyn's statistical analysis of the motivations for departure does not, in my opinion, produce useful results. In his text, Bailyn emphasizes that provincial emigrants left for negative reasons such as economic distress, while his summary description of the group emphasizes only their positive interest in acquiring land on the American frontier (*Voyagers to the West*, 198, 203). For his claim that extended families were uncommon among provincial emigrants, see ibid., 141–2.

9 See Greene, "Recent Developments," 143–77, and Cressy, *Coming Over*, especially 263–5.

10 For the story of Angus Macdonell's inheritance in Canada, see PAC RG1 L3, UCLP, M9 (1804–11), 106 (reel C-2196).

11 See the testimony of the Reverend N. McLeod, question and answer no. 921 in *Parliamentary Papers* 1841 (182) VI, Emigration, Scotland.

12 SCA, Blairs Papers, Alexander McDonell to Alexander Cameron, 14 June 1815.

13 Iain Liath Macdonald's "Oran" was published in the *Glengarry News*, an undated copy of which survives in a scrapbook of Gaelic poetry owned by John J. MacLeod of Glen Nevis, Lancaster Township. The poem was translated into English by Ian Paterson of the School of Scottish Studies at Edinburgh University. Anna McGillis's poem "Canada Ard" can be found in A.M. Sinclair, *Gaelic Bards*, 7–8, and in MacDonell's *Emigrant Experience*, 134–7. Archibald McMillan relished his freedom in Canada to hunt deer; see NA, MG24 I 183, letterbook, 1803–29, 210–15, 27 April 1805.

14 KAA, A12 C5, "Observations on the Scotch Settlements in British North America."

15 While not all of the 3,300 members of the nine group emigrations settled in Glengarry County, the number of those who settled elsewhere would be more than equaled by the clansmen who emigrated as individuals or in smaller groups, particularly after 1815.

16 For the population in 1832, see Upper Canada, House of Assembly.

Appendix to the journal of Assembly 1832–3, 184; for the population in 1852, see Canada. Board of Registration and Statistics. *Census of the Canadas* (1851–2), I. Since the ethnic origins of the 12,742 non-French natives of Canada are not given, I have taken the total number of those born in England, Ireland, Wales, and Scotland, and assumed that the percentage of these born in Scotland (85%) gave a reliable indicator of the percentage of Canadian-born people of Highland descent. This percentage probably underestimates somewhat the number of Canadians of the Highland ancestry, since the Highlanders settled in Glengarry earlier than other British groups; hence more people of Highland ancestry were likely to be Canadian-born by 1852. Moreover, individuals born in the Maritime provinces and the United States could also have Highland forebears. The census of clansmen in Glengarry was prepared by Col. Chisholm who had access to the manuscript census before it was forwarded to provincial officials; see Macdonell, *Sketches ... of Glengarry in Canada*, 156–8. As the list of clansmen found in Glengarry suggests, there was effectively no Lowland emigration to the county.

17 AAQ, Haut Canada, III-21, Alexander MacDonell (St. Raphael) to Bishop Plessis, 19 Nov. 1808.

18 NA, MG24 I 183, letterbook, Montreal, 27 April 1805, 212.

19 NA, MG29 C29, notebook, Donald Sutherland, 8.

20 Ibid. notebook with first page blank, James Duncan Macdonald's evidence is followed by loose notes; see the second of these notes.

21 Connor, *Man from Glengarry*. For "is Glengarry in Canada," see *Glengarry News*, 28 April 1933, account of Mr. Alston's visit to Montreal.

Bibliography

The following primary and secondary sources were found useful in the preparation of this book.

PRIMARY SOURCES

Manuscripts

SCOTTISH RECORD OFFICE

E721, E741, E768, E786, Forfeited and Annexed Estates papers.

GD44/25/28–30, Material relating to the Glengarry estate in the Duke of Gordon's papers.

GD51/1/844/3, copy of letter to Col. MacDonell, 27 October 1794.

GD128, Charles Fraser-Mackintosh collection, especially GD128/7 and 8, McDonell of Scotus, and GD128/65, Macdonell of Glengarry.

RH2/8/24, Blackadder's survey of Lord MacDonald's estates, 1799.

RH2/8/26, "Report of the Contents and Estimate Rents of part of the Annexed estate of Lochiel taken in 1772," by William Morison.

RH2/4/87, 151, letter from A. Macdonell, 21 March 1802.

RH2/4/89, 140–4, letter from Charles Hope, 3 Sept. 1804.

Great Britain, 1801 Census: Inverness-shire, Answers to questions with the census.

SCOTTISH CATHOLIC ARCHIVES, EDINBURGH

Blairs Papers, Correspondence from western Inverness-shire priests, 1765–1806.

Oban Papers, Correspondence, 1764–1819.

Preshome Letters, Letters and papers accumulated at Preshome by Bishop Kyle.

REGISTER HOUSE EDINBURGH
Parochial Register, Kilmallie, 520/1.

CAMERON OF LOCHIEL PAPERS, ACHNACARRY HOUSE,
INVERNESS-SHIRE
Copy of letter written by Nancy Jean Cameron to Mrs. Kenneth McPherson, 12 May 1785.

PUBLIC RECORD OFFICE, LONDON
T1/499, copy of letter from Customs House, Fort William, 13 December 1773.

NATIONAL ARCHIVES OF CANADA, OTTAWA
MG9/D7/6, St. Raphael's, Glengarry County, Parish Register.
MG9/D7/14, St. Andrews, Williamstown, Glengarry County, Parish Register.
MG9/D8/8, Court of the Quarter Sessions, Eastern District.
MG11 CO42 (and "Q" Series, transcripts), CO43, CO385: Great Britain, Colonial Office records (available on microfilm).
MG14 AO12, AO13: Great Britain, Audit Office records available on microfilm, including Loyalist claims.
MG21, "B" Series, Sir Frederick Haldimand papers, British Museum Additional Mss. 21661–21892 (available as transcripts and on microfilm).
MG23 GIII5, Lindsay-Morrison papers.
MG24 I3, John MacGillivray papers.
MG24 I183, Archibald McMillan and family papers.
MG24 J13, Rt. Reverend Alexander Macdonell, Bishop of Kingston, papers.
MG29 C29, Glengarry history notebooks, 1883–85 [George Sandfield Macdonald].
MG30 C22, Alexander McLean Macdonell papers.
RG1 L1, Quebec, Lower Canada, Upper Canada, Canada: Executive Council, Minute Books (Land Books), 1787–1867.
RG1 L3, Upper Canada and Canada: Petitions for land grants, 1791–1867; especially "M" and "MC."
RG1 L3L, Quebec et Bas Canada: Demandes de terres, 1637 à 1842.
RG1 L4, Upper Canada, Land Board minutes and records, 1765–1804, volume 10, 12, 13, and 15.
RG4 A1, "S" Series, Correspondence of Provincial and Civil Secretaries Offices, Quebec and Lower Canada, 1760–1841.
RG4 A3, Quebec and Lower Canada: Civil Secretary, registers and day books, 1762–1846, volume 3.
RG5 A1, Upper Canada Sundries, 1766–1841.
RG5 D1, Upper Canada Gazette.
RG7 G1, Governor General's Office: Despatches from the Colonial Office, 1784–1909, volume 54.

RG7 G16C, Governor General's Office: Civil Secretary's Letterbooks, Upper Canada, 1799–1841, volume 7.

RG8 C Series, British Military Records.

RG9 IB1, Adjutant General's Office, Upper Canada, Correspondence with Glengarry, Prescott and Stormont Militia, 1794–1840.

RG19, Department of Finance, vol. 4447, Loyalist victualling lists.

RG31, Manuscript Census, Glengarry County, 1851, 1861.

ARCHIVES OF ONTARIO, TORONTO

RG1, Department of Crown Lands.

Township Papers: Lancaster, Charlottenburgh, Lochiel and Kenyon townships.

Father Ewen John Macdonald papers.

Glengarry County Collection: Kippen families, and "Manuscript historical notes on Glengarry Co. by Angus Bhan McDonell."

KINGSTON ARCHDIOCESE ARCHIVES, KINGSTON

A12 C5 Papers of Bishop Alexander Macdonell, first bishop of Kingston.

ARCHIVES DE L'ARCHEVECHE DE QUEBEC, QUEBEC CITY

Correspondence with Alexander McDonell (Scotus), Roderick Macdonell, and Alexander Macdonell (the chaplain, later bishop of Kingston).

Maps

Scottish Record Office, Edinburgh, RHP 112, Plan of the Annexed Estate of Barisdale, William Morison, 1771.

Scottish Record Office, Edinburgh, RHP 11608, "Plan of the Intended Road from Loch Nevish Head to Loch Lochy Below Auchnacarrie By the north side of Loch Arkigg, Surveyed 1796 By Geo. Brown."

Scottish Record Office, Edinburgh, RHP Book 3424–76, William Morrison's surveys of the Barisdale and Lochiel farms, c. 1771.

National Archives of Canada, Ottawa, Patrick McNiff, "A Plan of the New Settlements" (1 Nov. 1786).

National Archives of Canada, Ottawa, Patrick McNiff, "Charlottenburgh Township," 1796, reel M-308, 756.

Government of Ontario, Department of Lands and Forests, plan of Lancaster by Lt. James McDonell, 2 Feb. 1791.

Interviews

Mrs. Mary Beaton, Ottawa, Ontario, 1977–81.

Mr. Alexander Fraser, Lancaster Township, Glengarry County, 1977.

Mrs. Florence Macdonell, The Glen Road, Charlottenburgh Township, Glengarry County, 1977–8.

Mrs. Harriet McKinnon, Alexandria, Ontario, 1977–81.

Mr. L. Raymond McLean, Ottawa, Ontario, 1977–89.

Mrs. Sybil McPhee, Dunvegan, Kenyon Township, Glengarry County, 1978–81.

PUBLISHED SOURCES

Adams, Margaret. "The Causes of the Highland Emigrations of 1783–1803." *Scottish Historical Review* 17 (1920).

– "The Highland Emigration of 1770." *Scottish Historical Review* 16 (1919).

Akenson, Donald. *The Irish in Ontario*. Kingston and Montreal: McGill-Queen's University Press, 1984.

Bailyn, Bernard. *The Peopling of British North America: An Introduction*. New York: Alfred A. Knopf, 1986.

– *Voyagers to the West: A Passage in the Peopling of America on the Eve of the Revolution*. New York: Alfred A. Knopf, 1986.

Belden's Illustrated Historical Atlas of Stormont, Dundas and Glengarry Counties, Ontario. Toronto: H. Belden, 1979; reprinted Belleville, Ont.: Mika, 1972.

Blegen, Theodore. *Norwegian Migration in America, 1825–1860*. Northfield, Minn.: Norwegian-American Historical Association, 1931.

Boswell, James. *Boswell's Journal of a Tour to the Hebrides*. F.A. Pottle and Charles H. Bennett, eds. New York: Macmillan, 1936.

Bumsted, J.M. *The People's Clearance: Highland Emigration to British North America*. Winnipeg: University of Manitoba Press, 1982.

– "Scottish Emigration to the Maritimes, 1770–1815: A New Look at an Old Theme." *Acadiensis* 10 (1981).

– "Sir James Montgomery and Prince Edward Island, 1767–1803." *Acadiensis* 7 (1978).

Campbell, D. and MacLean, R.A. *Beyond the Atlantic Roar*. Toronto: McClelland and Stewart, 1974.

Campbell, Mildred. "English Emigration on the Eve of the American Revolution." *American Historical Review* 61, no. 1 (1952).

Campbell, R.B. and McDermid, Douglas. *The Kennedys, MacDiarmids, McDermids, Munros and Other Glengarry–Stormont Pioneers*. Belleville, Ont.: Mika Publishers, 1986.

Campbell, William, *Annals of Tryon County*. New York: J. and J. Harper, 1831.

Canada. Board of Registration and Statistics. *Census of the Canadas, 1851–2*. Personal Census I. Quebec City: John Lovell, 1853.

Canadian Magazine and Literary Repository 4 (1825).

Carrothers, W.A. *Emigration from the British Isles*. London: P.S. King, 1929.

Chapman, L.J. and Putnam, D.F. *The Physiography of Southern Ontario*. Toronto: University of Toronto Press, 1951.

Clan MacLeod. *The Macleods of Glengarry*. Iroquois, Ont.: Clan MacLeod Society of Glengarry, 1971.

Clinton, George. *Public Papers of George Clinton*. Vols. 2–6. Albany, N.Y.: State of New York, 1900.

Connor, Ralph. *The Man from Glengarry*. London: Hodder and Stoughton, 1901.

– *Glengarry Schooldays*. Toronto: F.H. Revel, 1902.

Cowan, Helen. *British Emigration to British North America, 1783–1837*. Toronto: University of Toronto Press, 1928.

Craig, Gerald. *Upper Canada: The Formative Years*. Toronto: McClelland and Stewart, 1963.

Cregeen, Eric. "The Tacksmen and Their Successors," *Scottish Studies* 13 (1969).

Cressy, David. *Coming Over*. Cambridge, England: Cambridge University Press, 1987.

Darling, F. Fraser and Boyd, J. Morton. *The Highlands and Islands*. London: Collins, 1972.

Donaldson, Gordon. *The Scots Overseas*. London: Hale, 1966.

Dumbrille, Dorothy. *Braggart in My Step*. Toronto: Ryerson Press, 1956.

– *Up and Down the Glens*. Toronto: Ryerson Press, 1954.

Dunn, Charles. *Highland Settler*. Toronto: University of Toronto Press, 1953.

Elliot, Bruce. *Irish Migrants in the Canadas: A New Approach*. Kingston and Montreal: McGill-Queen's University Press, 1988.

Fighting Men of a Highland Catholic Jacobite Clan Who Fought in Canada to Gain It for and Preserve It to the Crown and for the Honour of the Name of Glengarry. Toronto: R.G. McLean, 1912.

Flinn, Michael. "Malthus, Emigration and Potatoes in the Scottish Northwest, 1770–1870," in *Comparative Aspects of Scottish and Irish Economic and Social History, 1600–1900*, L.M. Cullen and T.C. Smout, eds. Edinburgh: Donald, 1977.

– *Scottish Population History*. Cambridge, England: Cambridge University Press, 1977.

Forbes, F. and Anderson, W.J. "Clergy Lists of the Highland District, 1732–1828." *Innes Review* 17, no, 2 (1966).

Fortescue, John. *History of the British Army*. 13 Vols. New York: Macmillan, 1899–1930.

Fraser, Duncan, "Sir John Johnson's Rent Roll of the Kingsborough Patent." *Ontario History* 52 (1960).

Fraser-Mackintosh, Charles. *Antiquarian Notes*. 2d ser. Inverness, Scotland: n.p., 1897.

– *Letters of Two Centuries*. Inverness, Scotland: n.p., 1890.

- "The Macdonells of Scotos." *Transactions of the Gaelic Society of Inverness* 16.

Gaffield, Chad. "Canadian Families in Cultural Context: Hypothesis from the Mid-Nineteenth Century." Canadian Historical Association, *Historical Papers* 1979.

Gagan, David. *Hopeful Travellers: Families, Land and Social Change in Mid-Victorian Peel County*. Toronto: University of Toronto Press, 1981.

Gates, Lillian. *Land Policies of Upper Canada*. Toronto: University of Toronto Press, 1968.

Glengarry Historical Society. *Glengarry Life*. N.p., n.p. 1980.

Glengarry News (Alexandria, Ont.)

Goldring, Philip. "Lewis and the Hudson's Bay Company in the Nineteenth Century." *Scottish Studies* 24 (1980).

Graham, Ian C.C. *Colonists from Scotland*. Ithaca, N.Y.: Cornell University Press, 1956.

Grant, I.F. *The MacLeods*. London: Faber and Faber, 1959.

Grant, Rhodes. *The Story of Martintown*. N.p., n.p., 1974.

Gray, Malcolm. *The Highland Economy*. Edinburgh: Oliver and Boyd, 1957.

Great Britain. Parliament. House of Commons. *Parliamentary Papers* 1802–3 (80) IV, 129, "First Report from the Select Committee ... [on emigration]."

- *Parliamentary Papers* 1828 (569) VII, 375, "Report of the Select Committee on the Civil Government of Canada."

- *Parliamentary Papers* 1841 (182) VI, 1, "Report from the Select Committee Appointed to Inquire Into the Condition of the Population of the Islands and Highlands of Scotland, and Into the Practicability of Affording the People Relief by Means of Emigration."

Great Britain. War Office. *A List of Officers of the Army*. London: HMSO, 1786.

Green, Jack P. "Recent Developments in the Historiography of Colonial New England." *Acadiensis* 17, no. 2 (1988).

Grimble, Ian. "Emigration in the Time of Rob Donn, 1714–1778." *Scottish Studies* 7, part 2 (1963).

Guldan, Leroy. *The MacIssac MacDonald Story*. 2d ed. Norbert Ferre, ed. Cornwall, Ont.: privately published. 1978.

Handley, James. *Scottish Farming in the 18th Century*. London: Faber, 1953.

Hansen, Marcus Lee. *The Atlantic Migration, 1607–1860*. New York: Harper, 1961.

Harkness, John. *Stormont, Dundas and Glengarry*. Facsimile edition. Cornwall: United Counties of Stormont, Dundas, and Glengarry, 1972.

Harney, R.F. "Men Without Women: Italian Migrants in Canada, 1885–1930." *Canadian Ethnic Studies* 11, no. 1 (1979).

Hobsbawn, E.J. *The Age of Revolution*. London: Abacus, 1977.

Hunter, James. *The Making of the Crofting Community*. Edinburgh: John Donald, 1976.

Johnson, Sir William. *Sir William Johnson Papers*. Vols. 7–8, 11–12. Albany, N.Y.: University of the State of New York, 1921–65.

Johnston, Hugh. *British Emigration Policy, 1815–30*. Oxford: Clarendon Press, 1972.

Johnstone, G. Scott. *The Western Highlands*. Edinburgh: Scottish Mountaineering Trust, 1973.

Jones, Thomas. *History of New York*. 2 vols. New York: New York Historical Society, 1879.

Knox, John. *A Tour Through the Highlands and Hebrides*. London: J. Walter, 1787.

Macdonald, Donald A. "Fieldwork: Collecting Oral Literature," in *Folklore and Folklife: An Introduction*, ed. Richard M. Dorson. Chicago: University of Chicago Press, 1972.

Macdonald, Norman. *Canada, 1763–1841: Immigration and Settlement*. London: Longmans, 1939.

Macdonald, Rev. Roderick. "The Highland District in 1764." *Innes Review* 15, no. 2 (1964).

Macdonell, J.A. *Sketches ... of Glengarry in Canada*. Montreal: W.F. Brown, 1893.

MacDonell, Margaret. *The Emigrant Experience*. Toronto: University of Toronto Press, 1982.

MacGillivray, Carrie Homes. *The Shadow of Tradition*. Ottawa: Graphic, 1927.

MacGillivray, Royce and Ross, Ewan. *A History of Glengarry*. Belleville, Ont.: Mika, 1979.

MacKenzie, A.E.D. *Baldoon*. London, Ont.: Phelps, 1978.

MacLean, Raymond A., ed. *History of Antigonish*. 2 Vols. Antigonish, N.S.: Casket, 1976.

MacMillan, Rev. Somerled. *Bygone Lochaber*. Glasgow, 1971.

– *The Emigration of the Lochaber MacMillans to Canada in 1802*. Paisley, 1958.

MacTaggart, John. *Three Years in Canada*. 2 vols. London: H. Colburn, 1829.

MacWilliam, Rev. Alexander. "The Glasgow Mission, 1792–1799." *Innes Review* 4, no. 2 (1953).

Manion, John. *Irish Settlements in Eastern Canada*. Toronto: University of Toronto Press, 1974.

Masson, Raymond. *Généologie des familles de Terrebonne*. Vol. 3. Montreal: Therien, 1930–1.

Mathews, Hazel. *The Mark of Honour*. Toronto: University of Toronto Press, 1965.

McLean, Marianne. "Achd an Rhigh: A Highland Response to the Assisted Emigration of 1815." *Canadian Papers in Rural History* 5 (1986).

– "John McGillivray." *Dictionary of Canadian Biography* 8 (1985).

- "Peopling Glengarry County." Canadian Historical Association, *Historical Papers* (1982).

McLennan, John. "The Early Settlement of Glengarry," in *Transactions of the Celtic Society of Montreal*. Montreal: W. Drysdale, 1887.

The New Statistical Account of Scotland. By Ministers of the Respective Parishes. 15 vols. Edinburgh: Blackwood and Sons, 1845.

Old Statistical Account. See Sinclair, Sir John.

Ommer, Rosemary. "Highland Scots Migration to Southwestern Newfoundland: A Study of Kinship," in *The Peopling of Newfoundland*, J.J. Manion, ed. St. John's, Nfld.: Institute of Social and Economic Research, Memorial University of Newfoundland, 1977.

Phillipson, N. and Mitchison, R. *Scotland in the Age of Improvement*. Edinburgh: University of Edinburgh Press, 1970.

Pope, A.M. "A Scotch Catholic Settlement in Canada." *Catholic World* 34 (Oct. 1881).

Prebble, John. *The Highland Clearances*. Harmondsworth: Penguin, 1973.

- *Mutiny*. Harmondsworth: Penguin, 1977.

Pringle, J.F. *Lunenburgh*. Cornwall, Ont.: Standard, 1890.

Quebec Gazette (Quebec City).

Reid, W. Stanford, ed. *The Scottish Tradition in Canada*. Toronto: McClelland and Stewart, 1976.

Richards, Eric. *A History of the Highland Clearances*. London: Croom Helm, 1982, 1985.

- "How Tame Were the Highlanders During the Clearances?" *Scottish Studies* 17 (1973)

Robson, James. *General View of the Agriculture in the ... Western Part of Inverness-shire*. London, 1794.

Scotland. Record Office. *Statistics of the Annexed Estates*. Edinburgh: HMSO, 1973.

Selkirk, Thomas Douglas, Earl of. *The Collected Writings of Lord Selkirk, 1799–1809*. J.M. Bumsted, ed. Winnipeg: University of Manitoba Press, 1984.

- *Observations of the Present State of the Highlands of Scotland*. New York: Johnson Reprint, 1969.

- *Selkirk's Diary, 1803–1804*. New York: Greenwood, 1969.

Sellar, Robert. *History of Huntingdon, Chateauguay and Beauharnois*. Huntingdon, Que.: Canadian Gleaner, 1888.

Sinclair, Rev. Alexander Maclean. *The Gaelic Bards from 1825 to 1875*. Sydney, N.S.: Mac-Talla, 1904.

Sinclair, Sir John. *Statistical Account of Scotland*. (Also known as *Old Statistical Account*.) Vols. 4, 7, 8, 16, 17. Edinburgh: W. Creech, 1791–9.

Smout, T.C. *A History of the Scottish People*. London: Collins Fontana, 1972.

Statistics of the Annexed Estates. See Scotland.

Stewart, Charles. *The Service of British Regiments in Canada and North America.* Department of National Defence Library, pub. no. 2. Ottawa: Department of National Defence Library, 1962.

Sullivan, James. *Minutes of the Albany Committee of Correspondence.* Vol. 1. Albany, N.Y.: University of the State of New York, 1923.

Thomas, Cyrus. *History of Agenteuill, Que., and Prescott, Ont.* Montreal: John Lovell and Son, 1896.

Thomas, Peter. *Strangers from a Secret Land.* Toronto: University of Toronto Press, 1986.

– "Introduction to 'The Ballad of the *Albion.*'" *Acadiensis* 11, no. 1 (1981).

Thomas, W.I. and Znaniacki, F. *The Polish Peasant in Europe and America.* 5 vols. Boston, 1920.

Thomson, Derick. *An Introduction to Gaelic Poetry.* London: Gollancz, 1974.

Toomey, Kathleen. *Alexander Macdonell: The Scottish Years, 1762–1804.* Toronto: Canadian Catholic Historical Society, 1985.

Turnock, David. "Glenelg, Glengarry and Lochiel: An Evolutionary Study of Land Use." *Scottish Geographical Magazine* 83(1).

Upper Canada. House of Assembly. *Appendix to the Journal of Assembly* (1832–3). York, U.C.: Robert Stanton, 1833.

Vansina, Jan. *Oral Tradition: A Study in Historical Methodology.* London: Routledge and Kegan Paul, 1965.

Webster, Alexander. *Scottish Population Statistics, Including Webster's Analysis of Population, 1755.* James Kyd, ed. Edinburgh, 1952.

Willis, Virginia, ed. *Reports of the Annexed Estates, 1755–69.* Edinburgh, 1973.

Youngson, A.E. *After the Forty-five.* Edinburgh: University of Edinburgh Press, 1973.

Index

A date in brackets following an individual's name denotes the year of his or her emigration, if known. For convenience, individuals with identical names may be grouped; for example, "John Macdonald, 58, 138" may refer to two different John Macdonalds about whom nothing is known but their names.